A SHORT HISTORY OF AMERICAN LITERATURE

T0381698

A SHORT HISTORY

OF

AMERICAN LITERATURE

EDITED BY

WILLIAM PETERFIELD TRENT, JOHN ERSKINE,
STUART P. SHERMAN, AND CARL VAN DOREN

WITH AN INTRODUCTION BY
CARL VAN DOREN

Cambridge: at the University Press
New York : G. P. Putnam's Sons
1924

CAMBRIDGE
UNIVERSITY PRESS

University Printing House, Cambridge CB2 8BS, United Kingdom

Cambridge University Press is part of the University of Cambridge.

It furthers the University's mission by disseminating knowledge in the pursuit of education, learning and research at the highest international levels of excellence.

www.cambridge.org
Information on this title: www.cambridge.org/9781107554207

© Cambridge University Press 1924

First published 1924
First paperback edition 2015

A catalogue record for this publication is available from the British Library

ISBN 978-1-107-55420-7 Paperback

CONTENTS

iii

Contents

Contents

INTRODUCTION

IN calling this abridgment *A Short History of American Literature*, instead of *Chapters of American Literature* as was originally planned, the publishers and editors have had in mind chiefly the convenience of those students and general readers for whom the abridgment is intended and who might perhaps, had the discarded title been chosen, have failed to notice that the abridgment not only excerpts the chapters given to the principal figures in the four-volume *Cambridge History of American Literature* but also rearranges them in an order which illustrates the development of literature in the United States more simply than it was possible to do in the larger work. That larger work, the editors are aware, has the disadvantages as well as the advantages inherent in its method. Though no single writer could have spoken with the authoritative knowledge which the sixty-four different contributors brought to the undertaking, neither could so large a number of eyes have seen with the singleness of which one pair might have been capable, nor could so many pens have set down their observations with the unity of tone and style which one pen might have employed. Moreover, the years 1917–1921, during which the successive volumes passed through the press, were troubled years when it was not always practicable to follow programs laid down in quieter times; when editors and contributors had to do more of their work at long range than they desired; when this or that chapter had occasionally to wait so long upon its fellows that it needed revisions which it could not always get; and when parts of the material intended for the earlier volumes had to be left over to the later if they were not to be left out altogether. In the abridgment, however, it has been possible with a free hand to select and arrange those topics and chapters which seem best adapted to the need of the particular public which the abridgment aims to serve.

Exclusion has had to fall heavily, in a volume of this length, upon the underwoods and backgrounds of literature, to which the total work gives unprecedented attention.   The matter of space demanded that minor authors be slighted for the sake of those others who could not be slighted if any real principle of excellence were kept to.   Nor was it thinkable to cut the chapters on the ephemerides to the dimensions of encyclopœdic entries already to be found in numerous works of reference with which the *Short History* does not compete.   It seemed better to omit the lesser figures entirely than to dismiss them with scraps of information and bare critical epithets.   If an exception has been made in the case of the chapter on the short story, that is due to the special importance which the form has in American literature.   As a matter of fact, throughout the abridgment it will be noticed that the significance, the representativeness, of individual writers was taken into account when the question of their inclusion or exclusion came up.   Some strictly academic disposition might have urged that the principle of selection ought to consider only intrinsic excellence or only representative qualities; but the present editors, in view of their purpose, have denied themselves whatever sense of luxury might have come from the exercise of a disposition so strict.

So with the chapters concerned with the backgrounds which can be no more than hinted at in this briefer record.   *The Cambridge History of American Literature* has been called not only a history of one country's literature but a history as well of the moral, social, and intellectual development of that country. Of these two aspects of history the editors in the abridgment have felt obliged to confine themselves to one for fear of skimping either by attempting both, and they have chosen the one which, for this undertaking, seems to be essential to their function.   It happens, too, that the experience of many teachers confirms the belief that has helped to give the abridgment its general direction: the belief that literary history in its more technical concerns is a study which as a rule interests none but advanced students and which ought to wait upon the study of individual authors, taken up one by one, until students have the body of knowledge that is prerequisite to any real understanding of the schools and movements and tendencies and influences to which the historian of literature, as distinct from the critic, must give his time. Before New England transcendentalism, for instance, can mean a great deal to a student, he must, without too much attention to generalizations regarding its doctrines and policies, have gone directly to the lives and works of Emerson, Hawthorne, and Thoreau, upon whom, indeed, the most important generalizations regarding native transcendentalists must be based. Only after such fundamental inquiries is he ready for the wider range of reading and reflection that the topic offers him. Otherwise he will hold his opinions upon faith, without the concrete details which are the life of the matter. This *Short History of American Literature* undertakes to deal with the fundamental materials of its subject and leaves to the original work the task of presenting transitions and illustrations and elaborations for which there is here not enoug 1 space.

A special difficulty may seem to arise in connection with the colonial writers, of whom only Edwards and Franklin appear in the abridgment out of the many who are often mentioned and quoted in histories of literature of no greater bulk than this. The selection is deliberate. With no intention to undervalue the historians, theologians, travellers, and poets whom the colonies produced, one may still remember that many of them belong to the limbo of literature and that as a whole they have been greatly emphasized in countless textbooks and anthologies where they may be studied by any who want to go beyond the first principles with which this *Short History* deals. It happens, too, that in a particular degree the two are representative of the entire colonial era: Edwards of the old order which founded the northern colonies, established their culture, extended it over a large part of the country, and fought against the movement away from an order which in the end became a memory; Franklin of the new order which, in all the colonies, brought in modern theology, independent politics, worldly prudence, and secular attitudes in general. It happens, too, that they are both eminent writers, who may be read in a different age without the need of constant explanations as to how they could have been the kind of men they were, without the need of too much stress upon the significance of documents and of the curiosities of literature.

If the vigorous literature of the Revolution is here passed over, that is because most of it belongs in the domain of political controversy and because the abridgment, mindful of the great stress laid upon such matters in the *Cambridge History*, has chosen to follow more closely than its parent treatise the path of belles-lettres. The discussion broadens, however, when it reaches the early national period and the numerous figures who then emerged after the long post-Revolutionary generation of distraction and experiment which struggled to realize an indigenous culture and to give it adequate expression. Irving, who planted legends on the American soil, fixed a tradition for the past of his native city, and interpreted America to Europe and Europe to America in the suave language of a man of the world; Bryant, who, bred in New England like Franklin, like Franklin also carried his qualities into a blander region and there ripened in a conspicuous career; Cooper, who discovered the riches of the frontier and made them known to the world at large—these men flourished in New York and they have a chapter in the record. Poe, descended from Virginians, born in Boston, active in Baltimore, Philadelphia, and New York, has a separate chapter because he was, after all, an isolated figure not to be identified with any section of any country except the section of the country of art to which he belongs by virtue of his special traits. New England had its transcendental philosopher in Emerson, its transcendental romancer in Hawthorne, and its transcendental personality in Thoreau, who all lived in Concord, village of genius, and who deserve a chapter to themselves. And besides these there were the poets, essayists, and romancers, Longfellow, Whittier, Holmes, Lowell, Melville, and Mrs. Stowe, who in various parts of the United States, but mostly in New England, enlarged and enriched the field of letters as they enlarge and enrich this history in the chapter devoted to them.

Thereafter the *Short History* ventures to depart, advisedly, from the course pursued by most of the manuals on American literature. To Lincoln, orator and hero of the Civil War, and to Whitman, poet and prophet of the time, it gives a chapter each, calling attention to their great rôles and giving to them the distinctive place which it assigned them increasingly by fame as the slighter personages of their era pass from memory. A new emphasis is given, likewise, to the men of the Reconstruction by the chapter in which they appear: Mark Twain, humorist, who led a home-bred literary mode out of the waste of coarse fun which it had commonly inhabited; Howells, who preached the new code of realism in every season and practiced it with a new success; Henry James, who gave himself to international manners and found a fresh province for the imagination to revolve in; Lanier, who was the hopeful yet broken poet of the New South; Harris, who salvaged a folk-lore from the members of a racial minority before that minority could adapt itself to the conditions of the freedom that had been brought to them by the Civil War. And the chapter on the Short Story, making the exception already noted, calls attention to the process by which a form of art peculiarly characteristic of native literature advanced from its tentative beginnings under Irving to the height of its vogue and vernacularity under O. Henry.

In the chapter on Historians and Scholars will be found Prescott, Motley, Parkman, and Ticknor, who have had many chapters or parts of chapters assigned them in brief histories of American literature; but so also will be found Henry Adams, newly arrived at a reputation which must henceforth make it impossible to leave him out, and Whitney, heretofore neglected though one of the most notable of American savants. So also does the chapter on Preachers and Philosophers take account not only of Beecher and Brooks but also of those thinkers of a recent day, Royce and William James, who for some decades almost divided American thought between them. And finally, a chapter on the English Language in America now for the first time appears in a volume of the purpose of this one.

The desire to make the record as valuable as might be has not led the editors to include living writers in the *Short History*, even in the case of those whom the *Cambridge History*, in spite of its general policy, found it impossible to exclude altogether. The literature of the twentieth century, indeed, calls for investigation and will in time presumably receive it; but as that investigation has not yet been made it is too early for any manual to attempt to indicate the conclusions which only prolonged research can be expected to reach with authority. Nevertheless it is the hope of the editors of the *Cambridge History* and of the *Short History* that teachers and students will not forget that literary history is a continuous process and that eminence in literature is not merely a thing of the past. Meanwhile this abridgment, quarried from a work suitable for the most inquisitive specialist as well as for general readers, points the simpler way to an acquaintance with the most important American writers, discussed by many competent critics, arranged in a logical order, combined in a convenient form for readers of all classes.

C. V. D.

New York, Nov. 1, 1922.

A Short History
of
American Literature

CHAPTER I

Colonial Writers

1. JONATHAN EDWARDS

JONATHAN EDWARDS was born at Windsor, Connecticut, in 1703. He belonged, unlike his great contemporary Franklin in this, to the "Brahmin families" of America, his father being a distinguished graduate of Harvard and a minister of high standing, his mother being the daughter of Solomon Stoddard, a revered pastor of Northampton, Massachusetts, and a religious author of repute. Jonathan, one of eleven children, showed extraordinary precocity. There is preserved a letter of his, written apparently in his twelfth year, in which he retorts upon certain materialistic opinions of his correspondent with an easiness of banter not common to a boy; and another document, from about the same period, an elaborate account of the habits of spiders, displays a keenness of observation and a vividness of style uncommon at any age.

He studied at Yale, receiving his bachelor's degree in 1720, before his seventeenth birthday. While at college he continued his interest in scientific observations, but his main concern was naturally with theology and moral philosophy. As a sophomore he read Locke *On the Human Understanding*, with the delight of a "greedy miser" in "some newly discovered treasure." Some time after reading Locke and before graduation he wrote down a series of reflections, preparatory to a great metaphysical treatise of his own, which can be compared only with the *Commonplace Book* kept by Berkeley a few years earlier for the same purpose. In the section of "Notes on the Mind" this entry is found: "Our perceptions or ideas, that we passively receive by our bodies, are communicated to us immediately by God." Now Berkeley's *Principles* and his *Hylas and Philonous* appeared in 1710 and 1713 respectively, and the question has been raised, and not answered, whether this Berkeleian sentiment was borrowed from one of these books or was original with Edwards. Possibly the youthful philosopher was following a line of thought suggested by the English disciples of Malebranche, possibly he reached his point of view directly from Locke; in any case his life-work was to carry on the Lockian philosophy from the point where the Berkeleian idealism left off.

After graduation Edwards remained for two years at Yale, preparing for the ministry. In 1722 he was called to a Presbyterian church in New York. Here he preached acceptably for eight months, returning then to his father's house, and later to New Haven, where he held the position of tutor in the college. In 1727 he went to Northampton as colleague, and became in due time successor, to his grandfather. Almost immediately after ordination he married Sarah Pierrepont, like himself of the Brahmin caste, whom he had known as a young girl, and whose beauty of body and soul he had described in a passage of ecstatic wonder.

"They say," he began, being himself then twenty and the object of his adoration thirteen, "there is a young lady in New Haven who is beloved of that great Being who made and rules the world, and that there are certain seasons in which this great Being, in some way or other invisible, comes to her and fills her mind with exceeding sweet delight."

The marriage, notwithstanding this romantic rapture, proved eminently wise.

Like a good many other men of his age Edwards lived his inner life, so to speak, on paper. There is therefore nothing peculiar or priggish in the fact that at the beginning of his religious career he should have written out a set of formal resolutions, which he vowed to read over, and did read over, at stated intervals in order to keep watch on his spiritual progress. A number of these resolutions have been printed, as has also a part of the diary kept at about the same time. Neither of these documents, the time of their writing considered, contains anything remarkable. But it is quite otherwise with the private reflections which he wrote out some twenty years later (about 1743) at Northampton, apparently on some occasion of reading over his youthful diary. In these we have an autobiographical fragment that, for intensity of absorption in the idea of God and for convincing power of utterance, can be likened to the *Confessions* of St. Augustine, while it unites to this religious fervour a romantic feeling for nature foreign to the Bishop of Hippo's mind and prophetic of a movement that was to sweep over the world many years after Edwards's death. A few extracts from this document (not so well known as it would have been if it had not been printed with the works of a thorny metaphysician) must be given for their biographical and literary interest:

From my childhood up, my mind had been full of objections against the doctrine of God's sovereignty, in choosing whom he would to eternal life, and rejecting whom he pleased; leaving them eternally to perish, and be everlastingly tormented in hell. It used to appear like a horrible doctrine to me. But I remember the time very well, when I seemed to be convinced, and fully satisfied, as to this sovereignty of God. . . . I have often, since that first conviction, had quite another kind of sense of God's sovereignty than I had then. I have often since had not only a conviction, but a delightful conviction. The doctrine has very often appeared exceeding pleasant, bright, and sweet. Absolute sovereignty is what I love to ascribe to God. But my first conviction was not so.

The first instance that I remember of that sort of inward, sweet delight in God and divine things that I have lived much in since, was on reading those words, *Now unto the King eternal, immortal, invisible, the only wise God, be honour and glory for ever and ever, Amen.* As I read the words, there came into my soul, and was as it were diffused through it, a sense of the glory of the Divine Being. . . .

Not long after I first began to experience these things, I gave an account to my father of some things that had passed in my mind. I was pretty much affected by the discourse we had together; and when the discourse was ended, I walked abroad alone, in a solitary place in my father's pasture, for contemplation. And as I was walking there, and looking up on the sky and clouds, there came into my mind so sweet a sense of the glorious *majesty* and *grace* of God, that I know not how to express. I seemed to see them both in a sweet conjunction; majesty and meekness joined together; it was a sweet and gentle, and holy majesty; and also a majestic meekness; an awful sweetness; a high, and great, and holy gentleness.

This is not the Edwards that is commonly known, and indeed he put little of this personal rapture of holiness into his published works, which were almost exclusively polemical in design. Only once, perhaps, did he adequately display this aspect of his thought to the public; and that was in the *Dissertation on the Nature of Virtue*, wherein, starting from the definition of virtue as "the beauty of the qualities and exercises of the heart," he proceeds to combine ethics and aesthetics in an argument as subtle in reasoning as it is, in places, victorious in expression. One cannot avoid the feeling, when his writings are surveyed as a whole, that in his service to a particular dogma of religion Edwards deliberately threw away the opportunity of making for himself, despite the laxness of his style, one of the very great names in literature.

It should seem also that he not only suppressed his personal ecstasy in his works for the press, but waived it largely in his more direct intercourse with men. He who himself, like an earlier and perhaps greater Emerson, was enjoying the sweetness of walking with God in the garden of earth, was much addicted to holding up before his people the "pleasant, bright, and sweet" doctrine of damnation. Nor can it be denied that he had startling ways of impressing this sweetness on others. It is a misfortune, but one for which he is himself responsible, that his memory in the popular mind today is almost exclusively associated with certain brimstone sermons and their terrific effect. Best known of these is the discourse on *Sinners in the Hands of an Angry God*, delivered at Enfield, Connecticut, in the year 1741. His text was taken from Deuteronomy: "Their foot shall slide in due time"; and from these words he proceeded to prove, and "improve," the truth that "there is nothing that keeps wicked men at any moment out of hell, but the mere pleasure of God." He is said to have had none of the common qualities of the orator. His regular manner of preaching, at least in his earlier years, was to hold his "manuscript volume in his left hand, the elbow resting on the cushion or the Bible, his right hand rarely raised but to turn the leaves, and his person almost motionless"; but there needed no gesticulation and no modulation of voice to convey the force of his terrible conviction, when, to an audience already disposed to accept the dogma, he presented that dogma in a series of pictures like the following:

The God that holds you over the pit of hell, much as one holds a spider, or some loathesome insect, over the fire, abhors you, and is dreadfully provoked; his wrath towards you burns like fire; he looks upon you as worthy of nothing else, but to be cast into the fire; he is of purer eyes than to bear to have you in his sight.

The congregation of Enfield, we are told, was moved almost to despair; "there was such a breathing of distress and weeping" that the speaker was interrupted and had to plead for silence. Sincerity of vision may amount to cruelty, and something is due to the weakness of human nature.

The result was inevitable. The people of Northampton listened to Edwards for a time; were rapt out of themselves; suffered the relapse of natural indolence; grew resentful under the efforts to keep them in a state of exaltation; and freed themselves of the burden when it became intolerable. At first all went well. Stoddard, in whose declining years the discipline of the church had been somewhat relaxed, died in 1729, and the fervour of his successor soon began to tell on the people. In 1733, as Edwards notes in his *Narrative of Surprising Conversions*, there was a stirring in the conscience of the young, who had hitherto been prone to the awful sin of "frolicking." The next year the sudden conversion of a young woman, "who had been one of the greatest company keepers in the whole town," came upon the community "like a flash of lightning"; the Great Awakening was started, which was to run over New England like a burning fire, with consequences not yet obliterated. The usual accompaniments of moral exaltation and physical convulsions showed themselves. Edwards relates with entire approbation the morbid conversion of a child of four. The poor little thing was overheard by her mother in her closet wrestling with God in prayer, from which she came out crying aloud and "wreathing her body to and fro like one in anguish of spirit." She was afraid she was going to hell!

It was inevitable that such a wave of superheated emotion should subside in a short time. In fact the enthusiasm had scarcely reached its height when it began to show signs of perversion and decay. Immediately after the story of the young convert Edwards notes that "the Spirit of God was gradually withdrawing" and "Satan seemed to be let loose and raged in a dreadful manner." An epidemic of melancholy and suicidal mania swept over the community, and multitudes seemed to hear a voice saying to them: "Cut your own throat, now is a good opportunity." Strange delusions arose and spread, until common sense once more got the upper hand.

It was an old tale, told in New England with peculiar fury. The saddest thing in the whole affair is the part played by Edwards. Other leaders saw the danger from the first, or were soon awakened to it; but Edwards never, either at this time or later, wavered in his belief that the Awakening, though marred by the devil, was in itself the work of the Divine Spirit. His *Thoughts on the Revival of Religion* and his *Marks of a Work of the True Spirit* are both a thoroughgoing apology for the movement, as they are also an important document in his own psychology. The jangling and confusion he admits; he recognizes the elements of hysteria that were almost inextricably mixed up with the moral exaltation of conversion; but his defence is based frankly on the avowal that these things are the universal accompaniments of inspiration—they attended the founding of the church in the Apostolic age, they were to be expected at the instauration of religion. Often the reader of these treatises is struck by a curious, and by no means accidental, resemblance between the position of Edwards and the position of the apologists of the romantic movement in literature. There is the same directness of appeal to the emotions; the same laudation of sheer expansiveness, at the cost, if need be, of judgment or measure or any other restraint. Prudence and regularity may be desirable in the service of God, yet it is still true that "the cry of irregularity and imprudence" has been mainly in the mouths of those who are enemies to the main work of redemption. Perturbation, in truth, is not properly so called when it is the means of rousing the cold and indifferent from their lethargy; we are bound to suppose that not even the man "of the strongest reason and greatest learning" can remain master of himself if "strongly impressed with a sense of divine and eternal things." It comes in the end to this, that, notwithstanding his verbal reservations, Edwards had no critical canon to distinguish between the order and harmony governed by a power higher than either the imagination or the emotions, and the order and harmony that are merely stagnation.

One factor in his confidence was a belief that the discovery of America, coinciding as it did with the beginning of the Reformation, came by Providence for "the glorious renovation of the world"; nay more, that the humble town in which he was preaching might be the cradle of the new dispensation, from whence it should spread over the whole earth. His language may even seem to betray a touch of spiritual pride over the part he himself should be called upon to play as the instrument of Grace in this marvellous regeneration. That vice of the saints was indeed a subject much in his meditations, and one of the finest pieces of religious psychology in his works is the passage of the *Revival* in which he tracks it through the labyrinthine deceits of the human heart. It was a sin against which he had probably to keep particular ward in these years, but we should not say that he ever, in any proper sense of the word, lapsed from the virtue of Christian humility. If he seemed to set himself above other men as an exigent judge, this was rather due to a faulty sympathy, an inability to measure others except by the standard of his own great faculties. Thus, for all his emotionalism, he lived under the control of an iron will, and he could not comprehend how the over-stimulation of terror and joy in a weaker disposition would work moral havoc. Nor from his own constant height could he understand how brief and fitful any mood of exaltation must be among ordinary men in their ordinary condition. Hence he not only failed to see the gravity of the actual evils at the time of the Awakening, but failed also, with more grievous results for himself, to recognize the impossibility of flogging the dead emotion into new life.

The issue came on a point of church discipline. Edwards believed that religion was essentially a matter of the emotions or affections. A man might have perfect knowledge of divine things, as indeed the devil had, but unless the love of God was implanted in his heart by the free act of Grace he had no lot with the faithful. To develop this theme he wrote his great *Treatise Concerning Religious Affections*, a work which may without exaggeration be said to go as far as the human intellect can go in the perilous path of discriminating between the purely spiritual life and the life of worldly morality. Now even the simple statement of the difference between the condition of Grace and the condition of nature is hard for the natural man to follow; but when Edwards, with the acumen of a genius and the doggedness of a scholar, imposed his distinction on all the intricate feelings of life, the natural man was dazed; and when he attempted to make it the criterion of admission to the Lord's Table, the natural man who thought himself a Christian rebelled. Stoddard had held it right to admit to communion all those who desired honestly to unite themselves with the church. Edwards protested that only those who had undergone a radical conversion and knew the affections of supernatural love should enjoy this high privilege. His congregation sided with their old guide against him.

The quarrel was further embittered by another issue. It came to light that certain young folk of the church were reading profane books which led to lewd conversation. Edwards called for public discipline of the sinners; the congregation supported him until investigation showed that the evil was widespread and would bring discredit on most of the better families of the town, and then they blocked further proceedings. If tradition is correct in naming *Pamela* as one of the guilty books, we may admire the literary taste of youthful Northampton, yet think that their pastor was justified in condemning such reading as incendiary. However that may be, when, on 22 June, 1750, a public vote was taken whether Edwards should be dismissed from his pastorate, a large majority was counted against him. Northampton has the distinction of having rejected the greatest theologian and philosopher yet produced in this country. The behaviour of Edwards when the crisis actually came was simple, dignified, and even noble. His *Farewell Sermon*, with its dispassionate and submissive appeal from the tribunal of men to that final judgment which shall be given in knowledge and righteousness, cannot be read today without a deep stirring of the heart.

At the age of forty-six Edwards was thrust upon the world, discredited, in broken health, with a large family to support, but undaunted. Then befell a strange thing. This philosopher, whose thoughts and emotions ranged beyond the ken of most educated men, was sent to the frontier town of Stockbridge as a missionary to the Indians. There for six years he laboured faithfully and, at least in the practical management of affairs, successfully. It must have been one of the memorable sights of the world to see him returning on horseback from a solitary ride into the forest, while there fluttered about him, pinned to his coat, the strips of paper on which he had scribbled the results of his meditations. His days were little troubled, and not overburdened with work, peaceful it is thought; and now it was he wrote the treatise on the *Freedom of the Will* upon which his fame chiefly depends.

In 1757 his son-in-law, the Rev. Aaron Burr, died, and Edwards was chosen by the Trustees of the College of New Jersey to succeed him as president. Edwards hesitated, stating frankly to the Trustees his disabilities of health and learning, but he finally accepted the offer. He left his family to follow him later, and arrived in Princeton in January, 1758. Small-pox was in the town, and the new president was soon infected. His death took place on 22 March, in the fifty-fifth year of his age. His last recorded words were: "Trust in God and ye need not fear."

The child was indeed father of the man, and it was peculiarly fitting that he who from youth upward had been absorbed in the idea of God should have died with the sacred word on his lips. But what shall be said of the fearlessness—and there is no reason to question the perfect sincerity of his spiritual joy —in the breast of one who had made terror the chief instrument of appeal to men and had spent his life in fighting for a dogma which the genial author of *The One-Hoss Shay* thought no decent man could hold without going crazy? To understand that charge properly we must throw ourselves back into the age in which Edwards lived.

Now the Edwardian theology was a part of the great deistic debate which took its root in the everlasting question of the origin of evil in the world. It was a three-cornered contest. The Calvinists and the infidels both believed in a kind of determinism, but differed over the nature of the determining cause. The Calvinists found this cause in a personal Creator, omnipotent and omniscient, to whom they did not scruple to carry up all the evil as well as all the good of the universe—"c'est que Dieu," as Calvin himself states categorically, "non seulement a preveu la cheute du premier homme, et en icelle la ruine de toute sa posterité, mais qu'il l'a ainsi voulu." The deists, who at this time formed the fighting line of the infidels, while verbally acknowledging the existence of God and theorizing on the nature of evil, virtually regarded the universe as a perfectly working machine in which there was no room for a personal governor or for real sin. To the Arminians, including the bulk of the orthodox churchmen, the alliance between Calvinism and deism seemed altogether to outweigh the differences. As Daniel Whitby declares in the preface to his discourses *On the Five Points of Calvinism* (1710; reprinted in America), to hold God responsible for evil is to play directly into the hands of the atheists. And so the age-old dispute between Augustinian and Pelagian, and between Calvinist and Arminian, took on a new life from the deistic controversy, and there sprang up a literature which undertook to preserve the idea of an omnipotent personal Creator and at the same time to save his face, if the expression may be tolerated, by attributing to men complete free will and accountability for their actions.

It was in answer to Whitby's book and one or two others of the kind that Edwards composed his *Freedom of the Will*. His argument has a psychological basis. In the *Treatise Concerning Religious Affections* he had divided the soul into two faculties: one called the understanding, by which it discerns, views, and judges things; the other called the heart or will, being nothing else but the inclination of the soul towards or the disinclination from what is discerned and judged by the understanding. In the *Freedom of the Will* he starts with Locke's statement that "the Will is perfectly distinguished from Desire, which in the very same action may have a quite contrary tendency from that which our Wills set us upon." This theory Edwards analyses and rejects, and then proceeds to show that a man's desire and will are virtually the same faculty of the soul. It follows from this that the will at any moment is determined by the strongest motive acting upon the soul; we are free in so far as no obstacle is presented to our willing in accordance with our inclination, but our inclination is determined by what at any moment seems to us good. In his attack on the common arguments for the freedom of the will Edwards is magnificently victorious. If the psychology by which the Arminians sought to relieve God of the burden of evil in human life is pushed into a corner, it shows itself as nothing more than this: Man's will is a faculty absolutely indeterminate in itself and entirely independent of his inclinations. When, therefore, a man errs, it is because, the choice between evil with its attendant suffering and good with its attendant happiness being presented to him, the man, having full knowledge of the consequences and being impelled by no momentary preponderance of the one or the other from his innate disposition, deliberately and freely chooses what is evil and painful. Such an account of human action is monstrous, inconceivable; it offered an easy mark for so sharp a logician as Edwards.

But whence arise the conditions by which a man's inclination is swayed in one direction or the other? Edwards carries these unflinchingly up to the first cause,—that is, as a Christian, to God. Berkeley had made the world to consist of ideas evoked in the mind of man by the mind of God; Edwards accepts the logical conclusion, and holds God responsible for the inclination of the human will which depends on these ideas. Calvin did not hesitate to attribute, in the bluntest language, the source of evil to God's will, but at the same time he warned men against intruding with their finite reason into this "sanctuary of the divine wisdom." The mind of Edwards could not rest while any problem seemed to him unsolved. Confronted with the mystery of the divine permission of evil, he undertakes to solve it by applying his psychology of man to the nature of God. (He himself would put it the other way about: "Herein does very much consist that image of God wherein he made man.") The passage in which he develops this thesis, though generally overlooked by his critics, is of the first importance:

We must conceive of Him as influenced in the highest degree, by that which, above all others, is properly a moral inducement, viz., the moral good which He sees in such and such things: and therefore He is, in the most proper sense, a moral Agent, the source of all moral ability and Agency, the fountain and rule of all virtue and moral good; though by reason of his being supreme over all, it is not possible He should be under the influence of law or command, promises or threatenings, rewards or punishments, counsels or warnings. The essential qualities of a moral Agent are in God, in the greatest possible perfection; such as understanding, to perceive the difference between moral good and evil; a capacity of discerning that moral worthiness and demerit, by which some things are praiseworthy, others deserving of blame and punishment; and also a capacity of choice, and choice guided by understanding, and a power of acting according to his choice or pleasure, and being capable of doing those things which are in the highest sense praiseworthy.

In other words, the will of God is precisely like the will of man; it is merely the inclination, or *moral inducement*, to act as he is *influenced* by external power. The fatal mystery of good and evil, the true cause, lies above and beyond him; he is, like ourselves, a channel, not the source. The only difference is that God has complete knowledge of the possibilities of being, and therefore is not moved by threats and blind commands but, immediately, by what Edwards elsewhere calls the "moral necessity" of governing in accordance with the best of the "different objects of choice that are proposed to the Divine Understanding." By such a scheme God is really placed in about such a position as in the Leibnitzian continuation of Laurentius Valla's *Dialogue on Free Will and Providence*, where he is naïvely portrayed as looking upon an infinite variety of worlds piled up, like cannon balls, in pyramidal form before him, and selecting for creation that one which combines the greatest possible amount of good with the least possible admixture of evil.

From this pretty sport of the imagination Edwards would no doubt have drawn back in contempt, and indeed in his ordinary language God is merely the supreme Cause, without further speculation. One of the Leibnitzian inferences, moreover, is utterly excluded from his philosophy. He was no optimist, was in fact the last man to infer that, because this world is the best possible conceivable, evil is therefore a small and virtually negligible part of existence. On the contrary the whole animus of his teaching springs from a deep and immediate hatred of evil in itself and apart from any consideration of its cause.

"The thing," he says, "which makes sin hateful, is that by which it deserves punishment; which is but the expression of hatred. . . . Thus, for instance, ingratitude is hateful and worthy of dispraise, according to common sense; not because something as bad, or worse than ingratitude, was the cause that produced it; but because it is hateful in itself, by its own inherent deformity."

To the charge of the Arminians that the doctrine of predestination leaves no place for the punishment of sin, this is an adequate and practical reply. But the consequences of this principle of common sense are, in another way, peculiar and even disastrous to the Edwardian theology. If we are right, as we indubitably are right, in detesting evil in itself and wherever seen, and if we hold with Edwards that the will of God, like the will of man, is merely the inclination towards the best object presented to its choice, and there is no power either in God or in man above the will, in what essential way, then, does the act of God in creating a world mixed with evil differ from the act of Judas in betraying God, and how are we relieved from hating God for the evil of his work with the same sort of hatred as that which we feel for Judas? Edwards had terrified the people of Enfield with a picture of God treading down sinners till their blood sprinkled his raiment, and exulting in his wrath. The retort is obvious, and unspeakable. Nor can he, or any other Predestinarian, escape the odium of such a retort by hiding behind the necessity of things which all men must, in one way or another, admit. There is a war between the nations, he will say, and suddenly a bomb, dropping upon a group of soldiers, themselves innocent of any crime, horribly rends and mangles them. Here is a hideous thing, and by no twisting of the reason can we avoid carrying the responsibility for this evil back to the first great cause of all. Shall we be held impious for saying metaphorically that the blood of these soldiers is sprinkled on the raiment of that

Cause?—Aye, but the difference to us morally if we leave that cause in its own vast obscurity, unapproached by our reason, untouched by our pride; or if we make it into an image of ourselves, composed only of understanding and inclination like our own, and subject to our reprobation as surely as to our love!

Edwards had riddled and forever destroyed the arguments for free will commonly employed by the Arminians; is there no alternative for the human reason save submission to his theological determinism or to fatalistic atheism?

One way of escape from that dilemma is obvious and well known. It is that which Dr. Johnson, with his superb faculty of common sense, seized upon when the Edwardian doctrine came up in conversation before him. "The only relief I had was to forget it," said Boswell, who had read the book; and Johnson closed the discussion with his epigram: "All theory is against the freedom of the will, all experience for it." That is sufficient, no doubt, for the conduct of life; yet there is perhaps another way of escape, which, if it does not entirely silence the metaphysical difficulties, at least gives them a new ethical turn. Twice in the course of his argument Edwards refers to an unnamed Arminian[1] who placed the liberty of the soul not in the will itself, but in some power of suspending volition until due time has elapsed for judging properly the various motives to action. His reply is that this suspension of activity, being itself an act of volition, merely throws back without annulling the difficulty; and as the argument came to him, this refutation is fairly complete. But a fuller consideration of the point at issue might possibly indicate a way out of the dilemma of free will and determinism into a morally satisfying form of dualism within the soul of man himself. At least it can be said that the looseness of the Arminian reasoning leaves an easier loophole of escape into a human philosophy than does the rigid logic of the Predestinarians.

Yet for all that, though we may follow Edwards's logical system to the breaking point, as we can follow every meta-

---

[1] Edwards, it should seem, had immediately in mind the *Essay on the Freedom of Will in God and the Creature* of Isaac Watts; but the notion had been discussed at length by Locke (*Essay* II, xxi), and at an earlier date had been touched on with great acumen by John Norris in his correspondence with Henry More.

physical system, and though we may feel that, in his revulsion from the optimism of the deists, he distorted the actual evil of existence into a nightmare of the imagination,—yet for all that, he remains one of the giants of the intellect and one of the enduring masters of religious emotion. He had not the legal and executive brain of Calvin, upon whose *Institutes* his scheme of theology is manifestly based, but in subtle resourcefulness of reasoning and still more in the scope of his spiritual psychology he stands above his predecessor. Few men have studied Edwards without recognizing the force and honesty of his genius.

2. Franklin

IN a respectful and indeed laudatory notice of Franklin for
The Edinburgh Review of July, 1806, Lord Jeffrey employed
the case of the "uneducated tradesman of America" to support his contention that "regular education is unfavourable to
vigour or originality of understanding." Franklin attained his
eminence, so runs the argument, without academical instruction, with only casual reading, without the benefit of association with men of letters, and "in a society where there was no
relish and no encouragement for literature." This statement
of Franklin's educational opportunities is manifestly inadequate;
but it so pleasantly flatters our long-standing pride in our self-
made men that we are loath to challenge it. The hero presented to the schoolboy and preserved in popular tradition
is still an "uneducated tradesman of America": a runaway
Boston printer walking up Market Street in Philadelphia
with his three puffy rolls; directing his fellow shopkeepers the
way to wealth; sharply inquiring of extravagant neighbours
whether they have not paid too much for their whistle; flying
his kite in a thunderstorm; by a happy combination of curiosity
and luck making important contributions to science; and, to
add the last lustre to his name, by a happy combination of
industry and frugality making his fortune. This picturesque
and racy figure is obviously a product of provincial America,
the first great Yankee with all the strong lineaments of the
type: hardness, shrewdness, ingenuity, practical sense, frugality,
industry, self-reliance. The conception of the man here
suggested is perhaps sound enough so far as it goes, being derived mainly from facts supplied by Franklin himself in the
one book through which he has secured an eternal life in litera-

16

ture. But the popular notion of his personality thus derived is incomplete, because the *Autobiography*, ending at the year 1757, contains no record of the thirty-three years which developed a competent provincial into an able, cultivated, and imposing man of the world.

The Franklin now discoverable in the ten volumes of his complete works is one of the most widely and thoroughly cultivated men of his age. He had not, to be sure, a university training, but he had what serves quite as well: sharp appetite and large capacity for learning, abundance of books, extensive travel, important participation in great events, and association through a long term of years with the most eminent men of three nations. In touch as printer and publisher with the classic and current literature produced at home and imported from abroad, he becomes in Philadelphia almost as good a "Queen Anne's man" as Swift or Defoe. His scientific investigations bring him into correspondence with fellow-workers in England, France, Germany, Italy, Holland, and Spain. Entering upon public life, he is forced into co-operation or conflict with the leading politicians, diplomats, and statesmen of Europe. In his native land he has known men like Cotton Mather, White-field, Benjamin Rush, Benjamin West, Ezra Stiles, Noah Webster, Jay, Adams, Jefferson, and Washington. In England, where his affections strike such deep root that he considers establishing there his permanent abode, he is in relationship, more or less intimate, with Mandeville, Paine, Priestley, Price, Adam Smith, Robertson, Hume, Joseph Banks, Bishop Watson, Bishop Shipley, Lord Kames, Lord Shelburne, Lord Howe, Burke, and Chatham. Among Frenchmen he numbers on his list of admiring friends Vergennes, Lafayette, Mirabeau, Turgot, Quesnay, La Rochefoucauld-Liancourt, Condorcet, Lavoisier, Buffon, D'Alembert, Robespierre, and Voltaire. It is absurd to speak of one who has been subjected to the moulding of such forces as a product of the provinces. All Europe has wrought upon and metamorphosed the Yankee printer. The man whom Voltaire kisses is a statesman, a philosopher, a friend of mankind, and a favourite son of the eighteenth century. With no softening of his patriotic fibre or loss of his Yankee tang, he has acquired all the common culture and most of the master characteristics of the Age of Enlightenment—up to the point where the French Revolution injected into it a drop of madness: its emancipation from authority, its regard for reason and nature, its social consciousness, its progressiveness, its tolerance, its cosmopolitanism, and its bland philanthropy. Now this man deserves his large place in our literary history not so much by virtue of his writings, which had little immediate influence upon *belles-lettres*, as by virtue of his acts and ideas, which helped liberate and liberalize America. To describe his most important work is to recite the story of his life.

In reviewing his own career Franklin does not dwell on the fact that he who was to stand before kings had emerged from a tallow chandler's shop. To his retrospective eye there was nothing miraculous nor inexplicable in his origin. On the contrary he saw and indicated very clearly the sources of his talents and the external impulses that gave them direction. Born in Boston on 6 January, 1706, he inherited from his long-lived parents, Josiah and Abiah Folger Franklin, a rugged physical and mental constitution which hardly faltered through the hard usage of eighty-four years. He recognized and profited by his father's skill in drawing and music, his "mechanical genius," his "understanding and solid judgment in prudential matters, both in private and publick affairs," his admirable custom of having at his table, "as often as he could, some sensible friend or neighbour to converse with," always taking care "to start some ingenious or useful topic for discourse, which might tend to improve the minds of his children." Benjamin's formal schooling was begun when he was eight years old and abandoned, together with the design of making him a clergyman, when he was ten. He significantly remarks, however, that he does not remember a time when he could not read; and the subsequent owner of one of the best private libraries in America was as a mere child an eager collector of books. For the two years following his removal from school he was employed in his father's business. When he expressed a firm disinclination to become a tallow chandler, his father attempted to discover his natural bent by taking him about to see various artisans at their work. Everything that Franklin touched taught him something; and everything that he learned, he used. Though his tour of the trades failed to win him to any mechanical occupation,

it has ever since been a pleasure to me [he says] to see good workmen handle their tools; and it has been useful to me, having learnt
so much by it as to be able to do little odd jobs myself in my
house . . . and to construct little machines for my experiments,
while the intention of making the experiment was fresh and warm
in my mind.

Throughout his boyhood and youth he apparently devoured
every book that he could lay hands upon. He went through
his father's shelves of "polemic divinity"; read abundantly in
Plutarch's *Lives;* acquired Bunyan's works "in separate little
volumes," which he later sold to buy Burton's *Historical
Collections;* received an impetus towards practical improvements from Defoe's *Essay upon Projects* and an impetus
towards virtue from Mather's *Essays to do Good.* Before he
left Boston he had his mind opened to free speculation and
equipped for logical reasoning by Locke's *Essay Concerning
Human Understanding*, the Port Royal *Art of Thinking*,
Xenophon's *Memorabilia*, and the works of Shaftesbury and
Collins.

Franklin found the right avenue for a person of his "bookish
inclination" when his brother James, returning from England
in 1717 with a press and letters, set up in Boston as a printer,
and proceeded to the publication of *The Boston Gazette*, 1719,
and *The New England Courant*, 1721. Benjamin, aged twelve,
became his apprentice. It can hardly be too much emphasized
that this was really an inspiring "job." It made him stand
at a very early age full in the wind of local political and theological controversy. It forced him to use all his childish stock
of learning and daily stimulated him to new acquisitions. It
put him in touch with other persons, young and old, of
bookish inclination. They lent him books which kindled his
poetic fancy to the pitch of composing occasional ballads
in the Grub Street style, which his brother printed, and had
him hawk about town. His father discountenanced these
effusions, declaring that "verse-makers were generally beggars"; but coming upon his son's private experiments in
prose, he applied the right incentive by pointing out where the
work "fell short in elegance of expression, in method, and in
perspicuity." "About this time," says Franklin in a familiar
paragraph, "I met with an odd volume of the *Spectator*."

Anticipating Dr. Johnson's advice by half a century, he gave his days and nights to painstaking study and imitation of Addison till he had mastered that style—"familiar but not coarse, and elegant but not ostentatious"—which several generations of English essayists have sought to attain. All the world has heard how Franklin's career as a writer began with an anonymous contribution stealthily slipped under the door of his brother's printing-house at night, and in the morning approved for publication by his brother's circle of "writing friends." Professor Smyth[1] inclined to identify this contribution with the first of fourteen humorous papers with Latin mottoes signed "Silence Dogood," which appeared fortnightly in *The New England Courant* from March to October, 1722. In this year Benjamin was in charge of the *Courant* during his brother's imprisonment for printing matter offensive to the Assembly; and when, on repetition of the offence, the master was forbidden to publish his journal, it was continued in the name of the apprentice. In this situation James became jealous and overbearing, and Benjamin became insubordinate. When it grew evident that there was not room enough in Boston for them both, the younger brother left his indentures behind, and in 1723 made his memorable flight to Philadelphia.

Shortly after his arrival in the Quaker city, he found employment with the second printer in Philadelphia, Samuel Keimer, a curious person who kept the Mosaic law. In 1724, encouraged by the facile promises of Governor Keith, Franklin went to England in the expectation that letters of credit and recommendation from his patron would enable him to procure a printing outfit. Left in the lurch by the governor, he served for something over a year in two great London printing-houses, kept free-thinking and rather loose company, and, in refutation of Wollaston's *Religion of Nature*, upon which he happened to be engaged in the composing-room, published in 1725 his suppressed tract *On Liberty and Necessity*. Returning to Philadelphia in 1726, he re-entered the employ of Keimer; in

---

[1] *The Writings of Benjamin Franklin.* Collected and edited by Albert Henry Smyth. New York, 1907. Vol. II, p. 1. The Dogood Papers were claimed by Franklin in the first draft of his *Autobiography*, and they have been long accredited to him; but they were first included in his collected works by Professor Smyth.

1728 formed a brief partnership with Hugh Meredith; and in 1730 married and set up for himself. In 1728 he founded the famous Junto Club for reading, debating, and reforming the world—an institution which developed into a powerful organ of political influence. Shortage of money in the province prompted him to the composition of his *Modest Inquiry into the Nature and Necessity of Paper Currency* (1729), a service for which his friends in the Assembly rewarded him by employing him to print the money—"a very profitable job and a great help to me." Forestalled by Keimer in a project for launching a newspaper, Franklin contributed in 1728–9 to the rival journal, published by Bradford, a series of sprightly "Busy-Body" papers in the vein of the periodical essayists. Keimer was forced to sell out; and Franklin acquired from him the paper known from 2 October, 1729, as *The Pennsylvania Gazette*. To this he contributed, besides much miscellaneous matter, such pieces as the *Dialogue between Philocles and Horatio concerning Virtue and Pleasure*, the letters of "Anthony Afterwit" and "Alice Addertongue," *A Meditation on a Quart Mug*, and *A Witch Trial at Mount Holly*. In 1732 he began to issue the almanacs containing the wit and wisdom of "Poor Richard," a homely popular philosopher, who is only the incarnation of common sense, and who is consequently not, as has been carelessly assumed, to be identified with his creator.

By the time he was thirty Franklin gave promise of becoming, by a gradual expansion of his useful activities, the leading Pennsylvanian. In 1736 he was chosen clerk of the General Assembly, and in the following year was appointed postmaster of Philadelphia. He made both these offices useful to his printing business and to his newspaper. In compensation, he used his newspaper and his business influence to support his measures for municipal improvements, among the objects of which may be mentioned street-sweeping, paving, a regular police force, a fire company, a hospital, and a public library. As his business prospered, he expanded it by forming partnerships with his promising workmen and sending them with printing-presses into other colonies. In 1741 he experimented with a monthly publication, *The General Magazine and Historical Chronicle for all the British Colonies in America;* this monthly. notable as the second issued in America, expired with the sixth number. In 1742 he invented the stove of which he published a description in 1744 as *An Account of the New Invented Pennsylvanian Fire Places*. In 1743 he drew up proposals for an academy which eventually became the University of Pennsylvania, and in 1744 he founded the American Philosophical Society. In 1746 he witnessed Spence's electrical experiments in Boston, bought the apparatus, and repeated the experiments in Philadelphia, where interest in the new science was further stimulated that year by a present of a Leyden jar given to the Library Company by the English experimenter Peter Collinson. To this English friend Franklin made extended reports of his earlier electrical investigations in the form of letters which Collinson published in London in 1751 with the title *Experiments and Observations in Electricity, made at Philadelphia in America, by Mr. Benjamin Franklin*. In 1752 he showed the identity of lightning and electricity by his kite experiment, and invented the lightning rod. In 1748, being assured of a competency, he had turned over his business to his foreman David Hall, and purposed devoting the rest of his life to philosophical inquiries. But he had inextricably involved himself in the affairs of his community, which, as soon as it found him at leisure, "laid hold" of him, as he says, for its own purposes—"every part of the civil government, and almost at the same time, imposing some duty upon me." He was made a justice of the peace, member of the common council, and alderman, and was chosen burgess to represent the city of Philadelphia in the General Assembly. In 1753 he was appointed jointly with William Hunter to exercise the office of postmaster-general of America. In 1754 as a member of the Pennsylvania commission he laid before the colonial congress at Albany the "Plan of Union" adopted by the commissioners. In 1755 he displayed remarkable energy, ability, and public spirit in providing transportation for General Braddock's ill-fated expedition against the French; and in the following year he himself took command of a volunteer military organization for the protection of the north-west frontier. In 1757 he was sent to England to present the long-standing grievances of the Pennsylvania Assembly against the proprietors for obstructing legislation designed to throw upon them a fair share of the expense of government.

Though Franklin's political mission was not wholly successful, his residence in England from 1757 to 1762 was highly profitable to him. It developed his talent as a negotiator of public business with strangers; it enabled him to consider British colonial policies from English points of view; and it afforded him many opportunities for general self-improvement. After a fruitless effort to obtain satisfaction from the representatives of the Penn family, dismissing as impractical the hope of procuring for Pennsylvania a royal charter, he appealed to the Crown to exempt the Assembly from the influence of proprietary instructions and to make the proprietary estates bear a more equitable proportion of the taxes. To get the Assembly's case before the public, he collaborated with an unknown hand on *An Historical Review of the Constitution and Government of Pennsylvania*, published in 1759. The result was a compromise which in the circumstances he regarded as a victory. His interest in the wider questions of imperial policy he exhibited in 1760 by aspersing the advocates of a hasty and inconclusive peace with France in his stinging little skit, *Of the Meanes of disposing the Enemies to Peace*,[1] which he presented as an extract from the work of a Jesuit historian. In 1760, also, he was joint author with Richard Jackson of a notably influential argument for the retention of Canada, *The Interest of Great Britain Considered with Regard to Her Colonies;* to which was appended his *Observations Concerning the Increase of Mankind, Peopling of Countries*, etc. In the intervals of business, he sat for his portrait, attended the theatre, played upon the armonica, experimented with electricity and heat, made a tour of the Low Countries, visited the principal cities of England and Scotland, received honorary degrees from the universities, and enjoyed the society of Collinson, Priestley, Price, Hume, Adam Smith, Robertson, and Kames. He returned to America in the latter part of 1762. In 1763 he made a 1600-mile tour of the northern provinces to inspect the postoffices. In the following year he was again in the thick of Pennsylvania politics, working with the party in the Assembly which sought to have the proprietary government of the province replaced by a royal charter. In support of this movement he published in 1764 his *Cool Thoughts*

---

[1] See *Writings*, ed. Smyth, Vol. IV, pp. 89–95.

on the Present Situation of our Public Affairs and his *Preface to the Speech of Joseph Galloway*, a brilliant and blasting indictment of the proprietors, Thomas and Richard Penn.

In the fall of 1764 Franklin was sent again to England by the Assembly to petition for a royal charter and to express the Assembly's views with regard to Grenville's Stamp Act, then impending. On 11 July, 1765, after the obnoxious measure had been passed by an overwhelming majority, Franklin wrote to Charles Thomson:

Depend upon it, my good neighbour, I took every step in my power to prevent the passing of the Stamp Act. . . . But the Tide was too strong against us. The nation was provoked by American Claims of Independence, and all Parties joined in resolving by this act to settle the point. We might as well have hindered the sun's setting.

This letter and one or two others of about the same date express a patient submission to the inevitable. As soon, however, as Franklin was fully apprised of the fierce flame of opposition which the passage of the act had kindled in the colonies, he caught the spirit of his constituents and threw himself sternly into the struggle for its repeal. In 1766 he underwent his famous examination before the House of Commons on the attitude of the colonies towards the collection of the new taxes. The report of this examination, which was promptly published, is one of the most interesting and impressive pieces of dramatic dialogue produced in the eighteenth century. After the repeal, Franklin received recognition at home in the shape of new duties: in 1768 he was appointed agent for Georgia; in 1769, for New Jersey; in 1770, for Massachusetts. In the summer of 1766 he visited Germany; the following summer he visited Paris; and he was in France again for a month in 1769. His pen in these years was employed mainly in correspondence and in communications to the newspapers, in which he pointedly set forth the causes which threatened a permanent breach between the mother country and the colonies. In 1773 he published in *The Gentleman's Magazine* two little masterpieces of irony which Swift might have been pleased to sign: *An Edict by the King of Prussia* and *Rules by which a Great Empire may be Reduced to a Small*

One. In 1774, in consequence of his activity in exposing Governor Hutchinson's proposals for the military intimidation of Massachusetts, Franklin was subjected before the Privy Council to virulent and scurrilous abuse from Attorney-General Wedderburn. This onslaught it was, accentuated by his dismissal from the office of postmaster-general, which began to curdle in Franklin his sincere long-cherished hope of an ultimate reconciliation. It is a curiously ominous coincidence that in this year of his great humiliation he sent with a letter of recommendation to his son-in-law in Philadelphia one Thomas Paine, an obscure Englishman of whiggish temper, two years later to become the fieriest advocate of American independence. In disgrace with the Court, Franklin lingered in England to exhaust the last possibilities of amicable adjustment: petitioning the king, conferring with Burke and Chatham, and curiously arranging for secret negotiations with the go-betweens of the Ministry over the chessboard of Lord Howe's sister. He sailed from England in March, 1775, half-convinced that the Ministry were bent upon provoking an open rebellion. When he arrived in Philadelphia, he heard what had happened at Lexington and Concord. On 5 July, 1775, he wrote a letter to an English friend of thirty years' standing, William Strahan, then a member of Parliament; it was shortened like a Roman sword and sharpened to this point:

You and I were long Friends:—You are now my Enemy,—and I am
> Yours,
>> B. FRANKLIN.

As Franklin was sixty-nine years old in 1775, he might fairly have retreated to his library, and have left the burden of the future state to younger hands. He had hardly set foot on shore, however, before the Pennsylvania Assembly elected him delegate to the first Continental Congress, where his tried sagacity was enlisted in organizing the country's political, economic, and military resources for the great conflict. On 7 July, 1775, the old man wrote to Priestley:

My time was never more fully employed. In the morning at six, I am at the Committee of Safety, appointed by the Assembly to put the province in a state of defence; which committee holds till near nine, when I am at the Congress, and that sits till after four in the afternoon.

In the period slightly exceeding a year previous to his departure for France, he served on innumerable committees of the Congress, was made Postmaster-General of the colonies, presided over the Constitutional Convention of Pennsylvania, was sent on a mission to Canada, assisted in drafting the Declaration of Independence, and signed it.

In October, 1776, he sailed for France on a commission of the Congress to negotiate a treaty of alliance, which was concluded in February, 1778, after the surrender of Burgoyne had inspired confidence in the prospects of the American arms. In September, 1778, he was appointed plenipotentiary to the Court of France. Clothed with large powers, he transacted in the next few years an almost incredible amount of difficult business for his country. He obtained from the French government the repeated loans which made possible the carrying on of a long war; he made contracts for clothing and ammunition; he dissuaded or recommended to Congress foreign applicants for commissions in the colonial army; he arranged exchanges of prisoners-of-war; he equipped and to some extent directed the operations of privateers; he supplied information to many Europeans emigrating to America; he negotiated treaties of amity and commerce with Sweden and Prussia. With all this engrossing business on his hands, he found time to achieve an immense personal popularity. He was not merely respected as a masterly diplomat; he was lionized and idolized as the great natural philosopher, the august champion of liberty, and the friend of humanity. In the press of public affairs, never losing interest in scientific matters, he served on a royal French commission to investigate Mesmerism; sent to his foreign correspondents ingenious geological and meteorological conjectures; and transmitted to the Royal Society reports on French experiments in aeronautics. He entertained with a certain lavishness at his house in Passy; and he was a frequent diner-out, adored for his wit and good humour in the intimate coteries of Mme. Helvetius and Mme. Brillon. He set up for the amusement of himself and his friends a private press in Passy, on which he printed a number of *bagatelles* of an accomplished and charming levity: *The Ephemera* (1778), *The Morals of Chess* (1779), *The Whistle* (1779), *The Dialogue between Franklin and the Gout* (1780.) In 1784 he resumed work on his unfinished autobiography, and published *Advice to such as would remove to America* and *Remarks Concerning the Savages of North America*. In his residence in France he began seriously to feel the siege of gout, the stone, and old age. In 1781, in reply to repeated supplications for leave to go home and die, Congress had appointed him a member of the commission to negotiate a treaty of peace between England and the United States. This last great task was completed in 1785. In midsummer of that year he said a regretful farewell to his affectionate French friends, received the king's portrait set in four hundred diamonds, and in one of the royal litters was carried down to his point of embarkation at Havre de Grace.

Franklin arrived in Philadelphia in September, 1785, resolved to set his house in order. He was soon made aware that, like the hero in *The Conquest of Granada*, he had not "leisure yet to die." He was overwhelmed with congratulations; or, as he put it with characteristic modesty of phrase in a letter to his English friend Mrs. Hewson: "I had the happiness of finding my family well, and of being very kindly received by my Country folk." In the month after his arrival he was elected President of the State of Pennsylvania; and the honour was thrust upon him again in 1786 and in 1787. In a letter of 14 November, 1785, he says:

I had not firmness enough to resist the unanimous desire of my country folks; and I find myself harnessed again in their service for another year. They engrossed the prime of my life. They have eaten my flesh, and seem resolved now to pick my bones.

In 1787 he was chosen a delegate to the convention to frame the Constitution of the United States—an instrument which he deemed not perfect, yet as near perfection as the joint wisdom of any numerous body of men could bring it, handicapped by "their prejudices, their passions, their local interests, and their selfish views." In 1789, as President of the Abolition Society, Franklin signed a memorial against slavery which was laid before the House of Representatives; and on 23 March, 1790, less than a month before his death, he wrote for *The Federal Gazette* an ironical justification of the enslaving of Christians by African Mohammedans—quite in the vein of the celebrated *Edict of the King of Prussia*. As the shadows thickened about him, he settled his estate, paid his compliments to his friends, and departed, on the seventeenth day of April, 1790, in his eighty-fifth year.

In the matter of religion Franklin was distinctly a product of the eighteenth-century enlightenment. He took his direction in boyhood and early manhood from deistical writers like Pope, Collins, and Shaftesbury. At various periods of his life he drew up articles of belief, which generally included recognition of one God, the providential government of the world, the immortality of the soul, and divine justice. To profess faith in as much religion as this he found emotionally gratifying, socially expedient, and conformable to the common sense of mankind. He would have subscribed without hesitation to both the positive and negative dogmas of the *religion civile* formulated by Rousseau in the *Contrat Social*. In his later years he was in sympathetic relations with Paine, Price, and Priestley. He was, however, of a fortunately earlier generation than these English "heretics," and certain other circumstances enabled him to keep the temper of his heterodoxy sweet while theirs grew acidulous, and to walk serenely in ways which for them were embittered by the *odium theologicum*. His earlier advent upon the eighteenth-century scene made possible the unfolding and comfortable settlement of his religious ideas before deism had clearly allied itself with political radicalism and edged its sword for assault upon inspired Bible and established church as powers federate with political orthodoxy in upholding the ancient régime. Among the diverse denominational bodies in Pennsylvania his perfectly genuine tolerance and his unfailing tact helped him to maintain a friendly neutrality between parties which were far from friendly. Like Lord Chesterfield, he sincerely believed in the decency and propriety of going to church; and he went himself when he could endure the preachers. He advised his daughter to go constantly, "whoever preaches." He made pecuniary contributions to all the leading denominations in Philadelphia; respectfully acknowledged the good features of each; and undertook to unite in his own creed the common and, as he thought, the essential features of all. Man of the world as he was, he enjoyed the warm friendship of good Quakers, good Presbyterians, Whitefield, the Bishop of St. Asaph, and his French abbés. His abstention from theological controversy was doubtless due in part to a shrewd regard for his own interest and influence as a business man and a public servant; but it was due in perhaps equal measure to his profound indifference to metaphysical questions unrelated to practical conduct. "Emancipated" in childhood and unmolested in the independence of his mind, he reached maturity without that acrimony of free thought incident to those who attain independence late and have revenges to take. He was consistently opposed to the imposition of religious tests by constitutional authority. But in the Constitutional Convention of 1787 he offered a motion in favour of holding daily prayers before the deliberations of the assembly, for, as he declared, "the longer I live, the more convincing proofs I see of this Truth, *that* God *governs in the Affairs of Men.*" With his progress in eminence and years, he seems to have been somewhat strengthened in Cicero's conviction that so puissant a personality as his own could not utterly perish, and he derived a kind of classical satisfaction from the reflection that this feeling was in concurrence with the common opinions of mankind. A few weeks before his death he admitted, in a remarkable letter to Ezra Stiles, a doubt as to the divinity of Jesus; but he remarked with his characteristic tranquillity that he thought it "needless to busy myself with it now, when I expect soon an Opportunity of knowing the Truth with less Trouble." Not elate, like Emerson, yet quite unawed, this imitator of Jesus and Socrates walked in this world and prepared for his ease in Zion.

Franklin set himself in youth to the study of "moral perfection," and the work which only great public business prevented his leaving as his literary monument was to have been a treatise on the "art of virtue." His merits, however, in both the theory and practice of the moral life have been seriously called in question. It is alleged that his standards were low and that he did not live up to them. It must be conceded on the one hand that he had a natural son who became governor of New Jersey, and on the other hand that industry and frugality, which most of us place among the minor, he placed among the major virtues. When one has referred the *"errata"* of his adolescence to animal spirits, "free thinking," and bad company; and when one has explained certain laxities of his maturity by alluding to the indulgent temper of the French society in which he then lived; one may as well candidly admit that St. Francis made chastity a more conspicuous jewel in his crown of virtues than did Dr. Franklin. And when one has pointed out that the prudential philosophy of *Poor Richard's Almanac* was rather a collection of popular wisdom than an original contribution; and when one has called attention to the special reasons for magnifying economic virtues in a community of impecunious colonists and pioneers; one may as well frankly acknowledge that there is nothing in the precepts of the great printer to shake a man's egotism like the shattering paradoxes of the Beatitudes nor like the *Christian Morals* of Sir Thomas Browne to make his heart elate. Franklin had nothing of what pietists call a "realizing sense" of sin or of the need for mystical regeneration and justification—faculties so richly present in his contemporary Jonathan Edwards. His cool calculating reason, having surveyed the fiery battleground of the Puritan conscience, reported that things are properly forbidden because hurtful, not hurtful because forbidden. Guided by this utilitarian principle, he simplified his religion and elaborated his morality. His system included much more than maxims of thrift and prudent self-regard, and to insinuate that he set up wealth as the *summum bonum* is a sheer libel. He commended diligence in business as the means to a competency; he commended a competency as a safeguard to virtue; and he commended virtue as the prerequisite to happiness. The temple that he reared to Moral Perfection was built of thirteen stones: temperance, silence, order, resolution, frugality, industry, sincerity, justice, moderation, cleanliness, tranquillity, chastity, and humility—the last added on the advice of a Quaker. He wrought upon the structure with the method of a monk and he recorded his progress with the regularity of a bookkeeper. The presiding spirit in the edifice, which made it something more than a private oratory, was a rational and active benevolence towards his fellow-mortals in every quarter of the earth. The wide-reaching friendliness in Franklin may be distinguished in two ways from the roseate humanitarian enthusiasm in the Savoyard Vicar. It was not begotten by a theory of "natural goodness" nor fostered by millennial expectations, but was born of sober experience with the utility of good will in establishing satisfactory and fruitful relations among men. It found expression not in rhetorical periods but in numberless practical means and measures for ameliorating the human lot. By no mystical intuition but by the common light of reason the "prudential philosopher" discovered and acted upon the truth that the greatest happiness that can come to a man in this world is to devote the full strength of body and mind to the service of his fellow-men. Judged either by his principles or by his performance, Franklin's moral breadth and moral elevation have been absurdly underestimated.

It is perhaps in the field of politics that Franklin exhibits the most marked development of his power and his vision. A realistic inductive thinker, well versed in the rudiments of his subject long before the revolutionary theorists handled it, he was not rendered by any preconception of abstract rights indocile to the lessons of his immense political experience. He formulated his conceptions in the thick of existing conditions, and always with reference to what was expedient and possible as well as to what was desirable. He served his apprenticeship in the Philadelphia Junto Club, which at its inception was little more than a village improvement society, but which threw out branches till it became a power in the province, and a considerable factor in the affairs of the colonies. In this association he learned the importance of co-operation, mastered the tactics of organization, practised the art of getting propaganda afoot, and discovered the great secret of converting private desires into public demands. In proposing in 1754 his plan for a union of the colonies he was applying to larger units the principle of co-operative action by which he had built up what we might call to-day his "machine" in Pennsylvania. Writers like Milton and Algernon Sidney had reenforced his natural inclination towards liberal forms of government. But he had in too large measure the instincts and the ideas of a leader, and he had too much experience with the conflicting prejudices and the resultant compromises of popular assemblies, to feel any profound reverence for the "collective wisdom" of the people. "If all officers appointed by governors were always men of merit," he wrote in his *Dialogue Concerning the Present State of Affairs in Pennsylvania*, "it would be wrong ever to hazard a popular election." That his belief in popular representation was due as much to his sense of its political expediency as to his sense of its political justice is suggested by a passage in his letter on the imposition of direct taxes addressed to Governor Shirley, 18 December, 1754: "In matters of general concern to the people, and especially where burthens are to be laid upon them, it is of use to consider, as well what they will be apt to think and say, as what they ought to think." His sojourn in England widened his horizons, but not beyond the bounds of his nationality. As agent, he felt himself essentially a colonial Englishman pleading for the extension of English laws to British subjects across the sea, and playing up to the Imperial policy of crushing out the colonizing and commercial rivalry of France. The ultimate failure of his mission of reconciliation effected no sudden transformation of his political ideas; it rather overwhelmed him with disgust at the folly, the obstinacy, and the corruption rampant among English politicians of the period. He returned to the arms of the people because he had been hurled from the arms of the king; and he embraced their new principles because he was sure that they could not be worse applied than his old ones. His respect for the popular will was inevitably heightened by his share in executing it in the thrilling days when he was helping his fellow-countrymen to declare their independence, and was earning the superb epigraph of Turgot: *Eripuit fulmen coelo, sceptrumque tyrannis.* His official residence in France completely dissolved his former antagonism to that country. In the early stages of the conflict his wrath was bitter enough towards England, but long before it was over he had taken the ground of radical pacificism, reiterating his conviction that "there is no good war and no bad peace." He who had financed the Revolution had seen too much non-productive expenditure of moral and physical capital to believe in the appeal to arms. If nations required enlargement of their territories, it was a mere matter of arithmetic, he contended, to show that the cheapest way was purchase. "Justice," he declared, "is as strictly due between neighbour Nations as between neighbour Citizens, . . . and a Nation that makes an unjust War, is only a *great Gang*." So far as he was able, he mitigated the afflictions of noncombatants. He proposed by international law to exempt from peril fishermen and farmers and the productive workers of the world. He ordered the privateersmen under his control to safeguard the lives and property of explorers and men of science belonging to the enemy country; and he advocated for the future the abolition of the custom of commissioning privateers. In the treaty which he negotiated with Prussia he actually obtained the incorporation of an article so restricting the "zone of war" as to make a war between Prussia and the United States under its terms virtually impossible. His diplomatic intercourse in Europe and his association with the Physiocrats had opened his eyes to the common interests of all pacific peoples and to the inestimable advantages of a general amity among the nations. His ultimate political ideal included nothing short of the welfare and the commercial federation of the world. To that extent he was a believer in "majority interests." It may be further said that his political development was marked by a growing mastery of the art of dealing with men and by a steady approximation of his political to his personal morality.

For the broad humanity of Franklin's political conceptions undoubtedly his interest in the extension of science was partly responsible. As a scientific investigator he had long been a citizen of the world; and for him not the least bitter consequence of the war was that it made a break in the intellectual brotherhood of man. If he had not been obliged to supply the army of Washington with guns and ammunition, he might have been engaged in the far more congenial task of supplying the British Academy with food for philosophical discussion. He could not but resent the brutal antagonisms which had rendered intellectual co-operation with his English friends impossible, and which had frustrated his cherished hope of devoting his ripest years to philosophical researches. A natural endowment he certainly possessed which would have qualified him in happier circumstances for even more distinguished service than he actually performed in extending the frontiers of knowledge. He had the powerfully developed curiosity of the explorer and the inventor, ever busily prying into the causes of things, ever speculating upon the consequences of novel combinations. His native inquisitiveness had been stimulated by a young civilization's manifold necessities, mothering manifold inventions, and had been supplemented by a certain moral and idealizing passion for improvement. The practical nature of many of his devices, his interest in agriculture and navigation, his preoccupation with stoves and chimneys, the image of him firing the gas of ditch water or pouring oil on troubled waves, and the celebrity of the kite incident, rather tend to fix an impression that he was but a tactful empiricist and a lucky dilettante of discovery. It is interesting in this connection to note that he confesses his lack of patience for verification. His prime scientific faculty, as he himself felt, was the imagination which bodies forth the shapes and relations of things unknown—which constructs the theory and the hypothesis. His mind was a teeming warren of hints and suggestions. He loved rather to start than to pursue the hare. Happily what he deemed his excessive penchant for forming hypotheses was safeguarded by his perfect readiness to hear all that could be urged against them. He wished not his view but truth to prevail—which explains the winsome cordiality of his demeanour towards other savants. His unflagging correspondence with investigators, his subscription to learned publications, his active membership in philosophical societies, and his enterprise in founding schools and academies all betoken his prescience of the wide domain which science had to conquer and of the necessity for co-operation in the task of subduing it. Franklin was so far a Baconian that he sought to avoid unfruitful speculation and to unite contemplation and action in a stricter embrace for the generation of knowledge useful to man. But in refutation of any charge that he was a narrowminded utilitarian and lacked the liberal views and long faith of the modern scientific spirit may be adduced his stunning retort to a query as to the usefulness of the balloons then on trial in France: "What is the use of a new-born baby?"

Of Franklin's style the highest praise is to declare that it reveals the mental and moral qualities of the man himself. It is the flexible style of a writer who has learned the craft of expression by studying and imitating the virtues of many

masters: the playful charm of Addison, the trenchancy of
Swift, the concreteness of Defoe, the urbanity of Shaftesbury,
the homely directness of Bunyan's dialogue, the unadorned
vigour of Tillotson, and the epigrammatic force of Pope. His
mature manner, however, is imitative of nothing but the
thoroughly disciplined movement of a versatile mind which
has never known a moment of languor or a moment of un-
controllable excitement. Next to his omnipresent vitality,
his most notable characteristic is the clearness which results
from a complete preliminary vision of what is to be said, and
which in a young hand demands deliberate preconsideration.
To Franklin, the ordering of his matter must have become
eventually a light task as, with incessant passing to and fro
in his experience and with the daily habit of epistolary communication, he grew as familiar with his intellectual terrain as
an old field marshal with the map of Europe. For the writing
of his later years is marked not merely by clearness and force
but also by the sovereign ease of a man who has long understood the interrelations of his ideas and has ceased to make
revolutionary discoveries in any portion of his own nature. His
occasional wrath does not fluster him but rather intensifies
his lucidity, clarifies his logic, and brightens the ironical smile
which accompanies the thrust of his wit. The "decent plainness and manly freedom" of his ordinary tone—notes which
he admired in the writings of his maternal grandfather Peter
Folger—rise in parts of his official correspondence to a severity
of decorum; for there is a trace of the senatorial in the man,
the dignity of antique Rome. He is seldom too hurried, even
in a private letter, to gratify the ear by the turning and cadence
of sentence and phrase; and one feels that the harmony of his
periods is the right and predestined vesture of his essential
blandness and suavity of temper. His stylistic drapery, however, is never so smoothed and adjusted as to obscure the
sinewy vigour of his thought. His manner is steadily in
the service of his matter. He is adequate, not copious; for
his moral "frugality and industry" prompt him to eschew
surplusage and to make his texture firm. His regard for
purity of diction is classical; he avoids vulgarity; he despises
the jargon of scientific pedants; but like Montaigne he loves
frank and masculine speech, and he likes to enrich the language

of the well bred by discreet drafts upon the burry, homely, sententious, proverbial language of the people. Like Lord Bacon and like many other grave men among his fellow-countrymen, he found it difficult to avoid an opportunity for a jest even when the occasion was unpropitious; and he never sat below the Attic salt. When his fortune was made, he put by the pewter spoon and bowl of his apprenticeship; his biographers remind us that he kept a well stocked cellar at Passy and enjoyed the distinction of suffering from the gout. With affluence and years he acquired a "palate," and gave a little play to the long repressed tastes of an Epicurean whom early destiny had cast upon a rock-bound coast. The literary expression of his autumnal festivity is to be found in the *bagatelles*. *The Ephemera* proves that this great eighteenth-century rationalist had a fancy. It is no relative, indeed, of that romantic spirit which pipes to the whistling winds on the enchanted greens of Shakespeare. It is rather the classic Muse of eighteenth-century art which summons the rosy Loves and Desires to sport among the courtiers and philosophers and the wasp-waisted ladies in a *fête champêtre* or an *Embarkment for Cythera* of Watteau. The tallow chandler's son . who enters on the cycle of his development by cultivating thrift with Defoe, continues it by cultivating tolerance and philanthropy with Voltaire, and completes it with Lord Chesterfield by cultivating "the graces."

CHAPTER II

Knickerbocker Writers

1. IRVING

WASHINGTON IRVING was born in William Street, New York City, 3 April, 1783. As this was the year in which the colonies finally achieved the independence for which they had been fighting for seven years, Irving may be regarded as the first author produced in the new republic.

The writer recalls that he visited Sunnyside with his father a year or two before the death of Irving and heard him narrate, doubtless not for the first time, how, when he was a youngster a year old, his nurse had held him up in her arms while Washington was passing by on horseback, in order that the General might place his hand on the head of the child who bore his name. "My nurse told me afterwards," said Irving, "that the General lifted me in his arms up to the pommel of his saddle and bestowed upon me a formal blessing." The listening boy looked, with reverential awe, at the head that had been touched by the first president, but when later he told his father about Irving's words, the father said: "You did not see the spot that Washington touched." "And why not?" was the natural question. "You goose," came the retort, "do you not know that Mr. Irving wears a wig?"

Washington Irving was prevented by poor health from following his two elder brothers to Columbia College. His formal training was limited to a course of a few years in the public schools of the day. He had always, however, encouraged in himself a taste for reading and an interest in human affairs so that his education went on steadily from year to year. His father, a Scotchman by birth, had built up an importing business and ranked well among the leading merchants of the city. The family comprised in all five sons and two daughters. The relations to each other of these brothers and sisters were always closely sympathetic, and throughout the record of Irving's career the reader is impressed with the loyal service rendered, first, by the elder brothers to the younger, and later, when the family property had disappeared and the earnings of the youngster had become the mainstay of the family, by Washington himself to his seniors, and to his nieces.

In 1804, Irving, who had just attained his majority, made his first journey to Europe. His father had died some years earlier, and the direction of the family affairs was in the hands of the eldest brother William. The trip seems to have re-established Washington's health, which had been a cause of anxiety to his brothers. After a voyage of forty-two days he landed in Bordeaux, whence he journeyed to Paris. He then travelled by way of Marseilles to Genoa, from which point he went by stage-coach through some of the picturesque regions in Italy. It was on these trips that he secured his first impressions of the Italian hill country and of the life of the country folk, impressions that were utilized later in the *Tales of a Traveller*. From Naples, crossing to Palermo, he went by stage to Messina, and he was there in 1805 when the vessels of Nelson passed through the straits in their search for the combined French and Spanish fleet under Villeneuve, a search which culminated in the great victory at Trafalgar.

Journeying in Europe during those years of war and of national upheaval was a dangerous matter. Irving was stopped more than once, and on one occasion was arrested at some place in France on the charge of being an English spy. He seems to have borne the troublesome interruptions with a full measure of equanimity, and he used each delay to good purpose as an opportunity for a more leisurely study of the environment and of the persons with whom he came into touch. He returned to New York early in 1806, shortly after Europe had been shaken by the battle of Austerlitz.[1]

Irving was admitted to the bar in November, 1806, having previously served as attorney's clerk, first with Brockholst Livingston and later with Josiah Ogden Hoffman. The law

---

[1] During these journeys he took notes, wrote them out in a full journal, portions of which have recently been published, and utilized his material in elaborate letters to his relations.

failed, however, to exercise for him any fascination, and his practice did not become important. He had the opportunity of being associated as a junior with the counsel who had charge of the defence of Aaron Burr in the famous trial held in Richmond in June, 1807. The writer remembers the twinkle in the old gentleman's eye when he said in reply to some question about his legal experiences, "I was one of the counsel for Burr, and Burr was acquitted." In letters written from Richmond at the time, he was frank enough, however, to admit that he had not been called upon for any important service. During Irving's brief professional association with Hoffman, he was accepted as an intimate in the Hoffman family circle, and it was Hoffman's daughter Matilda who was the heroine in the only romance of the author's life. He became engaged to Matilda when he was barely of age, but the betrothal lasted only a few months, as she died suddenly at the age of seventeen. At the time of Irving's death it was found that he was still wearing on his breast a locket containing her miniature and a lock of hair that had been given to him half a century before. He never married.

The first literary undertaking to which Irving's pen was devoted, apart from a few ephemeral sketches for one of the daily papers, was a serial publication issued at irregular intervals during 1807–08, under the title of *Salmagundi*. In this work, Irving had the collaboration of his brother William and his friend James K. Paulding. The *Salmagundi* papers, reissued later in book form, possess, in addition to their interest as humorous literature, historical value as pictures of social life in New York during the first decade of the nineteenth century.

The famous *History of New-York* was published in 1809. The mystery surrounding the disappearance of old Diedrich Knickerbocker, to whom was assigned the authorship, was preserved for a number of months. The first announcement of the book stated that the manuscript had been found by the landlord of the Columbian Hotel in New York among the effects of a departed lodger, and had been sold to the printer in order to offset the lodger's indebtedness. Before the manuscript was disposed of, Seth Handaside, the landlord, inserted in New York and Philadelphia papers an advertisement describing

Mr. Knickerbocker and asking for information about him. When acknowledgment of the authorship of the book was finally made by Irving, it was difficult for his fellow New Yorkers to believe that this unsuccessful young lawyer and attractive "man about town" could have produced a work giving evidence of such maturity and literary power. He had secured an excellent position in New York society, a society which in the earlier years of the century was still largely made up of the old Dutch families. In the "veracious chronicle" of Mr. Knickerbocker free use was made of the names of these historic families, and it is related that not a few of the young author's Dutch friends found it difficult to accord forgiveness for the liberty that had been taken with their honourable ancestors in making them the heroes of such rollicking episodes.

After a brief editorial experience in charge of a Philadelphia magazine called the *Analectic*, to which he contributed some essays later included in *The Sketch Book*, Irving enjoyed for a few months the excitement of military service. He was appointed a colonel on the staff of Governor Tompkins, and during the campaign of 1814 was charged with responsibilities in connection with the defence of the northern line of New York.

In 1810, Irving had been taken into partnership with his two brothers, Peter and Ebenezer, who were carrying on business as general merchants and importers; and on the declaration of peace in 1814 he was sent by his firm to serve as its representative in Liverpool. If the business plans of that year had proved successful, it is possible that Irving might for the rest of his life have remained absorbed in commercial undertakings, but in 1818 the firm was overtaken by disaster and the young lawyer-merchant (never much of a lawyer and by no means important as a merchant) found himself adrift in England with small funds and with no assured occupation or prospects. He had already come into friendly relations with a number of the leading authors of the day, a group which included Scott, Moore, Southey, and Jeffrey. Scott had in fact sought him out very promptly, having years earlier been fascinated by the originality and the humour shown in *The History of New-York*.

After a couple of years of desultory travelling and writing, Irving completed a series of papers which were published in

New York in 1819–20 and in London in 1820, under the title of *The Sketch Book*. It is by this volume that he is today best known among readers on both sides of the Atlantic. The book has been translated into almost every European tongue, and for many years it served, and still serves, in France, in Germany, and in Italy as a model of English style and as a textbook from which students are taught their English. In this latter rôle, it took, to a considerable extent, the place of *The Spectator*.

The publication by Murray of *The Sketch Book*, and two years later of *Bracebridge Hall*, brought Irving at once into repute in literary circles not only in Great Britain, but on the Continent. In 1826, after a year or two chiefly spent in travelling in France, Germany, and Italy, he was appointed by Alexander Everett, at that time Minister to Spain, attaché to the Legation at Madrid, and this first sojourn in Spain had an important influence in shaping the direction of Irving's future literary work. In July, 1827, he brought to completion his biography of Columbus, later followed by the account of the *Companions of Columbus* (1831). The *Columbus* was published in London and in Philadelphia in 1828 and secured at once cordial and general appreciation. Southey wrote from London: "This work places Irving in the front rank of modern biographers"; and Edward Everett said that "through the Columbus, Irving is securing the position of founder of the American school of polite learning." Irving continued absorbed and fascinated with the examination of the Spanish chronicles. He made long sojourns in Granada, living for a great part of the time within the precincts of the Alhambra, and later he spent a year or more in Seville. He occupied himself collecting material for the completion of *The Conquest of Granada*, published in 1829, and for the *Legends of the Alhambra*, published in 1832.

In 1828, Irving declined an offer of one hundred guineas to write an article for *The Quarterly Review*, of which his friend Murray was the publisher, on the ground, as he wrote, "that the Review [then under the editorship of Gifford] has been so persistently hostile to our country that I cannot draw a pen in its service." This episode may count as a fair rejoinder to certain of the home critics who were then accusing Irving (as half a century later Lowell was, in like manner, accused) of having become so much absorbed in his English sympathies as to have lost his patriotism.

In 1829, Irving was made a member of the Royal Academy of History in Madrid, and having in the same year been appointed Secretary of Legation by Louis McLane, he again took up his residence in London. Here, in 1830, the Royal Society of Literature voted to him as a recognition of his "service to history and to literature" one of its gold medals. The other medal of that year was given to Hallam for his *History of the Middle Ages*. A little later Oxford honoured Irving with the degree of Doctor of Laws. The ceremony of the installation was a serious experience for a man of his shy and retiring habits. As he sat in the Senate Hall, the students saluted him with cries of "Here comes old Knickerbocker," "How about Ichabod Crane?" "Has Rip Van Winkle waked up yet?" and "Who discovered Columbus?"

In 1832, Irving returned to New York, having been absent from his country for seventeen years. His fellow citizens welcomed him, not a little to his own discomfiture, with a banquet given in the City Hall, where the orator of the evening addressed him as the "Dutch Herodotus." Later in the year, he made a journey through the territory of the Southwest, an account of which he published under the title of *A Tour on the Prairies* (1835). His description of St. Louis as a frontier post and of the great wilderness extending to the west of the Mississippi still makes interesting reading. Returning from his journey by way of New Orleans, he visited Columbia, South Carolina, where he was the guest of Governor Hamilton. The Governor, who had just transmitted to the legislature the edict of nullification, insisted that the author must repeat his visit to the state. "Certainly," responded the guest, "I will come with the first troops."

In 1834, Irving declined a Democratic nomination for Congress, and in 1838 he put to one side the Tammany nomination for mayor of New York and also an offer from President Van Buren to make him Secretary of the Navy. In 1842, he accepted from President Tyler the appointment of Minister to Spain. The suggestion had come to the President from Daniel Webster, at that time Secretary of State. The succeeding five years were in large part devoted to the collection of material relating to the history and the legends of Spain during the Moorish occupation.

On his return to New York in 1846, he met with a serious disappointment. His books were out of print, at least in the United States, and his Philadelphia publishers assured him that, as there was no longer any public demand for his writings, it would be an unprofitable venture to put new editions upon the market. They explained that the public taste had changed, and that a new style of authorship was now in vogue. The books had in fact been out of print since 1845, but at that time Irving, still absent in Spain, had concluded that the plan for revised editions might await his return. To be told now by publishers of experience that *The Sketch Book*, *Knickerbocker*, *Columbus*, and the other books, notwithstanding their original prestige, had had their day and were not wanted by the new generation, was a serious shock to Irving not only on the ground of the blow to his confidence in himself as an author, but because his savings were inconsiderable, and he needed the continued income that he had hoped to secure from his pen.

His personal wants were few, but he had always used his resources generously among his large circle of relatives, and having neither wife nor child he had made a home at Sunnyside for an aged brother Ebenezer, and at one time for no less than five nieces. Some western land investments, which in later years became profitable, were at this time liabilities instead of resources, and his immediate financial prospects were discouraging. He had taken a desk in the office of his brother John Treat Irving, and to John he now spoke, possibly half jestingly, of the necessity of resuming the practice of the law. He was at this time sixty-five years of age, and as it was forty years since he had touched a law book, it is hardly likely that he could have made himself of much value as a counsellor.

One morning early in 1848, he came into the office in a joyful frame of mind. He tossed a letter over to his brother saying: "John, here is a fool of a publisher willing to give me $2000 a year to go on scribbling." The "fool of a publisher" was the late George P. Putnam, who had recently returned from London where he had for eight years been engaged in the attempt to induce the English public to buy American books. Mr. Putnam now proposed to issue a uniform revised edition of all of Irving's writings, with which should be associated the books that he might later bring to completion, and to pay to the author a royalty on each copy sold, guaranteeing against such royalty for a term of three years a sum increasing with each year. It may be mentioned as evidence of the accuracy of the publisher's judgment that the payments during the years in which this guaranty continued were always substantially in excess of the amounts contracted for.

In 1849, the London publisher Bohn began to print unauthorized editions of the various books of Irving. A series of litigations ensued, as a result of which the authorized publishers, Murray and Bentley, discouraged with a long fight and with the great expense incurred in securing protection under the existing copyright regulations, accepted the offer of the pirate for the use, at a purely nominal price, of their publishing rights, and Irving's works came thus to be included in Bohn's Library Series. Copyright in Great Britain, as in the United States, was in 1850 in a very unsatisfactory condition, and it was not easy to ascertain from the provisions of the British statute just what rights could be maintained by alien authors. So far as American authors were concerned, this uncertainty continued until, through the enactment of the statute of 1891, an international copyright relation was secured.

As one result of the transfer to Bohn of the control of the English editions of Irving's earlier volumes, the author found that he could not depend upon any material English receipts for his later works. For the right to publish the English edition of the *Life of Washington* (a work comprised in five volumes) Bentley paid the sum of £50, which was a sad reduction from the £3000 that Murray had given him for the *Columbus*.

In December, 1852, Irving wrote to his American publisher a letter of thanks, which is notable as an expression both of the sense of fairness and of the modest nature of the man. That this expression of friendship was not a mere empty courtesy, he had opportunity of making clear a few years later. In 1857, partly because of the mismanagement of his financial partner and partly because of the general financial disasters of the year, Mr. Putnam was compelled to make an assignment of his business. Irving received propositions from a number of other publishers for the transfer of his books, the commercial value of which was now fully appreciated. From some of these propositions he could have secured more satisfactory returns than were coming to him under the existing arrangement. He declined them all, however, writing to his publisher to the effect that as long as a Putnam remained in the publishing business, he proposed to retain for his books the Putnam imprint. He purchased from the assignee the plates and the publishing agreements; he held these plates for a year or more until Mr. Putnam was in a position to resume the control of the publication, and he then restored them to his publisher. He waived the larger proceeds to which, as the owner of the plates, he would have been entitled, and insisted that the old publishing arrangement should be resumed. Such an episode is interesting in the long and somewhat troubled history of the relations of authors with publishers, and it may be considered equally creditable to both parties.

The final, and in some respects the greatest of Irving's productions, the *Life of Washington*, was completed on his seventy-sixth birthday, 1859, and a month or two later he had the pleasure of holding in his hands the printed volume. His death came on 29 November, of the same year, and he was laid to rest in the beautiful little graveyard of the Sleepy Hollow Church. The writer has in his memory a picture of the great weather-beaten walls of the quaint little church with the background of forest trees and the surroundings of the moss-covered graves. Beyond on the roadside could be seen the grey walls of the mill, in front of which Ichabod Crane had clattered past, pursued by the headless horseman. The roadside and the neighbouring fields were crowded with vehicles, large and small, which had gathered from all parts of the countryside. It was evident from the words and from the faces of those that had come together that the man whose life was closed had not only made for himself a place in the literature of the world, but had been accepted as a personal friend by the neighbours of his home.

Washington Irving occupied an exceptional position among the literary workers of his country. It was his good fortune to begin his writing at a time when the patriotic sentiment of the nation was taking shape, and when the citizens were giving their thoughts to the constructive work that was being done by

their selected leaders in framing the foundations of the new
state. It was given to Irving to make clear to his countrymen
that Americans were competent not merely to organize a state,
but to produce literature. He was himself a clear-headed and
devoted patriot, but he was able to free himself from the local
feeling of antagonism toward the ancient enemy Great Britain,
and from the prejudice against other nations, always based
upon ignorance, that is so often confused with patriotism.
Irving's early memories and his early reading had to do with
the events and with the productions of colonial days. Addison
and Goldsmith are the two English writers with whose works
his productions, or at least those relating to English subjects, have been most frequently compared. His biography of
Goldsmith shows the keenest personal sympathy with the
sweetness of nature and the literary ideals of his subject.
Irving's works came, therefore, to be a connecting link between
the literature of England (or the English-inspired literature of
the colonies) and the literary creations that were entitled to the
name American, and they expressed the character, the method
of thought, the ideals, and the aspiration of English folk on this
side of the Atlantic.

The greatest intellectual accomplishment to be credited to
New York during the first years of the republic was the production of *The Federalist*. It is fair to claim, however, that
with Irving and with those writers immediately associated with
his work during the first quarter of the nineteenth century,
began the real literature of the country. Partly by temperament and by character, and partly, of course, as a result of the
opportunities that came to him after a close personal knowledge
of England, with a large understanding of things Continental,
Irving, while in his convictions a sturdy American, became in
his sympathies a cosmopolitan. His first noteworthy production, *The History of New-York*, is so distinctive in its imagination and humour that it is difficult to class. It is purely local
in the sense that the characters and the allusions all have
to do with the Dutch occupation of Manhattan Island and the
Hudson River region, but, as was evidenced by the cordial
appreciation given to the book on the other side of the Atlantic,
the humour of Mr. Knickerbocker was accepted as a contribution to the literature of the world.

In the production of *The Sketch Book*, Irving was able not only to enhance his fame by a charming contribution to literature, but to render a special service to two countries, England and America. The book came into print at a time when the bitterness of the war which closed in 1814 was still fresh in the minds of both contestants. It was a time when it was the fashion in America to use Great Britain as a bugaboo, as a synonym for all that was to be abominated in political theories and in political action. The word "British" was associated in the minds of most Americans with an attempt at domination, while in England, on the other hand, references to the little Yankee nation were no more friendly, and things American were persistently decried and sneered at to the intense irritation of Americans.

It was of enormous value that at such a period, first in the list of patriotic Americans who through sympathetic knowledge of England have come to serve as connecting links between the two countries, Irving should have been a resident in England and should have absorbed so thoroughly the spirit of the best that there was in English life. It was in part because men honoured in Great Britain, writers like Scott, Southey, Rogers, Roscoe, Moore, men of affairs like Richard Bentley, John Murray, and many others, came not only to respect, but to have affectionate regard for, the American author, and it was in part because the books written by this man showed such sympathetic appreciation of things and of men English, that England was brought to a better understanding of the possibilities of America. If there could come from the States a man recognized as one of nature's gentlemen, and to be accepted as a companion of the best in the land, a man whose writings on things English won the highest approval of the most authoritative critics, it was evident that there were possibilities in this new English-speaking state. If one American could secure friendships in Great Britain, if one American could make a noteworthy contribution to the literature of the English tongue, the way was thrown open to other Americans to strengthen and widen the ties and the relations between the two countries. An American critic who might have been tempted to criticize some of the papers in *The Sketch Book* as unduly English in their sympathies and as indicating a surrender by the author of his American principles, was estopped from any such folly by the fact that the same volume contained those immortal legends of the Hudson, *Rip Van Winkle* and *The Legend of Sleepy Hollow*. In these stories, poems in prose, the author utilized, as the pathway and inspiration for his imagination, the great river of which he was so fond. If Irving's descriptions of rural England were to give fresh interest to American readers in the old home of their forefathers, the skill with which he had utilized the traditional legends of the Catskill Mountains and had woven fanciful stories along the roadway of Sleepy Hollow made clear to readers on the other side of the Atlantic that imagination and literary style were not restricted to Europe.

The work begun in *The Sketch Book* was continued in *Bracebridge Hall*. Here also we have that combination (possibly paralleled in no other work of literature) of things English and things American. Squire Bracebridge is, of course, a lineal descendant of Sir Roger de Coverley. It is not necessary, however, because Irving was keenly sympathetic with Addison's mode of thought, to speak of Irving's hero as an imitation. England has produced more than one squire, and Bracebridge and the family of the Hall were the creations of the American observer. The English home of the early nineteenth century is presented in a picture that is none the less artistic because it can be accepted as trustworthy and exact. In this volume we have also a characteristic American study, *Dolph Heyliger*, a fresh romance of Irving's beloved Hudson River.

The *Tales of a Traveller*, the scenes of which were laid partly in Italy, show the versatility of the author in bringing his imagination into harmony with varied surroundings. Whether the subject be in England, in France, or in Italy, whether he is writing of the Alhambra or of the Hudson, Irving always succeeds in coming into the closest sympathy with his environment. He has the artist's touch in the ability to reproduce the atmosphere in which the scenes of his stories are placed.

The *Life of Columbus* may be considered as presenting Irving's first attempt at history, but it was an attempt that secured for him at once a place in the first rank among historians. In this biography, Irving gave ample evidence of his power of reconstituting the figures of the past. He impresses upon the reader the personality of the great discoverer, the idealist, the man who was so absorbed in his own belief that he was able to impress this upon the skeptics about him. We have before us a vivid picture of the Spanish Court from which, after patient effort, Columbus secured the grudging support for his expedition, and we come to know each member of the little crew through whose service the great task was brought to accomplishment. Irving makes clear that the opposition of the clerics and the apathy of King Ferdinand were at last overcome only through the sympathetic support given to the project by Queen Isabella.

In the *Conquest of Granada*, the narrative is given in a humorous form, but it represents the result of very thorough historic research. By the device of presenting the record through the personality of the mythical priestly chronicler, Fray Agapida, blindly devoted to the cause of the Church, Irving is able to emphasize less invidiously than if the statements were made direct, the bitterness, the barbarism, and the prejudices of the so-called Christianity of the Spaniards. Through the utterances of Agapida, we come to realize the narrowness of Ferdinand and the priestly arrogance of Ferdinand's advisers. The admiration of the reader goes out to the fierce patriotism of the great Moorish leader, El Zagal, and his sympathies are enlisted for the pathetic career of Boabdil, the last monarch of Granada. *Granada* was Irving's favourite production, and he found himself frankly disappointed that (possibly on the ground of the humorous form given to the narrative) the book failed to secure full acceptance as history and was not considered by the author's admirers to take rank with his more popular work.

The *Alhambra*, which has been called the "Spanish Sketch Book," is a beautiful expression of the thoughts and dreams of the author as he muses amid the ruins of the Palace of the Moors. The reader feels that in recording the great struggle which terminated in 1492 with the triumph of Spain, Irving's sympathies are not with the conquering Christians but with the defeated Moslems.

The *Life of Mahomet* and the supplementary volume on the successors of Mahomet followed in 1849-50. The biographies constitute good narrative and give further examples of the author's exceptional power of characterization. If they fail to

4

reach the high standard of the *Columbus*, it is doubtless because Irving possessed no such close familiarity with the environment of his subjects.   In Spain he had made long sojourns and had become imbued with the atmosphere of the Spanish legends and ideals.   He knew his Italy, in like manner, from personal observation and from sympathetic relations with the peasants no less than the scholars, but Arabia was to him a distant land.

The writing of *Columbus* prepared the way for Irving's chief historical achievement.   The *Life of Washington* is not only a biography presenting with wonderful precision and completeness the nature and career of a great American, but a study, and the first study of importance, of the evolution of the republic. Irving had given thought and planning to the biography for years before he was able to put a pen to the work.   As early as 1832 he had confided to some of his nearer friends his ambition to associate his name with that of Washington and to devote such literary and historical ability as he possessed to the creation of a literary monument to the Father of the Republic.   The work had, of necessity, been postponed during his long sojourn in England and the later residence in Spain, but he never permitted himself to put the plan to one side.   As soon as the sales of the new Putnam edition of the earlier works and of the later volumes that he had been able to add to these freed him from financial care, he began the collection of material for the great history.   He had already travelled over much of the country with which the career of his hero was connected.   He knew by the observations of an intelligent traveller the regions of New England, New Jersey, Western Pennsylvania, and Virginia, while with the territory of New York he had from his youth been familiar.   The Hudson River, which had heretofore served as the pathway for Irving's dreams of romance, was now to be studied historically as the scene of some of the most critical of the campaigns of the Revolution.   Since the date of Irving's work, later historians have had the advantage of fuller material, particularly that secured from the correspondence in the homes of Revolutionary leaders, North and South, but no later historian has found occasion for any corrections of importance, either in the details of Irving's narrative, or in his analysis of the characters of the men through whom the great contest was carried on.   Irving possessed one qualification which is lacking in the make-up of not a few conscientious and able historians. His strain of romance and his power of imagination enabled him to picture to himself and to make vivid the scenes described, and the nature, the purpose, and the manner of thought of each character introduced. The reader is brought into personal association with the force and dignity of the great leader; with the assumption, the vanity, the exaggerated opinion of his powers and ability of Charles Lee; with the sturdy patriotism, the simple-hearted nature, persistence, and pluck of the pioneer fighter Israel Putnam; with the skill, leadership, and unselfishness of Philip Schuyler; with the pettiness and bumptiousness of Gates; with the grace, fascination, and loyalty of Lafayette; and with the varied attainments and brilliant qualities of that wonderful youth Alexander Hamilton. We are not simply reading descriptions, we are looking at living pictures, and the historic narrative has the quality of a vitascope.

The production of this great history constituted a fitting culmination to the literary labours of its author. When Irving penned the last word of the fifth volume of the *Washington*, he was within a few months of his death. The work on this volume had in fact been a strain upon his vitality, and there were times when he needed to exert his will power to the utmost in order to complete the task allotted to himself for the day. He said pathetically from time to time to his nephew and loyal aid Pierre and to his friend Putnam, "I do not know whether I may be spared to complete this history, but I shall do my best." In this his final work, the shaping of the fifth volume, he did his best.

It may fairly be contended for this American author, whose work dates almost from the beginning of the Republic, that his writings possess vitality and continued importance for the readers of this later century. His historical works have, as indicated, a distinctive character. They are trustworthy and dignified history, while they possess the literary charm and grace of the work of a true man of letters. For the world at large, Irving will, however, doubtless best be known by his works of imagination, and the students in the gallery in Oxford who chaffed "Diedrich Knickerbocker" as he was receiving his degree were probably right in selecting as the characteristic and abiding production of the author his *Rip Van Winkle*.

2. Bryant

TO the old-fashioned prayers which his mother and grandmother taught him, the little boy born in Cummington, Massachusetts, 3 November, 1794, a year before John Keats across the sea, was wont to add (so we learn from the Autobiographical Fragment),[1] his private supplication that he might "receive the gift of poetic genius, and write verses that might endure."

This inner urge and bent, witnessed so early and so long, could not be severed, early or late, from the unfathomable world. Bryant's was a boyhood and youth among the virginal woods, hills, and streams, among a farmer folk and country labours and pastimes, in a Puritan household, with a father prominent in the state as physician and legislator, whose independence and breadth are attested by a leaning toward that liberalism which was to develop into the American Unitarian movement and by his enlightened devotion, as critic and friend, to the boy's ambitions in rhyme. Private tutoring by unpretending clergymen, a year at poverty-stricken Williams College, law studies in an upland office, distasteful practice as a poor country lawyer, a happy marriage with her whose "birth was in the forest shades,"[2] death, season by season, of those nearest and dearest, travel down among the slave-holding states and out to the prairies of Illinois, where his brothers and mother were for a second time pioneers, with voyages on various

[1] Godwin, *Life*, vol. I, p. 26.
[2] *Poems*, p. 82. Roslyn edition (1913), from which all poetical quotations are cited in this chapter.

occasions to the West Indies, to Europe, and to the Levant, and
fifty years as a New York editor, who with the wisdom of a
statesman and the courage of a reformer made *The Evening
Post* America's greatest newspaper,—all this gives us a life of
many visions of forest, field, and foam, of many books in diverse
tongues, of many men and cities, of many problems in his own
career and in the career of that nation which he made so much
his own, a life not without its own adventures, struggles,
joys, and griefs. So it stands recorded, a consistent and eloquent and (fortunately) a familiar chapter in American biography, even as it passed before the visionary octogenarian
back in the old home, sitting "in the early twilight," whilst

> Through the gathering shade
> He looked on the fields around him
> Where yet a child he played.[1]

One might regard the events of this lifetime either as in
subtle and inevitable ways harmoniously contributory to the
poet-nature that was Bryant's (if not indeed often its persistent
and victorious creation), or as in the main a deflection, a check.
If no other American poet has written, year measured by year,
so little poetry, the poetry of no other so clearly defines at once
its author's character, environment, and country; if no other
American poet was apparently so much occupied with other
interests than poetry, not excepting the critic, diplomat, orator,
and humorist Lowell, none felt his high calling, it seems, with
as priestly a consecration,—no, truly, not excepting Whitman,
who protested thereon sometimes a little too much.

Bryant's public career as poet fulfilled the psalmist's three-
score years and ten, if we date from *The Embargo*, an anti-
Jefferson satire in juvenile heroics (1808). It began with the
year of Scott's *Marmion;* it was barely completed with *Sigurd
the Volsung* of William Morris; it included the lives of Byron and
Shelley and most that was best in those of Tennyson, Arnold,
Browning. It began the year following Joel Barlow's American
epic *The Columbiad,* and the publication of *The Echo* by the
Hartford Wits. Longfellow and Whittier were in the cradle,
Holmes and Poe unborn. Except Freneau, there were no poets

[1] *A Lifetime.*

in the country but those imitative versifiers of an already anti-
quated English fashion whom Bryant was himself to characterize[1] with quiet justice in the first critical appraisal of our
"literature," the first declaration of intellectual independence,
antedating Emerson's *American Scholar* by nineteen years.
He compassed the generations of all that was once or is still
most reputed in American poetry: the generations of Paulding,
Percival, Halleck, Drake, Willis, Poe, Longfellow, Whittier,
Emerson, Lowell, Whitman, Bret Harte.

Yet he was from very early, in imagination and expression,
curiously detached from what was going on in poetry around
him.   *The Embargo* is a boy's echo, significant only for precocious facility and for the twofold interest in verse and politics
that was to be lifelong.   Byron's voice is audible in the Spen-
serian stanzas and subject matter of the Phi Beta Kappa poem
of 1821, *The Ages*[2]*;* the New York verses, so painfully facetious
on Rhode Island coal and a mosquito, are less after Byron than
after the town wit Halleck and his coterie.   Wordsworth, at the
reading of whose *Lyrical Ballads* in 1811, "a thousand springs,"
Bryant said to Dana, "seemed to gush up at once in his heart,
and the face of Nature of a sudden to change into a strange
freshness and life," was the companion into the woods and
among the flowers who more than all others helped him to find
himself; but *Thanatopsis*, so characteristic of Bryant, was
written almost certainly some weeks before he had seen the
Lyrical Ballads,[3] and, even if Bryant's eminence as poet of
nature owed much to this early reinforcement, his poetry is
not Wordsworthian either in philosophy or in mood or in
artistry.   Wordsworth never left the impress on Bryant's
work that the realms of gold made upon the surprised and
spellbound boy Keats.   No later prophets and craftsmen,

[1] *North American Review*, July, 1818.

[2] Thomson's *Liberty* may have contributed something to the choice of theme.

[3] The time relations seem to have been as follows.   Bryant's father purchased
the *Lyrical Ballads* in Boston during 1810, when the son was at college (till May,
1811); Bryant "had picked it up at home" (Godwin, *Life*, vol. I, p. 104) to take
with him to Worthington (Dec., 1811), where it was that, as a young law student,
he first read it with such surprised delight.   *Thanatopsis* had been written between
May and December, apparently in the autumn (Godwin, *Life*, vol. I, pp. 97–99),
and if (as likely) before 3 November, then written when Bryant was still a lad of
sixteen.   See Van Doren, C., *The Growth of "Thanatopsis," Nation*, 7 October,
1915.

American, English, or continental, seem to have touched him at all.[1]

More obvious to the registrar of parallels are Bryant's literary relations to the poets he read, and read evidently with deeper susceptibility than has been realized, before 1811.[2] The reference is not alone to the well-known relation *Thanatopsis* bears to Blair's *Grave*, Porteus's *Death*,[3] Kirke White's *Time*, *Rosemary*, etc., and the whole Undertaker's Anthology so infinitely beneath the Lucretian grandeur of America's first great poem with its vision of

Dead men whose bones earth bosomed long ago.

The reference is equally to certain themes and moods and unclassified details in poems written long after *Thanatopsis*, all of which, though so characteristically Bryant's, make us feel him as much closer to the eighteenth century tradition than any of his contemporaries, even than Holmes with his deference to "the steel-bright epigrams of Pope"; so that we may appraise him much better by going forward from the moralizing, "nature" blank verse of Thomson, Cowper, Young, and Akenside, than backward from Wordsworth and Tennyson. In the eighteenth century tradition is the very preference for blank verse as the instrument for large and serious thought, and the lifelong preference itself for large and serious thought on Death, History, Destiny. The Biblical note too is of the former age. But the diction is, if anything, freer than the mature Wordsworth himself from eighteenth century poetic slang, and the peculiarities of this blank verse (to be mentioned later) have fewer cadences suggestive of Cowper than, perhaps, of the early poems of Southey, whose impression on those impressionable first years of Bryant's has apparently been overlooked.[4] With this early romanticism we may connect the sentimental element in the appeal of innocent and happy savages, whether

[1] Tennysonian blank-verse in *Sella* has been suggested—unconvincingly.
[2] See Autobiographical Fragment for a partial list.
[3] Winner of the Seaton Prize at Cambridge for 1759. *Death* may be found in *Musae Seatonianae*, Cambridge, 1808—a copy of which was apparently in Doctor Bryant's library.
[4] Compare Southey's *Inscriptions* (themselves imitated from Akenside), especially *In a Forest*, with *Inscription for the Entrance to a Wood*.

on Pitcairn's Island or in the pristine Indian summers; likewise the two or three tales of horror and the supernatural, in which he succeeded so poorly. But he arrived soon enough to contribute his own influence to the nineteenth-century poetry of nature.

He came to himself early, for one who had so many years in which to change, if he would change or could. The first volume, the forty-four pages of 1821, contains most, the second, 1832, certainly contains all, of the essential Bryant, the essential as to what he cared for in nature and human life, as to how he envisaged it in imagination and dwelt with it in intellect and character, and as to how he gave it expression. In the later years there is more of Bryant's playful fancy, perhaps more of ethical thinking and mood, a slight shift of emphasis, new constructions, not new materials. His world and his speech were already his: there is no new revelation and no new instrument in any one of the several succeeding issues of his verse (though there are many new, many high poems), as there are new revelations and new instruments in Byron, Tennyson, and Browning; indeed, Keats in the three years between the volumes of 1817 and 1820 lived a much longer, a more diversified life of steadily increasing vision and voice. It need hardly be remarked, then, that he experienced no intellectual and moral crisis,—neither from without, as did Wordsworth when his country took up arms against Liberty, Fraternity, and Equality and when shortly Liberty, Fraternity, and Equality danced, like the Weird Sisters, around the cauldron of horror; nor from within, like the expatriated husband and father Byron, and the political idealist Dante, and even the *flâneur* who wrote *The Ballad of Reading Gaol.*

He came, likewise, early to his fame. He was first and alone. The little world of the lovers of good things on the North Atlantic seaboard in those days, trained as it was in the English and ancient classics, quickly set the young man apart; Bryant became established, fortunately, somewhat before American literary criticism had become self-consciously patriotic, indiscriminate, vulgar. England, too, long so important an influence on American judgments of American products, early accorded him a measure of honour and thanks. It is well known that Washington Irving secured the English reprinting of the volume of 1832 in the same year, with a brief criticism by way of dedication to Samuel Rogers, whose reading of the contents was the delight of that old Maecenas and Petronius Arbiter. It has, however, apparently not been observed that the entire contents of the volume of 1821 were reprinted, indeed in the same order, in *Specimens of the American Poets* (London, 1822) with a noteworthy comment[1] on the lines *Thanatopsis* that "there are few pieces, in the works of even the very first of our living poets, which exceed them in sublimity and compass of poetical thought." And Bryant was spared from the beginning furor and contempt: he was never laurelled like Byron, never foolscapped like Keats by critics or public; his repute was always, like himself, dignified, quiet, secure. And so the critical problem is initially simplified, in two ways: there is no story of struggle for recognition, and the effects of that struggle on the workman; there is no story of evolution of inner forces. Thus the poetry of Bryant admits of treatment as one performance, one perception and one account of the world, in a more restricted sense than is generally applicable to poetic performance, where the unity is the unity of psychological succession in a changing temporal order: *Don Juan* is, perhaps, implied in the *English Bards* and *Childe Harold*, *Paradise Lost* in the *Nativity*, *Hamlet* in *Romeo and Juliet;* but, in a humbler sphere, *Among the Trees* and *The Flood of Years* are less implied than actually present in *A Forest Hymn* and *Thanatopsis*. If Bryant's poems need sometimes the reference of date, it is for external occasion and impulse, not for artistic registration. Three periods have been discovered for Chaucer, and four for Shakespeare; our modest American was without "periods."

The critical problem is simple, though not necessarily trivial or easy, in another way: this one performance was itself of a relatively simple character. Bryant's poems stress perpetually a certain few ideas, grow perpetually out of a certain few emotional responses, and report in a few noble imaginative modes a certain few aspects of man and nature, with ever recurring habits of observation, architectonics, and style. This absence of complexity is, again, emphasized by the elemental clarity and simplicity of those same few ideas, emotions, modes, methods. Within his range he is complete, harmonious, and,

[1] P. 190.

in a deeper sense than above, impressively one. It is for this, perhaps, that of all American poets he makes the strongest impression of an organic style, as contrasted with an individual, a literary style, consciously elaborated, as in Poe and Whitman. It is partly for this, perhaps, that the most Puritan of our poets is also the most Greek. Bryant's limitations, then, are intimately engaged in the peculiar distinction of his work; and it is ungracious, as well as superficial, to quarrel with them.

Bryant's ideas, stated in bald prose, are elementary,— common property of simple minds. His metaphysics was predominantly that of the Old Testament: God is the Creator and His works and His purposes are good. Bryant communicated, however, little sense of the loving fatherhood and divine guidance in human affairs: perhaps once only, in *To a Waterfowl*, which originated in an intensely religious moment of young manhood.[1] His ethics stress the austerer loyalties of justice and truth rather than those of faith, hope, and charity. His politics in his poems, however analytic and specific he might be as publicist, reiterate only the ideals of political freedom and progress, with ever confident reference to the high destinies of America, that "Mother of a Mighty Race." His assurance of individual immortality for all men, which scarcely touches the problem of sin, rests not on revelation, not on a philosophy of the transcendental significance of intellect, struggle, and pain, but mainly on primitive man's desire to meet the loved and lost, the father, the sister, the wife. There is nothing subtle, complex, or tricky here; there are no philosophers, apparently, on his reading desk; no Spinoza, Plotinus, Berkeley, Hartley, who were behind Coleridge's discursive verse; no Thomas Aquinas who was the propædeutic for *The Divine Comedy*. And of any intricate psychology, or pseudo-psychology, such as delighted Browning, there is of course not a bit. There is in these ideas, as ideas, nothing that a noble pagan, say of republican Rome, might not have held to, even before the advent of Stoic and Academician. But there is a further paganism in the emphasis on the phenomena of life as life, on death as death. Man's life, as individual and type, is what it is—birth and toil in time; and death is what it is, save when he mentions a private grief—for men and empires it is a passing away in a

[1] Godwin, *Life*, vol. I, pp. 143–145.

universe of time and change. The original version of *Thanatopsis* is more characteristic than its inconsistent introductory and concluding lines, now the oftenest quoted of all his writings. If Bryant was the Puritan in his austerity and morale, he was quite as much the Pagan in the universality of his ideas, and in his temperamental adjustment to brute fact.

On nature and man's relation to nature, one who reads without prepossession will find the American Wordsworth equally elemental. He raises his hymn in the groves, which were God's first temples,—venerable columns, these ranks of trees, reared by Him of old. And "the great miracle still goes on"; and even the "delicate forest flower" seems

> An emanation of the indwelling Life,
> A visible token of the upholding Love,
> That are the soul of this great universe.[1]

But more frequently nature is herself enough, in the simple thought that personifies and capitalizes: it is She herself that speaks to man, in his different hours, a various language. But it is only casually, as in *Among the Trees*, that he wonders if the vegetable world may not have some

> dim and faint
> . . . sense of pleasure and of pain,
> As in our dreams;

only casually, for conscious mysticism was foreign to Bryant's intellect, and the conception had yet to be scientifically investigated in the laboratories of the Hindoo botanist Bose. Here nature, as herself the Life, is simply an hypostasis of the racial imagination in which Bryant so largely shared, just like his intimate personifications of her phenomena, her flowers, her winds, and waters; it is not a philosophic idea, but a primitive instinct. "Nature's teachings" for men are simply the ideas that suggest themselves to Bryant himself (not inevitably to everyone) when he observes what goes on, or what is before him:

> The faintest streak that on a petal lies,
> May speak instruction to initiate eyes.[2]

[1] *A Forest Hymn.*   [2] *The Mystery of Flowers.*

But this apparently Wordsworthian couplet can be related to no system of thought or Wordsworthian instruction. These ideas are sometimes merely analogies, where in effect the flower (be it the gentian), or the bird (be it the waterfowl), is the first term in a simile on man's moral life; in this phase Bryant's thought of nature differs from that of Homer, the Psalmist, Jesus, or any sage or seer, Pagan or Christian, only in the appositeness, more or less, of the illustrative symbol. It implies no more a philosophy of nature than similes drawn from the action of a locomotive or a motor-boat would imply a philosophy of machinery. As a fact, Bryant's one abiding idea about nature is that she is a profound influence on the human spirit, chastening, soothing, encouraging, ennobling—how, he does not say; but the fact he knows from experience, and mankind knows it with him, and has known it from long before the morning when the sorrowful, chafed soul of Achilles walked apart by the shore of the many-sounding sea.

Every poet, like every individual, has of course his favourite, his recurrent ideas: Wordsworth, again and again, adverts to the uses of old memories as a store and treasure for one's future days, again and again he sees his life as divided into three ages; Browning again and again preaches the doctrine that it is better to aim high and fail than to aim low and succeed; Emerson that the soul must live from within. But with Bryant the recurrence is peculiarly insistent and restricted in variety.

But these ideas were involved in a temperament. The chief differences among men are not in their ideas, as ideas, but in the power of the ideas over their emotions, or in the ideas considered as the overflow of their emotions. In Bryant presumably the ideas became formulas of thought, clarified and explicit, through his feelings. A man of great reserve and poise, both in life and art, his "coldness," well established in our literary tradition by some humorous lines of Lowell and a letter of Hawthorne, is a pathetic misreading. There is no sex passion; if there was in Bryant any potentiality of the young Goethe or Byron, it was early transmuted into the quiet affections for wife and home. There is no passion for friends; without being a recluse, he never craved comradeship, like Whitman, for humanity's sake, nor, like Shelley, for affinity's sake, and was, in the lifelong fellowship with such men as the elder Dana, the literary mentor who is responsible for more of Bryant's revisions in verse than any one knows,[1] spared the shocks that usually stimulate the expression of the passion of friendship. But his feelings, for woman and friend, were deep if quiet—perhaps deeper because quiet. And the other primary feelings were equally deep: awe in the presence of the cosmic process and the movements of mankind, reverence for holiness, pity for suffering, brooding resentment against injustice, rejoicing in moral victory, patriotism, susceptibility to beauty of outline and colour and sound, with peculiar susceptibility to both charm and sublimity in natural phenomena. These emotions, in Bryant, ring out through his poetry, clear, without blur or fringe, like the Italian vowels. He had no emotional crotchets, no erratic sensibilities; among other things, he was too robust and too busy. He had the "feelings of calm power and mighty sweep" of which he himself speaks, as befitting the poet.[2]

The few aspects of man and nature he reported have, in a way, been necessarily already suggested. With senses more alert to observe details in the physiognomy and voice of nature than of man, his imagination continually sees the same general vision: the Indian, shadowy type of a departed world, accoutred with feathers and tomahawk, realized, however, in almost none of his actual customs and in none of his actual feelings save that of sorrow for tribal ruin; the warriors of freedom, especially of the American Revolution; the infinite and mysterious racial past on this earth with all its crimes, triumphs, mutations, rather than with its more ethical future which he believes in more than he visualizes, an act of his thinking rather than of his imagination; the earth itself as the sepulchre of man; and, like one great primeval landscape, the mountain, the sea, the wind, the river, the seasons, the plain, the forest that undergo small change from their reality, take on few subjective peculiarities, by virtue of an imagination that seems, as it were, to absorb rather than to create its objects,—in this more like the world of phenomena in Lucretius than, say, in Tennyson, or in the partially Lucretian Meredith, certainly than in Hugo, to whom

[1] See some correspondence between Bryant and Dana apropos the 1846 edition of the *Poems*, Godwin, *Life*, vol. II, p. 14 ff.

[2] *The Poet.*

nature becomes so often monstrous and grotesque. And yet
Bryant's imagination has its characteristic modes of relating
its objects. Three or four huge and impressive metaphors
underlie a great part of his poetry: the past as a place, an
underworld, [1] dim and tremendous, most poignantly illustrated
in the poem *The Past* with its personal allusions, and most
sublimely in *The Death of Slavery*, a great political hymn, with
Lowell's *Commemoration Ode*, and Whitman's *When Lilacs last
in the Dooryard Bloomed*, the highest poetry of solemn grandeur
produced by the Civil War; death as a mysterious passage-
way, whether through gate[2] or cloud,[3] with the hosts ever
entering and disappearing in the Beyond; mankind conceived
as one vast company, a troop, a clan; and, as suggested above,
nature as a multitudinous Life.

Bryant wonderfully visualized and unified the vast scope of
the racial movement and the range of natural phenomena. His
"broad surveys," as they have been called, are more than surveys: they are large acts of the combining imagination, presenting
the significance, not merely the catalogue. These acts take us
home to the most inveterate habit of his poet-mind. As method
or device they seem to suggest a simple prescription for writing
poetry; superficially, after one has met them again and yet
again in Bryant, one might call them easy to do, because easy
to understand. The task is, however, not to make a list, but to
make the right list; a list not by capricious association of ideas,
but by the laws of inner harmony of meaning. Again, in
Bryant the list is itself often a fine, far look beyond the immediate fact—the immediate fact with which all but the poet would
rest content. *The Song of the Sower* needed no suggestion from
Schiller's *Song of the Bell*, which, however, Bryant doubtless
knew;[4] it highly illustrates his own natural procedure:

[1] The figure is in Kirke White's *Time*:

> "Where are conceal'd the days which have elapsed?
> Hid in the mighty cavern of *the past*,
> They rise upon us only to appal,
> By indistinct and half-glimpsed images."

This is doubtless one of the many indications of how thoroughly Bryant's
early reading penetrated his subconsciousness and, with boyhood's woods and
mountains, contributed to his essential make-up in maturity.

[2] *Poems*, p. 260.   [3] *Ibid.*, p. 250.   [4] See *The Death of Schiller*.

Fling wide the golden shower; we trust
The strength of armies to the dust.

The grain shall ripen for the warrior. Then he goes on: 'O
fling it wide, for all the race: for peaceful workers on sea and
land, for the wedding feast, for the various unfortunate, for the
communion, for Orient and Southland'—and we live, as we
read, wise in the basic fact of agriculture and wise in the activities of humankind. The precise idea is handled more lightly
in *The Planting of the Apple Tree*. Often the "survey"—
the word is convenient—starts from some on-moving phenomenon in nature—again an immediate fact—and proceeds by
compassing that phenomenon's whence or whither, what it has
experienced or what it will do: let one re-read his tale of *The
River*, by what haunts it flows (like, but how unlike, Tennyson's
brook); *The Unknown Way*, the spots it passes (becoming a
path symbolic of the mystery of life); *The Sea*, what it does
under God (like and unlike Byron's apostrophe); *The Winds*,
what they do on sea and land; *A Rain-Dream*, imaging the
waters of the globe. Sometimes the phenomenon is static and
calls his imagination to penetrate its secret history, or what
changes it has seen about it, as when he looks at the fountain[1]
or is among the trees.[2] Sometimes the vision rides upon or
stands beside no force in Nature, but is his own direct report,
as in *Fifty Years*, on the changes in individual lives, in history,
in inventions, especially in these States, since his class graduated
at Williams. "Broad surveys" of human affairs and of the
face of earth, so dull, routine, bombastic as far as attempted in
Thomson's *Liberty*, in Blair's *Grave*, in White's *Time*, become
in Bryant's less pretentious poems the essential triumph of a
unique imagination. The mode remained a favourite to the
end: large as in *The Flood of Years*, intimate and tender in
A Lifetime. No American poet, except Whitman, had an
imagination at all like Bryant's, or, indeed, except Whitman and
Emerson, as great as Bryant's.

No reminder should be needed that Bryant, like Thoreau
and Burroughs, was a naturalist with wide and accurate knowledge. He knew the way of the mist on river and mountain-
crest, all tints of sunset, the rising and the setting of the

[1] *Poems*, p. 185. [2] *Ibid.*, p. 321.

constellations, every twig and berry and gnarled root on the
forest floor, all shapes of snow on pine and shrub, the commoner
insects and wild creatures, and especially the birds and the
flowers; and he knew the hums and the murmurs and the
boomings that rise, like a perpetual exhalation, from the breast
of earth.   A traveller from some other planet could take back
with him no more useful account of our green home than Bryant's honest poems of nature.   There is a group of his poems
that details the look, habits, and habitat of single objects:
The Yellow Violet (with an intrusive moral—but his "morals"
are, contrary to traditional opinion, seldom intrusive, being
part of the imaginative and emotional texture), and *Robert of
Lincoln* (which is besides most fetching in its playfulness and
Bryant's one success in dramatic portrayal).   He was a good
observer; he would never have placed, like Coleridge, a star
within the nether tip of the crescent moon.   There is an allied
group which impart the quality of a moment in nature, as
Summer Wind:

> It is a sultry day; the sun has drunk
> The dew that lay upon the morning grass;
> There is no rustling in the lofty elm . . .
> . . . All is silent, save the faint
> And interrupted murmur of the bee,
> Settling on the sick flowers . . . .
> . . . Why so slow?
> Gentle and voluble spirit of the air?

These, if not the most representative, are the most exquisite of
all his poems.

And no reminder should be needed that he knew best the
American scene, and was the first to reveal it in art.   Irving,
in the London edition of 1832, naturally emphasized this claim
to distinction; and Emerson, many years later, at an after-
dinner speech on the poet's seventieth birthday, dwelt on it
with a winsome and eloquent gratitude[1] that has made all subsequent comment an impertinence.

Apart from the characteristics outlined above, Bryant had,
as if a relief and release from the verities and solemnities, a love
of fairyland: he had found it already, for instance, in the snow

[1] Godwin, *Life*, vol. II, p. 216 ff.

world of the *Winter Piece;* he went to it more often and eagerly from the editorial desk and the noise and heat of the Civil War: in *The Little People of the Snow,* in *Sella* (the underwater maiden), and in the fragments, *A Tale of Cloudland* and *Castles in the Air.* Their flowing blank verse (each some hundreds of lines), unlike his early experiments in prose narrative (which in their wooden arrangement, dull plot, and stilted characterizations are of a piece with the American short story before Poe and Hawthorne), tells, in simple chronological order, of one simple type of adventure, a mortal penetrating beyond the confines of nature—again the repetition of theme and architectonics, and one more manifestation of the primitive in Bryant (for the fairy-tale is, as the anthropologists tell us, among the most primitive activities of man) as dreamer and poet.

Like Cowper and Longfellow, and so many others, Bryant turned, in later life, to a long task of translation, in his case Homer, as relief from sorrow. The literary interest was to see if he might not, by closeness to the original and simplicity of straightforward modern English, supersede the looseness and artificial Miltonic pomp of Cowper. His translation, by detailed comparison line for line with the Greek and with the English poet, will be found to be exactly what Bryant intended it. By block comparison of book for book, or version for version, it will be found to be the better translation, from the point of view of limpid and consequent story-telling—perhaps the best in English verse. Of Arnold's four Homeric characteristics, rapidity of movement, plainness of style, simplicity of ideas, nobility of manner, Bryant's translation is inadequate mainly in the first and the last, but the *Homer* is, in any case, a proof of intellectual alertness, scholarship, and technical skill. All his translations, many of them made before Longfellow's now widely-recognized activities as spokesman in America for European letters, are a witness to Bryant's knowledge of foreign tongues and literatures, to his part in the culturization of America, to the breadth of his taste and a certain dramatic adaptability (for the originals that attracted him had often not much of the specific qualities of his own verse), and to his all but impeccable artistry.

Of his artistry this study has scarcely spoken; yet it has

s

been throughout implied. His qualities of thought, feeling, imagination, were communicated, were indeed only communicable, because so wrought into his diction, his rhymes, cadences, and stanzas. Indeed, there is no separating a poet's feeling, say, for a beautiful flower from his manner of expressing it—for all we know about his feeling for the flower is what he succeeds in communicating by speech. It is tautology to say that a poet treats a sublime idea sublimely—for it is the sublimity in the treatment that makes us realize the sublimity of the idea. We can at most conceive a poet's "style" as a whole; as, along with his individual world of meditation and vision, another phase of his creative power—as his creation of music. Possibly it is the deepest and most wonderful of the poet's creations, transcending its manifestation in connection with any single poem. Perhaps, for instance, Milton's greatest creative act was not *Lycidas*, or the *Sonnets*, or *Paradise Lost*, but that music we call Miltonic. Certainly this is the more true the more organic the style is; and, as said before, Bryant's style was highly organic.

An astute and sympathetic mind who might never have seen a verse of Bryant's could deduce that style from what has been said in this chapter—if what has been said has been correctly said. Such a mind would not need to be told that Bryant's diction was severe, simple, chaste, narrower in range than that of his political prose; that his rhymes were dignified, sonorous, exact and emphatic rather than subtle or allusive, and narrow in range—not from artistic poverty but because the rhyme vocabulary of the simple and serious moods is in English itself narrow, and much novelty and variety of rhyme is in our speech possible only when, like Browning, one portrays the grotesque and the eccentric, or like Shelley the fantastic, or like Butler the comic, or like Chaucer the familiar. Such a mind would deduce Bryant's most fundamental rhythm, the iambic; his most fundamental metre, the pentameter; together with his preference for stanzaic, or periodic, treatment, whether in blank verse or in rhyme, rather than for couplets; yes, together with the most characteristic cadences,—like the curves of a distant mountain range, few and clear but not monotonous; like the waves of a broad river, slow and long but not hesitant or ponderous, never delighting by subtle surprises, nor jarring

by abrupt stops and shifts. Indeed, and would our critic not
likewise guess, especially if recently schooled at Leipzig under
Sievers, the very pitch of his voice in verse—strongest in the
lower octaves—as well as the intrinsic alliteration, [1]—an alliteration as natural as breathing, in its context unobtrusive as such
to the conscious ear because so involved in a diction which
is itself the outgrowth of very mood and meaning? In quite
different ways, Bryant is, with Poe, America's finest artist in
verse. Perhaps this is, with Bryant's genuineness of manhood,
a reason why Bryant was the one native contemporary that
Poe thoroughly respected.

What to puzzled readers seems "characteristically Bryant's
blank verse" is really the total impression of both materials
and manner, manner itself including diction as well as metrics.
But the metrics alone do have their peculiarities, which can,
however, hardly be examined here: line endings like "and the
green moss," caesuras at the end of the first and of the fourth
foot, the tendency to repeat the same caesura and cadence
through a succession of lines, a stanza group of five or more lines
with full stop followed by a single line or so, inverted accent at
the beginning of a line, and a differentiated, strong cadence at
the conclusion of the whole poem which gives the effect of a
completion, not of a mere stopping,—these are all contributing
factors.

Yet Bryant is not one of the world's master-poets. It is not
so much that he contributed little or nothing to philosophic
thought or spiritual revolution, not altogether that his range
was narrow, not that he never created a poem of vast and multitudinous proportions, drama, epic, or tale, not that he knew
nature better than human life and human life better than
human nature, not that he now and then lapsed from imaginative vision into a bit of sentiment or irrelevant fancy,—not
either that there is not a single dark saying, or obscure word,
construction, allusion, in all his verse, for the judicious to
elucidate at a club or in a monograph. He is not one of the
world's master-poets, because he was not pre-eminently endowed with intellectual intensity and imaginative concentration.
The character of his whole mind was discursive, enumerative,

---

[1] Largely on b and frequently in idiomatic pairs, as "bees and birds," "bled
or broke."

tending, when measured by the masters, to the diffuse. Thus, among other results, his report of things has given man's current speech but few quotations, of either epigrammatic criticism or haunting beauty. A book could be written on this thesis, but a paragraph must suffice. It is just as well: it is better to realize what Bryant was than to exploit what he was not.

And if he was and is a true poet, he belongs to our best traditions also as critic. He was never, to be sure, the professional guide of literary taste, like Arnold and Lowell. Apart from sensible but obvious memorial addresses on Irving, Halleck, and Cooper, his best known essay is introductory to his *Library of Poetry and Song;* it enunciates fewer keen judgments on individuals, fewer profound principles, than does Emerson's introduction to his *Parnassus,* but it does enunciate the primacy of "a luminous style" and of themes central to common man, in noble paragraphs that should not be forgotten, certainly not by any one who believes that criticism gains in authority when it is the concentrated deduction of experience. Of his services as editor of a leading metropolitan paper, through nearly two generations of crisis after crisis in the nation's life, only an historian should speak. Not even Godwin, his editorial colleague, has spoken, it seems, quite the definitive word. Why should it not be spoken? The fact is, no such man ever sat, before or since, in the editorial chair; in no one other has there been such culture, scholarship, wisdom, dignity, moral idealism. Was it all in Greeley? in Dana? What those fifty years may have meant as an influence on the American press, especially as counteracting the flamboyant and vulgar, the layman may only conjecture.

There is no space to speak of his letters beyond noting that, with all their elegance, courtesy, criticism, information, they do not belong, with Cicero's, Gray's, Cowper's, Byron's, Emerson's, Meredith's, to the literature of correspondence, because they are without zest for little details of human life (whether in others or in himself), or without informal spontaneity and flashes of insight—or without whatever it be that makes a private letter ultimately a public joy.

As a whole, Bryant's prose style has quality as well as qualities, but here a word only on its relation to the style of his poetry. Bryant more than once explicitly differentiated the functions of the two harmonies[1]; but Prescott[2] was not the only one who detected in both the same qualities of mind: obviously a man is not two different beings according to whether he is playing a violin or a cello, singing or talking. Bryant, as Dowden said of Burke, saw "the life of society in a rich, concrete, imaginative way"; and not unlike Burke he had, as politician, the poet's generalizing power. But the point here of special interest is the recurrence in his prose so often, when his prose rises to things in their significance (as apart from their mere relations), of the same imaginative procedure: there is the "broad survey," as in the account of the waters of the Mississippi[3] (themselves introduced as a simile to illustrate the fame of Homer); there are his fundamental metaphors, the grammar of his dialect, as that of the past as a place, occurring in the editorial[4] on the amendment abolishing slavery, which is besides in many details of imagery almost another version of the poem on the same theme, written, says Godwin, a little later. In a public address on the electric telegraph[5] he said:

My imagination goes down to the chambers of the middle sea, to those vast depths where repose the mystic wire on beds of coral, among forests of tangle, or on the bottom of the dim blue gulfs strewn with the bones of whales and sharks, skeletons of drowned men, and ribs and masts of foundered barks, laden with wedges of gold never to be coined, and pipes of the choicest vintages of earth never to be tasted. Through these watery solitudes, among the fountains of the great deep, the abode of perpetual silence, never visited by living human presence and beyond the sight of human eye, there are gliding to and fro, by night and by day, in light and in darkness, in calm and in tempest, currents of human thought borne by the electric pulse which obeys the bidding of man.

Is not this in imagination, mood, manner, even in the recurrent blank verse cadences, veritably as if an unpublished fragment of *A Hymn of the Sea*?

So we return to the Poet. Yet when all is said, it is the whole man that is ours and that should be ours. He is the Citizen of

[1] Godwin, *Prose*, vol. II, p. 22.   [2] Godwin, *Life*, vol. II, p. 36.
[3] Godwin, *Prose*, vol. II, p. 269.   [4] Godwin, *Life*, vol. II, p. 235.
[5] Godwin, *Prose*, vol. II, p. 259.

our tradition; not to us today so much for his hand in the founding of two political parties, nor for his counsels by personal letter and speech that Lincoln, the Statesman of our tradition, heard with such grave respect, nor for his civic activities in art, charity, and reform; but for that Mosaic massive head, those deep, peering, brooding eyes, those white shaggy brows, and the great beard over the old man's cloak that, in the engraving after Sarony's photograph, has been now for a generation familiar in so many homes of our land.

3. Cooper

A CERTAIN John Bristed, writing in 1818, maintained that the United States, without aristocracy, antiquity, and a romantic border, could not have a Scott. Seldom has time contradicted a prophet so fully and so soon as when Cooper, within three years, began to show that democracy has its contrasts, that two hundred years can be called a kind of antiquity, and that the border warfare between pioneer and Indian is one of the great chapters in the world's romance.

The task weighed less upon Cooper than it might had he been from boyhood at all bookish or, when he began his career, either scholar or conscious man of letters. But instead of this he had been trained in the world. Born at Burlington, New Jersey, 15 September, 1789, the son of Judge William Cooper and Susan Fenimore, James Cooper[1] was taken in November, 1790, to Cooperstown, the raw central village of a pioneer settlement recently established by his father on Otsego Lake, New York. Here the boy saw at first hand the varied life of the border, observed its shifts and contrivances, listened to tales of its adventures, and learned to feel the mystery of the dark forest which lay beyond the cleared circle of his own life. Judge Cooper, however, was less a typical backwoodsman than a kind of warden of the New York marches, like Judge Templeton in *The Pioneers*, and he did not keep his son in the woods but sent him, first to the rector of St. Peter's in Albany, who grounded him in Latin and hatred of Puritans, and then to Yale, where he wore his college duties so lightly as to be dis-

---

[1] The family name was changed to Fenimore-Cooper by act of legislature in April, 1826. Cooper soon dropped the hyphen.

missed in his third year. Thinking the navy might furnish better discipline than Yale, Judge Cooper shipped his son before the mast on a merchant vessel to learn the art of seamanship which there was then no naval academy to teach. His first ship, the *Sterling*, sailed from New York in October, 1806, for Falmouth and London, thence to Cartagena, back to London, and once more to America in September of the following year. They were chased by pirates and stopped by searching parties, incidents Cooper never forgot. In January, 1808, he was commissioned midshipman. He served for a time on the *Vesuvius*, and later in the same year was sent with a party to Lake Ontario to build the brig *Oneida* for service against the British on inland waters. He visited Niagara, commanded for a time on Lake Champlain, and in November, 1809, was ordered to the *Wasp*. In the natural course of events he would have fought in the War of 1812, but, having been married in January, 1811, to Miss Susan Augusta DeLancey, he resigned his commission the following May and gave up all hope of a naval career.

Thus at twenty-two he exchanged a stirring youth for the quiet, if happy, life of a country proprietor. He spent the next eleven years, except for a stay at Cooperstown (1814–17), in his wife's native county of Westchester, New York. There, in a manner quite casual, he began his real work. His wife challenged him to make good his boast that he could write a better story than an English novel he was reading to her. He attempted it and wrote *Precaution* (1820), which, as might have been expected from a man who, in spite of a juvenile romance and a few doggerel verses, was little trained in authorship, is a highly conventional novel. Its scene is laid in England, and no quality is more notable than stiff elegance and painful piety. Cooper was dissatisfied with his book. "Ashamed to have fallen into the track of imitation, I endeavoured to repay the wrong done to my own views, by producing a work that should be purely American, and of which love of country should be the theme."[1] He chose for his hero a spy who had served John Jay during the Revolution, according to Jay's own account, with singular purity of motive. The work was carelessly done and published at the author's risk, and yet

[1] *A Letter to his Countrymen*, 1834, p. 98.

with the appearance of *The Spy* (22 December, 1821), American fiction may be said to have come of age.

This stirring tale has been, for many readers, an important factor in the tradition which national piety and the old swelling rhetoric have built up around the Revolution. The share of historical fact in it, indeed, is not large, but the action takes place so near to great events that the characters are all invested with something of the dusky light of heroes, while the figure of Washington moves among them like an unsuspected god. Such a quality in the novel might have gone with impossible partiality for the Americans had not Cooper's wife belonged to a family which had been loyal during the struggle for independence. As it was, he made his loyalists not necessarily knaves and fools, and so secured a fairness of tone which, aside from all questions of justice, has a large effect upon the art of the narrative. It is clear the British are enemies worth fighting. Perhaps by chance, Cooper here hit upon a type of plot at which he excelled, a struggle between contending forces, not badly matched, arranged as a pursuit in which the pursued are, as a rule, favoured by author and reader. In the management of such a device Cooper's invention, which was great, worked easily, and the flights of Birch from friend and foe alike exhibit a power to carry on plots with sustained sweep which belongs only to the masters of narration. To rapid movement Cooper added the virtues of a very real setting. He knew Westchester and its sparse legends as Scott knew the Border; his topography was drawn with a firm hand. In his characters he was not uniformly successful. Accepting for women the romantic ideals of the day and writing of events in which, of necessity, ladies could play but a small part, Cooper tended to cast his heroines, as even that day remarked, into a conventional mould of helplessness and decorum. With the less sheltered classes of women he was much more truthful. Of his men, too, the gentlemen are likely to be mere heroes, though Lawton is an interesting dragoon, while those of a lower order have more marked characteristics. Essentially memorable and arresting is Harvey Birch, peddler and patriot, outwardly no hero at all and yet surpassingly heroic of soul. The skill with which Birch is presented, gaunt, weather-beaten, canny, mysterious—a skill which Brown lacked—should not make one overlook the half-supernatural spirit of patriotism which, like the daemonic impulses in Brown's characters, drives Birch to his destiny at once wrecking and honouring him. This romantic fate also condemns him to be sad and lonely, a dedicated soul who captures attention by his secrecy and holds it throughout his career by his adventures. No character in American historical fiction has been able to obscure this first great character, whose fame has outlasted every fashion for almost a century.

With *The Spy* Cooper proved his power to invent situations, conduct a plot, vivify history and landscape, and create a certain type of heroic character. His public success was instant. The novel reached a third edition the following March; it was approved on the stage; European readers accepted it with enthusiasm. Pleased, though perhaps surprised, at this reception of his work, Cooper threw himself into the new career thus offered him with characteristic energy. He removed to New York and hurried forward the composition of *The Pioneers*, which appeared in February, 1823, with Cooper's first bumptious preface. Technically this book made no advance upon *The Spy*. Cooper had but one method, improvisation, and the absence of any very definite pursuit deprives *The Pioneers*, though it has exciting moments, of general suspense. But it is important as his first trial at the realistic presentation of manners in America. Dealing as he did with the Otsego settlement where his boyhood had been spent, and with a time (1793) within his memory, he could write largely from the fact. Whatever romance there is in the story lies less in its plot, which is relatively simple, or in its characters, which are, for the most part, studied under a dry light with a good deal of caustic judgment, than in the essential wonder of a pioneer life. The novel is not as heroic as *The Spy* had been. Indian John, the last of his proud race, is old and broken, corrupted by the settlements; only his death dignifies him. Natty Bumppo, a composite from many Cooperstown memories, is nobler because he has not yielded but carries his virtues, which even in Cooper's boyhood were becoming archaic along the frontier, into the deeper forest. Natty stands as a protest, on behalf of simplicity and perfect freedom, against encroaching law and order. In *The Pioneers*, however, he is not yet of the proportions which he later assumed, and only at the end, when he withdraws from the field of his defeat by civilization, does he make his full appeal. Cooper may have felt that there were still possibilities in the character, but for the present he did not try to realize them. Instead, he undertook to surpass Scott's *Pirate* in seamanship and produced *The Pilot*, issued in January, 1824.[1] With this third success he practically ended his experimental stage. Like *The Spy*, his new tale made use of a Revolutionary setting; like *The Pioneers*, it was full of realistic detail based on Cooper's own experience. The result was that he not only outdid Scott in sheer narrative, but he created a new literary type, the tale of adventure on the sea, in which, though he was to have many followers in almost every modern language, he remains unsurpassed for vigour and variety. Smollett had already discovered the racy humours of seamen, but it remained for Cooper to capture for fiction the mystery and beauty, the shock and thrill of the sea. Experts say that his technical knowledge was sound; what is more important, he wrote, in *The Pilot*, a story about sailing vessels which convinces landsmen even in days of steam. The conventional element in the novel is its hero, John Paul Jones, secret, Byronic, always brooding upon a dark past and a darker fate. Thoroughly original is that worthy successor of Birch and Natty Bumppo, Long Tom Coffin, who lives and dies by the sea which has made him, as love of country made the spy and the forest made the old hunter.

Cooper had now become a national figure, although critical judgment in New England condescended to him. He founded the Bread and Cheese Club in New York, a literary society of which he was the moving spirit; he took a prominent part in the reception of Lafayette in 1824; in the same year Columbia College gave him the honorary degree of Master of Arts. He planned a series of *Legends of the Thirteen Republics*, aimed to celebrate each of the original states, which he gave up after the first, *Lionel Lincoln* (1825), for all his careful research failed to please as his earlier novels had done. During the next two years Cooper reached probably the highest point of his career in *The Last of the Mohicans* (February, 1826) and *The Prairie* (May, 1827). His own interest and the persuasion of his friends led him to continue the adventures of Natty Bumppo, and

[1] But dated 1823.

very naturally he undertook to show both the days of Natty's prime and his final fortunes. In each case Cooper projects the old hunter out of the world of remembered Otsego, into the dark forest which was giving up its secrets in 1793, or into the mighty prairies which Cooper had not seen but which stretched, in his mind's eye, for endless miles beyond the forest, another mystery and another refuge. Natty, called Hawkeye in *The Last of the Mohicans*, no longer has the hardness which marred his age in *The Pioneers*. With all his virtues of hand and head he combines a nobility of spirit which the woods have fostered in a mind never spoiled by men. He grows nobler as he grows more remote, more the poet and hero as the world in which he moves becomes more wholly his own. Chingachgook has undergone even a greater change, has got back all the cunning and pride which had been deadened in Indian John. But Hawkeye and Chingachgook are both limited by their former appearance; one must still be the canny reasoner, the other a little saddened with passing years. The purest romance of the tale lies in Uncas, the forest's youngest son, gallant, swift, courteous, a lover for whom there is no hope, the last of the Mohicans. That Uncas was idealized Cooper was ready to admit; Homer, he suggested, had his heroes. And it is clear that upon Uncas were bestowed some of the virtues which the philosophers of the age had taught the world to find in a state of nature. Still, after a century many smile upon the state of nature who are yet able to find in Uncas the perennial appeal of youth cut off in the flower. The action and setting of the novel are on the same high plane as the characters. The forest, in which all the events take place, surrounds them with a change-less majesty that sharpens, by contrast, the restless sense of danger. Pursuit makes almost the whole plot. The pursued party moving from Fort Edward to Fort William Henry has two girls to handicap its flight and to increase the tragedy of capture. Later the girls have been captured, and sympathy passes, a thing unusual in Cooper, to the pursuing rescuers. In these tasks Hawkeye and the Mohicans are opposed by the fierce capacity of Magua, who plays villain to Uncas's hero, in moral qualities Uncas's opposite. There is never any relaxation of suspense, and the scene in which Uncas reveals himself to the Delawares is one of the most thrilling moments in fiction.

The Prairie has less swiftness than *The Last of the Mohicans* but more poetry. In it Natty appears again, twenty years older than in *The Pioneers*, far away on the plains beyond the Mississippi. He owns his defeat and he still grieves over the murdered forest, but he has given up anger for the peace of old age. To him it seems that all his virtues are gone. Once valiant he must now be crafty; his arms are feeble; his eyes have so far failed him that, no longer the perfect marksman, he has sunk to the calling of a trapper. There is a pathos in his resignation which would be too painful were it not merely a phase of his grave and noble wisdom. He is more than ever what Cooper called him, "a philosopher of the wilderness." The only change is that he has left the perils and delights of the forest and has been subdued to the eloquent monotony of the plains. Nowhere else has Cooper shown such sheer imaginative power as in his handling of this mighty landscape. He had never seen a prairie; indeed, it is clear that he thought of a prairie as an ocean of land and described it partly by analogy. But he managed to endow the huge empty distances he had not seen with a presence as haunting as that of the populous forest he had known in his impressionable youth. And the old trapper, though he thinks of himself as an exile, has learned the secrets of the new nature and belongs to it. It is his knowledge that makes him essential to the action, which is again made up of flight and pursuit. Once more there are girls to be rescued, from white men as well as from Indians. There is another Magua in Mahtoree, another Uncas in the virtuous Hard-Heart. The Indians ride horses and are thus more difficult to escape than the Hurons had been. The flat prairies give fewer places of concealment. But the trapper is as ready as ever with new arts, and the flight ends as romance prescribes. The final scene, the death of the trapper in the arms of his young friends, is very touching and fine, yet reticently handled. For the most part, the minor characters, the lovers and the pedant, are not new to Cooper and are not notable. The family of Ishmael Bush, the squatter, however, make up a new element. They have been forced out of civilization by its virtues, as the trapper by its vices. They have strength without nobility and activity without wisdom. Except when roused, they are as sluggish as a prairie river, and like it they appear muddy and aimless.

Ishmael Bush always conveys the impression of terrific forces lying vaguely in ambush. His wife is nearly the most memorable figure among Cooper's women. She clings to her mate and cubs with a tigerish instinct that leaves her, when she has lost son and brother and retreats in a vast silent grief, still lingering in the mind, an inarticulate prairie Hecuba.

Possibly the novel owes some of its depth of atmosphere to the fact that it was finished in France and that Cooper was thus looking back upon his subject through a mist of regret. He had sailed for Europe with his family in June, 1826, to begin a foreign residence of more than seven years which had a large effect upon his later life and work. He found his books well known and society at large disposed to make much of him. In Paris he fraternized with Scott, who enjoyed and praised his American rival. Parts of his stay were in England, Holland, Germany, Switzerland, which delighted and astonished him, and Italy, which he loved. Most of his time, however, he passed at Paris, charmed with a gayer and more brilliant society than he could have known before. He did not cease to write. In January, 1828, he repeated the success of *The Pilot* with another sea tale, *The Red Rover*, which has always held a place among the most favoured of his books. The excitement is less sustained than in *The Pilot*, but portions of the narrative, notably those dealing with storms, are tremendous. The ocean here plays as great a part as Cooper had lately assigned to the prairie. One voices the calm of nature, one its tumult; both tend to the discipline of man. In 1829 he fared better than with *Lionel Lincoln* in another historical tale of New England, *The Wept of Wish-ton-Wish*, an episode of King Philip's War. It is a powerful novel, irregular and ungenial, not only because the Puritans represented were themselves unlovely, but because Cooper had an evident dislike for them which coloured all their qualities. This was followed in the next year by *The Water-Witch*, which Cooper thought his most imaginative book. It has a spirited naval battle, but it flatly failed to localize a supernatural legend in New York harbour.

Novels were not Cooper's whole concern during his years in Europe. Unabashedly, outspokenly American, he had secured from Henry Clay the post of consul at Lyons, that he might not seem, during his travels, a man without a country.

As consul, though his position was purely nominal, he felt called upon to resent the ignorance everywhere shown by Europeans regarding his native land, and he set out upon the task of educating them to better views. Cooper was not Franklin. His *Notions of the Americans* (1828), while full of information and a rich mine of American opinion for that day, was too obviously partisan to convince those at whom it was aimed. Its proper audience was homesick Americans. He indulged, too, in some controversy at Paris over the relative cost of French and American government which pleased neither nation. Finally, he applied his art to the problem and wrote three novels "in which American opinion should be brought to bear on European facts."[1] That is, in *The Bravo* (1831), *The Heidenmauer* (1832), and *The Headsman* (1833) he meant to show by proper instances the superiority of democracy to aristocracy as regards general happiness and justice. He claimed to be writing for his countrymen alone, some of whom must have been thrilled to come across a passage like "a fairer morning never dawned upon the Alleghanies than that which illumined the Alps," but he was not sufficiently master of his material, however stout and just his opinions, to make even *The Bravo*, the best of the three, as good as his pioneer romances.

Before he returned to New York in November, 1833, he was warned by his friend S. F. B. Morse that he would be disappointed. Cooper found himself, in fact, fatally cosmopolitan in the republic he had been justifying for seven years. Always critical, he sought to qualify too sweeping praise of America precisely as he had qualified too sweeping censure in Europe. But he had not learned tact while becoming a citizen of the world, and he soon angered the public he had meant to set right. The result was the long and dreary wrangling which clouded the whole remainder of his life and has obscured his fame almost to the present day. If he had attended the dinner planned in his honour on his return, he might have found his welcome warmer than he thought it. If he had been an observer keen enough, he would have seen that the new phases of democracy which he disliked were in part a gift to the old seaboard of that very frontier of which he had been painter and annalist. But he did not see these things, and so he carried on

[1] *A Letter to his Countrymen*, p. 12.

a steady fight, almost always as right in his contentions as he was wrong-headed in his manner. From Cooperstown, generally his residence, except for a few winters in New York, to the end of his life, he lectured and scolded. His *Letter to his Countrymen* (1834), stating his position, and *The Monikins* (1835), an unbelievably dull satire, were the first fruits of his quarrel. He followed these with five books dealing with his European travels and constantly irritating to the people of both continents. He indulged in a heated altercation with his fellow townsmen over some land which they thought theirs, although it was certainly his. In 1838 he published a fictitious record, *Homeward Bound* and its sequel *Home as Found*, of the disappointment of some Americans who return from Europe and find America what Cooper had recently found it. He proclaimed his political principles in *The American Democrat* (1838). Most important of all, he declared war upon the newspapers of New York and went up and down the state suing those that had libelled him. He won most of the suits, but though he silenced his opponents he had put his fame into the hands of persons who, unable to abuse, could at least neglect him.

His solid *History of the Navy of the United States of America* (1839) turned his attention once more to naval affairs, with which he busied himself during much of his remaining career. He wrote *Lives of Distinguished American Naval Officers* (1842–5), and *Ned Myers* (1843), the life of a common sailor who had been with him on the *Sterling*. The *History* led to a furious legal battle, but generally Cooper left his quarrels behind him when he went upon the sea. As a cosmopolitan, he seemed to feel freer out of sight of land, on the public highway of the nations. His novels of this period, however, are uneven in merit. *The Two Admirals* (1842) contains one of his best naval battles; *Wing-and-Wing* (1842) ranks high among his sea tales, richly romantic and glowing with the splendours of the Mediterranean. *Mercedes of Castile* (1840) has little interest beside that essential to the first voyage of Columbus. The two parts of *Afloat and Ashore* (1844), dealing powerfully as they do with the evils of impressment, are notable chiefly for sea fights and chases. *Jack Tier* (1846–8) is a lurid piratical tale of the Mexican War; *The Crater* (1847) does poorly what *Robinson Crusoe* does supremely; *The Sea Lions* (1849) has the distinction of marking the highest point in that religious bigotry which pervades Cooper's later novels as thoroughly as the carping spirit which kept him always alert for a chance to take some fling at his countrymen.

The real triumph of his later years was that he wrote, in the very midst of his hottest litigation, *The Pathfinder* (March, 1840) and *The Deerslayer* (August, 1841). One realizes, in reading them, that the forest more than the ocean was for Cooper a romantic sanctuary, as it was for Pathfinder the true temple, full of the "holy calm of nature," the teacher of beauty, virtue, laws. Returning to these solemn woods, Cooper was subdued once more to the spirit which had attended his first great days. The fighting years through which he had passed had left him both more mellow and more critical than at first. During the same time he had gone far enough from the original character of Leather-Stocking to become aware of traits which should be brought out or explained. It was too late to make his hero entirely consistent for the series, but Cooper apparently saw the chance to fill out the general outline, and he did it with such skill that those who read the five novels in the order of events will notice relatively few discrepancies, since *The Deerslayer* prepares for nearly all that follows. In *The Pathfinder*, undertaken to show Natty in love and to combine the forest and a ship in the same tale, Cooper was at some pains to point out how Pathfinder's candour, self-reliance, justice, and fidelity had been developed by the life he had led in the forest. Leather-Stocking, indeed, does not seem more conscious of these special gifts, but Cooper does. Still there is abundant action, another flight through the woods, a storm on Lake Ontario, a siege at a blockhouse. Chingachgook, unchanged, is with Pathfinder, who varies from his earlier character in little but his love for a young girl whom he finally surrenders to a more suitable lover. His love affair threatens for a moment to domesticate Natty, but the sacrifice restores him to his old solitude.

In the final book of the series, *The Deerslayer*, Cooper performed with full success the hard task of representing the scout in the fresh morning of his youth. Love appears too in this story, but Deerslayer, unable to love a girl who has been corrupted by the settlements, turns to the forest with his best devotion. The book is the tale of his coming of age.

6

Already a hunter, he kills his first man and thus enters the long career which lies before him. That career, however, had already been traced by Cooper, and the distress with which Deerslayer realizes that he has human blood on his hands becomes immeasurably eloquent. It gives the figure of the man almost a new dimension; one remembers the many deaths Natty has yet to deal. In other matters he is near his later self, for he starts life with a steady philosophy which, through all the many experiences of *The Deerslayer*, keeps him to the end as simple and honourable as at the outset.

The novel is thus an epitome of the whole career of the most memorable character American fiction has given to the world. Leather-Stocking is very fully drawn; Cooper's failure to write a sixth novel, as he at one time planned, which should show Natty in the Revolution, may be taken as a sign that he felt, however unconsciously, that the picture was finished. It is hard, indeed, to see how he could have added to the scout without taking something from the spy. More important still, the virtue of patriotism, if carried to the pitch that must have been demanded for that hero in that day, would surely have been a little alien to the cool philosopher of the woods. Justice, not partisanship, is Leather-Stocking's essential trait. In him Cooper exhibited, even better than he knew, his special idea that human character can be brought to a noble proportion and perfection in the school of pure nature. Now this idea, generally current in Cooper's youth, had an effect upon the Leather-Stocking tales of the greatest moment. Because their hero, as the natural man, had too simple a soul to call for minute analysis, it was necessary for Cooper to show him moving through a long succession of events aimed to test the firmness of his virtues. There was thus produced the panorama of the American frontier which, because of Cooper's incomparable fusion of strangeness and reality, at once became and has remained the classic record of an heroic age.

He wrote more border tales before his death. *Wyandotté* (1843) deals largely with the siege of a blockhouse near the upper Susquehanna, and *The Oak-Openings* (1848), the fruit of a journey which he made to the West in 1847, is a tale of bee hunting and Indian fighting on the shores of Lake Michigan. Full of border material, too, is the trilogy of *Littlepage Manu-*

scripts, Satanstoe (1845), *The Chainbearer* (1846), and *The Redskins* (1846). Having tried the autobiographical method with Miles Wallingford in *Afloat and Ashore*, Cooper now repeated it through three generations of a New York family. In the last he involved himself unduly in the question of anti-rentism and produced a book both fantastic and dull; the second is better by one of Cooper's most powerful figures, the squatter Thousandacres, another Titan of the brood of Ishmael Bush; the first, if a little beneath Cooper's best work, is so only because he was somewhat rarely at his best. No other novel, by Cooper or any other, gives so firm and convincing a picture of colonial New York. Even Cooper has no more exciting struggle than that of Corny Littlepage with the icy Hudson. But the special virtue of *Satanstoe* is a quality Cooper nowhere else displays, a positive winsomeness in the way Littlepage unfolds his memories (now sweetened by many years) and his humorous crotchets in the same words. There are pages which read almost like those of some vigorous Galt or Goldsmith. Unfortunately, Cooper did not carry this vein further. His comedy *Upside Down*, produced at Burton's Theatre, New York, 18 June, 1850, was a failure, and his last novel, *The Ways of the Hour* (1851), lacks every charm of manner. With his family and a few friends he lived his latter days in honour and affection, but he held the public at a sour distance and before his death, 14 September, 1851, set his face against a reconciliation even in the future by forbidding any biography to be authorized. The published facts of his life still leave his personality less known to the general world than that of any American writer of equal rank.

This might be somewhat strange, since Cooper was lavish of intrusions into his novels, were it not that he wrote himself down, when he spoke in his own person, not only a powerful and independent man, but a scolding, angry man, and thus made his most revealing novels his least read ones. One thinks of Scott, who, when he shows himself most, wins most love. The difference further characterizes the two men. In breadth of sympathies, humanity, geniality, humour, Cooper is less than Scott. He himself, in his review of Lockhart, said that Scott's great ability lay in taking a legend or historical episode, which Scotland furnished in splendid profusion, and reproducing it with marvellous grace and tact. "This faculty of creating a *vraisemblance*, is next to that of a high invention, in a novelist." It is clear that Cooper felt his own inferiority to Scott in "creating a *vraisemblance*" and that he was always conscious of the relative barrenness of American life; it is also tolerably clear that he himself aimed at what he thought the higher quality of invention. Cooper's invention, indeed, was not without a solid basis; he is not to be neglected as an historian. No man better sums up in literature the spirit of that idealistic, irascible, pugnacious, somewhat crude, and half aristocratic older democracy which established the United States. No one fixed the current heroic traditions of his day more firmly to actual places. No one else supplied so many facts to the great legend of the frontier. Fact no less than fiction underlies the character which, for all time, Cooper gave to the defeated race of red men, who, no longer a menace as they had been to the first settlers, could now take their place in the world of the imagination, sometimes idealized, as in Uncas and Hard-Heart, but more often credibly imperfect and uncivilized. It was his technical knowledge of ships and sailors which led Cooper to write sea tales, a province of romance in which he still takes rank, among many followers, as teacher and master of them all. True, Cooper had not Scott's resources of historical learning to fall back upon when his invention flagged, any more than he had Scott's resources of good-nature when he became involved in argument; but when, as in the Leather-Stocking tales, his invention could move most freely, it did unaided what Scott, with all his subsidiary qualities, could not outdo. This is to credit Cooper with an invention almost supreme among romancers. Certainly it is difficult to explain why, with all his faults of clumsiness, prolixity, conventional characterization, and ill temper, he has been the most widely read American author, unless he is to be called one of the most impressive and original.

CHAPTER III

Poe

THE saddest and the strangest figure in American literary history is that of Edgar Allan Poe. Few writers have lived a life so full of struggle and disappointment, and none have lived and died more completely out of sympathy with their times. His life has been made the subject of minute and prolonged investigation, yet there are still periods in his history that have not been satisfactorily cleared up. And the widest differences of opinion have existed as to his place and his achievements. But there are few today who will not readily concede to him a place among the foremost writers of America, whether in prose or in verse, and there are not wanting those who account him one of the two or three writers of indisputable genius that America has produced.

Poe was born at Boston, 19 January, 1809, the son of actor parents of small means and of romantic proclivities. Before the end of his third year he was left an orphan, his mother dying in wretched poverty at Richmond, Virginia, 8 December, 1811, and his father a few weeks later, if we may believe the poet's own statement. He was promptly taken under the protection of a prosperous tobacco exporter of Richmond, John Allan, in whose family he lived, ostensibly as an adopted child, until 1827. In his sixth year he attended for a short time the school of William Ewing in Richmond. In the summer of 1815 he went with his foster-father to England, and for the next five years, with the exception of a few months spent in Scotland shortly after reaching England, he lived in London, attending first a boarding school kept by the Misses Dubourg in Sloane Street, and later the academy of the Rev. John Bransby in Stoke Newington. He impressed Bransby as a "quick and clever boy," though embarrassed by "an extravagant amount of pocket-money"; and John Allan wrote of him in 1818 that he was "a fine boy" and read "Latin pretty sharply." In 1816 Allan described him as "thin as a razor," but in 1819 he wrote that he was "growing wonderfully."

On his return to Richmond in the summer of 1820, Poe entered an academy kept, first, by Joseph H. Clarke and, later, by William Burke, under whom he continued his work in the languages, earning the admiration of his fellows by his readiness at "capping verses" from the Latin and by his skill in declamation. He also wrote verses of his own, and it is said that a sheaf of his juvenilia was collected in 1822 or 1823 in the hope that they might be published in volume form. But before the end of 1824 he had somehow broken with his foster-father, and the breach between the two was never to be entirely healed. "The boy possesses not a spark of affection for us," wrote John Allan in November, 1824, "not a particle of gratitude for all my care and kindness towards him. . . . I fear his associates have led him to adopt a line of thinking and acting very contrary to what he possessed when in England." The immediate cause of the breach we do not know; but a parting of the ways between the two, who were radically dissimilar in tastes and ideals, was inevitable sooner or later.

The year 1826 Poe spent as a student at the University of Virginia. Here he made a creditable record in his classes, winning honourable mention in Latin and French; and he at no time fell under the censure of his instructors. At the end of the year, however, because of his having accumulated gambling debts of some twenty-five hundred dollars, he was withdrawn from college; and with the beginning of the next year he was placed by his adoptive father in his counting-house in Richmond, in the hope that he might develop a taste for a business career. But he had small leaning that way; besides, he had been disappointed in a love-affair, having become engaged before going to college to Miss Sarah Elmira Royster, of Richmond, who, in consequence of a misunderstanding, had jilted him in his absence and had betrothed herself to another. Smarting under this disappointment and completely out of sympathy with the life marked out for him by his foster-father, Poe now determined to run away; and at some time in March, 1827, he left Richmond for parts unknown. In May he appeared at Boston, and there, 26 May, he was mustered into the army of the United States. The next two years he served as a soldier in barracks, being stationed first at Boston, then at Charleston, South Carolina, and finally at Fortress Monroe. In the spring or summer of 1827 he brought out at Boston his first volume of poems, *Tamerlane and Other Poems*, a collection of ten fugitive pieces, all brief save one, and all plainly imitative either of Byron or of Moore.

In February, 1829, Mrs. Allan died, and in April Poe was discharged from the army, a substitute having been provided, and efforts were made to obtain for him an appointment to West Point. Some time intervened, however, before an appointment could be procured, and it was not until July, 1830, that he was admitted to the Academy. In the preceding December he had published at Baltimore a second volume of poems, made up largely of his earlier pieces revised, but containing his long poem *Al Aaraaf*, the most ambitious and the most promising of his earlier productions. At West Point he took high rank in his classes; but in October, 1830, John Allan had married a second time, and Poe, concluding that there was no longer any prospect of succeeding to a fortune, determined with the beginning of the new year to bring about his dismissal from the Academy. He adopted the very effective means of absenting himself from roll calls and from classes, was court-martialled in consequence, and 6 March, 1831, was formally expelled. In April a third volume of his poems appeared, containing some of the best work that he ever did, but in a state much inferior to that in which he ultimately left it.

During the ensuing four years Poe seems to have made his home in Baltimore, though it is impossible to trace his history with complete certainty throughout this period. Much of his time, no doubt, was given to his prose tales, five of which appeared in the Philadelphia *Saturday Courier*, in 1832,[1] and a sixth—for which he won a prize of fifty dollars—in the Baltimore *Saturday Visiter* in October, 1833; and he also worked at intervals during these years on a play, *Politian*, which, though published in part, was never completed. That

[1] These stories were originally submitted in competition for a prize—won, as it happens, by Delia Bacon.

he lived in poverty and in much obscurity is evident from the reminiscences of John Pendleton Kennedy, the novelist,[1] who had been one of the judges in the *Visiter's* contest in 1833 and who now proved his most helpful friend.

In the summer of 1835, Poe went to Richmond to assist in the editing of *The Southern Literary Messenger*, and before the end of the year he had been promoted to be editor-in-chief of that magazine. He was now fairly launched on his career as man of letters. In the columns of the *Messenger* he republished, with slight revisions, the tales that had already appeared, and in addition a number of new tales and poems, together with a long line of book reviews, which promptly won for the *Messenger* a popularity such as no other Southern magazine has ever enjoyed. In May, 1836, relying on his suddenly acquired prosperity, he married. His wife was Virginia Clemm,[2] a child of thirteen and the daughter of a paternal aunt, in whose home he had lived for a time in Baltimore. In the fall he was absent from his post for several weeks in consequence of illness brought on by excessive indulgence in drink; and though on his recovery he returned to his duties with his accustomed vigour, he was unable to satisfy his employer as to his stability of habit; and with the initial number of the *Messenger* for 1837 his resignation as editor was formally announced.

From Richmond he went to New York, where he hoped to find employment with *The New York Review*. In October, 1837, he was in Richmond again, posing as editor still of the *Messenger*, though we cannot be certain that he contributed anything to its columns at this time. At the end of the year he was again in New York; and in the following summer he moved to Philadelphia. In July he published at New York, in book form, the longest of his tales, *The Narrative of Arthur Gordon Pym*.

The next six years (1838–1844) he spent in Philadelphia. During the first year he was engaged largely in hack-writing, busying himself with a work on conchology (published in

[1] Tuckerman, *Life of Kennedy*, pp. 373 f.

[2] A license for marriage to Virginia Clemm was procured at Baltimore in September, 1835, but it has not been established that there was a wedding at that time.

1839) among other things, though he also composed at this time some of the best of his tales. In May, 1839, he became associate editor of *Burton's Gentleman's Magazine*, but a year later he quarrelled with Burton and lost his place. From April, 1841, to May, 1842, he edited *Graham's Magazine*. And in 1843 he had for a while some tacit connection with a Philadelphia weekly, *The Saturday Museum*. In *Burton's* and in *Graham's* he published a number of the ablest of his book-reviews and some of the most striking of his tales. At the end of 1839 he brought out at Philadelphia a collection of his tales, in two volumes; and in 1843 a further edition of his tales was projected, of which, however, only one fascicle, containing but two of his stories, was published. In the same year he won a prize of a hundred dollars for his story *The Gold Bug*. But at no time during these years was his income from his writings or from his editorial labours sufficient to enable him to live in comfort. During his later years in Philadelphia, moreover, his weakness for drink had grown on him, and he had as a result lost many of his friends; his wife, too, frail from childhood, had become an invalid in 1841 or in 1842; and so, early in 1844, the poet concluded to seek a new field.

In April, 1844, he moved with his family to New York; and there, either in the city or at Fordham, a few miles out, he lived during the remaining five years allotted to him. The year 1844 was uneventful, but the year 1845 proved to be the pivotal year of his history. At the end of January appeared in the New York *Evening Mirror*, on which he had held a minor editorial position for several months, *The Raven;* and he became at once the most talked of man of letters in America. In the summer he published a new volume of his tales, and in the fall, a collected edition of his poems, *The Raven and Other Poems*. Early in the year he became assistant editor of *The Broadway Journal;* in July he became sole editor, and in October editor and proprietor of this paper; and thus was enabled to realize an ambition that he had cherished for more than a decade, to edit a paper of his own. But owing to financial embarrassments arising from various causes, he was compelled to give up this paper at the end of the year. During the first half of 1846 he was ill, so he himself claimed, for several months. In the middle of the year (May to October) he published, in Godey's *Lady's Book*, his *Literati*, a series of bio-graphical-critical papers dealing with the chief living writers of Gotham; and the year was further made memorable by the controversy with Thomas Dunn English engendered by the publication of the *Literati*, and by a scandal growing out of his friendship with the poetess, Mrs. F. S. Osgood. Early in 1847 the poet's wife died, and throughout the year, as indeed during the preceding year, the family suffered keenly from the pinch of poverty. The year 1848 saw the culmination of two unhappy love-affairs—first, with Mrs. Shew, who had nursed the poet through a spell of illness following the death of his wife, and then with Mrs. Whitman, the Rhode Island poetess; and this year also witnessed the publication of his *Eureka*, a philosophical disquisition on the origin and composition of the universe.

The year 1849 opened auspiciously for the poet; during the first half he wrote at least one new tale, and several new poems, including the lines *For Annie, Eldorado*, a revised and much enlarged version of *The Bells*, and the last of his poems, *Annabel Lee*. In the summer of 1849 he went to Richmond, where he renewed his addresses to the sweetheart of his boy-hood, Miss Royster, now the widow Mrs. Shelton and wealthy, and they became engaged for a second time. Late in September Poe left Richmond for the North, intending to bring his mother-in-law, who remained loyal to him throughout the years, to the South for the marriage; but at Baltimore he was induced to break a temperance pledge that he had made in the summer, and as a result he fell into excesses from the effects of which he died 7 October, 1849. He lies buried in the churchyard of Westminster Presbyterian Church, Baltimore.

Such are the leading facts that have been established concerning Poe's life. But despite the labours of his biographers —and no American writer has had more and abler biographers —there are still certain periods of his life for which our knowledge is exceedingly meagre and unsatisfactory. We have, for instance, no specific knowledge as to how or where he spent the two months intervening between his departure from Richmond in March, 1827, and his mustering into the army at the end of May. We are likewise ignorant both as to his where-abouts and as to his activities during the year immediately preceding his winning of the *Visiter's* prize in October, 1833; and the entire period from 1831 to 1835 is obscure. He sinks out of sight again for six months in the middle of 1837. And a hiatus of several months also occurs in his history during the first half of the year 1846. For this obscurity Poe is himself mainly responsible. He took pleasure in mystifying his public about himself; and in a few instances he deliberately misstated the facts.[1]

As to Poe's character and personality the most divergent views have been expressed. According to Griswold, whom he chose as his literary executor, Poe was a "naturally unamiable character," arrogant, "irascible, envious," without "moral susceptibility" or sense of gratitude, and exhibiting "scarcely any virtue in either his life or his writings." According to the Richmond editor, John M. Daniel, who saw him frequently during the summer of 1849, he was sour of nature, capricious, selfish, a misanthrope, possessing "little moral sense." In the view of Lowell's friend, C. F. Briggs, with whom he was associated for several months in 1845 as co-editor of the *Broadway Journal*, he was "badly made up," a "characterless character," and "utterly deficient of high motive." And Horace Greeley was disturbed lest Mrs. Whitman should marry him, giving it as his opinion that such a union would be a "terrible conjunction." To N. P. Willis, on the other hand, who perhaps knew him better than any other outside of his immediate family during his last half-dozen years, there appeared, during several months of close association with him in 1844-1845, "but one presentment of the man,—a quiet, patient, industrious, and most gentlemanly person, commanding the utmost respect and good feeling by his unvarying deportment and ability"; and in subsequent years he saw, so he declares, nothing of the arrogance, vanity, and depravity of heart "that were commonly attributed to him." And George R. Graham, editor of the magazine that bore his name, testifies that, when he knew him best (in the first half of the forties), "he had the docility and kind-heartedness of a child," and that "no man was more quickly touched by a kindness, none more prompt to make return for an injury," and, further, that he was "the soul

[1] See, in particular, in this connection, an autobiographical memorandum sent to Griswold in 1841 (*Works of Poe*, ed. Harrison, Vol. I, pp. 344-346), in which most of the dates are inaccurately given, and in which we have one of several apocryphal accounts of a voyage to Europe in 1827.

of honour in all his transactions." Kennedy notes that he was "irregular, eccentric, and querulous," but adds—as if in set rejoinder to Griswold's charge that he was incapable of gratitude for service done—that "he always remembered my kindness with gratitude." As time has passed and we have come to know more about Poe's life, it has become more and more evident that the view of his character held by Griswold and those who sided with him was unduly harsh,[1] though it remains clear, nevertheless, that Poe was not without regrettable traits and serious weaknesses. It is plain, first of all, that he was abnormally proud and sensitive and impulsive; it is equally plain that he was thoroughly undignified and ungenerous in his attacks on certain of his contemporaries who had aroused his envy or incurred his dislike. We have already noted that he was not invariably accurate of statement, especially in matters pertaining peculiarly to himself; we know, too, that he was an incessant borrower, and that he neglected in some instances to make good his borrowings at the appointed time,—though there is no conclusive evidence of dishonesty of intent on his part. And all the world knows that he sometimes drank to excess. But it is also clear—contrary to the popular assumption—that Poe was not a confirmed inebriate: the volume and the quality of his writings sufficiently demonstrate this; and it is not to be denied that he made repeated and manful efforts to shake off the tyranny of drink. Nor can we read his letters —in which we see the true Poe more plainly than elsewhere— without being convinced that he also possessed amiable traits and noble impulses. In any estimate of his character, moreover, it is but just to take into account—as, indeed, most of his recent biographers have done—the influences exerted on his character by heredity and by his early environment[2]; and it should also be borne in mind that he suffered during most of his later career from serious physical infirmities.[3]

[1] It is due to Griswold, however, to say that his account of Poe's life, though inaccurate at many points and jaundiced throughout, is more to be relied on than is now commonly assumed. For exposing most of Griswold's inaccuracies we are indebted to Poe's English biographer, the late John H. Ingram.

[2] His father before him was highly impulsive and was over-fond of drink, and his foster-father was not only given to wine-bibbing but was an arch-hypocrite besides.

[3] The clash of opinion with respect to Poe's character appears to be due

It was as critic that Poe first attracted widespread attention.   As editor of the *Messenger* and *Burton's* and *Graham's*
his chief function was that of book-reviewer; and much of the
work that he did for other periodicals was of the nature of
book-reviews and gossip about books and authors.   The bulk
of his work in this field is journalistic in style and of ephemeral
interest, much of it being the merest hack-writing; but there
remains a small body of critical matter that possesses genuine
worth and distinction, and that entitles Poe to an honourable
place among the literary critics of America.[1]   Assuredly no
other American critic of his day, save Lowell, may take rank
above him.   This residue of good work comprises a score of
masterly book-reviews, including the memorable notices of
Longfellow's *Ballads*, Hawthorne's *Twice-Told Tales*, and
Dickens's *Barnaby Rudge;* some half-dozen essays in the
theory of criticism, of which the earliest is his *Letter to B——*,
and the most significant is his *Poetic Principle;* and a series of
obiter dicta, collected under the title *Marginalia*, which have
justly been held to contain much of his best work as critic.[2]

His most distinctive gifts as critic were clearness of intellect and a faculty for analysis.   Few Americans of his time
had finer intellectual endowments.   He also had the poet's
"faculty of ideality," on which he laid great stress in his judgments of others.   And he was the most independent and fearless of critics, disdaining not to attack either high or low.   He
had not read very widely; but he knew his Milton well, and
probably his Shakespeare and his Pope, and he was familiar

---

mainly, as Willis suggested, to the fact that most of the contemporary judgments
adverse to him were based on his conduct during his spells of inebriation, at
which times (as he pathetically admitted more than once) he was largely irresponsible. Most of these estimates, too, are based, naturally, on the poet's
later years, after both body and mind had become enfeebled. Poe himself
urged, in partial explanation of his irregularities in his later years, the plea of
insanity; and there is reason to believe that he was at one time addicted to the
use of opium.

  [1] "Poe's critical writing was so much superior to the best of what had preceded it," remarks William Morton Payne (*American Literary Criticism*, 1904,
p. 14), "that one might almost be pardoned for saying that this department of
our literature began when, in 1835, *The Southern Literary Messenger* engaged
his services."

  [2] F. C. Prescott, *Selections from the Critical Writings of Edgar Allan Poe*, p.
xix; J. M. Robertson, *New Essays towards a Critical Method*, p. 117.

with the chief Romantic poets of the age immediately preceding his own; while as editor and magazinist he kept in close touch with contemporary literature. On the other hand, he was prone to exaggerate technical blemishes and to underestimate ethical and philosophical significance. And his taste was not always impeccable. By his contemporaries he was thought of as inexcusably harsh in his criticisms: by one of them he is dubbed the "tomahawk man," by another the "broad-axe man"; and Lowell remarks, in his sketch of him, that he seemed "sometimes to mistake his phial of prussic-acid for his inkstand." What is more to his discredit, he stooped now and then to log-rolling both on his own account and on behalf of his friends, and his unfavourable judgments appear to have been actuated in some instances by animus and jealousy. But most of his critical judgments have been sustained by time. And despite the arrogance charged against him by Griswold and others, it is to be set down to his credit that he ungrudgingly conceded to Longfellow and Lowell the primacy among the American poets of his time and that he generously proclaimed Hawthorne to be without a peer in his peculiar field. His chief hobbies as critic were originality— and, *per contra*, imitation and plagiarism—"unity or totality of effect," consistency and "keeping," verisimilitude, "the heresy of the didactic," provinciality, metrical imperfections of whatever sort, and verbal inaccuracies and infelicities; some of which hobbies—as plagiarism—he rode over-hard. But his influence in an age when wholesale adulation was the rule, and when art counted for but little, was naturally wholesome.

Among the best known of his critical *dicta* is his characterization of the short story in his notice of Hawthorne's *Twice-Told Tales* (1842). Probably no other passage in American literary criticism has been quoted so often as the following extract from this review:

A skilful literary artist has constructed a tale. If wise, he has not fashioned his thoughts to accommodate his incidents; but having conceived, with deliberate care, a certain unique or single *effect* to be wrought out, he then invents such incidents—he then combines such events as may best aid him in establishing this preconceived effect. If his very initial sentence tend not to the outbringing of this effect, then he has failed in his first step. In the whole composition there should be no word written, of which the tendency, direct or indirect, is not to the one pre-established design. And by such means, with such care and skill, a picture is at length painted which leaves in the mind of him who contemplates it with a kindred art, a sense of the fullest satisfaction. The idea of the tale has been presented unblemished, because undisturbed; and this is an end unattainable by the novel.[1]

Scarcely less famous are some of his deliverances on the meaning and the province and aims of poetry. Poetry he defined as the "rhythmical creation of beauty," holding with Coleridge, his chief master as critic, that its "immediate object" is "pleasure, not truth"; and that "with the intellect or with the conscience it has only collateral relations." "Poetry and passion" he held to be "discordant." And humour, also, he believed to be "antagonistical to that which is the soul of the muse proper." Sadness he declared to be the most poetic of moods; and "indefinitiveness" one of the chief essentials of lyric excellence. A long poem he held, with Bryant, to be a "contradiction in terms."

Poe's critical doctrines find their best exemplification in his own poems. He is, first of all, a poet of beauty, paying little heed to morality or to the life of his fellow-men. He is, in the second place, a master-craftsman, who has produced a dozen poems of a melody incomparable so far as the western world is concerned; and he has achieved an all but flawless construction of the whole in such poems as *The Raven*, *The Haunted Palace*, and *The Conqueror Worm;* while in *The Bells* he has performed a feat in onomatopœia quite unapproached before or since in the English language. He is, moreover, one of the most original of poets. And the best of his verse exhibits a spontaneity and finish and perfection of phrase, as well as, at times, a vividness of imagery, that it is difficult to match elsewhere in American poetry.

But his poems of extraordinary worth are exceedingly few —scarcely above a score at most—in which must be included the earlier lines *To Helen, Israfel, The City in the Sea, The Sleeper,*

[1] *Works of Poe*, ed. Harrison, Vol. XI, p. 108.

The Haunted Palace, Dream-Land, The Raven, Ulalume, For Annie, and *Annabel Lee.* And most of his earlier verses are manifestly imitative, Byron and Moore and Coleridge and Shelley being his chief models; while much of his earlier work, including all of the volume of 1827, and some of his latest— notably the verses addressed to Mrs. Osgood and Mrs. Shew and Mrs. Lewis—are either fragmentary and "incondite" or mere "verses," or both. It has been justly said that "there is almost no poet between whose best and worst verse there is a wider disparity."[1] His range, too, is narrower than that of any other American poet of front rank. Consistently with one of his theories already adverted to, he wrote no long poem, save the juvenile *Tamerlane* and *Al Aaraaf,* both of them extremely crude performances (though *Al Aaraaf* contains excellent passages and played a large part in his development as poet), and an abortive play, *Politian,* which he never saw fit to publish in its entirety; so that he lives as poet solely by reason of his lyrics. And within the realm of the lyric he confined himself to the narrowest range of ideas. Nature he employed merely as ornament or as symbol or to fill in the background; and nowhere in his poems does he deal with the life about him, except in so far as he writes of friends and kindred. His most constant theme—if we exclude the poet himself, for few writers have so constantly reflected themselves in their work—is either the death of a beautiful woman and the grief occasioned thereby, or the realm of shades—the spirit-world —a subject to which he was strongly attracted, especially in his middle years. Hence, although most European critics have accorded him first place among American poets, most American critics have hesitated to accept their verdict.

Much of the excellence of his best poems arises from the never-ending revisions to which he subjected them. *The Raven,* for example, exists in upwards of a dozen variant forms, and some of his earlier verses were so radically altered as to be scarcely recognizable in their final recast. His melody, especially in his later poems, grows in large measure out of his all but unexampled use of parallelism and of the refrain.[2] Not a little of his charm, moreover, both in his earlier and in

[1] J. M. Robertson, *New Essays,* p. 76.
[2] C. A. Smith, *Repetition and Parallelism in English Verse,* pp. 44 f.

his later work, results from his use of symbolism. It is idle to complain that his best verses—as *Israfel* or *The Haunted Palace* —are superficial; and it is futile to contend that such poems as *Annabel Lee* or the sonnet *To My Mother* are not sincere, or that his poems, one and all, lack spontaneity. But it is not to be denied that some of his best-known poems—as *Lenore* and *The Raven*—exhibit too much of artifice; that *The Conqueror Worm* and passages in still other poems approach too near to the melodramatic; and that, with many readers, his verses must suffer by reason of their sombreness of tone.

Poe's tales, which exceed in number his fully authenticated poems, have been held by some of the most judicious of his critics to constitute his chief claim to our attention.[1] There are those who will not subscribe to this view, but it is plain that he was the most important figure in the history of the short story during his half-century. Hawthorne alone may be thought of as vying with him for this distinction; but although the New Englander is infinitely Poe's superior in some respects—as in the creation of character and in wholesomeness and sanity—he must yield place to him in the creation of incident, in the construction of plot, and in the depicting of an intensely vivid situation. Whether or not we allow Poe the distinction of having invented the short story will depend on our interpretation of terms; but at least he invented the detective story, and more than any other he gave to the short story its vogue in America.

Like his poems, his tales are notably unequal. Some of his earlier efforts—especially his satirical and humorous extravaganzas, as *Lionizing* and *Bon-Bon*—are properly to be characterized as rubbish; and he was capable in his later years of descending to such inferior work as *The Sphinx, Mellonta Tauta,* and *X-ing a Paragrab.* One feels, indeed, that Lowell's famous characterization of him:

Three fifths of him genius and two fifths sheer fudge,

applies with entire justice to him as a maker of short stories. The best of his narrative work is to be found in his analytical

[1] E. C. Stedman in the Stedman-Woodberry edition of Poe, Vol. x, p. xiii; and Robertson, *l. c.,* p. 75.

tales, as *The Gold Bug* or *The Descent into the Maelstrom*, in certain stories in which he combines his analytical gift with the imaginative and inventive gift, as *The Cask of Amontillado* and *William Wilson*, or in certain studies of the pure imagination, as *The Fall of the House of Usher* and *The Masque of the Red Death*. In all of these he displays a skill of construction and of condensation surpassed by few if any other workers in his field. In some—as in *The Masque of the Red Death*, or in *Eleonora*, or in his landscape studies—he shows himself a master of English style; and in two of his briefer studies—*Shadow* and *Silence*—he approaches the eloquence and splendour of De Quincey.

His main limitations as a writer of the short story are to be found in the feebleness and flimsiness of his poorer work; in his all but complete lack of healthy humour; in his incapacity to create or to depict character; in his morbidness of mood and grotesqueness of situation.[1] He suffers also in comparison with other leading short-story writers of America and England in consequence of his disdain of the ethical in art (though neither his tales nor his poems are entirely lacking in ethical value); he suffers, again, in comparison with certain present-day masters of the short story in consequence of his lack of variety in theme and form; and he was never expert in the management of dialogue.

By reason of his fondness for the terrible and for the *outré*, he is to be classed with the Gothic romancers: he makes constant use of Gothic machinery, of apparitions, cataleptic attacks, premature burial, and life after death. In several of his stories—as also in his long poems, *Tamerlane* and *Al Aaraaf* —he follows in the steps of the Orientalists. On the other hand, in some of his tales of incident he achieves a realism and a minuteness of detail that betray unmistakably the influence of Defoe. And it is easy to demonstrate an indebtedness to divers

[1] His friend, P. P. Cooke, wrote of him in 1847: "For my individual part, having the seventy or more tales, analytic, mystic, grotesque, arabesque, always wonderful, often great, which his industry and fertility have already given us, I would like to read one cheerful book made by his *invention*, with little or no aid from its twin brother *imagination*, . . . a book full of homely doings, of successful toils, of ingenious shifts and contrivances, of ruddy firesides—a book healthy and happy throughout" (*Southern Literary Messenger*, January, 1848, p. 37).

of his contemporaries, as James and Bulwer and Disraeli and Macaulay. It has been proved also that he knew the German romancer, E. T. A. Hoffmann, if not in the original, at least in translation, and that he caught his manner and appropriated his themes.[1] For the rest, he drew for his materials largely on the magazines and newspapers of his day, finding in a famous newspaper sensation of the forties the suggestion of his *Mystery of Marie Rogêt* (as he had found in another sensation, of the twenties, the plot of his *Politian*), and taking advantage of certain contemporary fads in his myth-making about mesmerism, ballooning, premature burial, and the like; and he boldly pilfered from government reports, scientific treatises, and works of reference such material as he found serviceable in some of his tales of adventure. Hence his originality may be said to consist rather in combination and adaptation than in more obviously inventive exercises of the fancy.

Poe's influence has been far-reaching. As poet, he has had many imitators both in his own country and abroad, but especially in France and England.[2] As romancer he has probably wielded a larger influence than any English writer since Scott. And as critic it is doubtful whether any other of his countrymen has contributed so much toward keeping the balance right between art-for-art's-sake and didacticism. His fame abroad is admittedly larger than that of any other American writer, and his vogue has been steadily growing among his own people.

[1] Palmer Cobb, *The Influence of E. T. A. Hoffmann on the Tales of Edgar Allan Poe*. Woodberry, *Life of Poe*, vol. I, pp. 379–381, and *passim*.

[2] In the view of Edmund Gosse, "there is hardly one [of the later English poets] whose verse-music does not show traces of Poe's influence" (*Questions at Issue*, p. 90). On Poe's influence and vogue in France, see L. P. Betz, *Edgar Poe in der franzoesischen Litteratur: Studien zur vergleichenden Litteraturgeschichte der neueren Zeit* (1902), pp. 16–82; C. H. Page in *The* [New York] *Nation* for 14 January, 1909; and G. D. Morris, *Fenimore Cooper et Edgar Poe*, pp. 67 f. (Paris, 1912).

CHAPTER IV

Transcendentalists

1. EMERSON

IT becomes more and more apparent that Emerson, judged by an international or even by a broad national standard, is the outstanding figure of American letters. Others may have surpassed him in artistic sensitiveness, or, to a criticism averse to the stricter canons of form and taste, may seem to be more original or more broadly national than he, but as a steady force in the transmutation of life into ideas and as an authority in the direction of life itself he has obtained a recognition such as no other of his countrymen can claim. And he owes this pre-eminence not only to his personal endowment of genius, but to the fact also that, as the most perfect exponent of a transient experiment in civilization, he stands for something that the world is not likely to let die.

Ralph Waldo Emerson, born in Boston, 25 May, 1803, gathered into himself the very quintessence of what has been called the Brahminism of New England, as transmitted through the Bulkeleys, the Blisses, the Moodys, and the direct paternal line. Peter Bulkeley, preferring the wilderness of Satan to Laudian conformity, founded Concord in 1636; William Emerson, his descendant in the fifth generation, was builder of the Old Manse in the same town and a sturdy preacher to the minute-men at the beginning of the Revolution; and of many other ministerial ancestors stories abound which show how deeply implanted in this stock was the pride of rebellion against traditional forms and institutions, united with a determination to force all mankind to worship God in the spirit. With William, son of him of Concord and father of our poet, the fires of zeal began to wane. Though the faithful pastor of the First Church (Unitarian) of Boston, it is recorded of him that he entered the ministry against his will. Yet he too had his un-fulfilled dream of "coming out" by establishing a church in Washington which should require no sort of profession of faith. He died when the future philosopher was a boy of ten, leaving the family to shift for itself as best it could. Mrs. Emerson cared for the material welfare of the household by taking in boarders. The chief intellectual guidance fell to the Aunt Mary Moody Emerson, of whom her nephew drew a portrait in his *Lectures and Biographies*. "She gave high counsels," he says. Indubitably she did; but a perusal of her letters and of the extracts from her journals leaves the impression that the pure but dislocated enthusiasms of her mind served rather to push Emerson in the direction of his weaker inclination than to fortify him against himself. When a balloon is tugging at its moorings there may be need of low counsels.

In 1817, Emerson entered Harvard College, and in due course of time graduated. Then, after teaching for a while in his brother's school in Boston, he returned to Cambridge to study for the ministry, and was in the autumn of 1826 licensed to preach. Three years later he was called, first as assistant to Henry Ware, to the Second Church of Boston. His ministra-tion there was quietly successful, but brief. In 1832, he gave up his charge on the ground that he could not conscientiously celebrate the Communion, even in the symbolic form customary among the Unitarians. He was for the moment much adrift, his occupation gone, his health broken, his wife lost after a short period of happiness. In this state he went abroad to travel in Italy, France, and England. One memorable incident of the journey must be recorded, his visit to Carlyle at Craigenput-tock, with all that it entailed of friendship and influence; but beyond that he returned with little more baggage than he took with him. He now made his residence in Concord, living first with his mother and then with his second wife. Thence-forth there was to be no radical change in his life, but only the gradual widening of the circle. The house that he now bought he continued to inhabit until it was burned down in 1872; and then his friends, in a manner showing exemplary tact, sub-scribed money for rebuilding it on the same lines. For a number of years he preached in various pulpits, and once even considered the call to a settled charge in New Bedford, but

he could not overcome his aversion to the ritual of the Lord's
Supper and to regular prayers.

Meanwhile, by the medium of lectures delivered here and
there and by printed essays, he was making of himself a kind
of lay preacher to the world. His method of working out the
more characteristic of these discourses has long been known:
he would commonly select a theme, and then ransack his note-
books for pertinent passages which could be strung together
with the addition of such developing and connecting material
as was necessary. But since the publication of his *Journals*
it has been possible to follow him more precisely in this procedure and to see more clearly how it conforms with the inmost
structure of his mind. These remarkable records were begun
in early youth and continued, though at the close in the form of
brief memoranda, to the end of his life. The first entry preserved (not the first written, for it is from *Blotting Book No.
XVII*) dates from his junior year at college and contains
notes for a prize dissertation on the Character of Socrates.
Among the sentences is this:

What is God? said the disciples, and Plato replied, It is hard
to learn and impossible to divulge.

And the last page of the record, in the twelfth volume, repeats
what is really the same thought:

The best part of truth is certainly that which hovers in gleams
and suggestions unpossessed before man. His recorded knowledge
is dead and cold. But this chorus of thoughts and hopes, these
dawning truths, like great stars just lifting themselves into his
horizon, they are his future, and console him for the ridiculous
brevity and meanness of his civic life.

There is of course much variety of matter in the *Journals*—
shrewd observations on men and books, chronicles of the day's
events, etc.—but through it all runs this thread of self-com-
munion, the poetry, it might be called, of the New England
conscience deprived of its concrete deity and buoying itself
on gleams and suggestions of eternal beauty and holiness. Of
the same stuff, not seldom indeed of the same words, are those
essays of his that have deeply counted; they are but a repetition
to the world of fragments of this long inner conversation.

Where they fail to reach the reader's heart, it is not because they are fundamentally disjointed, as if made up of sentences jostled together like so many mutually repellent particles; but because from the manner of his composition Emerson often missed what he might have learned from Plato's *Phaedrus* was the essence of good rhetoric, that is to say, the consciousness of his hearer's mind as well as of his own. We hear him, as it were, talking to himself, with no attempt to convince by argument or enlighten by analysis. If our dormant intuition answers to his, we are profoundly kindled and confirmed; otherwise his sentences may rattle ineffectually about our ears.

Emerson's first published work was *Nature* (1836), which contains the gist of his transcendental attitude towards the phenomenal world, as a kind of beautiful symbol of the inner spiritual life, floating dreamlike before the eye, yet, it is to be noted, having discipline as one of its lessons for the attentive soul. The most characteristic and influential of his books are the two volumes of *Essays*, issued respectively in 1841 and 1844. In the former of these are those great discourses on *Self-Reliance*, *Compensation*, and *The Over-Soul*, into which was distilled the very quintessence of the volatile and heady liquid known as Emersonianism. Other volumes followed in due course. The latter publications, however, beginning with *Letters and Social Aims* (1875), are made up mainly of gleanings from the field already harvested, and were even gathered by hands not his own.

Two of his addresses (now both included in the volume with *Nature*) deserve special notice for the attention they attracted at the time. The first of these is the oration before the Phi Beta Kappa Society of Harvard, in 1837, a high but scarcely practical appeal to the American scholar to raise himself above the dust of pedantries, even out of the routine of what is "decent, indolent, complaisant," and to reach after the inspiration of "the Divine Soul which also inspires all men." The other lecture was delivered the next year before the senior class in Divinity College, Cambridge, and held up to the prospective preacher about the same ideal as was presented to the scholar. Historical Christianity is condemned because "it is not the doctrine of the soul, but an exaggeration of the personal, the positive, the ritual. It has dwelt, it dwells, with noxious exaggeration about the *person* of Jesus." The founder of Christianity saw, indeed, "with open eye the mystery of the soul," but what as a man he saw and knew of man's divinity cannot be given to man to-day by instruction, but only on the terms of a like intuition. The Unitarians of Massachusetts had travelled far from the Calvinistic creed of the Pilgrim Fathers, but Emerson's suave displacement of the person of Jesus for the "chorus of thoughts and hopes" in any human soul, perhaps even more his implicit rejection of all rites and institutions, raised loud protest among the worshippers of the day. For the most part he answered the criticism by silence, but in a letter replying to one of the more courteous of his opponents he used these significant words:

> I could not give an account of myself, if challenged. I could not possibly give you one of the "arguments" you cruelly hint at, on which any doctrine of mine stands; for I do not know what arguments are in reference to any expression of a thought.

There may be some guile in this pretence to complete intellectual innocence, but it is nevertheless a fair statement of a literary method which seeks, and obtains, its effect by throwing a direct light into the soul of the hearer and bidding him look there and acknowledge what he sees.

Of the events of these years there is not much to relate. A journey to Europe, in 1847, resulted in the only two of his books which may be said to have been composed as units: *Representative Men* (published in 1850, from a series of lectures delivered in London), which displays Emerson's great powers as an ethical critic, in the larger use of that phrase, and *English Traits* (1856), which proves that his eyes were observing the world about him with Yankee shrewdness all the while that he seemed to be gazing into transcendental clouds. Into the question of slavery and disunion which was now agitating the country, he entered slowly. It was natural that one to whom the power and meaning of institutions had little appeal and to whom liberty was the all-including virtue, should have been drawn to the side of the Abolitionists, but at first there was a philosophical aloofness in his attitude. Only after the passing of the Fugitive Slave Law and Webster's defection were his passions deeply engaged. Then he spoke ringing words:

There is infamy in the air. I have a new experience. I awake in the morning with a painful sensation, which I carry about all day, and which, when traced home, is the odious remembrance of that ignominy which has fallen on Massachusetts, which robs the landscape of beauty, and takes the sunshine out of every hour.

And the war came to him as a welcome relief from a situation which had grown intolerable.

A third trip to Europe was made in 1872, when his central will was already loosening and his faculties were losing their edge. It was at this time that Charles Eliot Norton talked with Carlyle, and heard the old man, eight years older than Emerson, expatiate on the fundamental difference in their tempers. And on the voyage home in the same boat, Norton, who so fully represents the judgment of New England, had much conversation with Emerson, and recorded his opinion in words that, whether welcome or not, should not be forgotten:

Emerson was the greatest talker in the ship's company. He talked with all men, and yet was fresh and zealous for talk at night. His serene sweetness, the pure whiteness of his soul, the reflection of his soul in his face, were never more apparent to me; but never before in intercourse with him had I been so impressed with the limits of his mind. His optimistic philosophy has hardened into a creed, with the usual effects of a creed in closing the avenues of truth. He can accept nothing as fact that tells against his dogma. His optimism becomes a bigotry, and, though of a nobler type than the common American conceit of the preeminent excellence of American things as they are, has hardly less of the quality of fatalism. To him this is the best of all possible worlds, and the best of all possible times. He refuses to believe in disorder or evil. . . . But such inveterate and persistent optimism, though it may show only its pleasant side in such a character as Emerson's. is dangerous doctrine for a people. It degenerates into fatalistic indifference to moral considerations, and to personal responsibilities; it is at the root of much of the irrational sentimentalism in our American politics, of much of our national disregard of honour in our public men, of much of our unwillingness to accept hard truths, and of much of the common tendency to disregard the distinctions between right and wrong, and to excuse guilt on the plea of good intentions or good nature.[1]

For some time there had been a gradual relaxation of Emerson's hold on life. Though always an approachable man and fond of conversation, there was in him a certain lack of human warmth, of "bottom," to use his own word, which he recognized and deplored. Commenting in his *Journal* (24 May, 1864) on the burial of Hawthorne, he notes the statement of James Freeman Clarke that the novelist had "shown a sympathy with the crime in our nature," and adds: "I thought there was a tragic element in the event, that might be more fully rendered,—in the painful solitude of the man, which, I suppose, could not longer be endured, and he died of it." A touch of this romantic isolation, though never morose or "painful," there was in himself, a failure to knit himself strongly into the bonds of society. "I have felt sure of him," he says of Hawthorne in the same passage, "in his neighbourhood, and in his necessities of sympathy and intelligence,—that I could well wait his time,—his unwillingness and caprice,—and might one day conquer a friendship. . . . Now it appears that I waited too long." Eighteen years later, standing by the body of Longfellow, he was heard to say: "That gentleman was a sweet, beautiful soul, but I have entirely forgotten his name." Such forgetfulness, like a serene and hazy cloud, hovered over Emerson's brain in his closing years. A month afterwards, on 27 April, 1882, he himself faded away peacefully.

To one who examines the events of Emerson's quiet life with a view to their spiritual bearing it will appear that his most decisive act was the surrender of his pulpit in 1832. Nearly a century earlier, in 1750, the greatest of American theologians had suffered what now befell the purest of American seers; and though the manner of their parting was different (Jonathan Edwards had been unwillingly ejected, whereas Emerson left with good will on both sides), yet there is significance in the fact that the cause of separation in both cases was the administration of the Lord's Supper. Nor is there less significance in the altered attitude of the later man towards this vital question. Both in a way turned from the ritualistic

[1] *Letters of Charles Eliot Norton*, vol. I, pp. 503 and 506.

and traditional use of the Communion, and in this showed themselves leaders of the spirit which had carried the New England Fathers across the ocean as rebels against the Laudian tyranny of institutions. Edwards had revolted against the practice of Communion as a mere act of acquiescence in the authority of religion; he was determined that only those should approach the Table who could give evidence of a true conversion, by conversion meaning a complete emotional realization of the dogma of divine Grace and election. The eucharist was not a rite by conforming with which in humility men were to be made participators in the larger religious experience of the race, but a jealously guarded privilege of the few who already knew themselves set apart from the world. He was attempting to push to its logical issue the Puritan notion of religion as a matter of individual and inward experience, and if he failed it was because life can never be rigidly logical and because the worshippers of his day were already beginning to lose their intellectual grasp on the Calvinistic creed. By Emerson's time, among the Unitarians of Boston, there could be no question of ritualistic grace or absolute conversion, but his act, nevertheless, like that of Edwards, was the intrusion of unyielding consistency among those who were content to rest in habit and compromise. In his old age Emerson gave this account of his conduct to Charles Eliot Norton, who subsequently repeated it:

He had come to the conviction that he could not administer the Lord's Supper as a divinely appointed, sacred ordinance of religion. And, after much debate with himself, he told his people that he could henceforth conduct the service only as a memorial service, without attributing to it any deeper significance. A parish meeting was held; the parish, though most kindly affected to him, could not bring themselves to accept his view,—it would be tantamount to admitting that they were no longer Christians. He resigned his charge, but an effort was made to induce him to remain, he administering the Lord's Supper in his sense, the people receiving it in theirs. But he saw that such an arrangement was impossible, and held to his resignation. [1]

Emerson had come to the inevitable conclusion of New England individualism; he had, in a word, "come out." Ed-

---

[1] *Letters of Charles Eliot Norton*, vol. 1, p. 509.

wards had denied the communal efficacy, so to speak, of rites, but had insisted on inner conformity with an established creed. Emerson disavowed even a conformity in faith, demanding in its stead the entire liberty of each soul to rise on its own spiritual impulse. He was perspicacious and honest enough to acknowledge to himself the danger of such a stand. "I know very well," he wrote in his journal at the time of his decision, "that it is a bad sign in a man to be too conscientious, and stick at gnats. The most desperate scoundrels have been the over-refiners. Without accommodation society is impracticable." But, he adds, he could "not go habitually to an institution which they esteem holiest with indifference and dislike"; and again, looking deeper into his heart, "This is the end of my opposition, that I am not interested in it."

Emerson's act of renunciation was not only important as determining the nature of his career, but significant also of the transition of New England from theological dogmatism to romantic liberty. Much has been written about the influences that shaped his thoughts and about the relation of his transcendentalism to German metaphysics. In his later years it is clear that the speculations of Kant and Schelling and Fichte were known to him and occasionally coloured his language, but his *Journals* prove conclusively enough that the whole stamp of his mind was taken before these sources were open to him. Indirectly, no doubt, something of the German spirit came to him pretty early through Carlyle, and a passage in his *Journal* for 13 December, 1829, shows that he was at that time already deeply engaged in the Teutonized rhapsodies of Coleridge. But it would be easy to lay too much stress even on this indirect affiliation. Long before that date, as early as his senior year in college, he is yearning "to separate the soul for sublime contemplation till it has lost the sense of circumstances," and otherwise giving implicit expression to the full circle of transcendental faith. He was in fact a product of the great romantic movement that was sweeping over the world as it listed; his ideas, so far as they came to him from books, go back mainly to the Greek philosophers and the poets and preachers of seventeenth-century England, as these were interpreted under the light of the new movement. When he declared, in *Nature*, that "the vision of genius comes by renouncing the too officious activity of the understanding, and giving leave and amplest privilege to the spontaneous sentiment," he was stating in precise terms an idea familiar to Blake and to the romanticists of every land—the elevation of enthusiasm above judgment, of emotion above reason, of spontaneity above discipline, and of unlimited expansion above centripetal control. But there was another element as strongly formative of Emerson's disposition as was the current of romanticism, and that was his ancestral inheritance. Romantic spontaneity moved in various directions in accordance with the field in which it worked; in an Emerson, with all the divinity of Massachusetts in his veins, it might move to repudiate theological dogma and deny Jehovah, but it could not get out of hearing of the question "What is God?" It could not fall into the too common confusion of spiritual aspiration with the sicklier lusts of the flesh; it could never, for all its centrifugal wandering, overstep the bounds of character. Emersonianism may be defined as romanticism rooted in Puritan divinity.

In literary form and style the privilege of spontaneous sentiment showed itself with Emerson not in that fluency which in many of his contemporaries meant mere longwindedness, but in the habit of waiting for the momentary inspiration to the neglect of meditated construction and regularity. He has indeed succeeded in sustaining himself to the end in three or four poems of some compass, but his noblest work in verse must be sought in those quatrains which need no context for their comprehension and might be called spiritual ejaculations. Matthew Arnold has quoted for approval the two familiar stanzas,

> So nigh is grandeur to our dust,
>   So near is God to man,
> When Duty whispers low, *Thou must*,
>   The youth replies, *I can.*

and,

> Though love repine and reason chafe,
>   There came a voice without reply:
> "'Tis man's perdition to be safe,
>   When for the truth he ought to die."

These quatrains are, he says, "exceptional" in Emerson. They are that, and something more: they are exceptional in literature. One would have to search far to find anything in English equal to them in their own kind. They have the cleanness and radiance of the couplets of Simonides. They may look easy, but as a matter of fact the ethical epigram is an extremely difficult *genre*, and to attain this union of gravity and simplicity requires the nicest art. Less epigrammatic in tone but even more exquisitely finished are the lines entitled *Days*, pre-eminent in his works for what may truly be called a haunting beauty:

> Daughters of Time, the hypocritic Days,
> Muffled and dumb like barefoot dervishes,
> And marching single in an endless file,
> Bring diadems and faggots in their hands.
> To each they offer gifts after his will,
> Bread, kingdoms, stars, and sky that holds them all.
> I, in my pleachèd garden, watched the pomp,
> Forgot my morning wishes, hastily
> Took a few herbs and apples, and the Day
> Turned and departed silent. I, too late,
> Under her solemn fillet saw the scorn.

And as his verse, so is his prose. Though in one sense, so far as he writes always with two or three dominant ideas in his mind, he is one of the most consistent and persistent of expositors, yet he is really himself only in those moments of inspiration when his words strike with almost irresistible force on the heart, and awake an echoing response: "This is true; this I have myself dimly felt." Sometimes the memorable paragraph or sentence is purely didactic; sometimes it is highly metaphorical, as is the case with the closing paragraph of the *Conduct of Life:*

There is no chance, and no anarchy, in the universe. All is system and gradation. Every god is there sitting in his sphere. The young mortal enters the hall of the firmament; there is he alone with them alone, they pouring on him benedictions and gifts, and beckoning him up to their thrones. On the instant, and incessantly, fall snowstorms of illusions. He fancies himself in a vast crowd which sways this way and that, and whose movement and doings he must obey: he fancies himself poor, orphaned, insignificant. The mad crowd drives hither and thither, now furiously commanding this thing to be done, now that. What is he that he should resist their will, and think or act for himself? Every moment, new changes, and new showers of deceptions, to baffle and distract him. And when, by and by, for an instant, the air clears, and the cloud lifts a little, there are the gods still sitting around him on their thrones,—they alone with him alone.

There is, it need scarcely be said, a good deal in the works of Emerson—literary criticism, characterization of men and movements, reflection on the state of society—which lies outside of this ethical category; but even in such essays his guiding ideas are felt in the background. Nor are these ideas hard to discover. The whole circle of them, ever revolving upon itself, is likely to be present, explicit or implicit, in any one of his great passages, as it is in the paragraph just cited—the clear call to self-reliance, announcing that "a man should learn to detect and watch that gleam of light which flashes across his mind from within"; the firm assurance that, through all the balanced play of circumstance, "there is a deeper fact in the soul than compensation, to wit, its own nature"; the intuition, despite all the mists of illusion, of the Over-Soul which is above us and still ourselves: "We live in succession, in division, in parts, in particles; meanwhile within man is the soul of the whole; the wise silence; the universal beauty . . .; the eternal *One*."

Emerson's philosophy is thus a kind of reconciled dualism, and a man's attitude towards it in the end will be determined by his sense of its sufficiency or insufficiency to meet the facts of experience. One of Emerson's biographers has attempted to set forth this philosophy as "a synthesis and an anticipation." It is a synthesis because in it we find, as Emerson had already found in Plato and Plotinus, a reconciliation of "the many and the one," the everlasting flux and the motionless calm at the heart of things:

An ample and generous recognition of this transiency and slipperiness both in the nature of things and in man's soul seems more and more a necessary ingredient in any estimate of the universe which shall satisfy the intellect of the coming man. But it seems equally true that the coming man who shall resolve our problems will never content himself with a universe a-tilt, a universe in cascade, so to speak; the craving for permanence in some form cannot be jauntily evaded. Is there any known mind which foreshadows the desired combination so clearly as Emerson's? Who has felt more profoundly the evanescence and evasiveness of things? . . . Yet Emerson was quite as firm in his insistence on a single unalterable reality as in his refusal to believe that any aspect or estimate of that reality could be final.[1]

The necessity of the dualism that underlies Emerson's philosophy could scarcely be put more neatly, and the kind of synthesis, or reconciliation, in which Emerson floated is admirably expressed. But it is not so plain that this synthesis anticipates the solution of the troublesome problems of life. There will be those who will ask whether the power of religion for mature minds does not depend finally on its feeling for evil. How otherwise, in fact, shall religion meet those harder questions of experience when its aid is most needed? And in like manner they will say that the power of philosophy as the *dux vitae* depends on its acquaintance with the scope and difficulties of scepticism. Both religion and philosophy would seem, in such a view, to rest not only on a statement of the dualism of good and evil, knowledge and ignorance, but on a realization of the full meaning and gravity, practical and intellectual, of this dualism. Now Emerson certainly recognizes the dualism of experience, but it is a fair question whether he realizes its full meaning and seriousness. He accepts it a trifle too jauntily, is reconciled to its existence with no apparent pang, is sometimes too ready to wave aside its consequences, as if a statement of the fact were an escape from its terrible perplexities. Carlyle meant something of the sort when he worried over Emerson's inability to see the hand of the devil in human life. Hence it is that Emerson often loses value for his admirers in proportion to their maturity and experience. He is above all the poet of religion and philosophy for the young; whereas men, as they grow older, are inclined to turn from him, in their more serious moods, to those sages who have supplemented insight with a firm grasp of the darker facts of human nature. That is undoubtedly true; nevertheless, as time passes, the deficiencies of this brief period of New England, of which

[1] O. W. Firkins, *Ralph Waldo Emerson*, p. 364.

Emerson was the perfect spokesman, may well be more and more condoned for its rarity and beauty. One of the wings of the spirit is hope, and nowhere is there to be found a purer hope than in the books of our New England sage; rather, it might be said that he went beyond hope to the assurance of present happiness. The world had never before seen anything quite of this kind, and may not see its like again.

2. Hawthorne

THE romances of Hawthorne can hardly be understood apart from the current of Transcendentalism in which his genius was formed. Most foreigners and many of his countrymen have thought of him as an affectionate student of the New England past, in a small way comparable to Scott with his love of Border history, and especially they have thought of him as a kind of portrait painter, who magically resharpened for us the already fading lineaments of Puritanism. Reflection might suggest, however, that the portrait he restored bears an unlucky resemblance in its sombreness and its unloveliness to the portrait of Edward Randolph in the *Twice Told Tales*, and a little further thought would perhaps convince us that Hawthorne usually treats Puritanism, not as the central theme in his canvas, but as a dark background for the ideas and for the experiences which more deeply concern him. Those ideas and experiences have little to do with Puritanism except by contrast; they were partly furnished to his imagination by the enthusiastic but uncritical thinkers among his acquaintance who kindled rapturously at Alcott's conversations or basked in the indefiniteness of Emerson's lectures, and partly they were furnished by his own contact with Alcott and Emerson and with their writings. Like them, he was less a Puritan than a lover of the present, and if he seemed often to deal with things long past, it was only because he had the faculty, more than other men, of recognizing in the present whatever had served its purpose or was worn out or dead.

But if as a Transcendentalist he stood aloof from Puritanism, his temperament forced him to stand aloof also from the other

Transcendentalists. Although their philosophy, as they liked to say, was a "questioning" of life, he differed from them all in being a true skeptic. To be quite precise, let us say that he drew the inspiration of his romances not so much from their ideas as from the neglected but inevitable conclusions of their ideas. Alcott and Emerson uttered between them a set of doctrines so full of apparent contradictions as to seem almost double-faced. They preached the sacredness of fact as against the authority of tradition; they made much of physical heredity, of evolution, of fate; they pointed out the inadequacy of any moral scheme to comprehend all the surprises of nature; yet being inveterate optimists, both of them, and both at certain moments curiously mystical, and both enjoying an outward orthodoxy of manners and culture, they soothed their hearers and seemed less dangerous than they were. Their sincerity, of course, was unquestionable, but they obscured even to themselves the startling conclusions of their own surmises, and having shaken their moral world to its foundation, they allowed the structure to settle again, and all this in such a glamour of temperamental cheerfulness that those who felt only the eloquence of their mood could depart conscious of spiritual uplift, and none but the few who attended to the implications of their specific ideas went away troubled. How few these critics were is attested by the lonely position in which their spokesman, Hawthorne, seems to stand. He was no mystic; what attracted him in Transcendentalism was its free inquiry, its radicalism, its contact with actual life. In his stories, therefore, he was a philosophical experimenter, in whose method was no room for optimism nor for prepossessions of any kind; he had recourse to life in order to try out the efficacy or the consequences of Transcendental ideas, and if the result was hardly what he expected, he still pursued the hypothesis to the bitter end. He was really the questioner, the detached observer, that other Transcendentalists thought they were. The soul, Emerson had said, "accepts whatever befalls, as part of its lesson. It is a watcher more than a doer, and it is a doer only that it may the better watch." The description is truer of Hawthorne's soul than of Emerson's. In accepting whatever befalls, Emerson was convinced, as he says in the essay on *Circles*, that there is a saccharine principle in all things; small wonder that Hawthorne seems an alien among such cheerful sages. When Emerson says that either love or crime leads all souls to the good, that there is no straight line in nature, that evil in the end will bless, Hawthorne examines the doctrine somewhat dubiously in Hepzibah and Clifford Pyncheon and in Donatello; and when the cheerful philosopher tells us to trust ourselves, to follow our own nature, to live from the Devil if we are the Devil's children, Hawthorne projects the advice experimentally in *The Scarlet Letter* and in *The Blithedale Romance*.

Those who classify Hawthorne in a loose way as the romancer of Puritanism sometimes speak of him also as a psychologist. The term needs defining. To him, as to other Transcendentalists, the fortune of a human soul was the most critical of experiences; comparatively negligible were the doings of society as a whole or the outward panorama of events and scenes. If to be thus interested in the soul is to be a psychologist, then Hawthorne was one, as to some extent are all who write of human nature. But if the term denotes attention to motives and to fine mental processes, to the anatomy, as it were, of character, then Hawthorne was no such psychologist as, let us say, Henry James or George Meredith. It is important to realize how broad and general his ideas and his art were, how completely he avoided the special and the minute. He studied no subtle character, nor any character subtly. He was a moralist rather than a psychologist. Were it not sufficiently evident in the stories themselves, the notes preserved in his journals would show that his imagination was engaged first by a moral idea, which he afterwards incorporated in plot and in persons. When he is most successful the plot seems actually to occur, and the persons really live; when his imagination fails him, the incidents seem allegorical and the figures become shadowy; but in either case the abstract idea from which he started is likely to be clear enough, and his own personality will probably be felt as standing outside the story, looking on. Since he is neither novelist nor preacher, but only an investigator of moral ideas, it is equally beside the mark to expect of him Balzac's sense of the social panorama, or Bunyan's certitude of faith.

A writer who pictures life chiefly in order to project abstract ideas is not likely to reveal in his art more of himself than his general disposition. Hawthorne's biography makes rich and human reading, for he was an admirable man in all ways and his private life was in the best sense fortunate; if at first he endured poverty, he earned success later, and even in the obscure years he had the admiration of loyal friends. But only in a few instances does his biography aid directly in the understanding of his works, and then for the most part by explaining his contact with Transcendental ideas. Of the non-literary events in his life it is enough to say that he was born in Salem, Massachusetts, 4 July, 1804, of an old New England family; that after his father's death he was educated by his mother's brothers, and in 1825 he was graduated from Bowdoin College; that among his classmates he made three lifelong friends—Longfellow, the poet, Franklin Pierce, later President of the United States, and Horatio Bridge, who first appreciated his genius; that chiefly through Bridge's thoughtfulness he was made weigher and gauger at the Boston Custom House, 1839–1841, and surveyor at the Salem Custom House, 1846–1850; that President Pierce appointed him to the consulship of Liverpool, 1853–1857; that he lived in Italy for two years, 1857–1859, and that while travelling for his health, attended by Pierce, he died at Plymouth, New Hampshire, 18 May, 1864.

The facts of his literary record are hardly more numerous, but they invite more comment. His college letters to his mother and his sisters show how early he mastered his superb style. Indeed, they are much better written than his first published story, *Fanshawe* (1828), which was probably composed, in part at least, during his college days. From 1825 to 1837 he lived at home in Salem, laboriously perfecting his short stories and sketches, and publishing them anonymously or under assumed names, chiefly in Goodrich's annual, *The Token*, and in *The New England Magazine*. He gives an idealized account of this period in his sketches *The Devil in Manuscript* and *The Journal of a Solitary Man*. In 1837, again through Bridge's good offices, a publisher was found for the *Twice Told Tales* (enlarged edition in two volumes, 1842). With this practical beginning of his reputation coincided his first acquaintance with the Peabody family. In all the biographies his love for Sophia Peabody has naturally filled a large place, but no sufficient estimate has perhaps been made of the intellectual enrichment his love brought him. It was through the Peabodys that he became really alive to the philosophical currents of his time. Transcendentalism had, of course, enfolded him, as it had the average New Englander, in its general atmosphere, and its temper is felt in some of his earliest writings, but it can hardly be said to have possessed his thought as it did later, and he had been in personal contact with none of the leaders. The Peabodys, however, were on intimate terms with Emerson, the young rhapsodist of *Nature*, whose recent triumph in *The American Scholar* had more recently been rendered equivocal by his *Divinity School Address;* and Alcott, Emerson's inspirer, they knew still better, for Elizabeth and to some extent Sophia had assisted at his Temple school in Boston, and Elizabeth had published in her *Records of a School* (1835) verbatim reports of Alcott's conversations with his pupils. When *The Dial* was founded in 1840, Elizabeth Peabody, who by that time had organized a remarkable book store, became its publisher. It was not extraordinary, therefore, that Hawthorne was drawn, though with some mental qualms, into the full tide of Transcendentalism, nor that upon the termination of his service in the Boston Custom House, in 1841, he joined the Brook Farm venture, in the hope of establishing a home there. His note-books tell us the most interesting aspects of this passage in his life. At the end of a year and a half, completely disillusioned with the community experiment, he married and settled at Concord, in the Old Manse, where for neighbours he had Emerson, Alcott, and Thoreau, all busy with *The Dial*, and where Thoreau was shortly to undertake his Walden solitude. In Concord most of the stories were written which Hawthorne published in 1846 as *Mosses from an Old Manse*. A still later collection, *The Snow Image* (1852), gathered up practically all of the remaining sketches which he cared to preserve. His longer romances show a tendency to rework or develop this earlier material, or to draw upon actual scenes and events for their narrative fabric; the controlling problems, however, which the romances deal with are more obviously than in the shorter stories suggested by Transcendental ideas. *The Scarlet Letter* (1850), is developed from a brief description in *Endicott and the Red Cross*, one of the *Twice Told Tales*. In *The House of the Seven Gables* (1851), Hawthorne makes use of such a curse as was pronounced on his own ancestor, John Hawthorne, or Hathorne, a severe magistrate in witchcraft times. In *The Blithedale Romance* (1852) it is hard not to identify Hawthorne's Brook Farm experience, though he warned us against the temptation. The outward details of *The Marble Faun* (1860) are clearly the result of observations which he made during his two years in Italy.

Besides the short stories and the romances, Hawthorne wrote several important books for children—the series called *Grandfather's Chair* (1841–1842) and the two *Wonderbooks* (1852–1853). He also edited his friend Bridge's *Journal of an African Cruiser* (1845), wrote a campaign life of his friend Pierce (1852), and published some of his notes on England under the title of *Our Old Home* (1863).

If it is just to see in the early writings a picture of his native temper before he was consciously engaged with Transcendental doctrines, it is also true that from the first his mind was of another order than Alcott's or Emerson's, and that though he might be interested in the same ideas, he would treat them very differently. Most philosophers can be classed roughly among those who conceive of the ideal ends of life as already existing in heaven, in some order or pattern which may be imitated on earth, or among those who think of the ideal as of something which does not yet exist, but which is implicit in the universe, and toward which the universe evolves. A philosopher of the first or Platonic type, if he notices facts at all, is likely to be disconcerted by them, since they rarely conform to his ideal or serve to authorize it; his comfort is in rising superior to actual life—that is, in ignoring it. Alcott was an almost pure example of this type. The other kind of philosopher is likely to entertain a respect amounting almost to reverence for any concrete existing condition, because as two points determine a straight line, so a recent moment observed against the past gives indication of the order to come. Emerson was partly, like Alcott, a Platonist, but he had also a profound and inconsistent disposition toward this other way of thought; having two points of view at once, therefore, he is not only perplexing at times, but really contradictory, and it is not strange that he should have proved in one aspect of his genius inspiring to Maeterlinck and in the other aspect acceptable to Nietzsche. Hawthorne belonged altogether to the second type of thinker. Concerned primarily with the actual world before him, he found a natural use for the past in the explanation it might give of the present, but the present was to him just as naturally the more important moment, and most interesting of all was the occasional hint or prophecy of that to which time through its past and present changes might be tending. He was a radical, therefore, but he saw clearly that this particular present will soon be no more sacred than any other moment of the past, and that to devote oneself to any cause as though it were a final remedy of circumstances, promising rest thereafter, is merely to postpone stagnation for a while. With this insight he could not readily give his faith to any reform or reformer; even the crusade for abolition and the war for the Union left him cold, for he wisely doubted whether measures conceived in the root-and-branch spirit might not raise more evils in the state than they were intended to cure. True reform, the only kind that could enlist his sympathy, must work hand in hand with nature's slowly evolving but inevitable order, and so long as that order can be but partially or infrequently discerned, it is best to do nothing violent, nothing headlong. Even when we discern the order, from time to time, we should become humble, observing how little it resembles our own morality, our own dreams of perfection.

It needs no fine perception to discover these principles or attitudes in Hawthorne, for they are displayed quite simply on the surface of his early stories. The significance he attached to the present world, whatever it might be, can be seen in the important group of essay sketches such as *A Rill from the Town Pump, David Swan, Sights from a Steeple*, and *Main Street*. Some resemblance has been found between this department of his work and the essays of Addison and of Irving, and certainly Addison's cheerfulness is here, and often something more than Irving's fancy. But neither *The Spectator* nor *The Sketch Book* would suggest that Addison or Irving was in the habit of keeping a diary; whereas Hawthorne's

simple studies, of the group just referred to, are in form nothing more than episodes in a journal. The fact is of some consequence in understanding his genius. When the American
and European notebooks were finally included in the complete
editions of his writings, they took their place, not as an appen-
dix or illustration of more perfect things, but on equal terms
with his other works; for the journal manner was suited to his
realistic, unprejudiced search into the world about him, and
his lifelong preoccupation with his diary was not, as with most
novelists, for the sake of books to be written later, but was
itself the satisfaction of a primary literary interest. Like the
journals, the essay sketches take the scene as they find it,
extract from it all that observation can, and then discard it,
having proved no point and exhibited no characters in continuous interplay, but having uncovered possibilities, hints,
causes, coincidences. In the simpler essays Hawthorne observed these possibilities and coincidences in a kind of sta-
tionary cross-section, and left them undeveloped; but in more
elaborate stories he played with the ironic contrasts between
the order which we foresee in life and the order which time
brings to pass. Emerson often came out of his mysticism and
contemplated the "beautiful necessity," the inevitable consequence of things, to which man must submit himself before
he has either happiness or power. Hawthorne was inclined
to stress rather man's inability to submit himself to this necessity, since he seldom guesses correctly what it would be. *Mr.
Higginbotham's Catastrophe* is a lighter treatment of this theme
of consequences; *Edward Fane's Rosebud* and *The Wives of the
Dead* are in a darker tone. Or sometimes Hawthorne would
turn the irony in another direction, by emphasizing the incredible swiftness with which the present becomes the past,
and the insidiousness with which antiquity begins to show its
symptoms even in what seems youthful and emancipated.
The May-pole of Merry Mount brings this idea home, less in the
overthrow of the maskers at Merry Mount than in the expressed faith of the stern Puritan leader that the troubles of
life come soon and unexpectedly—a confession which somehow
brings a chill over his own righteous success. A still better
illustration is *Endicott and the Red Cross*, which shows the
Puritans, who crossed the ocean for freedom of conscience

and who in the moment of the story proclaim themselves champions of religious liberty, as having nevertheless instituted already the pillory and the stocks for those who disagree with them.

The Transcendental ideas which chiefly occupied Hawthorne's thought in the long romances were the doctrines of self-reliance, of compensation, and of what Emerson expressed in his essay on *Circles*. The ideal of self-reliance was that a man should live according to his own nature, by listening to the dictates of the over-soul as revealed in his impulses; to this end he should keep himself free of the imprisoning past, and of conventional society, which embodies the past. To Alcott or to Emerson this doctrine was so obviously sound that they stated it with every emphasis of rhetoric and with no qualifications. "Whoso would be a man must be a nonconformist." Hawthorne doubtless felt the truth of the doctrine as keenly as any one, but he was alive also to the unsocial results which might follow a narrow practice of it. A man consciously and entirely free of the past and on his guard against it might indeed possess his soul, but he might also miss the essence of culture, and having renounced the finer instruments of the art of life, he might so isolate himself from his fellows as to become ineffective in his noblest virtues. Since nature is unfolding a necessary order in and around us, an order which we apprehend with difficulty, the great danger of asserting ourselves is that we may thereby place ourselves outside of our true development, and never return to it. This danger of stepping out of the order, of doing violence to our proper destiny, gave Hawthorne the theme of such stories as *Wakefield*, *The Prophetic Pictures*, and *Rappaccini's Daughter*. The doctrine of compensation, in one form or another, was peculiarly dear to Transcendental optimism. Every action carries its reward or punishment with it. The thief is punished, though the police never find him, for the price of theft is loss of innocence, fear of arrest, suspicion of other men. What compensation is destined for the victim of the thief, optimistic Transcendentalism preferred not to investigate, but it was into just such a neglected area of morals that Hawthorne liked to push his inquiry. His observations brought him into a certain agreement with the doctrine; because a natural order constantly unfolds in the world, he believed in the efficacy of mere time to break down conventions and to reveal a nobler law, and in his historical scenes—*Howe's Masquerade*, for example, or *The Gray Champion*—he liked to show a fossilized past at the moment when it is shattered. He could believe that life does so far make restitution, but in daily life he could find no compensation for the injuries suffered by the innocent, nor could he persuade himself that a noble bearing of wrongs will necessarily lead to spiritual profit. Indeed, though Emerson's sunny temperament had spread its glamour over his discussion of this theory, to Hawthorne the theory seemed, so far as it was true, one of the darkest and most perplexing. Still less could he agree with Emerson's exaggeration of the same doctrine in *Circles*. Optimism here, taking the bit in its teeth, contended that as there is in experience no such thing as a straight line, so there is practically no such thing as evil—a prophetic application, it would seem, of Riemannian geometry to morals; that what seems hopelessly bad will in the end be found to contain the good principle; and, quite illogically, that what seems to be good will actually prove to be so.

> In vain produced, all rays return;
> Evil will bless and ice will burn.

In a famous passage in *Circles*, Emerson acknowledges the awkwardness of this position, and explains that his temperament dictates it. Hawthorne could not undertake any such cheerfulness, but he was profoundly concerned with the moral phenomena by which Emerson may have justified his faith. Here springs that paradox of experience, that mystery of sin, the question as to what sin is, which threw its shadow over three at least of the four romances. Since we rarely discern our true destiny, the human being who steps out of what seems the moral order may really have chanced upon a sounder morality; through what appears to be sin, therefore, may sometimes come the regeneration of a soul—not through repentance, be it observed, but through sincere adherence to the sin. Conversely, though a man should devote himself to the highest ideal he is aware of, if that ideal does not lie in the true order of nature, his devotion may bring him to an evil end. These possibilities, together with the implications of self-reliance and compensation, furnish the moral problems of Hawthorne's romances.

Hester Prynne, for example, in *The Scarlet Letter*, illustrates self-reliance in a way that some Emersonians may have found not altogether comfortable. Since her love for Dimmesdale was the one sincere passion of her life, she obeyed it utterly, though a conventional judgment would have said that she was stepping out of the moral order. There is nothing in the story to suggest condemnation of her or of the minister in their sin; the only blame attaches to Dimmesdale's cowardice, his lack of self-reliance, his unreadiness to make public acknowledgment of his love. The passion itself, as the two lovers still agree at the close of their hard experience, was sacred, and never caused them repentance. The doctrine of compensation is illustrated in Chillingworth, who, having determined on a fiendish revenge, becomes himself a fiend. There is a kind of comment on Emerson's cheerful doctrine in the fact that this gloomy soul, marked for perdition, is a firm believer in compensation; he wronged Hester's youth by marrying her, and therefore he bears her no ill will for wronging him, but he argues that since the minister had never received a justifying harm at his hands, the secret lover should therefore be punished by the injured husband. As Chillingworth discusses the matter with Hester, compensation seems to be at one moment sheer fatalism, at another moment a primitive exacting of an eye for an eye, but never does it come to a happy issue. The optimistic turn in the doctrine is illustrated by Hester—or perhaps it is better to say that she illustrates the optimism of *Circles*. She has sinned, but the sin leads her straightway to a larger life. Like Adam and Eve driven out of Paradise, she finds she has a career at last. Social ostracism first gives her leisure for meditation and a just angle from which to attack social problems, and then it permits her to enter upon a life of mercy and good works which would have been closed to a conventional woman. Hawthorne had described the original wearer of the scarlet letter in *Endicott and the Red Cross* as a woman who braved her shame by embroidering the guilty "A" into an elaborate and beautiful emblem; so in the romance he lets the sin elaborate itself, so far as Hester's nature is concerned, into nothing but beauty. She becomes more loving, more sympathetic, more tender; and intellectually she becomes emancipated from the narrowness of her age, so that even now she seems prophetic of what the noblest women may be. Thoughts were her companions which, says Hawthorne, would have been held more dangerous than the sin of the scarlet letter, had they been seen knocking at her door. She saw how completely the social scheme must be altered before woman can enjoy a true equality with man, and she suspected the losses in the best of manhood and womanhood which might be the incidental or temporary price of the belated justice.

The greatness of *The Scarlet Letter*, on repeated readings, seems to lie in this social interest, this inexorable study of the world as it is, which distinguishes Hawthorne from other Transcendentalists. The Puritan environment is represented as already dying, young as it was in the new world; at the outset of the story Hawthorne shows us that these courageous founders of religious liberty in the wilderness felt the necessity at once of building a prison and of setting up a pillory. The ideals which a little while before were an inner light for the community, carrying inevitable conviction, were now stiffened into convention and leaned upon force. In making the point that Hawthorne was no special admirer of Puritanism, we must add that neither was he a special critic of it; he used the Puritan moment in our history merely to illustrate the truth of all moments, that society conventionalizes its ideals and becomes cruel, and that time, which annihilates one set of conventions, substitutes another. But some specific criticism of Puritan New England, of New England in his own day, may be discerned in the fortunes of Hester, and may be still more clearly felt in Zenobia and in Miriam, the later heroines; these are all represented as physically beautiful, and as in some way estranged from life, and we wonder whether it was not their beauty rather than their conduct that alienated them from their environment. What career has a beautiful woman in New England?—Hawthorne seems to ask, and he seems to imply that if she is conventional she may live down the handicap of beauty, but meantime she is dangerous to others and to herself. The danger to herself is indicated by the fact that Hester, Zenobia, and probably Miriam, were all married for their beauty, when they were very young, to men who could not appreciate their greatness of soul, and whom therefore they were forced to divorce or to desert.

The House of the Seven Gables is so quiet a story that Hawthorne's characteristic criticism of self-reliance or of compensation is not at first disturbing, but in none of his books does he take more essential issue with Alcott and Emerson. On the surface of the romance lies the theme of long-delayed retribution—the curse of old Maule falling on each generation of the usurping Pyncheons. But what punishment does after all overtake the thoroughly bad man who allows his innocent cousin to rest in jail for years? He dies of apoplexy, as he would have died had he been the innocent cousin. And what happens to his victims? It is easy to guess how Emerson might have treated Clifford and Hepzibah; the innocence of the imprisoned brother would somehow have been its own reward, and the loyalty of the devoted sister, waiting for his release, would have ennobled her character. But confinement in prison is not likely to sweeten even innocence; Hawthorne shows Clifford on his return to the old house a broken man, irritable and unappreciative. Hepzibah's long waiting proved for her a solitude almost as complete as prison confinement; Hawthorne shows her as a shrivelled old maid, angular and grim, with hardly a grace remaining. He had no more wish than Emerson would have had to decry the ethical beauty of her patient loyalty, but he could not help seeing that she, like Clifford, was the victim of gross wrong, and that it is disastrous to be even an innocent victim. Similarly he insists on a precise account of self-reliance in Holgrave, the descendant of old Maule. Emerson himself could not have portrayed a more thorough-going critic of the past.

"Shall we never, never get rid of this Past?" asks Holgrave. "It lies upon the Present like a giant's dead body. In fact, the case is just as if a young giant were compelled to waste all his strength in carrying about the corpse of the old giant, his grandfather, who died a long while ago, and only needs to be decently buried. . . . A dead man, if he happen to have made a will, disposes of wealth no longer his own; or, if he die intestate, it is distributed in accordance with the notions of men much longer dead than he. A dead man sits on all our judgment-seats; and living judges do but search out and repeat his decisions. We read in dead men's books! We laugh at dead men's jokes, and cry at dead men's pathos! We are sick of dead men's diseases, physical and moral, and die of the same remedies with which dead doctors killed their patients! We worship the living Deity according to dead men's forms and creeds. Whatever we seek to do, of our own free motion, a dead man's icy hand obstructs us! Turn our eyes to what point we may, a dead man's white, immitigable face encounters them, and freezes our very heart! And we must be dead ourselves before we can begin to have our proper influence on our own world, which will then be no longer our world, but the world of another generation, with which we shall have no shadow of a right to interfere."

How far Hawthorne agrees with Holgrave we cannot tell, but there is no doubt what sort of character he thought would result from a sincere practice of such philosophy. Holgrave is free of the past, and thereby he is practically free of the present too; his honesty and his emancipation attract the reader, yet he has little or no influence. Few men really wish to detach themselves so far. Even Phœbe, the young girl whom he marries, who has the natural freshness of innocence, seems curiously social in comparison with this conscientious rover whose one dread is that he may take root somewhere.

Hawthorne showed an increasing disposition to discuss these philosophical questions in frank comment outside the plot of his romances. Hollingsworth, in *The Blithedale Romance*, illustrates his fear of tampering with the natural order of things, especially by organized reform; and Zenobia illustrates his reflections on self-reliance, especially where woman is concerned. Hollingsworth was a determined social reformer; he wished to reform criminals through an appeal to their higher instincts. Hawthorne observed that such philanthropy, admirable in its intention, often proceeded on slight knowledge of the facts. "He ought to have commenced his investigation of the subject by perpetrating some huge sin in his proper person, and examining the condition of his higher instincts afterwards." As a matter of fact, Hollingsworth does ruin two lives, Zenobia's and Priscilla's, in the selfish pursuit of his philanthropic ideal, and, if he had chosen, might well have furnished the state of his own heart for examination. Hawthorne comments again, making his familiar point that a good ideal brings a man to a good end only if it does not lead him out of the natural sympathies of life:

> The moral which presents itself to my reflections, as drawn from Hollingsworth's character and errors, is simply this—that, admitting what is called philanthropy, when adopted as a profession, to be often useful by its energetic impulse to society at large, it is perilous to the individual whose ruling passion, in one exclusive channel, it thus becomes. It ruins, or is fearfully apt to ruin, the heart, the rich juices of which God never meant should be pressed violently out and distilled into alcoholic liquor by an unnatural process, but should render life sweet, bland, and gently beneficent, and insensibly influence other hearts and other lives to the same blessed end.

Zenobia is a modern and conscious Hester—or rather, her experience is the reverse of Hester's, for she is a woman naturally emancipated who is ruined by disappointed love. It is this difference in their problems that makes her seem less noble than Hester, less tragic than pitiful. But in portraying her, Hawthorne raises more especially the question he had suggested in *The Scarlet Letter:* is not such a woman, so beautiful and so intellectual, an exotic creature in our society? Here is the modern woman whom Hester dreamed of, but the old misfortune still overtakes her; like Hester, she has married one who could not appreciate her, but she has never found the lover who should have been her mate, and she has no true companionship with other women. She seems to be a foreigner, and in the New England thought of Hawthorne's time foreigners had the right to be, like Zenobia, physically beautiful.

The Marble Faun repeats in Miriam the problem of Hester and of Zenobia, and in Hilda, the simple Puritan girl who finds peace in the Roman Catholic confessional, the story illustrates beautifully Hawthorne's faith that some of our most unconventional impulses lead us to a practical morality. But the philosophy of the book centres in Donatello, that wonderful creature who begins life with the animal-like innocence which radical thought seems often to desire for man, and who develops an immortal soul by committing an impulsive murder. The doctrine of *Circles* has its most elaborate illustration here; here is the evolution of good out of sin—not out of repentance for sin. But if the doctrine is sound, our theology needs thorough revision, and Hawthorne suggests the logical change in our conception of sin:

> Is sin then—which we deem such a dreadful blackness in the universe—is it, like sorrow, merely an element of human education, through which we struggle to a higher and purer state than we could otherwise have attained? Did Adam fall that we might ultimately rise to a far higher Paradise than his?

These problems, suggested by the Transcendental philosophy, occupied Hawthorne to the last. It was not in his disposition to suggest answers to them. His distinction in American literature is the extent to which he projected them experimentally into life, and the sincerity with which he modified them to conform to stubborn and perplexing facts.

9

3. Thoreau

THE life of a village community is not seldom enriched by the inclusion of a rebel, an original who refuses obstinately to conform to type, and succeeds in following out his idea, in contrast to the humdrum routine of his fellows. When the community happens to be Concord, the picturesque and historic village where the Revolution began, the Weimar of American literature, and when the rebel happens to be an American faun, the conjunction must result in no ordinary enrichment. There on 12 July, 1817, just after the second war with Britain, David Henry Thoreau was born to a small farmer and artisan who kept a shop and painted signs. The French-looking surname came by way of the Channel Islands, for the author's grandfather was born in Jersey, and, in spite of his British origin, had served as a sailor in a Continental privateer. Thoreau passed his life in the village of his birth, and now his name is indissolubly associated with it.

For a generation which plumes itself upon its "breadth," no slight effort is needed to picture the life of a typical New England village before the Transcendental movement had broken up the hard old Puritanic crust. It was a rigid and limited life made up of work, thrift, duty, and meetings. Caricatured and ridiculed though it be, that old stern life moulded men and women of the toughest moral and intellectual fibre. Puritanism was an intellectual creed, and led directly to the cultivation of the intellect. The minister and the schoolmaster were twin ruling powers. None questioned the value of education; it was almost a fetish. So as a child in a Puritan community, Henry Thoreau followed the regular routine of the common school until he was ripe for the university.

Thoreau became a man of letters, but he was also a wild man, a faun; he became Emerson's man, and—although it is rather difficult to fit into the picture—he was a Harvard man. He went up at sixteen and took his degree at twenty. His portrait at this time shows a smooth, grave face dominated by a Roman nose and overhung by a bush of fine brown hair. What benefit he derived from his college years is a matter both of record and of inference. "What I was learning in college was chiefly, I think, to express myself," he writes five years after leaving Harvard. Perhaps the most significant memorial of his college career is the Latin letter he wrote to his sister Helen, in 1840. It gave him pleasure to use the language of Virgil and Cicero, for one of the many paradoxes in Thoreau's life was the union of true American contempt for tradition with an unaffected love of the classics. After a diatribe against the narrow religiosity of New England, he draws breath to praise "the Ionian father of the rest," with the enthusiasm of Keats.

There are few books which deserve to be remembered in our wisest hours, but the Iliad is brightest in the serenest days, and embodies still all the sunlight that fell in Asia Minor. No modern joy or ecstasy of ours can lower its height, or dim its lustre, but there it lies in the east of literature, as it were the earliest and latest production of the mind.

From the wildwood simplicity of Walden, he startles the reader with deliverances which might have come from the Bodleian.

Those who have not learned to read the ancient classics in the language in which they were written must have a very imperfect knowledge of the history of the human race. . . . Homer has never been printed in English, nor Æschylus, nor Virgil even,—works as refined, as solidly done, as beautiful almost as the morning itself; for later writers, say what we will of their genius, have rarely if ever equalled the elaborate beauty and finish and the lifelong and heroic literary labours of the ancients.

Thoreau translated the *Prometheus Vinctus* and tried his hand at Pindar. His pages are sown with classical allusions and quotations. The sunset at Cape Cod brings a line of Homer into his memory "with a rush," as the shining torch of the sun falls into the ocean. He has words of just appreciation for Anacreon. His odes

charm us by their serenity and freedom from exaggeration and passion, and by a certain flower-like beauty, which does not propose itself, but must be approached and studied like a natural object.

Such genuine admiration for Greek genius is rare at any time, and certainly not many American hands could have been busy translating Æschylus, Pindar, and Anacreon in the hurried forties and fifties of the nineteenth century. This large and solid academic basis for Thoreau's culture is not generally observed. His devotion to the Greeks rings truer than his various utterances on Indian literature and philosophy. Besides, he was well seen in the English classics from Chaucer downwards. A few pages of *A Week* yield quotations from Emerson, Ovid, Quarles, Channing, *Relations des Jesuits*, Gower, Lydgate, Virgil, Tennyson, Percy's *Reliques*, Byron, Milton, Shakespeare, Spenser, Simonides. As Lowell remarks, "His literature was extensive and recondite." The truth is, Thoreau was a man of letters, whose great ambition was to study and to write books.

During and after his college career, Thoreau taught school, like the hero of *Elsie Venner*. He is quite frank about this episode. "As I did not teach for the good of my fellow-men, but simply for a livelihood, this was a failure." Brief as was his apprenticeship to the schoolmaster trade, one might possibly conjecture that it left some mark upon him. The many citations of recondite literature do not escape the suspicion of parade and pedantry. There is a certain gusto with which he inserts the botanical name of a plant after the picturesque vernacular, and distinguishes between *Rana palustris* and *Rana pipiens*. In general, the tone he adopts towards the world is that of the pedagogue dealing habitually with inferior minds.

After his college days comes an episode which his biographers seem inclined to slur over, perhaps from a false sense of the dignity of biography, and that is the two years, from 25 April,

1841, to May, 1843, which Thoreau spent under Emerson's roof. By the time Thoreau left Harvard, Emerson had become a power in the spiritual life of America. His brief career as a Unitarian minister was already far behind him; he had made his pilgrimage to Europe; he had penetrated the wilds of Scotland to Craigenputtock because one Thomas Carlyle, another unrecognized genius, lived there. He had given in Boston those lectures on *Great Men* and *The Philosophy of History* which foreshadow the great address commonly called the declaration of independence for American literature. He had brought out his Scottish friend's odd book, *Sartor Resartus*, a publication which accelerated the Transcendental movement. Emerson discovered the youth Thoreau as a true poet, and communicated the discovery in a letter to Carlyle. Thoreau became a member of Emerson's household, apparently as general "help," a relationship which all Americans will understand but which will be the despair of all Europeans.

The most practical and handy person in all matters of every day life, a good mechanic and gardener, methodical in his habits, observant and kindly in the domestic world,

is the character Emerson gives him. There must have been a cash nexus, but the essence of the relationship was the tie uniting master and pupil, sage and disciple. This long and close association with the great literary force of that time had no slight effect in moulding Thoreau's character and determining his bent.

His biographer, who knew him personally, says that he imitated Emerson's tones and manners so that it was annoying to listen to him.

The imitation of Emerson in Thoreau's writing is equally apparent. Lowell saw and condemned it in his criticism of *A Week*. In prose there is the sentence which reads like an oracle. It may be the profoundest wisdom, or it may be the merest matter of moonshine. When Thoreau writes "Ancient history has an air of antiquity," or, "Give me a sentence which no intelligence can understand," the critic can only fall back on the Gilbertian comment upon the young man who "expresses himself in terms too deep for me." The imitation of Emerson's poetry is even more marked and results in what Lowell calls Thoreau's "worsification." He had no candid friend to tell him what Dryden told "Cousin Swift." There was, on the other hand, no little benefit in mere contact with such a personality as Emerson, much more in continual and close intercourse with him. The stimulus to thought must have been most potent, and Emerson's influence could not but stiffen Thoreau in his natural independence and confirm him in his design of living his own life.

The village rebel who will not conform rebels first against the local religion. It is the obvious thing to rebel against. What Thoreau dissented from was New England Puritanism, as is plainly shown in "Sunday" of *A Week*. The atmosphere of that lost religion hangs about the letter of his roommate at Harvard, who became a minister in due course. One thinks of the letters young Mr. Tennyson of Trinity was exchanging with other Cambridge "Apostles" about the same time. The salutation is "Friend Thoreau," which seems to have been the accepted convention at the time. Perhaps the most significant sentence in it runs:

I hear that you are comfortably located in your native town, as the guardian of its children, in the immediate vicinity, I suppose, of one of our most distinguished apostles of the future, R. W. Emerson, and situated under the ministry of our old friend Reverend Barzillai Frost, to whom please make my remembrances.

It does not appear that Thoreau after reaching manhood was ever "situated under the ministry" of the Reverend Barzillai Frost. In "Civil Disobedience," he writes:

Some years ago, the State met me on behalf of the Church and commanded me to pay a certain sum toward the support of a clergyman, whose preaching my father attended, but never I myself. "Pay" it said, "or be locked up in jail." I declined to pay. But unfortunately, another man saw fit to pay it.

The recusant even rendered the authorities a reason in writing for his recusancy.

Know all men by these presents that I Henry Thoreau do not wish to be regarded as a member of any incorporated society which I have not joined.

Opposition to the State followed naturally on opposition to the Church. To his honour, Thoreau took a stand against slavery when it was anything but popular to do so, even in the State of Massachusetts. In all his words on this theme there is a fire not to be found elsewhere. What roused him was the spectacle of fugitive slaves escaping to the free North, and, through the action of Northern courts, dragged back into slavery. The State was clearly in the wrong; Thoreau, in his own phrase, "declared war on the State," by refusing to pay his poll-tax. He believed that such passive resistance by a number of taxpayers would bring about the abolition of slavery. He was therefore quite consistent with himself when he stood forth from the crowd as the champion of John Brown in his history-making raid on Harper's Ferry. Public opinion, North and South, condemned the raid as the outrage of a fanatic attempting to kindle a servile war. Thoreau was of the remnant who saw its true bearing.

It was in the first year of his Walden hermitage that Thoreau was arrested and lodged in jail for refusing to pay his poll-tax. He tells how he was going to the cobbler's, with a shoe to be mended, when the Law laid hold of him, how he spent the evening very pleasantly with the other inmates of the lock-up, how he was released next morning, and immediately started off with a berry-picking party. This "grand refusal" struck the imagination of Stevenson, who considers it the most significant act of Thoreau, and more important than his retreat in Walden. A parallel might be found in Stevenson's account of his brief incarceration in a French prison in the epilogue to *An Inland Voyage*. Again, some friend paid Thoreau's poll-tax for him, but he never wavered in his reasoned policy of passive resistance to an unjust, slavery-supporting State. At the same time, he never refused to pay the highway tax, because, "I am as desirous of being a good neighbour as I am of being a bad subject." "I simply wish," he continues, "to refuse allegiance to the State, to withdraw and stand aloof from it effectually."

His next step was a more remote withdrawal, an attempt to stand aloof from his kind. It was an attempt to live by himself and to himself, in fact, to turn modern hermit. Apparently the idea had long been germinating in his mind. On that far-off Harvard commencement of 1837, he took part in a "conference," an obsolete academic exercise resembling a medieval "disputation." He took one side of an argument and a fellow-student, afterwards a judge, maintained the opposite. The subject debated was "The Commercial Spirit." In his set speech, the grave, shock-headed graduate from Concord suggested that

the order of things should be somewhat reversed; the seventh should be man's day of toil, wherein to earn his living by the sweat of his brow; and the other six his Sabbath of the affections and the soul— in which to range this widespread garden, and drink in the soft influences and sublime revelations of Nature.

The young collegian's division of time may have provoked a smile, but the day was to come when he was to make the actual experiment. Thoreau had turned against the Church, he had turned against the State, and now he turned against organized society. He perceived that man was bound to the wheel of circumstance, he was the passive, unquestioning slave of a vain and sordid routine. One man at least would wrench himself free from the mill at which he saw his fellows ceaselessly toiling. He would carry out his boyhood's dream, and, by reorganization of his life, obtain freedom for the things that matter. By making life more simple, he would cheat circumstance and really begin to live.

I dream of looking abroad summer and winter, with free gaze from some mountainside, while my eyes revolve in an Egyptian slime of health—I to be nature looking into nature with such easy sympathy as the blue-eyed grass in the meadow looks in the face of the sky. From such recess, I would put forth sublime thoughts daily, as the plant puts forth leaves.

It only remained to choose his "recess."

Apparently the suggestion as to the particular recess came from his friend, Channing, who writes,

I see nothing for you in this earth but that field which I once christened "Briars"; go out upon that, build yourself a hut, and there begin the grand process of devouring yourself alive.

Thoreau was a natural ascetic. He ate little flesh meat, but subsisted almost entirely on vegetable food; he drank nothing but water; he never married. He refers in a letter to a nameless lady who wished to marry *him*, and he calls the inverted courtship "tragic." In the Age of Faith he would have fled to the wilderness for the same reason that he built his hut by Walden pond, in order to save his soul. Salvation for him meant escape from endless labour for the acquisition of useless things. By another paradox of his career, he freed himself from New England thrift by being still more thrifty. By denying himself and faring more scantily than his neighbours, he secured leisure for pursuits they could not comprehend. Thoreau is a prophet of the simple life, perhaps the first in America. He uses the very term.

I do believe in simplicity. When the mathematician would solve a difficult problem, he first frees the equation from all encumbrances, and reduces it to its simplest terms. So simplify the problem of life, distinguish the necessary and the real.

He was preaching to his friend Blake what he had already practised. He had felled the pines with his borrowed axe, and dug his cellar, and built his

tight shingled and plastered house, ten feet wide by fifteen long, and eight feet posts, with a garret and a closet, a large window on each side, two trap-doors, one door at the end, and a brick fireplace opposite.

It was a little smaller than the room he occupied at Harvard. The materials cost less than twenty-nine dollars; and by cultivating beans and other vegetables he was able to support himself at an annual expense of a little more than eight dollars. This was removing the encumbrances from the equation, with a vengeance, but Thoreau could make a "dinner" of berries. The experiment lasted from March, 1845, until September, 1847, and then having satisfied himself that the thing could be done, he gave it up.

Two years later, Thoreau published his first book, *A Week on the Concord and Merrimack Rivers*. The actual voyage was performed by the two brothers Henry and John in the late summer of 1839 in a boat of their own making, "painted green below with a border of blue, with reference to the two elements in which it was to spend its existence." During his Walden retirement, Thoreau worked over the original record of his pleasant outing, expanding it greatly by the inclusion of very various material, and had it published at his own risk by Monroe in 1849. It was the year of the Argonauts, of the gold-rush to California, and such literary treasure as the odd book contained was not much regarded. Though favourably reviewed by Ripley and by Lowell, it did not please the public, and over seven hundred copies out of an impression of one thousand were thrown back on the author's hands. It is another of the paradoxes of Thoreau's career that since his death, this failure has been edited with almost benedictine care.

Lowell's praise of *A Week* can hardly be termed excessive. After dwelling on its weak points, its lack of unity, its imitation of Emerson, its dolorous verse, he continues,

the prose work is done conscientiously and neatly. The style is compact and the language has an antique purity like wine grown colourless with age.

The truth is that Thoreau with all his genuine appreciation of the classics never learned their lessons of proportion, restraint, "nothing too much." Nor was the example of his master Emerson likely to correct his own tendency to formlessness. The principle of selection is absent. The week's excursion is only an excuse for including Emersonian essays on friendship and chastity, or dissertations on the Laws of Menu, or translations of Anacreon, till the reader asks resentfully what they are doing in this dory-modelled *galère*, painted green below with a border of blue, on the Merrimack and Concord, lucid streams. If he had possessed the artistic instinct of Stevenson, or had undergone Stevenson's rigid self-imposed discipline in the writer's craft, he might have made *A Week* as complete a little masterpiece as *An Inland Voyage*. *A Week* fails on account of its scattering aim. It is neither a record of a week's excursion, nor a book of essays, but a jumble of the two. Thoreau's American contempt for tradition accounts for the artistic failure.

Where Thoreau is not the transcendental essayist, but the first-hand observer of nature, he is delightful. When discoursing on such a theme as the common sunfish, the reader wishes he would never end.

The breams are so careful of their charge that you may stand close by in the water and examine them at your leisure. I have stood over them half an hour at a time, and stroked them familiarly without frightening them, suffering them to nibble my fingers harmlessly, and seen them erect their dorsal fins in anger when my hand approached their ova, and have even gently taken them out of the water with my hand. . . . As you stand thus stooping over the bream in its nest, the edges of the dorsal and caudal fins have a singular dusty golden reflection, and its eyes, which stand out from its head, are transparent and colourless. Seen in its native element, it is a very beautiful and compact fish, perfect in all its parts, and looks like a brilliant coin fresh from the mint.

If the whole book had been of this texture, it would be a classic. Another element in the book which Thoreau valued slightly— those incidental glimpses of a vanished America—will be prized by later generations. His accounts of the mountain people he discovered, of the girl combing her black hair, of his surly host, Rice, and his strange inn, of the old farmer praying in the dim morning pasture, of the canal boatmen, of the lockmen's house, and the small-voiced but sincere hospitality of the Yankee housewife offering the obsolete refreshment of "molasses and ginger," read like pages Irving forgot to put into *The Sketch Book*. These things are seen with the naturalist's clear grave eyes and recorded in plain words with no attempt at oracular profundity. For the sake of more such true pictures of reality, how gladly would the modern reader forego the disquisitions on Persius and Ossian.

The next year, 1850, Thoreau and his friend Channing made a brief raid across the border into Quebec, though the record of his experience was not published until 1866, with the title *A Yankee in Canada*. Stevenson found the book dull.

Still, it has an interest of its own for the light it sheds on Thoreau's peculiar temperament, and particularly on his robust Americanism, a sentiment based on traditional dislike of Britain and on contempt for monarchy as an effete institution. Patriotism is a curious passion. It does not seem possible to love one's own country except by hating some other country. Emerson defines Thoreau almost in these terms:

> No truer American existed than Thoreau. His preference of his country and condition was genuine, and his aversation from English and European manners and tastes almost reached contempt.

With no great love for the institutions of his own land, he showed his instinctive preference for them during his one brief sojourn under an alien flag. His attitude throughout is one of consistent patronage to all he sees and hears. The red-coats in the citadel at Quebec have the manhood drilled out of them. Britain, he believes, is "red in the knuckles" with holding on to the Canadas, and must soon relax her grasp. Towards the great mystery of historical Christianity, he is equally contemptuous. The devout worshippers in the Cathedral at Montreal, absorbed in prayer and regardless of gazing strangers, suggest the parallel of his fellow Yankees going to meeting on a week-day, after the cattle-fair. The Sisters of Charity whom he saw in the street looked as if they had cried their eyes out, "insulting the daylight with their presence." That the soldier and the religious had something valuable to which he was a stranger, never occurred to him. In other words, he was blind to the romance of war and the poetry of faith. Even the natural courtesy of the *habitants* seems to him mere servility. For the American of Thoreau's generation, history began with the musketry of the embattled farmers at Concord bridge. Before that day, there was only a dark welter of wicked kings and mad tories. These limitations prevented him from realizing, as Parkman did, the epic struggle which ended on the Plains of Abraham. He indeed transcribes the inscription on the monument to Wolfe and Montcalm, but the splendour and pathos of their fate leave him unmoved. Still, this rigid and narrow provincialism gives salt to his books and explains his revolt against convention.

It was his Americanism which drove Thoreau to realize himself in his own way.

In 1854, Thoreau published the book by which he will always be best known, *Walden, or Life in the Woods*. It is by far the deepest, richest, and most closely jointed of his books. It shows Thoreau at his best, and contains all that he had to say to the world. In fact, he is a man of one book, and that book is *Walden*. In plan, it is open to the same objection as *A Week*, and might almost plead guilty to the charge of obtaining a hearing under false pretences. "Life in the woods" suggests the atmosphere of *As You Like It* and the Robin Hood ballads, but not moralizings on economy and the duty of being yourself. The reader who takes up the book with the idea that he is going to enjoy another *Robinson Crusoe* will not be pleased to find that every now and then he will have to listen to a lay sermon, or a lyceum lecture.

Still it is the adventurous, *Robinson Crusoe* part that is imperishable. How a man resolved to live in a new way, how he borrowed an axe and began felling pines on the ground that sloped southward to a wonderful pond, how he trimmed his rafters, dug his cellar, bought an Irish labourer's shanty, transported the materials to a new site and raised the frame, appeal to the open-air instinct of every man. Even how he maintained the fire on the hearth, and grubbed out the fat pine roots to feed it, are matters of absorbing interest. His struggle with the weeds and poor soil of the two-acre patch on which he raised his beans and potatoes, every item of his various accounts, his food, his daily routine, his house-cleaning, have the fascination of a narrative by Defoe. The reader follows the solitary in his swim across the lake, or through the wood to the village, or about the hut, or along the rows of beans, with a zest he can hardly explain to himself. The reason is that Henry Thoreau in Walden wood is the same as the mariner of York on the Island of Desolation; he represents once more the struggle of primitive man to obtain food and shelter, in fact the epic of civilization. The interest of the theme is perennial.

Walden is also the memorial of an American faun, of a wild man who lived in the woods, who carried an umbrella like Robinson Crusoe, to weatherfend his head, and used a microscope to study insects with. About the same time, just after leaving Harvard, Thoreau found his first arrowhead and began his first journal, and the two streams of tendency ran side by side in his nature till the end. Intercourse with nature was even more necessary to Thoreau than intercourse with books. Intercourse with human beings he thought he did not need, but he was always tramping off to the village for a chat. He was not a real solitary, for visitors were always coming to view the progress of the odd experiment in living. Still Thoreau differed widely from the ordinary gregarious man in that he could manage to be alone for long periods with the woods and the sky. A friend called him a poet-naturalist; but the description is not exact. He hardly views nature as a poet, and he is surpassed by not a few observers of nature, who have had the stimulus of Darwin. The merely pictorial in nature does not much interest him, probably because he had seen no pictures. To Thoreau nature is no divinity as she is to Wordsworth; she is simply the pleasantest of companions, or rather the pleasantest environment for a natural man. In a house, in a town, he is like a creature caged. It is characteristic that after swimming across the lake, he would sit in his doorway all morning, "in a wise passiveness," as Wordsworth would term it. So wild creatures live in the wild, when not hunger-driven. The wild things found him to be of their own kind; a mouse made friends with him, a hen partridge led her brood about his hut, he could take a fish out of the water in his hand. Thoreau is perhaps the first to suggest the pleasure of hunting animals without a gun, of learning about them without any desire to kill. He was not influenced by Darwin, or such a conception as the struggle for existence. Nature to him was not red in tooth and claw with ravin; it was a gentle, friendly, peaceful alternative to the mean greed and futile toil of man. The atmosphere of Walden is always serene and free from cloud or storm. Rain and winter come in their season; but they never seem to touch him; the rain does not wet, and the winter does not chill. There may be a thousand nooks in New England more beautiful than Walden, but they remain unknown, while the pine-clad slope which this strange being discovered and haunted for two years is charted as a permanent addition to the world-wide map of Romance.

Thoreau has two styles, the oracular and the simple; and

in *Walden* the simple prevails. Like the water of the pond, it is clear, colourless and wholesome. Thoreau is a careful writer, with an instinct for the right word which was developed and strengthened by a lifelong devotion to the best books. His love of the classics must have tended to purify his style and increase its natural dignity. *Walden* is generally free from oracular phrases and grotesque locutions like "eyes revolve in an Egyptian slime of health." It must always retain the deep unfailing value of all autobiography, personal memoirs, "confessions." The record of a life will never fail of an audience. When a man declares, "Thus I did, thus I thought, thus I felt," other men are always eager to attend his tale.

The Walden experiment was not unlike the other Transcendental experiment of Brook Farm. Both were declarations of independence; both were attempts to place life on a new basis; both broke down. The Greek dog-sage in his tub, the English Quaker in his suit of leather, the Yankee land-surveyor in his wooden hut are three object lessons to the world of the ancient truth that "a man's life consisteth not in the abundance of the things that he possesseth." The Walden experiment is open to all the criticism of Lowell: "it presupposed all the complicated civilization which it theoretically abjured." Even for Thoreau it was not a success. In the first year, his Homer lay open on the table, but he was so busy that he could only read it by snatches; in the second year, he was forced to set up a prosaic stove in the place of the romantic fire-place. Thoreau's ideal of a world of book men, or contemplatives, is a dream. Still, the experience of the ascetic always shames the grossness of the worldly wiseman. If a man can live for a year for eight dollars, we certainly spend too much on things we could do without. Thoreau's experiment will always have its appeal to hot, ambitious spirits on their first awakening to the intricacy of life. The hero of *Locksley Hall* longs to escape from civilization to summer isles of Eden. At least one American man of letters has followed Thoreau's example by going into retreat.

After living in his hut for two years, Thoreau supported himself for three more by cultivating his garden, like Candide. Thus he obtained the freedoms he desired, the leisure to think, and to read, and to write, and to be himself. Then he went back to his land-surveying, his communing with the spirits of the wild, and the compilation of his voluminous journals. From the latter, several volumes have been quarried for the definitive edition of his works. They must always be of more interest to the admirer of Thoreau and the student of literature than to the general reader.

Then came the break-down of his health. It was the irony of fate that the man who lived according to nature, who obeyed the dictates of spare temperance, who never seemed to tire, should die of tuberculosis, the scourge of civilized life. His latest portrait, a daguerreotype taken in New Bedford, seven months before his death, shows a hairy, innocent, pathetic face; the eyes have the mute appeal of the consumptive. In 1861, the stricken man made a trip to the West, in the vain hope of restoration to health by change of air. He died in his birth-place, Concord, on 2 May, 1862, in the second year of the Civil War. He has been blamed for expressing his sense of detachment from that terrible conflict, but if, like Mercutio, he cries, "A plague on both your houses!" it must be remembered that, like Mercutio, he was a dying man. His last letter, dictated to his sister, concludes, "I am enjoying existence as much as ever, and regret nothing."

Emerson has written an appreciation of Thoreau with intimate knowledge and tender humanity. To that estimate, little can be added, or taken away. Lowell and Stevenson have appraised his character and his work, none too gently. Of himself he said, "I am a mystic, a Transcendentalist, and a natural philosopher."

CHAPTER V

Poets, Essayists, Romancers

I. LONGFELLOW

HENRY WADSWORTH LONGFELLOW was born in Portland, Maine, 27 February, 1807. In view of what America as a whole then was and of what he was destined to accomplish for the literature of the country, it is difficult to see how he could have been more fortunately circumstanced with respect to stock and environment. Both the Longfellows and his mother's people, the Wadsworths, were well-to-do, and they represented the best New England, particularly Massachusetts, traditions, which, with the spread of Unitarianism, were losing some of their rigidity. Thus the child experienced little that was specially straitening, and he received a training well adapted to bring out the talents that soon manifested themselves. His native town furnished the influence of the sea and sea-faring men; the virgin District soon to be the State of Maine afforded other impressive features of nature; and the frontier situation, even if it could not make strenuous a constitutionally gentle and refined disposition, at least inculcated feelings of sympathy with a pioneer, rugged, prevailingly practical population, which were to be of great use to a poet who in after years could point to his successful fulfilment of the threefold function of transmitter of Old World culture to the New, shaper into verse of aboriginal, colonial, and Revolutionary material, both legendary and historical, and lyric interpreter of the simple thoughts and feelings of an unsophisticated people. His career was well foreshadowed when he published anonymously at the age of thirteen, in a local newspaper, a Revolutionary battle-lyric.

After a good schooling and an introduction to the best reading old and new, including Irving's *Sketch Book*, Longfellow, in the autumn of 1822, entered Bowdoin College as a sophomore, having Nathaniel Hawthorne as a classmate. Here, as at home, he continued to come under unpretentious, wholesome influences, to which were added those of rural seclusion. Before he graduated in 1825, he was writing verse rather copiously, and some of it was published in a literary journal just founded in Boston. As is not surprising, it was overpraised by a provincial public, but for a wonder, in view of the vogue of Byron, it was not stormily romantic. His success gave point to his plans for leading a literary life, but his more experienced father held out for the law, although he was willing to give his son a year of grace to be spent in less uncongenial studies at Harvard. This plan was abandoned because it was found feasible for Longfellow to fit himself to become the first incumbent of a chair of modern languages to be established at Bowdoin.

Travel and study in Europe were essential to such a design, and the middle of June, 1826, saw the youth of nineteen beginning at Havre a European sojourn of a little more than three years. Temperament and immaturity, combined doubtless with a shrewd perception of the fact that great erudition was not a prerequisite to successful language-teaching in Maine, made it natural that Longfellow should become rather a sentimental pilgrim than a delving student or a philosophical observer, and that he should make but slight use of Ticknor's recommendation of Göttingen as a centre and source of the exact scholarship so much needed in America. German sentiment and romance were later to mean much to the poet; but Latin colour and picturesqueness meant more to the young traveller. France, Spain, where he met Irving, and Italy, from whose greatest writer his mature and declining years derived their chief solace, were in turn visited, their manners noted, their literatures studied, their languages in more than polite measure mastered. Then several months were given to Germany, including a little studying at Göttingen, and in August, 1829, the neophyte professor was back in America ready to take up the duties of his chair.

Those duties occupied him until his second visit to Europe, which took place nearly six years later. He was a conscientious and successful teacher and compiler of text-books, he lectured on literary history, he wrote for *The North American*

Review essays flavoured with scholarship, he gave a pledge to society by taking to himself, in 1831, a wife, Mary Storer Potter, of Portland. Except for some verse translations from the Spanish and certain traces of the poet to be discovered in a series of travel-sketches, which appeared in a volume entitled *Outre-Mer: a Pilgrimage beyond the Sea* (1835), one might have been justified in supposing that without doubt the undergraduate whose heart was set on "future eminence in literature" would end his life as a distinguished academic personage, not as the most popular poet of his generation. His fate seemed sealed with his acceptance of the Smith Chair of Modern Languages at Harvard, in succession to Ticknor, and with his departure for Europe in April, 1835, in order that by study of the northern literatures he might the better qualify himself for his important post.

His second period of training in Europe, although shorter, rendered Longfellow a greater service than his first. As he was more mature, his genius was better prepared to receive a definitive bent, and his experiences determined that that bent should take an emotional rather than an emphatically intellectual direction. After a short visit to England he spent some months in Sweden and Denmark studying their literatures with results obvious to the reader of his later poetry. Then he went to Holland, where his wife fell ill and died in the autumn. This meant that the ensuing winter at Heidelberg saw no notable progress made by the young professor in his German studies, but did see a deep absorption of the spirit of German romanticism by the young widower and the future poet. The sentimental prose romance *Hyperion* and the collection of poems entitled *Voices of the Night*, both published in 1839, show what bereavement and the new environment, physical as well as mental and spiritual, had brought to the man entering his fourth decade. We track the footsteps of the naïve hero of *Hyperion* with less confiding delight than our grandfathers and grandmothers probably experienced, but then we are less sentimental and more widely travelled than they were, facts which of course do not warrant us in arrogating to ourselves a taste necessarily superior to theirs. *Hyperion* doubtless meant more to the author and his countrymen than a scholarly monograph would have meant, for what

America needed just then, apparently, was some one who, like Longfellow, could carry on the work begun by Irving of interpreting the Old World to the New.   The younger man was not only better endowed with the faculty of specific poetic utterance, but he was naturally more fully qualified than his predecessor to gratify the taste of a generation that was be, ginning to be affected by the work of the newer English roman- tic poets.   Thus we are not surprised to find the Smith Professor writing poems on European subjects instead of gram- mars and histories of literature, and editing in place of text- books a small collection of poems entitled *The Waif* (1843), a similar volume, *The Estray* (1847), and the comprehensive and useful *Poets and Poetry of Europe* (1845).   Even the thirty-one volumes of the much later *Poems of Places* (1876–1879) with which Longfellow's name is more or less associated, bear wit- ness to the influence of the teacher-poet's second sojourn in Europe both upon him and upon American culture.

But the greatest influence of that sojourn, exhibited after he took up his duties at Harvard in December, 1836, is to be seen in the simple, wholesomely emotional, and unblushingly didactic poems with which Longfellow now began to win the hearts of his provincial readers.   *The Psalm of Life* is perhaps the best known and the best chosen example of these "house- hold poems," shall we call them?   With its companion pieces *The Reaper and the Flowers*, *The Light of Stars*, and *Footsteps of Angels*, it is undoubtedly amenable to some of the harsh criticism it has received from those persons who seem to imagine that taste thrives only on its own exigency.   But it is hard to see how verses of subtler quality would have so sung themselves through the length and breadth of young America, or could have laid so broad and deep a foundation for the fame of the most heartily loved poet of his generation.

Long before that poet had reached the zenith of his reputa- tion the professor had grown weary of his chair.   At first he worked hard enough to justify weariness, particularly at the uncongenial task of supervising the instruction in the elemen- tary language courses given by his assistants; but gradually, whatever enthusiasm he may have had for a scholarly, academic career wore itself out, and toward the end of his eighteen years of service—he resigned in 1854—he was almost querulous in his attitude toward a calling without the aid of which he would probably have remained a somewhat local and minor writer, his disposition scarcely prompting him to draw inspiration from Transcendentalism or the anti-slavery movement, and his genius not qualifying him to probe the heart or to wander in shadowland.

Whatever its irksomeness, however, his position at Harvard brought with it compensations. He soon secured a congenial habitat—the now famous Craigie House—he gathered about him a group of sympathetic friends, he became a distinguished figure in the most cultured community in America, the Cambridge of Lowell's essay and of Colonel Higginson's books, he added to his happiness and his income by a second marriage— to Miss Frances Elizabeth Appleton in 1843—and he found time and incentive to write whatever he had in his mind and heart to say. Reading his letters and his diaries, putting together the biographical details furnished by others, and constructing as best one can the man's life and spirit from his writings, one is forced to the conclusion that except for a single great tragedy—the accidental burning to death of his wife in 1861—Longfellow's is one of the most serenely fortunate careers ever led by a man of letters. Some of his critics have wished that it might have been otherwise, apparently supposing that, if he had been more unfortunate, his poetry would have been more to their liking. It is not, however, on record that any critic has deliberately wooed infelicity in order to qualify himself for a fuller enjoyment of Longfellow's placid verses.

In 1842 a third visit was made to Europe, this time a short one for the sake of health. It was preceded by the *Ballads and Other Poems* (1841), and followed by the *Poems on Slavery* (1842). These justly enhanced his reputation, but the meritorious anti-slavery verses proved no prelude to active participation in the great conflict that was leading up to the Civil War. The prior volume with such pieces as *The Village Blacksmith, God's Acre, Maidenhood,* and the egregiously anabatic *Excelsior,* strengthened his hold upon the popular heart, and in the successful ballads proper, such as *The Wreck of the Hesperus* and *The Skeleton in Armor,* it gave him, in addition, some incentive to address his readers in narrative verse, the form of poetry in which, during his middle period, he made himself easily the chief American master. Neither in these earlier volumes, to which may be added *The Belfry of Bruges and Other Poems* (1846), nor in *Evangeline* (1847) and succeeding tales in verse, did Longfellow show himself to be a consummate metrical and verbal artist of the highest order or a poet of sustained imaginative flight; nor was he, in compensation, one of those writers who produce a strong effect through their subtle knowledge of human character or their exceptional ability to describe and interpret nature or their profound understanding of a country or a period. Yet even in these particulars he was capable of exhibiting distinguished merit—witness his command of the simpler rhythms, his wide-reaching metrical experimentation, his feeling for the sea, his sympathetic attitude toward the Middle Ages displayed in *The Golden Legend* (1851), his presentation of the larger natural features of America in *Evangeline*—and in his lyrical appeal, especially through his semi-didactic poems of reflection and sentiment, as well as in his general narrative power, he was during his life, and he still remains, unapproached by any other American poet.

The years immediately preceding his second marriage in 1843 were partly devoted to the composition of a poetical drama in three acts, *The Spanish Student*, which was published serially in 1842, and the next year was issued in book form. It is generally and justly regarded as a failure, since Longfellow exhibited neither in it nor in later poems cast in similar form —*The New England Tragedies* (1868), *Judas Maccabaeus* (1872), and *Michael Angelo* (1883),—the slightest trace of dramatic genius. A poet of literary derivation, so to phrase it, inspired by his own wide reading, and a useful transmitter of culture he could not help being from first to last, and his growing reputation naturally prompted him to undertake elaborate works in a form of art practised by preceding poets in every age. His countrymen were not exigent critics, and were inclined to resent it when he was accused, as by Poe and by Margaret Fuller, of unoriginality; latter-day readers are likely to skim, or else altogether to neglect the dramas that are protected from complete oblivion by the venerated and still venerable name. If they desire any justification for their conduct, such prudent readers may ejaculate "*habent sua fata libelli*," or may recall the facts that Dr. Samuel Johnson wrote *Irene* and William Wordsworth, *The Borderers.*

In all probability, neither of these ominous dramatic productions was in Longfellow's mind when he was writing *The Spanish Student*, or planning his presumptive masterpiece, *Christus: A Mystery*, which finally saw the light in 1872, more than twenty years after the first appearance of its second part, *The Golden Legend*, one of the most attractive and yet one of the least widely read of its author's books. Poems Swedish and German, ominous in no bad sense, were in his mind when he wrote his sentimental idyllic narrative in hexameters, *Evangeline*, not perhaps the best of his longer poems, but certainly the most popular both at home and abroad. Hawthorne, from whom Longfellow secured the theme of the Acadian maiden's vain search for her lover, might have made more of the pathetic story, but he would have done it for fewer readers. Other writers might have improved the local colour of the poem, still others might have laboured more heroically to keep the hexameters from making forays across the borders of prose, but it may be doubted whether any contemporary could have written, on the whole, a better *Evangeline*, at least one more suited to the taste of the period. Few of his contemporaries, however, have left behind a more negligible prose romance than the story of an impossible New England village which Longfellow published in 1849 under the title *Kavanagh; A Tale.*

The end of the fifties saw the culmination of his genius in the appearance of *The Courtship of Miles Standish and Other Poems* (1858). This narrative poem, another experiment in hexameters, seems to surpass Longfellow's other successful achievements in the same category because it is more racy of New England, fuller of humour, superior in movement and in characterization. It is less popular than *Evangeline*, partly no doubt because it is less sweet, and it seems to have made less impression than its predecessor the Indian epic *Hiawatha* (1855)—another metrical experiment, this time in rhymeless trochaic tetrameters—partly because it is less ambitious and exotic. The popularity of *Hiawatha* is not undeserved, however, since novelty and quaintness may well be set over against facility and factitiousness, and since, being in a certain sense

American, the poem may justly make more of a local appeal than such a work as *The Golden Legend* based on *Der Arme Heinrich*. Yet it may be doubted whether either *Hiawatha* or *Miles Standish* did as much to establish Longfellow as the most admired poet of his time as some of the unpretentious poems contained in the collection entitled *The Seaside and the Fireside* (1850), such poems, for example, as the tender *Resignation*, to say nothing of the patriotic close of *The Building of the Ship*.

From the date of the tragic accident to his wife—July, 1861—to his death 24 March, 1882, at his home in Cambridge, Longfellow's life takes on dignity without losing its quiet charm, and his genius—shall we say, mellows, or slowly abates in energy? There was no marked falling off in the number of published volumes, in the range of his interests, in his hold upon his intimate friends, such as Charles Eliot Norton and James Russell Lowell, in his endeavours, conscious and unconscious, to deserve the affectionate gratitude of his countrymen. Even in the South, for a time rent away from the rest of the country politically, and for a longer period estranged in sentiment, his was a Northern name not anathema to the rising generation, and in Great Britain he rivalled in popularity Tennyson himself. But, as might have been expected, these years saw the production of little, except for some excellent sonnets, that adds permanently to his fame as a poet.

True, he added considerably to the mass of his narrative poetry by the three series of *Tales of a Wayside Inn*, the first of which appeared under its own name in 1863, the second and third of which were included respectively in *Three Books of Song* (1872—along with *Judas Maccabaeus*), and in *Aftermath* (1874), but save for the spirited *Paul Revere's Ride* and the *Saga of King Olaf*, of the first series, these tales in verse have made only a mild impression. This is about all that may justly be said with regard to the twelve poems collected in *Flower-de-luce* (1867); it is more than should be said of *The New England Tragedies*, the third part of *Christus*, consisting of *John Endicott* and *Giles Cory of the Salem Farms*. These, with the first part of the ambitious trilogy, *The Divine Tragedy* (1871), constitute what may best be ambiguously denominated "efforts." Longfellow was more fortunately employed when he put himself in the company of Cowper and Bryant, and sought solace for his private woes in an extensive piece of poetical translation. Perhaps his true genius as a translator, seen early in the *Coplas de Manrique* (1833), is better exemplified in his numerous renderings of lyrics, particularly, as in Uhland's *The Castle by the Sea*, from the German, than in the faithful, meritorious version of *The Divine Comedy*, which appeared in three volumes between 1867 and 1870; but, despite a certain lack of metrical charm resulting from the facile character of the rhymeless lines printed in threes, the version of the masterpiece to which Longfellow gave so many years of love and study seems worthy of his pains and of the praise it has received from other admirers of Dante.

After the appearance of the translation of Dante and of the *Christus*, two works *de longue haleine* which show that the retired professor of nearly twenty years' standing was not open to the charge of idleness, Longfellow had still about a decade to live and to continue his writing. Some of the titles of his collections of verse have been already given; others are *The Masque of Pandora, and Other Poems* (1875), *Kéramos; and Other Poems* (1878), *Ultima Thule* (1880), and *In the Harbor* (1882—posthumous). The first of these volumes contained one of the most dignified and impressive of all his poems, one of the best occasional poems in American literature, the *Morituri Salutamus*, written for the semi-centennial of the poet's class at Bowdoin. It also contained *A Book of Sonnets*, fourteen in all, considerably extended in number in later editions of the poetical works. Some notable sonnets had been published with the translation of Dante, and to these Longfellow's later achievements in the same form are worthy pendants. High praise has been given to them by many critically minded readers of a later generation, who have wished, in default of admiration for Longfellow's earlier work, to combine patriotism with acumen in their praise of a poet whose reputation seemed to require rather delicate handling. Both the sonnets and their American encomiasts are fortunately unamenable to comments lacking in amiability, although it is open to doubt whether even such a pathetic sonnet as *The Cross of Snow*, written at the close of the poet's life in memory of his unfortunate second wife, will ever mean to the great public what *The Bridge* and *The Day is Done* have meant. It is perhaps more to the purpose to express satisfaction that the poet was capable of making the double appeal—to the reader who thinks he knows what to think and to the reader who knows he knows how to feel.

It may be gathered from this brief survey of a long life and a productive career that Longfellow's reputation, in the opinion of the present writer, was amply deserved in the poet's day, and rested in the main on his gifts as a story-teller in verse, on his power to transplant to American literature some of the colour and melody and romantic charm of the complex European literatures he had studied, and, more especially, on his skill in expressing in comparatively artless lyrics of sentiment and reflection homely and wholesome thoughts and feelings which he shared with his countrymen of all classes throughout a broad land the occupation of which proceeded apace during his own span of years. Whatever he accomplished beyond this as teacher and editor and writer of prose, and as self-conscious poet seeking success in the more elaborate traditional forms of his art, is worthy, to say the least, of as much praise as the similar work of his predecessors, contemporaries, and successors among American poets, and is not clearly doomed to a speedier death than the elaborate productions of his contemporaries and successors among the British poets. His place is not with the few eminent poets of the world, or even of his century, as the admiration of the mass of his countrymen and the critical lucubrations of some of them might be held to imply; but it is, legitimately and permanently, in the forefront of the small band of important writers in verse and in prose who during the first century of the republic's existence laid firmly and upon more or less democratic lines the foundations of a native literature.

2. Whittier

IT was in 1638, when the great Puritan emigration to Massachusetts was beginning to slacken, that Thomas Whittier, a youth of eighteen, possibly of Huguenot extraction, landed in New England and made a home for himself on the shores of the Merrimac River. The substantial oak farmhouse which, late in life, he erected for his large family near Haverhill, is still standing. Descended from him in the fourth generation, John Greenleaf Whittier, the poet, was born in this house, 17 December, 1807. This is the homestead described with minute and loving fidelity in *Snow-Bound*, and it is typical of the many thousands of its sort that dotted the New England country-side, rearing in the old Puritan tradition a sturdy pioneer stock that was to blossom later in the fine flower of political and ethical passion, of statesmanship and oratory and letters. Though Whittier's family tree was originally Puritan, a Quaker scion was grafted upon it in the second American generation, when Joseph Whittier, the youngest son of the pioneer, married Mary Peaslee, whose father had been an associate and disciple of George Fox. The descendants in this line remained faithful to the doctrines of the Society of Friends, and the poet, although he persisted in the characteristic and quaint (although ungrammatical) use of the second person singular pronoun in address, found the principle of non-resistance something of a strain in the days when his fondest hopes were bound up in the holy cause for which his friends were bearing arms and laying down their lives upon the battle-field.

The levelled gun, the battle brand
    We may not take,
But, calmly loyal, we can stand
And suffer for our suffering land
    For conscience' sake.

The temperament of the New England Quaker was not unlike that of the New England Puritan.   The one could be as cantankerous as the other, on occasion, but when the early Puritan intolerance of the sect had been smoothed away, the Quaker was found to be a man whose ideals were essentially those of the founders of Massachusetts, contributing to those ideals his own element of kindly sympathy, his own insistence upon the dignity of the individual, and his own uncompromising spirit of democracy.   These traits were permanently stamped upon Whittier's character, and all rested upon a foundation of unshakable faith in the spiritual order of the world.   Christianity has perhaps never assumed a purer or lovelier guise than it took in the lives of those New England Quakers of whom Whittier was the type.

The life of the household in which the poet grew to manhood is reproduced in *Snow-Bound* with a fidelity which makes of that poem, for its truthfulness and sincerity, one of the imperishable things in American literature—a document whose significance is becoming fully apparent only now that the phase of life it describes has all but vanished from American life, whether in New England or elsewhere.   The home which *Snow-Bound* describes was a comfortable one, as New England farmsteads went, and, in poetical retrospect, its gracious human aspects are raised to a prominence which somewhat obscures the hard facts of the daily life of the household.   It was a life of toil, with meagre opportunities for recreation, and the young Whittier did not have the constitution needed for its requirements.   The physical disabilities under which he laboured all his life were doubtless traceable to the hardships of these early years on the farm.

Whittier had but little education of the formal sort.   There were sessions of the district school for a few weeks every year, and these he attended off and on.   In his twentieth year, an academy was opened in Haverhill, and in this institution he

was enrolled as a student for two terms, earning the money to
pay for his tuition. Meanwhile, he had been acquiring the
best kind of education by devouring every book that he could
lay his hands on, including the few on the family shelf—mostly
the writings of pious Quakers—and

> The Bible towering o'er the rest,
> Of all other books the best.

One evening the district school teacher, Joshua Coffin, brought
to the house a volume of Burns, and read from it to the family.
This reading was a revelation to the boy of fourteen, who
eagerly sought permission to keep the book for a while. The
Scotch poet aroused in him the poetical stirrings which were
to occupy his mind from that time on, and marked an epoch
in the intellectual development of his boyhood. It was Burns,
as he confessed many years later, who made him see

> through all familiar things
> The romance underlying;
> The joys and griefs that plume the wings
> Of Fancy skyward flying,

and so shaped his imaginings that he became, in a more exact
sense than is usually connoted by such literary analogies, the
Burns of his own New England country.

From this time on, Whittier was an industrious scribbler
of rhymes. Most of them have been lost, but enough remain
to reveal a promise which may perhaps be characterized as
similar to that of the *Poems by Two Brothers*, or the *Poems by
Victor and Cazire*. The first of his verses to appear in print
were sent, unknown to the author, by his sister Mary to *The
Free Press*, a weekly paper just established by William Lloyd
Garrison in Newburyport. The boy's surprise was great
when he read his own composition in an issue of the paper
that was delivered at the Whittier farm in the summer of 1826.
Other pieces followed, and one day shortly afterward, Garrison
made a journey to the farm for the purpose of hunting up his
promising contributor. He found Whittier at work in the
field, urged the poet's father to send him to the academy, and
thus began what was to be the life-long friendship of these

two remarkable personalities. During the next two years Whittier published in the Haverhill *Gazette* nearly one hundred poems, besides prose articles on *Burns, War,* and *Temperance.* In 1828, a volume to be entitled *The Poems of Adrian* was projected, but this venture was abandoned. In the summer of that year his schooldays came to an end, and he began to look about for a means of earning his living. An offer was made him of the editorship of *The Philanthropist,* a paper devoted to the cause of what is called "temperance" in the current perverted sense of that term, but this offer he declined in a letter containing this significant confession: "I would rather have the memory of a Howard, a Wilberforce, and a Clarkson than the undying fame of Byron." By this time, he had acquired a considerable local reputation as a young writer of promise, and various modest openings already lay in his path.

During the next four years of his life (1828–32), Whittier was the editor of papers in Boston and Haverhill, and of *The New England Review,* in Hartford, Connecticut, besides contributing to many others. He became a partisan of Clay and the protective system, and looked askance at Jackson, "the blood-thirsty old man at the head of our government." The death of the elder Whittier in 1830 kept him for some time in Haverhill for the settlement of the family affairs. His interest in politics became more and more pronounced, and he thought seriously of standing for an election to Congress in 1832 but gave up the idea because he would, at the time of the election, be a few weeks short of the legal age requirement. When he identified himself, the next year, with the unpopular cause of the abolitionists, he gave up all hopes of political advancement.

Whittier's first published book was entitled *Legends of New England, in Prose and Verse.* It appeared in 1831, and was followed in 1832 by a pamphlet containing *Moll Pitcher.* Both these publications he afterwards did his best to suppress. Reform still appealed to him even more than poetry, and he wrote upon one occasion: "I set a higher value on my name as appended to the Antislavery Declaration of 1833 than on the title-page of any book." This Declaration was issued by the Convention held in Philadelphia, in 1833, to which Whittier was a delegate. In taking this momentous decision, he builded better than he knew, for the poet in him was aroused, and the *Voices of Freedom* which from that time flowed from his pen were the utterances of a deeply-stirred soul, as different as possible from the imitative exercises which had hitherto engaged him.

The incidents of Whittier's life during the following few years may be briefly summarized. In 1835 he served a term in the Massachusetts Legislature. In 1836, the Haverhill homestead was sold, and he bought in Amesbury, a few miles down the Merrimac, the cottage which was to be his home for the rest of his life. He occupied various editorial positions, which, together with activities in connection with the abolitionist agitation, kept him moving about until 1840, when he found his health badly broken and returned to Amesbury, there to remain for the greater part of the half-century that was still vouchsafed to him. In his abolitionist activities he proved his mettle, often suffering indignities at the hands of mobs and being on several occasions in no small physical peril. His shrewd and persuasive political activities made him a force to be reckoned with, and he kept in close touch with the leaders and movements of the time, allying himself with the Liberty Party of 1840, which, like the scriptural mustard seed, was destined to wax into so great a tree.

In 1836, Whittier published *Mogg Megone*, and, in the following year, a collection of his miscellaneous poems. In 1849, a comprehensive collection of his poems appeared, followed a year later by *Songs of Labor and Other Poems*. The first English edition of his collected poems also appeared in 1850. These volumes included all that he thought worth preserving of the work of twenty years. In 1857, the "blue and gold" collected edition of the poems was published in Boston. From this time onward small volumes of new poems appeared at intervals of about two years down to the year of the author's death, *At Sundown*, the last of the series, bearing the date of that very year (1892). Of special significance are the idyl entitled *Snow-Bound* (1866) and the cycle called *The Tent on the Beach* (1867). These two volumes marked a broadening of Whittier's fame, a higher recognition of his standing as an artist, and a noticeable measure of release from the financial difficulties under which he long had struggled. For the rest, the ballads, lyrics, and occasional pieces which made him most famous are scattered somewhat indiscriminately through the score or more of his volumes. For upwards of half a century verse flowed profusely from his pen, and his career did not fall into the distinctive periods that it is the task and the delight of the critic to define and to characterize in the work of many other poets.

From 1840 onward Whittier made Amesbury his home, although he allowed himself many protracted visits to friends and relatives, to Danvers and Newburyport, to the waters and mountains of New Hampshire, to Maine and the Isles of Shoals. From 1847 to 1860 he was associated, at long distance, with *The National Era*, a weekly paper published at Washington, and best remembered as the periodical in which *Uncle Tom's Cabin* was first given to the world. This paper was the chief medium for his expression until the establishment of *The Atlantic Monthly* in 1857, in whose pages a large part of his later work appeared. His seventieth birthday, in 1877, was made the occasion of a celebration more elaborate than had before been the reward of any American poet. He attended the Boston dinner then given in his honour, feeling

> Like him who in the old Arabian joke
> A beggar slept and crownéd Caliph woke.

His eightieth birthday was also celebrated, bringing to him a striking memorial signed by all the members of the Supreme Court bench, nearly all the members of both houses of Congress, and many private citizens of the highest distinction, making it clear that the nation held him in love and veneration as one of its greatest spiritual assets. He was visiting at the house of a friend, a few miles from Amesbury just over the New Hampshire border, when a cerebral hemorrhage brought him to a peaceful death, 7 September, 1892. "Love to all the world," were the words that played upon his lips just before the end.

In the classification of Whittier's work, the narrative poems are the first to call for consideration. "Of all our poets he is the most natural balladist," says E. C. Stedman, and throughout his entire life he was always ready to turn from the strenuous exactions of the causes which claimed his most ardent sympathies to the delightful relaxation of story-telling. From childhood he was steeped in the legendry of New England, its tales of Indian raids, of Quaker persecutions, of picturesque pioneers, and of romantic adventure; while the wide reading which made Whittier in later life a cultivated man fed his narrative faculty with old-world themes, ranging all the way from the Norse to the Oriental. The grim tragic economy of the folk-ballad, as it sprang from the heart of the people in England, Denmark, or Germany, never imparted its secret to him, although in *The Sisters* he came near to plucking the heart out of that mystery; but the ballad was to him the occasion for a rambling narration, diffuse in its unfolding and unrestrained in its form, often with decorative illustrations drawn from quite unexpected sources, and usually shaped to the point of a rather obtrusive moral. Such pieces as *Maud Muller* and *Barclay of Ury* would doubtless have been better poems without the moralizing tags which conclude them, but probably they would also have been less popular. Whittier's public expected a certain element of sermonizing in his verse and the America of his time paid scant heed to the cry that "art for art's sake" should be the guiding principle of poetic practice. The best of Whittier's ballads, nevertheless, are comparatively unburdened with didacticism. Among these may be mentioned *Pentucket,* with its memories of old-time Indian raids along the Merrimac; *Cassandra Southwick,* a tale of the Quaker persecutions; *The Angels of Buena Vista,* an echo from the battle-fields of the Mexican War; *The Garrison of Cape Ann,* which tells how the New Englander of old vanquished the powers of darkness; *Skipper Ireson's Ride,* a spirited song of the vengeance wrought by the women of Marblehead upon a sea-captain thought to have abandoned the crew of a sinking ship; *Mabel Martin,* an idyl of the days of witchcraft, and *Amy Wentworth,* a dainty romance of the old colonial time. Upon these ballads, and many others, New England childhood has been nurtured for a century, gaining from them its special sense of a heritage of no mean spiritual content, rich also in picturesque associations and romantic memories.

The high-water mark of Whittier's artistic achievement was undoubtedly reached in the years that gave birth to *Snow-*

Bound and *The Tent on the Beach.* The latter and less important of these two works is a cycle of narratives in verse, linked together in the fashion of Longfellow's *Tales of a Wayside Inn.* The company are three in number, "Fields the lettered magnate and Taylor the free cosmopolite" being foregathered on Salisbury Beach with Whittier, who thus describes himself:

> And one there was, a dreamer born,
> Who, with a mission to fulfil,
> Had left the Muses' haunts to turn
> The crank of an opinion-mill,
> Making his rustic reed of song
> A weapon in the war with wrong.

The poems which make up the cycle fall into the general class of Whittier's narrative verse; the thousand lines of octosyllabic rhyme which are entitled *Snow-Bound* are almost in a class by themselves. This idyllic description of the Whittier household shut in for a week by

> The chill embargo of the snow,

which bids us

> pause to view
> These Flemish pictures of old days,

is not only a poem but a social document of the highest value. In the words of T. W. Higginson,

Here we have absolutely photographed the Puritan Colonial interior, as it existed till within the memory of old men still living. No other book, no other picture preserves it to us; all other books, all other pictures combined, leave us still ignorant of the atmosphere which this one page re-creates for us; it is more imperishable than any interior painted by Gerard Douw.

It has been said of Whittier that he could never be concise—and a diffuse style is undoubtedly one of the greatest artistic defects of the body of his verse—but the criticism falls flat in the presence of the lines which describe the fireplace on that winter evening.

This poem has often been compared with *The Cotter's Saturday Night* and it means to the American all and more than Burns's famous poem means to the Scotsman. There is also much aptitude in a comparison with Crabbe, but it has qualities of wistful sentiment and tender reminiscence that are not to be found in the poet of *The Village* and *The Borough*. Akin to *Snow-Bound*, and to be mentioned as offering a foretaste of its subtle charm, is the short poem *The Barefoot Boy*, dated some ten years earlier, and cast in the same mould of retrospective yearning for the happy and wholesome days of childhood.

The most considerable section of Whittier's verse in point of volume is that in which the poet voices the burning indignation fanned in his breast by the curse of negro slavery in America. His fellow-poets—Holmes, Longfellow, Lowell, and Emerson—were all enlisted in the warfare against this monstrous evil, and did yeoman service in the cause of freedom, but Whittier alone gave himself heart and soul to the crusade, from early manhood until the cause was won, from the time of his first association with Garrison to the time when his jubilant *Laus Deo* acclaimed the writing into the fundamental law of the republic of the ban upon slavery throughout the extent of its domain. Every step in the history of the conflict, which is the history of the United States for the period of a full generation, was seized upon by Whittier as a pretext for poetical expression—the terrorizing of the pioneer abolitionists, the war which the annexation of Texas made inevitable, the efforts of Clay and Webster'to heal the wounds of dissension by compromise, the outrage of the Fugitive Slave Law, the struggle for freedom in the Territory of Kansas, the growth of the modern Republican party, and the holocaust of the Civil War. The majority of the poems occasioned by these themes are too entirely of and for the moment to have any lasting value, but their immediate effect was potent in strengthening the mighty moral resolve of the nation, and they made Whittier perhaps the best beloved of contemporary American poets. When this mass of work is sifted by criticism, only a few pieces seem to preserve much of the fire which made them so effective at the time of their publication. We may still be stirred by the stanzas of *Le Marais du Cygne* and the marching-song of *The Kansas Emigrants:*

> We cross the prairies as of old
>   The pilgrims crossed the sea,
> To make the West, as they the East,
>   The homestead of the free!

The ballad of *Barbara Frietchie* still has power to thrill its readers, and the terrible *Ichabod*, occasioned by Webster's willingness to make terms with the abhorred evil of slavery, has lost little or none of its original force. "It is a fearful thing," says Swinburne, paraphrasing the Scriptures in praise of Victor Hugo, "for a malefactor to fall into the hands of an ever-living poet." And nowhere in the *Châtiments* of the French poet is there to be found a greater finality of condemnation than that with which Whittier stamped the subject of this truly great poem.

It will have been observed that many of the pieces already mentioned belong to the class of occasional or personal compositions. This class constitutes a large fraction of the total of Whittier's work. The long list of his friendly tributes and poems written for occasions includes many that are merely trivial or without any special appeal to readers for whom the incidents or personalities commemorated have no longer any meaning. Whittier had neither the wit nor the erudition that have preserved many of the occasional pieces of Holmes and Lowell from decay. The tributes to Garrison, Sumner, and a few others still stand out as significant from this mass of metrical exercises, and when a great occasion inspired Whittier to song, the result was likely to be memorable, as in the verses which celebrate the Emancipation Proclamation, the Thirteenth Amendment to the Federal Constitution, the Chicago Fire of 1871, and the Centennial Exhibition of 1876.

The deep and sincere religious feeling of the *Centennial Hymn* is characteristic of the entire body of Whittier's verse, and not merely of the poems specifically religious in their subject-matter. His consciousness was shot through with a sense of the divine, and the essential spirituality of his thought suffuses his expression like the sunlight in cloud-banked western skies. But his religious faith was far from being of the dogmatic type. "I regard Christianity as a life rather than as a creed," he once said, and the whole of his writing exemplifies the statement. He found in the doctrines of the Society of Friends exactly the framework which his nature needed, saying that "after a candid and kindly survey" of all the other creeds, "I turn to my own Society, thankful to the Divine Providence which placed me where I am; and with an unshaken faith in the one distinctive doctrine of Quakerism —the Light Within—the immanence of the Divine Spirit in Christianity." In this doctrine, he says elsewhere, "will yet be found the stronghold of Christendom, the sure, safe place from superstition on the one hand and scientific doubt on the other." The perfect expression of this simple and serene faith is found in *The Eternal Goodness*, and still again in the very last of all his poems. The sunset song of Tennyson's soul, just before "crossing the bar" that divides the harbour of Time from the ocean of Eternity, illustrates no better than do these final lines of Whittier the matchless beauty that may crown the simplest modes of expression, if only they are based upon perfect faith and perfect sincerity.

While Whittier was primarily a poet, his activities as a reformer and philanthropist, and his editorial work in connection with the many papers that claimed his services, made him an important writer of prose. The amount of his prose writing is very great, and, although the larger part of it is too ephemeral to have any place in the history of American literature, the part which has been thought worthy of inclusion in the standard edition of his collected works fills three of the seven volumes. Much of this writing is controversial in character, like the early tract on *Justice and Expediency*, but the greater part of it belongs to the permanent literature of New England history and thought. The most important titles are *The Stranger in Lowell*, *The Supernaturalism of New England*, *Leaves from Margaret Smith's Journal in the Province of Massachusetts Bay*, and *Literary Recreations and Miscellanies*. The story of Margaret Smith is almost a work of fiction. It recounts the imagined observations of a young woman who comes from England on a visit to the Bay Colony in its early

days. She meets the chief worthies of the time, describes the
landscape and the crude pioneer life, and writes of witch-
hunting, Quaker-baiting, and Indian warfare. G. R. Carpenter says of this work that "no single modern volume could be
found which has so penetrated the secret of colonial times in
Massachusetts, for it is almost line by line a transcript
and imaginative interpretation of old letters, journals, and
memoirs." Its Quaker authorship, moreover, gives it just the
detachment needed to save it from the danger of accepting
too unreservedly the view of New England colonial life that
the leaders of the Puritan theocracy so zealously sought to
perpetuate.

In the history of English literature in the larger sense,
Whittier is probably no more than a poet of the third rank.
His native endowment was rich, but it was supplemented by
neither the technical training nor the discipline required for
the development of the artist. He was extremely careless about
his rhymes—"good Yankee rhymes, but out of New England
they would be cashiered," he once said of them. The construction of his stanzas was diffuse and often slovenly. The
organ voice and the lyric cry were not, except at rare moments,
his to command. But no American who lived in the shadow
of slavery and internecine strife, none who grew to manhood
in the generation succeeding those epic days, would dream of
measuring his love and veneration for Whittier by the scale
of absolute art. Whittier's verse is so inwrought with the
nation's passion during that period of heightened consciousness that preserved the Union and redeemed it from the curse
of slavery that it cannot be coldly and critically considered
by any one who has had a vital sense of the agonies and exalta-
tions of that critical time. To such, the invocation of Stedman's *Ad Vatem* will always be a truer expression of their
feeling than any critical judgment, for they can never forget
their debt to him for

> righteous anger, burning scorn
> Of the oppressor, love to humankind,
> Sweet fealty to country and to home,
> Peace, stainless purity, high thoughts of heaven,
> And the clear, natural music of [his] song.

Fifty years ago, the verdict of thoughtful Americans acclaimed Whittier as the foremost American poet, with the possible exception of Longfellow, and while now there would be more dissentients from that judgment than there were then, his fame still rests upon a very solid basis of acceptance and esteem. And especially to those who have sprung from the soil of New England, he will always be the incomparable poet of their childhood home, of its landscape, its legendry, and the spiritual essence of its history.

3. Holmes

ONE of the best known passages in *Elsie Venner* is that in which Holmes asserted the existence of an aristocracy in New England, or at least a caste, which "by the repetition of the same influences, generation after generation," has "acquired a distinct organization and physiognomy." This caste is composed of those whose ancestors have had the advantage of college training and have practised one or another of the three learned professions. The young man born in this selected group is commonly slender, with a smooth face and with features regular and of a certain delicacy. "His eye is bright and quick,—his lips play over the thought much as a pianist's fingers dance over their music,—and his whole air, though it may be timid, and even awkward, has nothing clownish." Teachers discover that he "will take to his books as a pointer or setter to his field work." He may be intended for the bar while his father was a minister and his grandfather a physician; and by the very fact of this heredity he "belongs to the Brahmin caste of New England."

The man who thus described this caste was himself a Brahmin of the strictest sect, endowed with its best qualities, and devoid of its less estimable characteristics,—the tendency to anæmia and to the semi-hysterical outlook of the dyspeptic reformer. He was energetic, wholesome to the core, sound and sane, unfailingly alert, fundamentally open-minded, never tempted to crankiness or freakishness. He was born in an illustrious year, 1809, which saw the birth of Darwin and Lincoln, of Tennyson and Gladstone, of Chopin, Mendelssohn, and Edgar Allan Poe. It was toward the end of August that the Rev. Abiel Holmes, author of the *Annals of America,* made a brief entry at the foot of a page in his almanac, "—29. son b." The son was named Oliver Wendell Holmes, the Wendell being the maiden name of his mother, descended from an Evert Jansen Wendell who had been one of the early settlers of Albany; and thus her son could claim a remote relationship with the Dutch poet Vondel:

And Vondel was a Wendell who spelt it with a V.

Through his father, the Calvinist minister, and his grandfather, a physician who had served in the Revolution with the Continental troops, Holmes was descended from Anne, daughter of Thomas Dudley, governor of Massachusetts Bay, and wife of Simon Bradstreet, twice governor of the province— herself the first poetess of her province and nation. The author of the *Autocrat* shared with R. H. Dana, author of *Two Years before the Mast,* the honour of descent from this literary ancestress. Holmes was born in Cambridge, in an old gambrel-roofed house that had served as General Ward's headquarters at the outbreak of the Revolution: "The plan for fortifying Bunker's Hill was laid, as commonly believed, in the southeast room, the floor of which was covered with dents, made, it is alleged, by the butts of the soldiers' muskets." Holmes's mother, it may be recorded here, to account in a measure for the veracity and the vigour of his *Grandmother's Story of Bunker-Hill Battle,* was only a little girl of six when she was hurried off from Boston, then taken by the British, who were preceded by rumours that "the redcoats were coming, killing and murdering everybody as they went along." Legends of the Revolution were thick around his youth.

It was in Cambridge that Holmes grew to boyhood, playing under the Washington Elm. He was sent to what was then known as a "dame's school." He had an early inclination to verse, and composed rhyming lines in imitation of Pope and Goldsmith before he knew how to write; and Pope and Goldsmith remained his masters in metrical composition to the end of his long life. His father had a library of between one and two thousand volumes, and in this the son browsed at will, reading in books rather than through them. "I like books," he told us later; "I was born and bred among them and have the easy feeling when I get into their presence, that a stable boy has among horses." When he was fifteen he was sent to Phillips Academy at Andover; and at sixteen he entered Harvard, graduating in 1829, eight years after Emerson and nine before Lowell. Among his classmates were James Freeman Clarke and S. F. Smith, the author of *America* (1832). He wrote freely for the college papers, both in prose and verse, preserving in his collected works only a very few of his earlier humorous lyrics, though these are of a quality which might have made him willing to preserve others.

Upon his graduation he hesitated as to his profession, spending a year at the Dana Law School without awakening any liking for the law, and confessing later that "the seduction of verse-writing" had made this period "less profitable than it should have been." Yet it was while he was supposed to be studying law, and when he was just twenty-one, that he wrote the first of his poems to achieve an immediate and lasting popularity. This was the fiery lyric on *Old Ironsides*, protesting against the breaking up of the frigate *Constitution*, victor in the naval duel with the *Guerrière*. The glowing stanzas were written in a white heat of indignation against the proposed degradation of a national glory; they were published in 1830 in the Boston *Advertiser;* they were copied in newspapers all over the country; they were reprinted on broadsides; and they accomplished their purpose of saving the ship, which did not go out of commission for more than half a century after Holmes had rhymed his fervent appeal for its preservation.

At last he turned from the law to medicine, the profession of his grandfather. He studied for a while at the private school of Dr. James Jackson; and then he crossed the Atlantic to profit by the superior instruction to be had in Paris. Half a century later he recorded:

I was in Europe about two years and a half, from April, 1833, to October, 1835. I sailed in the packet ship "Philadelphia" from New York to Portsmouth, where we arrived after a passage of twenty-four days. . . . I then crossed the channel to Havre, from which I went to Paris. In the spring and summer of 1834 I made my principal visit to England and Scotland. . . . I returned in the packet ship "Utica," sailing from Havre, and reaching New York after a passage of forty-two days.

On his return to America he settled in Boston as a practising physician, taking as his motto "the smallest fevers thankfully received." He was twenty-seven when he obtained the degree of doctor of medicine and when he issued his earliest volume of poems. Nothing that he had written before or that he was to write later was more characteristic than one of the lyrics in this book,—*The Last Leaf*. He won several prizes for dissertations upon medical themes, published together in 1838; and the next year he was appointed professor of anatomy and physiology in the medical school of Dartmouth College, a position which he held for only a brief period. In 1840 he married Amelia Lee Jackson. He had resumed his practice in Boston, and he continued to contribute freely to the literature of his profession. He was always justly proud of his share in diminishing the danger from puerperal fever and of his trenchant attack upon *Homeopathy and its Kindred Delusions* (1842). Then in 1847 he was called to Harvard as professor of anatomy and physiology; and this position he was to fill with distinction for thirty-five years.

The career of Holmes was placid and uneventful even beyond the average of literary careers. Nothing happened to him other than the commonplaces of life; he took part in nothing unusual; he practised medicine for a few years and he taught medical students for many years; he wrote prose and verse in abundance; and in the fulness of years he died. The only dates that call for record here are those of the publication of his successive books. Until he was almost at the summit of his half-century he was known to the general public only as a writer of verse. He used prose for his discussions of medical questions; and whenever he was moved to express his opinions on other themes he chose the medium of metre. Those were the fertile years of the Lyceum System, and Holmes went the rounds of the lecture-halls like many others of the New England authors who were his contemporaries; but even as a lecturer he preferred rhyming verse to the customary colloquial prose.

Then quite unexpectedly, when he was forty-eight, an age when most men shrink from any new departure disconcerting to their indurated habits, he revealed himself in an entirely new aspect. *The Atlantic Monthly* was started in 1857 with Lowell as its editor; and to its early numbers Holmes contributed *The Autocrat of the Breakfast-Table.* Lowell had insisted as a condition precedent to his acceptance of the editorship that Holmes should be a constant contributor, awakening him "from a kind of lethargy in which" he was "half-slumbering."

Much of the vogue of the new magazine was due to the novel flavour of Holmes's series of papers; and he was persuaded to follow up his first success with kindred volumes entitled *The Professor at the Breakfast-Table* (1860), *The Poet at the Breakfast-Table* (1872), and *Over the Teacups* (1890). For the same monthly he wrote many disconnected essays, some of which he sent forth in 1863 under the appropriate name *Soundings from the Atlantic.* In the several volumes of the Breakfast Table series there is a thin thread of story and the obligatory wedding winds them up at the end; and in his three attempts at fiction, *Elsie Venner* (1861), *The Guardian Angel* (1867), and *A Mortal Antipathy* (1885), the thread is only a little strengthened and there is no overt abandonment of the leisurely method of the essayist. From the telling of fictitious biographies to the writing of the lives of two of his friends was only a step; and he published a memoir of John Lothrop Motley in 1878 and a study of Emerson in 1884.

It was in 1883, when he was seventy-four, that he resigned his professorship; and it was in 1886, when he was seventy-seven, that he paid his second visit to Europe. He spent the summer mainly in England, and in London he was "the lion of the season." It was almost exactly half a century since his first voyage across the ocean; and on his return from this second voyage he wrote out a pleasantly personal narrative of *Our Hundred Days in Europe.* At intervals, for nearly sixty years, he had sent forth volumes of verse; the latest to appear (in 1888) was aptly entitled *Before the Curfew,*—as Longfellow had called his final volume *In the Harbor* and Whittier had felicitously styled his last book *At Sundown.* On 7 October, 1894, Holmes died at the ripe age of eighty-five, unusual even among the long-lived American poets of his generation, of whom he was the last to survive.

During his second visit to London, Holmes was the guest of honour at a dinner of the Rabelais Club, founded to cherish the memory of an earlier humorist who was also a practitioner of medicine; and in his letter accepting the invitation he took occasion to confess his regard for another physician-author, Ambroise Paré, whom he termed "good, wise, quaint, shrewd, chatty." And all five of these characteristics he possessed himself. He was a gentleman and a scholar—to revive the fine old phrase—who was also a physician learned in the lore of the healing art and keenly interested in its history. He was a gentleman and a scholar, who was also a man of the world, in the best sense of that abused term,— a man of the world holding a modest place as a man of science. And at bottom he was a Yankee, with a true Yankee inventiveness,—the hand-stereoscope he devised being the outward and visible sign of this native gift, which was exhibited incessantly in his writings, notably in *The Physiology of Verse* and in *The Human Wheel, its Spokes and Felloes*. In prose and in verse he disclosed an unfailing Yankee cleverness, whittling his rhymes and sharpening his phrases with an innate dexterity.

"The secret of a man who is universally interesting is that he is universally interested," William Dean Howells has told us; "and this was above all the secret of the charm Doctor Holmes had for every one." There is zest and gusto in all that he wrote, and the reader can share the writer's own enjoyment. Especially was the writer interested in himself, as the true essayist must be. His delight in talking about himself was complacent, contagious, and innocent. "I have always been good company for myself," Holmes once confessed; and this is one reason why he has been pleasantly companionable to countless readers who found in him a friendly quality which took them captive. His egotism was as patent as Montaigne's, even if it was not so frank in its expression nor so searching in its analysis. The more of himself he revealed, the more he won the hearts of his fellow men, who relished the gentleness and the firmness of the character so openly disclosed, its kindliness, its urbanity and amenity, its lack of all acerbity or acridity, its total free-

dom from the rennet of meanness which curdles the milk of
human kindness.

In a letter which Whittier wrote for a celebration of
Holmes's seventy-fifth birthday, the Quaker poet singled out
for praise the Boston bard's "genial nature, entire freedom from
jealousy and envy, quick tenderness, large charity, hatred of
sham, pretence and unreality, and his reverent sense of the
eternal and permanent." This is keen criticism. Holmes was
a wit, but there was no bitterness in his laughter, because it
lacked scorn; and there was in it no echo of the cruel sterility of
Voltaire's irony. We can say of Holmes what Moore said of
Sheridan, that his wit

> ne'er carried a heart-stain away on its blade.

We can say this with the weightier emphasis when we
recall the cheerful courtesy with which he met the vindictive
and virulent retorts evoked by his dissolvent analysis of the
abhorrent and horrible aspects of Calvinism, a disestablished
code inherited from a less civilized past. Holmes's influence
was civilizing and humanizing; and it was more important
than we are likely now to recognize. He had in a high degree
the social instinct which has given grace to French life and
which was perhaps accentuated in him during his two years'
stay in Paris in his malleable youth. He was the constant
exponent of good manners and of right feeling, at a period in
the evolution of American society when the need for this was
even more evident than it is now.

It was in a score of his poems and in the successive volumes
of the *Breakfast-Table* series that Holmes most completely
disclosed himself. His two biographies and his three novels
are far less important,—in fact, these other prose writings are
important chiefly because they are the work of the "Autocrat"; and it may be well to deal with them briefly before
considering his major work, in which he is expressing the
essence of his cheerful optimism. The less significant of his
two memoirs is that of Motley, a labour of love undertaken
in the months that followed hard upon the death of the historian. "To love a character," said Stevenson, "is the only
heroic way of understanding it." Possibly an author could

write a vigorous life of a man he hated, since hatred is the other side of love. But no author could paint a vital portrait of a personality which left him indifferent; to his biographer at least a man must be a hero; and no valet has yet written an acceptable account of his master's life. But love needs to be controlled by judgment; and Holmes, at the time he composed his memoir, felt too keenly the injustice from which Motley had suffered to be able to survey the career and to estimate the character of the eminent historian with the detachment necessary to the painting of a portrait for posterity. What he did was to put forward an apology for Motley, with undue insistence upon the temporary griefs of the man and with less adequate consideration of the histories by which his fame is supported.

The biography of Emerson is far better, even if it also is not wholly satisfactory. It is in no sense an apology, for there was nothing in Emerson to extenuate. It is less personal, more detached, more disinterested, more comprehensive. It is admirably planned, with the adroitly articulated skeleton which we have a right to expect from a professor of anatomy. It is rich in appreciation and abundant in phrases of unforgettable felicity, for Holmes was ever the neatest of craftsmen. But when all is said, we cannot repress the conviction that he was out of his natural element when he undertook to deal with a figure so elusive as Emerson's. Holmes's very qualities, his concreteness, his sense of reality, his social instinct, tended to unfit him for interpreting an intangible personality like Emerson. He was characteristically witty when he compared Emerson to those "living organisms so transparent that we can see their hearts beating and their blood flowing through their transparent tissues"; but he did not altogether succeed in making us feel the ultimate purpose for which Emerson's heart beat and his blood flowed. The interest of the biography— and it has its full share of the interest which animated all that Holmes wrote—is kept alive rather by the adroitness of its author than by the revelation of its subject.

Such also is the interest of his three novels; they appeal to those who relish the flavour of Holmes's personality rather than to those who expect a work of fiction to be first of all a story, and secondly a story peopled with accusable characters.

In one of the prefaces to *Elsie Venner* Holmes cited the remark of a dear old lady who spoke of the tale as "a medicated novel"; and he declared that he was "always pleased with her discriminating criticism." It is not unfair to say that all three novels were conceived by a physician and composed by an essayist. Holmes, so Leslie Stephen asserted, lacked the "essential quality of an inspired novelist," which is "to get absorbed in his story and to feel as though he were watching instead of contriving the development of a situation."

Of *Elsie Venner* Holmes himself said that the "only use of the story is to bring the dogma of inherited guilt and its consequences into a clearer point of view"; and he declared that his "heroine found her origin not in fable or romance, but in a physiological conception, fertilized by a theological dogma." In other words, *Elsie Venner* is a novel-with-a-purpose; it is a fiction devised by a nineteenth-century physician to attack eighteenth-century Calvinism. Perhaps a born story-teller could have so constructed his narrative as to fascinate the reader in spite of the argument it was intended to carry, but Holmes was not a born story-teller. He described characters and places, not for their bearing on the story itself, and not even for suggesting the appropriate atmosphere of the action, but mainly if not solely for their own sake, and quite in the manner of the character-writers who had blazed the trail for the early essayists. By the side of figures thoroughly known and delicately delineated, there are others, not a few, outlined in the primary colours and trembling on the very verge of caricature. In this we can discover the unfortunate influence of Dickens, as we can perceive the fortunate influence of Hawthorne in the treatment of the abnormal heroine. And equally obvious is the influence of Thackeray, who also began and ended his career as an essayist. Thackeray, even if he had a bias toward moralizing, confessed to the Brookfields that he found his ethical lectures very convenient when he had to pad out his copy to fill the allotted number of pages in the monthly parts in which his larger novels originally appeared. But Thackeray, after all, was a born story-teller, an inspired novelist, who got absorbed in his story and felt as though he were watching and not inventing his situations. Holmes lingered by the way and chatted with the reader, not from any external necessity, but because digression and even disquisition is to the essayist the breath of life.

In *The Guardian Angel*, the heroine is a composite photograph of half a dozen warring ancestors of whom now one and now another emerges into view to insist upon the reappearance of his or her identity in Myrtle Hazard. Yet, when all deductions are made, both *Elsie Venner* and *The Guardian Angel* have many a chapter that only Holmes could have written, rich in wisdom, in wit, in whimsy, and in knowledge of the world. But this can scarcely be said of *A Mortal Antipathy*, the latest of the medicated fictions and the feeblest, written when its author had long passed threescore years and ten. The physiological theme is too far-fetched, too unusual, too abnormal, to win acceptance even if it had been handled by a master of fiction; and we may doubt whether even Balzac could have dealt with it triumphantly. As Holmes dealt with it, it did not justify itself; the narrative was too fragmentary for fiction and too forced, while the intercalary papers lacked the freshness of view and the unpremeditated ease of Holmes's earlier manner as an essayist.

"The prologue of life is finished at twenty; then come five acts of a decade each, and the play is over, with now and then a pleasant or a tedious afterpiece, when half the lights are put out, and half the orchestra is gone." When Holmes wrote this, he could not foresee that he would be able to keep in their seats more than half of the spectators, if not the most of them, to the very end of his pleasant afterpiece. He was not forty when he first discoursed as the "Autocrat" and he was twice forty when he gossiped "Over the Teacups." In the octogenarian book he may be a little less spontaneous and a little more self-centred than in its predecessor of twoscore years earlier; and the shadowy figures who take part in its conversations may seem to talk a little because they are aware that they were created on purpose to converse, instead of talking freely for the fun of it as the solider persons who met around the breakfast table were wont to do. Yet the latest of the group, even if its wit be less pungent, has almost as many samples of shrewd sagacity as adorned the two books that came after the *Autocrat*. "Habits are the crutches of old age," Holmes tells us; and he never lost the habit of cheerfulness. There is no hypocritic praising of past times; on the contrary there is a blithe and buoyant recognition of the gains garnered in eighty years.

Over the Teacups may be a little inferior to *The Poet at the Breakfast-Table* but only as the *Poet* is a little inferior to the *Professor* and the *Professor* to the *Autocrat*, because the freshness had faded and because we were no longer taken by surprise. The *Autocrat* struck the centre of the target and the hit was acclaimed with delight; the later books went to the same mark, even if they were not winged by an aim as unerring. No doubt, a part of the immediate success of the *Autocrat* was due to its novelty,—novelty of form and novelty of content. Holmes was characteristically shrewd when he declared that "the first of my series came from my mind almost with an explosion, like the champagne cork; it startled me a little to see what I had written and to hear what people said about it. After that first explosion the flow was more sober, and I looked upon the product of my wine-press more coolly"; and he added, "continuations almost always sag a little." Perhaps the novelty of form was more apparent than real, since Steele and Addison had given us a group of characters talking at large as they clustered about Sir Roger de Coverley. But there is this salient difference, that in *The Spectator* the talk is mainly for the purpose of creating character, whereas in the *Autocrat* the characters have been created that they might listen.

Yet in so far as the *Autocrat* has a model, this is plainly enough the eighteenth-century essay, invented by Steele, improved by Addison, clumsily attempted by Johnson, and lightly varied by Goldsmith. Steele is the originator of the form, since the earlier essay of Montaigne and of Bacon makes no use of dialogue; it has only one interlocutor, the essayist himself, recording only his own feelings, his own opinions, and his own judgments. Steele was probably influenced by the English character-writers, perhaps also by the lighter satires of Horace, and quite possibly by the comedies of Molière,— notably by the *Précieuses Ridicules* and the *Femmes Savantes*. The outline Steele sketched the less original Addison filled with a richer colour. As Holmes had begun when a child by imitating the verse of Pope and Goldsmith, so as a man when he wrote prose he followed the pattern set by Steele and Addison. Although he was not born until the ninth year of the nineteenth century, he was really a survivor from the eighteenth century; and his prose like his verse has the eighteenth-century characteristics, despite the fact that he himself was ever alert to apprehend the new scientific spirit of the century in which he lived.

The real novelty of the *Autocrat* was in its content, that is to say, in Holmes himself, the master talker of the Breakfast-Table, in the skill with which the accent of conversation is caught. The other characters are responsible for an occasional remark not without individuality and point; but the Autocrat himself tends to be a monopolist and to intermit his discourse only that his adversary in the verbal combat may lay himself open to a series of sharp thrusts in retort. This is as it should be, since the others who gather about the breakfast table were but ordinary mortals, after all, whereas the Autocrat was an extraordinary mortal, an artist in conversation, gifted by nature and trained by long experience, a man who had thought widely if not deeply about life, who had read the records of the past and who could revive them to shed light on the present, a physician abreast of modern science and swift to bring its new discoveries to bear on the old problems of life. In reading the *Breakfast-Table* series in swift succession the reader cannot help remarking the frequency with which Holmes draws on his professional experience; he sees men and women through the clear spectacles of the family physician;—and perhaps one reason why he arrogates to himself the major part of the conversation is in revenge for the silence imposed on the practitioner by the tedious and interminable talk of his patients about themselves to which the family physician has perforce to submit. Holmes used medical analogies and dropped into the terminology of the anatomist and physiologist with the same frequency that Shakespeare employed the vocabulary of the theatre, even in incongruous situations finding material for figures of speech in his own experience on the stage.

Holmes is not only a man of science and a man of the world, he is also a humorist and a wit,—a wit who has no antipathy even to the humble but useful pun,—a humorist abounding in whimsy. And as a result of this fourfold equipment his talk is excellent merely as talk. It has the flavour of the spoken word; it is absolutely unacademic and totally devoid of pedantry. Therefore it is not only delightful but stimulating; it continually makes the reader think for himself and turn back upon himself. Despite its acuteness, its liveliness, its briskness, its vivacity, it never lacks seriousness, without ever becoming ponderous.

It may be that Holmes does not attain to the high seriousness, the deep seriousness, of enduring philosophy; and it cannot be denied that there are pages here and there which are not as valid today as when they were written. It would be doing the Autocrat an ill-service to compare him with his remote and mighty predecessors Montaigne and Bacon. And it may be admitted that there is more or less warrant for the remark of John Burroughs, to the effect that Holmes always reminded him "of certain of our bird songsters, such as the brown thrasher or the cat-bird, whose performances always seem to imply a spectator and to challenge his admiration." Holmes seems "to write with his eye upon his reader, and to calculate the advance upon his reader's surprise and pleasure." To admit this would be only to acknowledge the truth of the French saying that every man has the defects of his qualities. But it cannot be admitted if it implies that Holmes was unduly self-conscious or affected or pretentious. In fact, much of the charm of the Autocrat is due to the entire absence of affectation and to the apparent spontaneity of the talk which pours so easily from his lips and which discloses so abundantly the winning personality of Holmes himself. "Every book is, in an intimate sense, a circular letter to the friends of him who writes it," so Stevenson has told us; and Holmes was fortunate in that his circular letter made a friend of every one who received it.

The qualities which give charm to Holmes's prose are those which please us also in his verse. He has left a dozen or a score of lyrics secure in the anthologies of the future. But he wrote too easily and he wrote too much to maintain a high average in the three hundred double-columned pages in which his complete poems are collected. No poet or prose man can take down to posterity a baggage wagon of his works, and he is lucky if he can save enough to fill a saddle-bag. Holmes's reputation as a poet will rise when his verses are winnowed and garnered into a thin volume of a scant hundred pages wherein *Old Ironsides* and *The Last Leaf*, *The Chambered Nautilus* and *Homesick in Heaven*, *The Wonderful "One-Hoss Shay"* and *The Broomstick Train*, *Grandmother's Story of Bunker-Hill Battle*, and a handful more are unincumbered by the hundreds of occasional verses which were each of them good enough for its special occasion and yet not good enough to demand remembrance after the event.

There are a few of Holmes's loftier poems in which we feel that the inspiration is equal to the aspiration; but there are only a few of them, with *The Chambered Nautilus* at the head, accompanied by *Homesick in Heaven*,—not overpraised by Howells when he called it one of the "most profoundly pathetic of the language." And Stedman was right also when he suggested that Holmes's serious poetry had scarcely been the serious work of his life. Even at its best this serious poetry is the result of his intelligence rather than of his imagination. It lacks depth of feeling and largeness of vision. It has a French felicity of fancy, a French dexterity of craftsmanship, a French point and polish; and also a French inadequacy of emotion. "Assuredly we love poetry in France," said Anatole France when he was discussing the verse of Sainte-Beuve; "but we love it in our own fashion; we insist that it shall be eloquent, and we willingly excuse it from being poetic." *Old Ironsides*, fiery as its lines ring out, is eloquent rather than truly poetic.

Here again Holmes declares himself as a survival from the eighteenth century, when English literature conformed to French principles. His favourite reading as a child was Pope's *Homer*, the couplets of which "stimulated his imagination in spite of their formal symmetry." And even their formal symmetry was not displeasing to his natural taste:

> And so the hand that takes the lyre for you
> Plays the old tune on strings that once were new.
> Nor let the rhymester of the hour deride
> The straight-backed measure with its stately stride;
> It gave the mighty voice of Dryden scope;
> It sheathed the steel-bright epigrams of Pope;
> In Goldsmith's verse it learned a sweeter strain,
> Byron and Campbell wore its clanking chain;
> I smile to listen while the critic's scorn
> Flouts the proud purple kings have nobly worn.

The even merit of its occasional verse is one of the obvious qualities of the eighteenth century which we find also in Holmes. Late in life he admitted that he had become rather too well known in connection with "occasions." He was intensely loyal to Boston; and he felt that he had no right to refuse the summons to stand and deliver whenever the city received an honoured guest or when an honoured citizen died or went away or came back. As he explained in one of these occasional pieces,

> I'm a florist in verse, and what *would* people say
> If I came to a banquet without my bouquet?

Late in life Holmes admitted that "many a trifling performance has had more good honest work put into it than the minister's sermon of that week had cost him"; he confessed to strenuous effort over his copy of verses, insisting that "if a vessel glides off the ways smoothly and easily at her launching, it does not mean that no great pains have been taken to secure the result"; and he proudly reminded his readers that "Pindar's great odes were occasional poems . . . and yet they have come down among the most precious bequests of antiquity to modern times." The noblest example of English prose in the nineteenth century, Lincoln's Gettysburg address, was also evoked by an occasion. Even if Holmes's occasional verse has not the lofty elevation of Pindar's odes or the pathetic simplicity of Lincoln's little speech, it has almost always an exquisite propriety to the event itself, an unfailing happiness of epithet, a perfect adequacy to the moment of local importance. Its chief fault, if not its only defect, is that there is too much of it, even if its average is higher than might reasonably be expected.

In a letter to Lowell, Holmes declared, speaking of Bostonians in particular and yet perhaps also of Americans in general, that "we Boston people are so bright and wide-awake . . . that we have been in danger of thinking our local scale was the absolute one of excellence—forgetting that 212 Fahrenheit is but 100 centigrade." There is one department of poetry in which Holmes can withstand without any danger of shrinking the application of the centigrade scale; this is the department of *vers de société*, so called, although it is never merely society verse. Perhaps Cowper's term best describes it, "familiar verse," the lyric commingled of humour and pathos, brief and brilliant and buoyant, seemingly unaffected and unpremeditated, and yet—if we may judge by the infrequency of supreme success—undeniably difficult, despite its apparent ease. Dr. Johnson, who was himself quite incapable of it, too heavy-footed to achieve its lightness, too polysyllabic to attain its vernacular terseness, was yet shrewd enough to see that it is

less difficult to write a volume of lines, swelled with epithets, brightened with figures, and stiffened by transpositions, than to produce a few couplets, grand only by naked elegance and simple purity, which require so much care and skill that I doubt whether any of our authors have yet been able for twenty lines together nicely to observe the true definition of easy poetry.

In this "easy poetry," which is the metrical equivalent of the essay in its charm, in its grace and in its colloquial liberty, Holmes has few rivals in our language. It was with strict justice that Locker-Lampson, in the preface to the first edition of *Lyra Elegantiarum* (1867)—to this day the most satisfactory anthology of *vers de société*,—declared that Holmes was "perhaps the best living writer of this species of verse." It may be recorded also that Locker-Lampson paid Holmes the even sincerer compliment of imitation, borrowing for two of his delightful lyrics not only the spirit but also the stanza Holmes had invented for *The Last Leaf*. With characteristic frankness the London lyrist once told an American admirer that this stanza might seem easy but it was difficult, so difficult that no one had handled it with complete success—except Holmes and himself.

Locker-Lampson derived directly from Praed, whose verses have an electric and dazzling brilliance, whereas in Holmes the radiance is more subdued and less blinding. Of all the writers of familiar verse no one has ever surpassed Holmes in the delicate blending of pathos with humour, as exemplified most strikingly in *The Last Leaf*, in which fantasy plays hide and seek with sentiment. Scarcely less delightful in its eighteenth-century quaintness is the family portrait, *Dorothy Q;* and close to those two masterpieces are lesser lyrics like *Contentment, Bill and Joe*, and the lines *On Lending a Punch Bowl* and *To an Insect:*

I love to hear thine earnest voice,
    Wherever thou art hid,
Thou testy little dogmatist,
    Thou pretty Katydid!
Thou mindest me of gentlefolks,—
    Old gentlefolks are they,—
Thou say'st an undisputed thing
    In such a solemn way.

These are only a few of the best of his lighter lyrics, now sprightly and sparkling, and now softer and more appealing, often evoking the swift smile, although never demanding the loud laugh, and sometimes starting the tear on its way to the eyelid; and in them Holmes proved that Stedman was only just when he declared that familiar verse may be "picturesque, even dramatic," and that it may "rise to a high degree of humor and of sage and tender thought."

4. Lowell

NEITHER Lowell's poetry nor prose has that obvious unity of effect which characterizes the work of so many nineteenth century writers. His work does not recall, even in the minds of its admirers, a group of impressions so distinct and fixed as those summoned by the poetry of Whittier, Poe, or Whitman, or by that of Swinburne, Morris, or Browning, or by the prose of Thoreau or Emerson, of Ruskin or Arnold. His work, indeed, does not have the marks of a dominant or of a peculiar personality; nor does it add to literature a new group of ideas or a new departure in workmanship. Though its volume is large, and though a number both of his poems and his essays have won a wide familiarity, there is difficulty in summarizing their qualities of form or matter in a way that will indicate with justice his importance in American literature.

This somewhat miscellaneous appeal made by his writing may be ascribed in part, no doubt, to a lack of literary power that prevented him from winning the triumphs that belong to the great conquests of the imagination, but it is also due in large measure to the variety of responses which his rich personality made to the changing movements of American life. Other writers were surer of their message or of their art, but perhaps the career of no other affords a more varied and interesting commentary on the course of American letters, or responds as constantly to the occasions and needs of the nation's experience. It is impossible to consider him apart from his time and environment, or to judge his writing apart from its value for the United States. It has left something for posterity, but its best energy was expended in the manifold tasks which letters must perform as a builder of national civilization.   It is this service which makes him an eminent and in some ways our most representative man of letters.

The briefest summary of the events of his life will indicate the variety of his interests and occupations.   Born in 1819 in Cambridge, Massachusetts, in the colonial house where he was to spend most of his life, he went to Harvard College, studied law—and abandoned it for a career of letters.   He contributed verses and sketches to the magazines, edited a few numbers of an unsuccessful literary journal, *The Pioneer*, brought out his first volume of poems, *A Year's Life*, in 1841, a second volume in 1843, and a collection of essays, *Conversations on Some of the Old Poets*, in 1844.

In December of this year he was married to the poetess Maria White.   The nine years of their married life until her death in 1853 mark a distinct period in Lowell's literary work. He contributed constantly both prose and verse to various journals, at first largely for those of the anti-slavery propaganda; and the Mexican War gave the opportunity for *The Biglow Papers*, the first of which appeared in *The Boston Courier* of 17 June, 1846.   In 1848 appeared a second collection of poems, the completed *Biglow Papers*, and *The Fable for Critics*.   Lowell had won, in both popular and critical regard, an assured place in what was already an important national literature.   The fifteen months which the family spent in Europe in 1851–52 seem to have increased his desire to widen the range of his poetry, but the ambitions that thronged with the return to America were interrupted by the death of his wife. A period of uncertainty followed his bereavement, and circumstances gave him a new occupation.

In 1855 he delivered in Boston a course of twelve lectures (unpublished) on English poetry, and as a result of their success was appointed to succeed Longfellow as Smith Professor of the French and Spanish Languages and Literatures and Professor of Belles Lettres in Harvard College.   A few months were spent in Dresden in preparation for a course on German literature, and in the fall of 1856 he began twenty years work as a teacher.   In the following year he was married to Frances Dunlap and resumed life in Elmwood.   His professorship turned his mind to criticism and scholarship, but did not hasten that stronger poetic flight for which he had felt himself preparing. A brief-lived literary magazine, *Putnam's Monthly*, in 1853–54 had given place to one or two of his best known essays, and a new literary enterprise, *The Atlantic Monthly*, in 1857 gave further opportunity for his prose. Lowell was editor of the new magazine for two years and a regular contributor of reviews and articles until 1863, when he joined with Charles Eliot Norton in editing *The North American Review*. For the next dozen years his essays both political and literary appeared mainly in this review.

During the Civil War, Lowell's chief contributions to poetry were the new series of *Biglow Papers* which began in the *Atlantic* in 1861. It was not until the war was over that the great themes of national triumph through sacrifice called forth the four memorial odes. Miscellaneous verse of the preceding twenty years was collected in *Under the Willows* (1868); but the odes and longer poems, as *The Cathedral* (1870), *Agassiz* (1874), best represent both the emotional impulses that followed the war and the maturity of Lowell's art.

The political interests which had engaged much of his prose writing before and during the war had not interrupted his increasing devotion to the study and criticism of literature. He had been directing his attention less to contemporary letters and more to the masters of English and to a few of the masters of foreign literature, notably Dante. The result of these studies was a long succession of essays which make up the volumes *Among My Books* (1870), *My Study Windows* (1871), and *Among My Books, Second Series* (1876). It is these books which are his main contributions to literary criticism.

Lowell and his wife spent two years (1872–74) in Europe, and after a brief resumption of his professorship he was appointed minister to Spain in 1877, and in 1880 was transferred to England. After his retirement in 1885 he spent a considerable part of his time in England until his death in 1891. The mission was a recognition of his distinction not merely as a man of letters but as a representative of the best American culture, and this distinction Lowell maintained in a number of addresses on both literary and political themes, represented by the volume *Democracy and Other Addresses* (1886). Although his poetry became infrequent there was enough for a final volume, *Heartsease and Rue*, in 1880.

To all these varied activities as poet, essayist, humorist, editor, teacher, scholar, and diplomat, must be added that of letter writer.   For Lowell's letters, in addition to their annals of his personal experiences and friendships, contribute something to literature and history which perhaps has ceased with the day of the typewriter—a record of the intimate association of the high-minded.   His work as a man of letters may be considered most readily by the main divisions of verse and prose; but the separation is not always significant.   The poetry is mostly bounded by the years 1840 and 1870, and the best of the essays by 1860 and 1890; but there is hardly a year of his half century which did not see both prose and verse.   Nor can the subject matter be divided by the two forms, for both require attention from the historian of either the literary or the political progress of the half-century.   Both respond to the changing events of his own life, and to the greater changes that transformed the nation of 1840 into that of 1890.

Lowell's youth was spent among books.   Before he left college he had become a wide if desultory reader, and the study of law failed to detach him from what was to become a life-long devotion to the easy chair and the library.   To the inheritance of English blood, law, language, and religion that bound New England to the mother country, he added an enthusiastic appreciation for English literature.   Naturally this appreciation was directed by the Romanticism which had reached its full flower in English letters, by its leaders, Wordsworth, Keats, Lamb, or by the gods of its idolatry, Shakespeare, Spenser, and Dante.   His feeling was like that which Keats had experienced twenty years before, when English poetry had opened out a new world inviting to fresh beauty and new enterprise. And this world of British letters had added since then the clarion voice of Carlyle and the exquisite art of Keats himself and of Tennyson.   It is easy to trace in Lowell's early verse imitation and reminiscence of the English poets of the preceding half-century; but even more important was his acceptance of their faith in poetry.   With Wordsworth he believed that it was to be the moral guide and spiritual inspirer, with Keats he saw it opening new doors to the abode of beauty.   He shared the assurance of *Sartor Resartus* that literature was to supply the new priesthood that was to direct the new age.

There were also new ideas and impulses astir in the New England of Lowell's youth. The narrow Puritanism had given way to Unitarianism and Transcendentalism and literature. During the first twenty years of Lowell's life, American literature had taken a bulk and character which might risk comparison with the literature of any European nation during that period. In his teens he was reading Emerson, Longfellow, Holmes, Whittier, Hawthorne, and Prescott, and most of these men were his neighbours and ready to welcome and direct his first attempts at letters. There is a sense of an intellectual and imaginative dawn to be found in Lowell's essays and verse, a dawn that is to gladden the granite and pines of his native land. With a loving admiration for the old literature, there is a loyal national pride in the new; or, rather, there is a sectional pride; for the patriotism is mainly a sectional patriotism, a fervour for the New England hills and men. Boston was then a long way from New York and Philadelphia—although Lowell's literary adventures carried him to both cities—and the rest of the nation was separated by barriers of manners and habit. He was patriotically American because his beloved and awakened New England was expected to lead the nation into new spiritual adventures.

Lowell's early poems do not show much novelty of theme or manner. They are on about the same subjects that all men were writing verse upon in the forties, and written with the same vocabulary, images, and rhythms. Love, nature, liberty, idealism, classic story, personal moods are the themes, but there is some novelty in the ingenuity of the phrases and in the new fauna and flora. If he was following the English romanticists he was transferring their worship of beauty to a New England landscape and their religious musings to the turmoil of idealism that stirred the youth of Massachusetts. He writes of the dandelion and the pine-tree, and his seasons are the riotous June or the Indian summer of Cambridge, his landscape that of Beaver Brook. All is descriptive or reflective; there is no narrative except when it is the mere text for sentiment and moral.

Some union of art and morality, of Keats and Carlyle, Poe and Emerson—that was the poet's endeavour. He wrote to Briggs in 1846:

Then I feel how great is the office of Poet, could I but even dare to hope to fill it.   Then it seems as if my heart would break in pouring out one glorious song that should be the gospel of Reform, full of consolation and strength to the oppressed, yet falling gently and restoringly as dew on the withered youth-flowers of the oppressor.   That way my madness lies.[1]

It is easy to smile at this youthful fervency, as Lowell himself smiled a year or two later in *The Fable for Critics*.

There is Lowell, who's striving Parnassus to climb
With a whole bale of isms tied together with rhyme.
The top of the hill he will ne'er come nigh reaching
Till he learns the distinction 'twixt singing and preaching.

But, with most nineteenth-century poets, Lowell was a preacher as well as a singer.   Poverty, tyranny, doubt, industrialism, are the themes that for England distracted the attention of the Muse; in the United States, the mid-century vision of beauty was clouded by the presence of slavery.   And if Lowell was conscious that the isms, even that of the anti-slavery cause, burdened his climb up Parnassus, there was never any doubt of the imperative nature of the summons of moral reform.

The American reader should indeed have a special sympathy for this avowal of high purpose; for is not this gospel of reform the better genius of our nation?   The material advance which has conquered a continent has made us self-confident, disregardful of the past, and careless of reflection, but it has inspired us with a faith in our power to rebuild and move on. The evils which beset us do not daunt us, and the virtues we possess we would fain impose upon others.   We believe in propaganda, we are uneasy without some cause to further, some improvement to promote.   If we ever determine what the American idea is, we shall evangelize the world.

It was perhaps this spirit of reform which Lowell had sought to express in his *Prometheus* and which he had in mind when in another letter to Briggs he declares "I am the first who has endeavoured to express the American Idea, and I shall be popular by and by."[2]   Popularity came first, however, when

---

[1] Scudder, *Life*, Vol. 1, p. 267.   [2] *Ibid.*

fervour was linked with wit and humour in *The Biglow Papers* with their racy Yankee dialect and their burning zeal against the aggressiveness of the slave-holding South.

The art of these verses has no resemblance to the art of Keats, and their gospel of reform is not a glorious song of consolation; but their rapid fire of wit and common sense was perhaps a better expression of Lowell's temperament than any of his more studied measures. Certainly no poems have ever more distinctly revealed the New England temper. When collected they were imbedded in a paraphernalia of apparatus in which the wit is often laboured, and some of them are no more than clever journalism; but the best have become a lasting part of our popular literature. If this is due in part to their vernacular homeliness, and in part to their wit, it is also due to the moral fire of their democracy. As Horace Scudder insisted, there is a connection between them and another popular success of a different kind, *The Vision of Sir Launfal*. There "it is the holy zeal which attacks slavery issuing in this fable of a beautiful charity."[1]

In 1850 Lowell wrote to Briggs:

I begin to feel that I must enter a new year of apprenticeship. My poems have thus far had a regular and natural sequence. First, Love and the mere happiness of existence beginning to be conscious of itself, then Freedom—both being the sides which Beauty presented to me—and now I am going to try more after Beauty herself. Next, if I live, I shall present Life as I have seen it.

But, as often, Life proved a jealous mistress who would not yield the field to Beauty. Change and bereavement followed, and his professorship and editorship gave little incentive for verse. The moral exaltation which had seemed the promise of America found itself involved with all the turmoil of emotions that accompany terrific war. For these, Hosea's dialect was scarcely an adequate vehicle of expression, and the second series of *Biglow Papers*, if not inferior in skill, somehow lacks the entire sufficiency of the first; even when, as in the tenth paper, both the pathos and valour of the great conflict sound through the verse. The passions that the war aroused were

[1] Scudder, *Life*, Vol. I, p. 268.

too overpowering for poetry except the brief expression of
dominant feeling, as in the fine stanza written in October,
1861.

> God, give us peace! not such as lulls to sleep,
> But sword on thigh, and brow with purpose knit!
> And let our Ship of State to harbor sweep,
> Her ports all up, her battle-lanterns lit,
> And her leashed thunders gathering for their leap!

In the poems written in the decade after the war there is
a greater depth of thought and a maturity of feeling. The
cause which he served broadened into the issue of the life of a
national democracy; and he was called upon to sing its victories
and the sacrifice by which they were won. The odes are so
noble in sentiment and so splendid in parts that one cannot
forbear to regret that they do not bring an even more perfect
beauty to their great theme. The far-fetched figure, the halting
measure, the forced rhythm occasionally intrude on verse
where the feeling demands all the majesty of poetic mastery.
And yet, national anniversaries have rarely if ever aroused
such pæans as these in which New England mourns her slain
but passes on her heritage to the larger nation. Eloquence
rises again and again to passionate melody, yet the feeling
never loses the restraining guide of thought. Lowell never
attains greater mastery than in the thoughtful analysis and
noble beauty of the stanzas on Lincoln in the *Commemoration
Ode.*

The war and its aftermath left Lowell's poetic faculty somewhat spent. Now and then a theme would arouse his imagination to its earlier spontaneity. Chartres revisited summoned
back the recollections of its first impressions and stirred him to
search again the mysteries and confusions of faith. The death
of Agassiz recalled the Cambridge of old and its brave spirits.
But the visits of the Muse grew rarer, and Lowell came to find
his most characteristic expression in the prose essay. As the
close of the war relieved him from the pressing necessity of
political writing, he naturally returned to literature.

Mrs. Browning, in one of her letters to her husband,
complains of the *Conversations on Some of the Old Poets*, which
she has just been reading, that Lowell is saying over again the

same things that every one knows. There is, no doubt, a
certain truth in the charge, even when applied to his maturer
essays. Lowell introduces no new principle or methods into
literary criticism and he makes no search after novelties. In
these respects and in the part that his essays have played in
changing the direction of literary criticism, they may be
regarded as less important than those which Matthew Arnold
was writing during the same decade. But this is mainly due
to the fact that Arnold's literary criticism was a part of a
definite propaganda. When he gave up poetry and turned to
prose, it was with the pronounced intention of getting at the
British public, of entering on controversy, of preaching a new
gospel, that of Culture, which was to have its main ally in
criticism. Lowell's increasing use of prose was made from no
such incentive. The great cause to which he had been devoted
had been won. It was in part as a relief from controversy
and propaganda that he turned from political subjects to the
leisurely appreciation of his favourite authors. The essays
have no reforms to propose. They are the summing up of
many hours spent in his library and his class-room.

The influence of the college makes itself felt in various
ways. Agassiz in science and Child in letters were among
Lowell's colleagues, and his years as a professor had given him
both an opportunity for wide reading and an acquaintance
with the sterner exactions of scholarship. In some cases, as in
the careful review of Richard Grant White's edition of Shakespeare, the criticism is precise and textual. In all cases the
reflections about the great masters formed through years of
intimacy have undergone the seasoning discipline of a broad
and adequate scholarship. Lowell did not write on a subject
unless he knew a good deal about it, nor did he fail to avail
himself of the best that scholarship had accumulated; and such
habits have not been matters of course among literary critics.
Not only Lowell's thoroughness and accuracy, but his very
freedom from the bias of propaganda and from the desire for
novelty give his criticism an enduring sanity, a sanity which is
happily united with a rich and discriminating sympathy.

Lowell's essays indeed may be warmly defended from any
charge of ineffectuality. If he did not proclaim a definite
evangel, yet scarcely less potently than Arnold he preached

the gospel of culture. To a nation torn by war and largely engaged in the indispensable work of economic reconstruction, he taught by both precept and example the value of criticism. In the renewed task of making a nation, he turned confidently to literature as the record of human activity that contains most that is vital for the spirit. The cause of culture, indeed, called for a different service in the two countries. For Arnold in England, literature was to be given a renewed allegiance in the face of industrialism and science, and literature itself was to be directed away from the dangers of romanticism into a wiser and better poised criticism of conduct. For Lowell in the United States, the nation was to be reminded of the value for it of the great traditions of the old world and the need of linking both conduct and letters to the best that the past could offer.

One example may further suggest the different tasks of literary criticism in the two countries. It was unnecessary for Arnold to preach the value of medieval art. The Middle Ages were still very much present in England, and they had been summoned for various purposes by Scott, Carlyle, Tennyson, Ruskin, and Morris. In the United States, the Middle Ages are as remote as Persia or Egypt, and their significance for us discernible mainly through literature. Lowell took occasion later to defend his land against the implication in Ruskin's remark that he could not live in a country that had neither castles nor cathedrals. But for "our past well-nigh desolate of æsthetic stimulus" his essays were supplying the past of Milton and Spenser, of Chaucer and Dante. The essays on the two medieval poets are among his best and have done their part in stimulating among thoughtful Americans a study and appreciation of the great centuries of human progress that preceded Columbus's discovery.

The personal essay as a literary form seems to require maturity of mind, breadth of experience and reading, a responsive humour, and intensity and discrimination in taste. These qualities Lowell brought to his essay writing, whether the subject be drawn from nature or society or the world of books. Nowhere else, unless in his letters, is his personality more fully and charmingly revealed. The essays are full of good things. Allusion and quotation, epigram and description, whimsical epithet and graphic phrase crowd one another along the page, but all move in the train of Wit and Wisdom, our constant companions along the way.

The glimpses of New England village life that one receives in the essays will appeal to some readers with a charm like that of personality. The village has often been celebrated in literature from Sweet Auburn to Spoon River, but full justice has scarcely been done to the individuality and distinction of the New England village of the mid-nineteenth century. Cambridge was one of the best representatives of the type, but there were many of them. Each was likely to have a college, or at least an academy, one orthodox and one Unitarian church, a few pleasant colonial houses, and many elms. Everyone who lived in the village had been born there, was proud of that accident, loved whatever natural beauty its trees and meadows afforded, and enjoyed a conscious satisfaction that it was not like other places. Among the residents there might be a great personage, or even a poet, and there were certain to be enough teachers, ministers, doctors, judges, and writers to make up a coterie where ideas circulated. During the long winters, in fact, every one did considerable reading and thinking.

It was for the cultivated men and women of these villages that Lowell wrote. They of all persons delighted in his essay *On a Certain Condescension in Foreigners*, with its urbane reproof of criticism of our lack of urbanity; for the village cherished some dignity of manners and would accept a predestined hell easier than condescension from anybody. The old villages have faded, but their June gardens and winter nights, their serious talk and eager reading, their self-reliance, mitigated by a sense of humour, live again in Lowell's prose.

Wit becomes less exuberant and sagacity is the leading spirit in Lowell's later writing. Village society is disappearing, Cambridge is becoming a large city and Harvard a university, and Lowell is in Europe. Both as a poet and an essayist, he had appeared in part as a mediator or ambassador between the culture of the old world and the new, between the ideals of England and of the United States. In continuing this function as a foreign minister, he did not escape some censure that he was losing his faith in American democracy. To the reader today of his later addresses, that criticism must seem groundless. To be sure, his long residence abroad increased his liking for England and Englishmen; and the course of American politics was a rather dismal sequel to the *Gettysburg Address* and the *Commemoration Ode*. After vanquishing slavery, the nation found itself facing still more dangerous evils, and was somewhat loth to gird its loins for the struggle. Lowell had greeted the dawn that was brightening the New England of his youth, and had seen the noonday of heroic effort in the Civil War. Now, as his own days were lengthening, he could be excused if he saw only a dubious twilight in the America of the eighties.

As a matter of fact there is little doubt and no indifference in these later writings. The maturing years had widened Lowell's perspective without vanquishing the idealism of his youth. He could look back on the course of the industrial revolution which had transformed his New England as well as older lands; and he could foresee the impending revolution that science had already begun in men's standards and processes. The effect of these movements on his own thought are manifest in his poetry and essays mainly by implication and suggestion; but in the utterances of the last decade of his life he often looks upon both his own career and the American purpose directly from this more modern point of view.

In his address at Manchester, in 1884, on Democracy, he declared:

By temperament and education of a conservative turn, I saw the last years of that quaint Arcadia which French travellers saw with delighted amazement a century ago, and have watched the change (to me a sad one) from an agricultural to a proletary population.

Nevertheless, though opposing the single tax and State Socialism, he could see with hopefulness the portents in the air and even believe that democracy was to be the fulcrum for a Socialism possessing "the secret of an orderly and benign construction." He is willing to rebuild his house and believes that it can be builded better. The forward call is to be found in those speeches as well as in the ardent verse of youth, the call of "the radiant image of something better and nobler and more enduring than we are."

This moral earnestness, this desire for perfection, this zeal to reform a changing but evil world, characterizes English literature of the years 1830–1880, and American literature of the same epoch. Literature in those years has preached many creeds and many reforms, and it has lost something in simplicity and certainty because it has been so much in earnest. So Lowell's writing loses in certainty of art and unity of effect from its very responsiveness to the shifting opportunities for usefulness. But its contribution to civilization is not lessened, for it has done its best to teach a new people to guide their steps by the great men and great ideas of the past.

In the address on Democracy, Lowell held forth as arguments in favour of our national institutions two of their products, Lincoln and Emerson. We surely need not despair of our democracy so long as it can produce men of letters like Lowell and utilize them in the service of the common weal.

5. Melville

WITH the Transcendentalists might have been discussed a writer who, though not allied to the group, and in contact with any of them only through a robust friendship for Hawthorne, yet fell under the influence of certain Transcendental moods and ideas, from whomever caught, and was by them deflected from a path which at the moment seemed to promise him every honour as a romancer. Herman Melville, grandson of the conservative old gentleman upon whom Holmes wrote *The Last Leaf*, and son of a merchant of New York, was born there, 1 August, 1819. The early death of his father and the loss of the family fortune having narrowed Melville's chances for higher schooling to a few months in the Albany Classical School, he turned his hand to farming for a year, shipped before the mast to Liverpool in 1837, taught school from 1837–40, and in January, 1841, sailed from New Bedford on a whaling voyage into the Pacific. Upon the experiences of that voyage his principal work is founded. The captain of the *Acushnet*, it seems, treated the crew badly, and Melville, with the companion whom he calls Toby, escaped from the ship to the Island of Nukuheva [Nukuhiva] in the Marquesas and strayed into the cannibal valley Typee [Taipi], where the savages kept Melville for four months in an "indulgent captivity." Rescued by an Australian whaler, he visited Tahiti and other islands of the Society group, took part in a mutiny, and once more changed ship, this time setting out for Honolulu. After some months as a clerk in Hawaii, he joined the crew of the frigate *United States* and returned by the Horn to Boston, October, 1844. "From my twenty-fifth year," he told Hawthorne, "I date my life." Why he held 1844 so important is not clear; he may then first have turned to authorship. Though he had kept no notes of his journeying, within a year he had completed his first book, *Typee*, the record of his captivity. This was followed the next year by *Omoo*,[1] which completes his island adventures. In 1849 came *Redburn*, based on his earlier voyage to Liverpool, and in 1850 *White-Jacket*, an account of life on a man-of-war.

The first two had a great vogue and aroused much wonder as to the proportion of fiction and fact which might have gone to their making. Murray published *Typee* in England in the belief that it was pure fact. There were others to rank it with Richard Henry Dana's *Two Years before the Mast* (1841) as a transcript of real events. But though little is known of Melville's actual doings in the South Seas, it is at least clear that *Typee* and *Omoo* are no more as truthful as *Two Years before the Mast* than they are as crisp and nautical as that incomparable classic of the sea. Melville must be ranked less with Dana than with George Borrow. If he knew the thin boundary between romance and reality, he was still careless of nice limits, and his work is a fusion which defies analysis. *White-Jacket*, of these four books, is probably nearest a plain record; *Redburn* has but few romantic elements. *Omoo*, as a sequel, has not the freshness of *Typee*, nor has it such unity. *Typee*, indeed, is Melville at all but his best, and must be classed with the most successful narrations of the exotic life; after seventy years, when the South Pacific seems no longer another world, the spell holds. The valley of Taipi becomes, in Melville's handling, a region of dreams and languor which stir the senses with the fragrance and colour of the landscape and the gay beauty of the brown cannibal girls. And yet Melville, thoroughly sensitive to the felicities of that life, never loses himself in it but remains the shrewd and smiling Yankee.

The charge that he had been writing romance led Melville to deserve the accusation, and he wrote *Mardi* (1849), certainly one of the strangest, maddest books ever composed by an American. As in *Typee*, two sailors escape from a tyrannical captain in the Pacific and seek their fortune on the open sea, where they finally discover the archipelago of Mardi, a para-

[1] The word is Polynesian for "rover."

dise more rich and sultry than the Marquesas, which becomes, as the story proceeds, a crazy chaos of adventure and satirical allegory. In *Mardi* for the first time appear those qualities which made a French critic call Melville "un Rabelais améri- cain," his welter of language, his fantastic laughter, his tumultu- ous philosophies. He had turned, contemporaries said, from the plain though witty style of his first works to the gorgeous manner of Sir Thomas Browne; he had been infected, say later critics, with Carlylese. Whatever the process, he had surely shifted his interest from the actual to the abstruse and symboli- cal, and he never recovered from the dive into metaphysics which proved fatal to him as a novelist. It was, however, while on this perilous border that he produced the best of his, and one of the best of American, romances; it is the peculiar mingling of speculation and experience which lends *Moby Dick* (1851) its special power.

The time was propitious for such a book. The golden age of the whalers was drawing to a close, though no decline had yet set in, and the native imagination had been stirred by tales of deeds done on remote oceans by the most heroic Yankees of the age in the arduous calling in which New England, and especially the hard little island of Nantucket, led and taught the world. A small literature of whaling had grown up, chiefly the records of actual voyages or novels like those of Cooper in which whaling was an incident of the nautical life. But the whalers still lacked any such romantic record as the frontier had. Melville brought to the task a sound knowledge of actual whaling, much curious learning in the literature of the subject, and, above all, an imagination which worked with great power upon the facts of his own experience. Moby Dick, the strange, fierce white whale that Captain Ahab pursues with such relentless fury, was already a legend among the whalers, who knew him as "Mocha Dick."[1] It remained for Melville to lend some kind of poetic or moral significance to a struggle ordinarily conducted for no cause but profit. As he handles the story, Ahab, who has lost a leg in the jaws of the whale, is driven by a wild desire for revenge which has maddened him and which makes him identify Moby Dick with the very spirit of evil and hatred. Ahab, not Melville, is to blame if the story seems an allegory,

[1] See Reynolds, J. N., *Mocha Dick, Knickerbocker Magazine*, May, 1839.

which Melville plainly declares it was not; but it contains, nevertheless, the semblance of a conflict between the ancient and unscathable forces of nature and the ineluctable enmity of man. This is the theme, but description can hardly report the extraordinary mixture in *Moby Dick* of vivid adventure, minute detail, cloudy symbolism, thrilling pictures of the sea in every mood, sly mirth and cosmic ironies, real and incredible characters, wit, speculation, humour, colour. The style is mannered but often felicitous; though the book is long, the end, after every faculty of suspense has been aroused, is swift and final. Too irregular, too bizarre, perhaps, ever to win the widest suffrage, the immense originality of *Moby Dick* must warrant the claim of its admirers that it belongs with the greatest sea romances in the whole literature of the world.

Married in 1847, Melville lived for three years in New York and then for thirteen years in a farmhouse near Pittsfield, Massachusetts. Although he did not cease to write at once, *Moby Dick* seems to have exhausted him. *Pierre* (1852) is hopelessly frantic; *Israel Potter* (1855) is not markedly original; neither are *The Piazza Tales* (1856), and *The Confidence Man* (1857). The verses which he wrote in his later years, his sole output, are in a few instances happy, but far more often jagged and harsh. Whatever the causes of his loss of power, he fretted under it and grew more metaphysical, tortured, according to Hawthorne, his good friend, by uncertainty as to a future life. That way, for Melville, was madness; his earlier works should have taught him that he was lost without a solid basis in fact. He moved restlessly about, lecturing on the South Seas during the years 1857–1860 in many cities of the United States and Canada. He visited Europe and Palestine. Finally, having returned to New York, he was appointed to a place in the Custom House in 1866, and served there for twenty years, living a private life of almost entire, though voluntary and studious, seclusion. His death, 28 September, 1891, after nearly forty silent years, removed from American literature one of its most promising and most disappointing figures. Of late his fame is undergoing an energetic revival in both America and England.

6. Mrs. Stowe

HARRIET BEECHER, born in Litchfield, Connecticut, 14 June, 1811, passed her childhood and girlhood, indeed practically her entire life, in an atmosphere of piety which, much as she eventually lost of its original Calvinistic rigour, not only indoctrinated her with orthodox opinions but furnished her with an intensely evangelical point of view and a sort of Scriptural eloquence. Her youth was spent in a more diversified world than might be thought: from her mother's people, who were emphatically High Church and, in spite of the Revolution, some of them still Tory at heart, she learned a faith and ritual less austere than that of her father, Lyman Beecher; she had good teaching at the Litchfield Academy, especially in composition; like all her family, she was highly susceptible to external nature and passionately acquainted with the lovely Litchfield hills; she read very widely, and not only theology, of which she read too much for her happiness, but the accepted secular authors of the eighteenth century, as well as Burns and Byron and Scott. At the same time, she justified her Beecher lineage by her ready adaptation to the actual conditions under which she lived during Lyman Beecher's pastorates in Litchfield and Boston, and during her own career as pupil and then teacher in the school conducted at Hartford by her strong but morbid sister Catherine. Although Harriet Beecher was still a thorough child of New England when she went, in 1832, to live in Cincinnati, to which her father had been called as president of the Lane Theological Seminary, and although her earliest sketches and tales, collected in a volume called *The Mayflower* (1843), deal largely with memories of her old home set down with an exile's affection, she grew rapidly in knowledge and experience. Married in 1836 to Professor Calvin E. Stowe of the Seminary, mother by 1850 of seven children, she returned in that year to Brunswick, Maine, where Professor Stowe had accepted a position in Bowdoin College. There, deeply stirred by the passing of the Fugitive Slave Law, she began *Uncle Tom's Cabin; or, Life among the Lowly*, which ran as a serial in *The National Era* of Washington from June, 1851, to April, 1852, and then, on its appearance in two volumes in March, 1852, met with a popular reception never before or since accorded to a novel. Its sales went to the millions. Over five hundred thousand Englishwomen signed an address of thanks to the author; Scotland raised a thousand pounds by a penny offering among its poorest people to help free the slaves; in France and Germany the book was everywhere read and discussed; while there were Russians who emancipated their serfs out of the pity which the tale aroused. In the United States, thanks in part to the stage, which produced a version as early as September, 1852, the piece belongs not only to literature but to folklore.

That *Uncle Tom's Cabin* stands higher in the history of reform than in the history of the art of fiction no one needs to say again. Dickens, Kingsley, and Mrs. Gaskell had already set the novel to humanitarian tunes, and Mrs. Stowe did not have to invent a type. She had, however, no particular foreign master, not even Scott, all of whose historical romances she had been reading just before she began *Uncle Tom*. Instead she adhered to the native tradition, which went back to the eighteenth century, of sentimental, pious, instructive narratives written by women chiefly for women. Leave out the merely domestic elements of the book—slave families broken up by sale, ailing and dying children, negro women at the mercy of their masters, white households which at the best are slovenly and extravagant by reason of irresponsible servants—and little remains. To understand why the story touched the world so deeply it is necessary to understand how tense the struggle over slavery had grown, how thickly charged was the moral atmosphere awaiting a fatal spark. But the mere fact of an audience already prepared will not explain the mystery of a work which shook a powerful institution and which, for all its defects of taste and style and construction, still has amazing power. Richard Hildreth's *The Slave; or Memoirs of Archy Moore* (1836) and Mrs. M. V. Victor's once popular "dime novel" *Maum Guinea; or, Christmas among the Slaves* (1861) no longer move. They both lack the ringing voice, the swiftness, the fullness, the humour, the authentic passion of the greater book.

It has often been pointed out that Mrs. Stowe did not mean to be sectional, that she deliberately made her chief villain a New Englander, and that she expected to be blamed less by the South than by the North, which she thought peculiarly guilty because it tolerated slavery without the excuse either of habit or of interest. Bitterly attacked by Southerners of all sorts, however, she defended herself with *A Key to Uncle Tom's Cabin; Presenting the Original Facts and Documents upon which the Story is Founded* (1853), and then, after a triumphant visit to Europe and a removal to Andover, essayed another novel to illustrate the evil effects of slavery especially upon the whites. *Dred; A Tale of the Great Dismal Swamp* (1856)[1] has had its critical partisans, but posterity has not sustained them. Grave faults of construction, slight knowledge of the scene (North Carolina), a less simple and compact story than in *Uncle Tom's Cabin*, and a larger share of disquisition,—these weigh the book down, and most readers carry away only fragmentary memories, of Dred's thunderous eloquence, of Tom Gordon's shameless abuse of his power as master, and of Old Tiff's grotesque and beautiful fidelity.

After *Dred* Mrs. Stowe wrote no more anti-slavery novels, although during the Civil War she sent to the women of England an open letter reminding them that they, so many of whom now sympathized with the defenders of slavery, had less than ten years ago hailed *Uncle Tom's Cabin* as a mighty stroke for justice and freedom. A considerable part of her later life (she died 1 July, 1896) was spent in Florida, where she had taken a plantation on the St. John's River for the double purpose of establishing there as a planter one of her sons who had been wounded at Gettysburg and of assisting the freedmen, about whom and their relation to the former masters she had more

[1] Also known as *Nina Gordon* from the English title.

enlightened views than were then generally current in the North. Now an international figure, she let her pen respond too facilely to the many demands made upon it: she wrote numerous didactic and religious essays and tales, particularly attentive to the follies of fashionable New York society, in which she had had little experience; she was chosen by Lady Byron to publish the most serious charges ever brought against the poet. In another department of her work, however, Mrs. Stowe stood on surer ground, and her novels of New England life—particularly *The Minister's Wooing* (1859), *The Pearl of Orr's Island* (1862), *Oldtown Folks* (1869), *Poganuc People* (1878)—cannot go unmentioned.

Weak in structure and sentimental she remained. Her heroines wrestle with problems of conscience happily alien to all but a few New England and Nonconformist British bosoms; her bold seducers, like Ellery Davenport in *Oldtown Folks* and Aaron Burr in *The Minister's Wooing*, are villains to frighten schoolgirls; she writes always as from the pulpit, or at least the parsonage. But where no abstract idea governs her she can be direct, accurate, and convincing. The earlier chapters of *The Pearl of Orr's Island* must be counted, as Whittier thought, among the purest, truest idyls of New England. It is harder now to agree with Lowell in placing *The Minister's Wooing* first among her novels, and yet no other imaginative treatment so well sets forth the strange, dusky old Puritan world of the later eighteenth century, when Newport was the centre at once of Hopkinsian divinity and the African slave trade. Mrs. Stowe wisely did not put on the airs of an historical romancer but wrote like a contemporary of the earlier Newport with an added flavour from her own youthful recollections. This flavour was indispensable to her. When her memory of the New England she had known in her girlhood and had loved so truly that Cotton Mather's *Magnalia* had seemed "wonderful stories . . . that made me feel the very ground I trod on to be consecrated by some special dealing of God's providence,"—when this memory worked freely and humorously upon materials which it was enough merely to remember and set down, she was at her later best. These conditions she most fully realized in *Poganuc People*, crisp, sweet, spare (for her), never quite sufficiently praised, and in *Oldtown Folks*, like the other a series of sketches rather than a novel, but—perhaps all the more because of that—still outstanding, for fidelity and point, among the innumerable stories dealing with New England.

CHAPTER VI

Lincoln

THE man of many minds who upon the surface, at least, is variable is not thought of ordinarily as a great leader. And yet in some of the greatest of men a surface variableness has not in the long run prevented a consummate achievement. There is Cæsar, to be pondered upon by all who consider such men second rate. And in American history, there is Lincoln. His life as man of action brings this out well enough. He wavered during many years, hesitating between politics and law, not drivingly conscious of his main bent. Still more clearly is this brought out by his personal life and by those literary and mystical phases that are linked so intimately with the personal. The changes of his mood are at times bewildering. He is often like a wayfarer passing through successive strata of light and darkness, the existence of which does not seem to be explained by circumstance, of whose causes neither he nor his observers have explanation. Did they arise from obscure powers within? Were they the reaction of an ultra-sensitive nature to things without that most people were not able to perceive? He speaks of himself in one of his letters as superstitious. Should the word give us a hint? Whatever theory of him shall eventually prevail, it is sure to rest on this fact: he was a shrouded and a mysterious character, a man apart, intensely reticent, very little of whose inner life has been opened to the world.

It is significant that he was not precocious. The touching picture, preserved in several memories—the lonely, illiterate boy with a passion for reading, indulging the passion at night by a cabin fire—this picture has nothing of early cleverness. Of the qualities that appear after his advent, it is the moral not the mental ones that were clearly foreshadowed in his youth. The simplicity, the kindliness, the courage, the moderation of the matured man have their evident beginnings in the boy. His purely mental characteristics appeared so gradually, so unostentatiously, that his neighbours did not note their coming. Today, seen in the perspective of his career, their approach is more discernible. To one who goes carefully through the twelve volumes of the chronological edition of Lincoln's writings, though the transition from characterlessness to individuality is nowhere sudden, the consciousness of a steady progress in mental power, of a subtle evolution of the literary sense, is unmistakable. The revelation gains in celerity as one proceeds. But there is no sunburst, no sudden change of direction. And yet, for all the equivocality of the early years, one ends by wondering why the process has seemed vague. It is like that type of play whose secret is not disclosed until just before the curtain but which, once disclosed, brings all preceding it into harmony.

So of the literary Lincoln. Looking back from the few great performances of his fruition, why did we not earlier foresee them? There are gleams all along that now strike us as the careless hints of a great unseen power that was approaching. But why—considering the greatness of the final achievement—were they no more than gleams?

Here is an original literary artist who never did any deliberate literary work, who enriched English style in spite of himself under pressure of circumstances. His style is but the flexibility with which his expression follows the movements of a peculiar mind. And as the mind slowly unfolds, becomes overcast, recedes, advances, so, in the main, does the style. The usual symptoms of the literary impulse are all to seek. He is wholly preoccupied with the thing behind the style. Again the idea of a nature shrouded, withdrawn, that dwells within, that emerges mysteriously. His youth, indeed, has a scattered, unemphatic intimation of something else. What might be called the juvenilia of this inscrutable mind include some attempts at verse. They have no literary value. More significant than his own attempts is the fact that verse early laid a strong hold upon him. Years later, when the period of his juvenilia may be counted in the past, as late as 1846, in denying the authorship of a newspaper poem he added: "I would give all I am worth and go in debt to be able to write so fine a piece." Even in the first period of his maturity he could still lapse into verse. A visit to his former home in 1844 called forth two poems that have survived. One was a reverie in the vein of

> O Memory! thou midway world
>   Twixt earth and Paradise,
> Where things decayed and loved ones lost
>   In dreamy shadows rise.

The other was a description of an idiot, long a familiar village figure. Commenting on this poem, Lincoln refers to his "poetizing mood." His official biographers tell us that his favourite poets were Shakespeare, Burns, Byron, and Tom Hood, and add that his taste was "rather morbid." Byron's *Dream* was one of his favourites. It is a commonplace that he never tired of the trivial stanzas beginning

> Oh why should the spirit of mortal be proud.

When his writings come to be edited as literary remains—not merely as historical data—the period of his juvenilia will close with the year 1842. The first period of his maturity will extend to the close of his one term in Congress. Or, it may be, these two periods will be run together. To repeat, there are no sharp dividing lines across this part of his life. He was thirty-three in 1842; forty when he retired from Congress. Either age, in such a connection, is strangely removed from the precocious. In his writings before the end of his thirty-third year there is nothing that would have kept his name alive. However, even as early as twenty-three, in an address to the "People of Sangamon County" submitting himself as a candidate for the legislature, Lincoln revealed two, at least, of the characteristics of his eventual style—its lucidity and its sense of rhythm. Boy as he was, he was little touched by the bombastic rhetoricality of his day. On this side, from the first, he had purity of taste. His sense of rhythm—faintly to be sure—was also beginning to assert itself in 1832. Lincoln's sense of rhythm was far deeper, far more subtle, than mere cadence. In time it became a marvellous power for arranging ideas in patterns so firmly, so clearly, with such unfaltering disposition of emphasis that

14

it is impossible to read them into confusion—as is so easy to do with the idea-patterns of ordinary writers. And with this sense of the idea-pattern grew up at last a sense of cadence most delicately and beautifully accompanying, and reinforcing, the movement of the ideas. In 1832 there were but gleams of all this—but genuine gleams.

The ten years following, sterile from the point of view of production, are none the less to the student of Lincoln's mind most important. As to literary workmanship in these years, what he did to develop his power of expression—in all but the vaguest outline the story is gone. That he read insatiably, that he studied and practised law, that he won local fame as an oral story-teller and as an impromptu debater, these details are preserved. With these is another tradition borne out by his writing. He was a constant reader of the Bible. This introduces the most perplexing question of his inner life. What was his religion? The later Lincoln—the one to whom, perhaps, we get the clue in these ten years between twenty-three and thirty-three—is invariably thought of in popular local tradition as a man of piety. But on this point what do we know? Lincoln has left us no self revelation. His letters, with the exception of one group, are not intimate. His native taciturnity, in this respect, was unconquerable.

Though born in a family of Baptists, he never became a member of the Baptist or of any church. Except for one amazing fragment he has left no writings that are not more or less obscure where they touch on religious themes. It is a curious fact that in the index to the voluminous official *Life* the word religion does not occur. As against this singular negative evidence there are anecdotes of a religious attitude. But the historian learns to question the value of all anecdotes. Nevertheless the tradition of Lincoln's piety—of his essentially religious nature —will not down. A rooted tradition, almost contemporary, is more significant than anecdotes, less susceptible of that constant dramatic heightening which makes the anecdote in retelling more and more positive. Now, the traditional Lincoln is a man overshadowed, a man of infinite gentleness whose pity seems to be more than mere friendliness or generosity. His own world, though uninformed as to his specific beliefs, persistently conceived of him as a mystic, as a walker apart with God. For evidence to support this impression we naturally look to his intimate letters. If we may judge by the surviving correspondence, this man, of whose friendliness ten thousand authentic instances testify, seems none the less to have lived and died solitary. The one mitigating experience appears in his early friendship for Joshua F. Speed. Cordial, trustful, sympathetic he was with many friends. The group of letters written to Speed in 1842 are in a vein that sets them apart. Both men had suffered through their emotions, and each in an analytical, self-torturing way. Upon Lincoln the sudden death of Ann Rutledge, with whom he thought himself in love at twenty-three, is supposed to have had, for the time at least, a deeply saddening effect. A second love affair was lukewarm and ended happily in divergence. The serious matter, his engagement to Miss Mary Todd, led to such acute questioning of himself, such painful analysis of his feeling, such doubt of his ability to make her happy, that the engagement was broken off. Within a month he had written: "I am now the most miserable man living. If what I feel were equally distributed to the whole human family, there would not be one cheerful face on earth." (23 January, 1841.) Two years were to elapse before the harm was repaired and Lincoln and Miss Todd married. Meanwhile Speed, becoming engaged, suffered a similar ordeal of introspection, of pitiless self-analysis. He too doubted the reality of his feeling, feared that he would be wronging the woman he loved by marrying her. Lincoln's letters to his unhappy friend are the most intimate utterances he has left. Sane, cheerful,—except for passing references to his own misfortune,—thoughtful, they helped to pull Speed out of the Slough of Despond.

As nothing in these letters has the least hint of the perfunctory their reverent phrases must be accepted at face value. That a belief in God, even in God's personal direction of human affairs, lies back of these letters, is not to be doubted. Nevertheless the subject remains vague. Lincoln's approach to it is almost timid. There is no hint of dogma. But the fact that he here calls himself superstitious sends us back to his earliest days, to his formative environment, seeking for clues to the religious life he may have inherited.

Loneliness was the all-pervading characteristic of that life. The pioneer cabin, whether in Kentucky, Indiana, or Illinois, was an island in a wilderness. The pioneer village was merely a slightly larger island. Both for cabin and for village, the near horizon encircled it with the primeval. This close boundary, the shadow of the old gods, is a mighty, neglected factor in all the psychological history of the American people. In the lives of the pioneers, scattered over the lonely West, it is of first magnitude. It bore in upon them from every point of the compass, the consciousness of a world mightier than their own, the world of natural force. To a sensitive, poetic spirit, temperamentally melancholy, that encircling shadow must have had the effect of the night on Browning's David, though without producing the elation of David. That the mysticism of the primitive should have developed to full strength in a dreamer of these spiritual islands, but that it should not have risen victorious out of the primeval shadow, is explicable, perhaps, by two things—by the extreme hardness of pioneer life and by the lack of mental fecundity in these men whose primitive estate was a reversion not a development. While their sensibilities had recovered the primitive emotions, their minds, like stalled engines, merely came to a pause. Except for its emotional sensing of the vast unseen, the religious life of the pioneer islands lay most of the time dormant. It is a fact of much significance that the Western pioneers were not accompanied by ministers of religion—which is one detail of the wider fact that their migration was singly, by families, not communal. What a vast difference between the settlement of a colonial community, bringing with it organized religion, and these isolated, almost vagrant, movements into the West with organized religion left behind! Most of the time, in the places where Lincoln's boyhood was passed, there were no public religious services. Periodically a circuit-rider appeared. And then, in a terrific prodigality, the pent-up religious emotion burst forth. The student of Dionysus who would glimpse the psychology of the wild women of the Ecstasies, if he is equal to translating human nature through widely differing externals, may get hints from the religious passion of the pioneer revival. Conversely, Dionysus will help him to understand the West. That there was not much Christianity in all this goes without saying. It was older, simpler, more elemental. But it was fettered mentally in a Christian phraseology. Out of this contradiction grew its incoherency, its mean-

inglessness. With the passing of one of these seasons of storm-
ful ecstasy, there was left in its wake often a great recharge of
natural piety but nothing—or hardly anything—of spiritual
understanding.

And out of these conditions grew the spiritual life of Lincoln.
He absorbed to the full its one great quality, the mystical
consciousness of a world transcending the world of matter. He
has no more doubt of this than all the other supreme men have
had, whether good or bad; than Napoleon with his impatient
gesture toward the stars, that night on shipboard, and his
words, "There must be a God." But when it comes to giving
form to what he feels encompassing him, then Lincoln's lucid
mind asserts itself, and what has imposed on his fellow-villagers,
as a formulation, fades into nothing. And here is revealed a
characteristic that forms a basal clue. His mind has no bent
toward this sort of thinking. Before the task of formulating
his religion he stands quite powerless. His feeling for it is
closer than hands or feet. But just what it is that he feels im-
pinging on him from every side—even he does not know. He
is like a sensitive man who is neither a scientist nor a poet in
the midst of a night of stars. The reality of his experience
gives him no power either to explain or to express it.

Long afterward, in one of his most remarkable fragments,
the reality of his faith, along with the futility of his religious
thinking, is wonderfully preserved. It was written in September, 1862. The previous February the death of one of his
children had produced an emotional crisis. For a time he was
scarcely able to discharge his official duties. This was followed
by renewed interest in religion, expressing itself chiefly by constant reading of Scripture. Whether any new light came to him
we do not know. But in the autumn he wrote this.

The will of God prevails. In great contests, each party claims
to act in accordance with the will of God. Both may be, and one
must be wrong. God cannot be for and against the same thing at
the same time. In the present Civil War it is quite possible that
God's purpose is something quite different from the purpose of
either party; and yet the human instrumentalities working just as
they do, are the best adaptation to effect His purpose. I am almost
ready to say that this is probably true; that God wills this contest
and wills that it shall not end yet. By His mere great power on the

minds of the now contestants, He could either have saved or destroyed the Union without a human contest.   Yet the contest began.   And, having begun, He could give the final victory to either
side any day.   Yet the contest proceeds.

Six months later one of the great pages of his prose called
the nation to observe a day of "national humiliation, fasting,
and prayer."   That the Dionysian and circuit-riding philosophy
had made no impression on his mind is evinced by the silences
of this singular document.   Not a word upon victory over enemies—eagerly though, at the moment, he was hoping for it—
but all in the vein of this question:

And insomuch as we know that by His divine law nations, like
individuals, are subjected to punishment and chastisement in this
world, may we not justly fear that the awful calamity of civil war
which now desolates the land may be a punishment inflicted upon
us for our presumptuous sins, to the needful end of our national
reformation as a whole people?

The context shows that he was not—as the abolitionists wished
him to do—merely hitting at slavery over the Lord's shoulder.
The proclamation continues the fragment.   This great mystic,
pondering what is wrong with the world, wonders whether all
the values, in God's eyes, are not different from what they seem
to be in the eyes of men.   And yet he goes on steadfast in the
immediate task as it has been given him to understand that
task.   So it was to him always—the inscrutable shadow of the
Almighty for ever round about him; the understanding of His
ways for ever an insistent mystery.

To return to Lincoln's thirty-third year.   Is it fanciful to
find a connection between the way in which his mysticism develops—its atmospheric, non-dogmatic pervasiveness—and the
way in which his style develops?   Certainly the literary part of
him works into all the portions of his utterance with the grad-
ualness of the daylight through a shadowy wood.   Those seven
years following 1842 show a gradual change; but it is extremely
gradual.   And it is to be noted that the literary quality, so far
as there is any during these years—for it comes and goes—is
never incisive.   It is of the whole, not of the detail.   It does not
appear as a gift of phrases.   Rather it is the slow unfolding of

those two original characteristics, taste and rhythm. What is growing is the degree of both things. The man is becoming deeper, and as he does so he imposes himself, in this atmospheric way, more steadily on his language.

Curiously enough it is to this period that his only comic writings belong. Too much has been said about Lincoln's humour. Almost none of it has survived. Apparently it was neither better nor worse than the typical American humour of the period. Humorously, Lincoln illustrated as an individual that riotous rebound which so often distinguishes the nature predominantly melancholy; and as a type, he illustrates the American contentment with the externals of humour, with bad grammar, buffoonery, and ironic impudence. His sure taste as a serious writer deserts him at times as a reader. He shared the illusions of his day about Artemus Ward. When he tried to write humorously he did somewhat the same sort of thing—he was of the school of Artemus.

A speech which he made in Congress, a landmark in his development, shows the quality of his humour, and shows also that he was altogether a man of his period, not superior in many small ways to the standards of his period. The Congress of the United States has never been distinguished for a scrupulous use of its time; today, however, even the worst of Congresses would hardly pervert its function, neglect business, and transform itself into an electioneering forum, with the brazenness of the Congresses of the middle of the last century. In the summer of 1848, with Zachary Taylor before the country as the Whig nominee for president, Lincoln went the way of all flesh political, squandering the time of the House in a jocose electioneering speech, nominally on a point before the House, really having no connection with it—in fact, a romping burlesque of the Democratic candidate, Cass. As such things went at that day, it was capital. It was better than most such speeches because, granting the commonplace thing he had set out to do, Lincoln's better sense of language gave even to his romp a quality the others did not have.

We come now to the year 1849, to Lincoln's fortieth birthday, and probably to another obscure crisis in his career. For thirteen years at least, politics had appeared to contain his dominant ambition. Amid bursts of melancholy of the most

intense sort, in spite, it would seem, of occasional fits of idleness, he seems in the main to have worked hard; he had made
headway both in politics and in law; he had risen from grinding
poverty to what relatively was ease. Now, he made the surprising decision to abandon politics. The reasons remain obscure. However, he carried his decision into effect. What the
literary student might call his second period extends from his
abandonment of politics to his return, from 1849 to 1855—or
perhaps through the famous Douglas controversy in 1858.

It was a period of slight literary production—even including
the speeches against Douglas—but of increasingly rapid literary development. One curious detail perhaps affords a clue
worth following up. Shortly after his return from Congress
Lincoln, with several other middle-aged men, formed a class
that met in his law office for the study of German. Was this an
evidence that his two years in the East had given him a new
point of view? Was this restless mind, superficially changeable,
sensitive to its surroundings, was it impressed—perhaps for the
moment, overawed—by that Eastern culture of the mid-century, of the time—so utterly remote it seems today!—when
German was the soul's language in New England? Lincoln had
visited New England, on a speech-making invitation, as a consequence of his romp against Cass. He was made much of by
the New England Whigs—perhaps for what he was, perhaps
as a Western prodigy uncouth but entertaining. From New
England, and from his two years in Congress, he came home to
forsake politics, to apply himself with immense zeal to the law,
to apply himself to the acquisition of culture. The latter purpose appears before long to have burned itself out. There was
a certain laziness in Lincoln alongside his titanic energy. It
would seem that the question whether he could keep steadily
at a thing depended not on his own will but on the nature of
the task. With those things that struck deep into the parts of
him that were permanent he was proof against weariness. But
with anything that was grounded on the surface part of him,
especially on his own reactions to the moment, it was hit or
miss how long he would keep going. Whatever it was that
started him after formal education in 1849, it had no result.
In the rapid development of the next few years his new-found
enthusiasm disappears. It is the native Lincoln moving still

upon his original bent, though with swiftly increasing mentality, who goes steadily forward from the able buffoonery of the speech against Cass to the splendid directness of the speeches against Douglas.

In these years he became a very busy man. At their close he was one of the leading lawyers of the state. Two things grew upon him. The first was his understanding of men, the generality of men. He always seemed to have known men's hearts. This was the gift of his mysticism—the gift which mysticism has often bestowed upon natures predisposed to kindness. Almost inevitably this gift produces sadness. Lincoln did not form an exception. The pity of men's burdens, the vision of the tears of the world falling for ever behind its silences, was as real in this peasant dreamer of our rude West as in that clerkly mediæval dreamer whom Walter Pater has staged so magically in the choir at Amiens. But the exquisite melancholy of the singer in the high church with its glorious windows can easily slide down smooth reaches of artistic contemplation into egoism. The rough, hard world of the West, having less of refuge for the dreamer, made the descent less likely. Nevertheless its equivalent was possible. To stifle compassion, or to be made unstable by compassion, was a possible alternative before the rapidly changing Lincoln of the early years of this period. What delivered him from that alternative, what forced him completely around, turning him permanently from all the perils of mysticism while he retained its great gift, may well have been his years of hard work, not in contemplating men but in serving them. The law absorbed his compassion; it became for him a spiritual enthusiasm. To lift men's burdens became in his eyes its aim. The man who serves is the one who comes to understand other men. It is not strange, having such native equipment for the result, that Lincoln emerged from this period all but uncannily sure in his insight into his fellows.

The other thing that grew upon him was his power to reach and influence them through words. The court room was his finishing academy. The faculty that had been with him from the start—directness, freedom from rhetoric—was seized upon in the life-and-death-ness of the legal battle, and given an edge, so to speak, that was incomparable. The distinction between pure and applied art, like the distinction between pure and applied mathematics, is never to be forgotten. Applied art, the art that must be kept in hand, steadily incidental to an ulterior purpose, affords, in a way, the sharpest test of artisticality. Many a mere writer who might infuse himself into an imaginative fantasy would fail miserably to infuse himself into a statement of fact. To attend strictly to business, and yet to be entirely individual—this is a thrilling triumph of intellectual assimilation. This is what Lincoln in these years of his second period acquired the power to do. When he emerges at its close in the speeches against Douglas, at last he has his second manner, a manner quite his own. It is not his final manner, the one that was to give him his assured place in literature. However, in a wonderful blend of simplicity, directness, candour, joined with a clearness beyond praise, and a delightful cadence, it has outstripped every other politician of the hour. And back of its words, subtly affecting its phrases, echoing with the dreaminess of a distant sound through all its cadences, is that brooding sadness which was to be with him to the end.

Another period in Lincoln's literary life extends from his return to politics to the First Inaugural. Of all parts of his personal experience it is the most problematic. At its opening there rises the question why he returned to politics. Was there a crisis of some sort about 1855 as, surely, there was about 1849? His official biographers are unsatisfying. Their Lincoln is exasperatingly conventional—always the saint and the hero, as saint-heroes were conceived by the average American in the days when it was a supreme virtue to be "self-made." That there was some sort of failure of courage in the Lincoln who gave up politics in 1849 is of course too much for official biography to be expected to consider. But it might perceive something besides pure devotion to the public weal in Lincoln's return. That this successful provincial lawyer who had made a name for conscientiousness should be deeply stirred when politics took a turn that seemed to him wicked, was of course quite what one would expect. And yet, was the Lincoln who returned to the political arena the same who had withdrawn from it? Was there not power in him in 1855 that was not in him in 1849? May it not be that he had fled from his ambition in an excess of self-distrust, just as in his love affair doubt of

himself had led him for a time to forsake what he most desired?
And may not the new strength that had come to him have
revived the old ambition, blended it with his zeal for service,
and thus in a less explicit way than his biographers would have
us think, faced him back toward politics. Be that as it may,
his literary power, which took a bound forward in the excitement following the Nebraska Bill, holds itself at a high level for
several years, and then suddenly enters into eclipse. Beginning
with the speech at Springfield on the Dred Scott case, including
the "house divided" speech, the Douglas speeches, and closing
with the Cooper Union speech in February, 1860, there are a
dozen pieces of prose in this second manner of Lincoln's that
are all masterly. If they had closed his literary career we
should not, to be sure, particularly remember him today. In
his writing as in his statesmanship it was what he did after
fifty—the age he reached 12 February, 1859—that secures his
position. None the less for surety of touch, for boldness, for
an austere serenity with no hint of self-distrust, these speeches
have no superiors among all his utterances, not even among the
few supreme examples of his final manner. Reading these
speeches it is hard to believe that this man in other moods had
tasted the very dregs of self-distrust, had known the bitterest
of all fear—that which rushes upon the dreamer from within,
that snatches him back from his opportunity because he doubts
his ability to live up to it.

The confident tone of these speeches makes all the more
bewildering the sudden eclipse in which this period ends. The
observer who reaches this point in Lincoln's career, having pondered upon his previous hesitation, naturally watches the year
1860 with curious eyes, wondering whether 1841 and 1849 will
be repeated, whether the man of many minds will waver, turn
into himself, become painfully analytical, morbidly fearful, on
the verge of a possible nomination for the Presidency. But the
doubtfulness of the mystics—who, like Du Maurier's artists,
"live so many lives besides their own, and die so many deaths
before they die"—is not the same thing as the timidity of the
man afraid of his fate. Hamlet was not a coward. The impression which Lincoln had recently made upon the country was
a true impression—that he was a strong man. However, not
his policies, not his course of action, had won for Lincoln his

commanding position in his party in 1860, but his way of saying things. In every revolution, there is a moment when the man who can phrase it can lead it. Witness Robespierre. If the phraser is only a man of letters unable to convert literature into authority, heaven help him. Again witness Robespierre. Although if we conclude that the average American in the spring of 1860 was able to read through Lincoln's way of handling words deep enough into his character to perceive his power to handle men, we impute to the average American an insight not justified by history, yet that average man was quite right in hearing such an accent in those speeches of the second manner as indicated behind the literary person a character that was void of fear—at least, of what we mean by fear when thinking of men of action. That Lincoln wanted the nomination, welcomed it, fought hard for his election, only the sentimental devotees of the saint-hero object to admitting. Nor did his boldness stop at that. Between the election and New Year's Day, the secession of South Carolina and the debates in Congress forced the Republicans to define their policy. The President-elect, of course, was the determining factor. Peace or war was the issue. There is no greater boldness in American history than Lincoln's calm but inflexible insistence on conditions that pointed toward war. No amiable pacifism, no ordinary dread of an issue, animated the man of the hour at the close of 1860.

Then, in the later winter, between his determination of the new policy and his inauguration, came the eclipse. All the questions roused in the past by his seasons of shadow, recur. Was it superstition? Was it mystical premonition? Was there something here akin to those periods of intense gloom that overtook the Puritans of the seventeenth century? In a few respects there are points of likeness between Lincoln and Cromwell. In most respects, the two men are widely dissimilar. But in their susceptibility to periodic and inexplicable overshadowing they are alike. With Cromwell, besides his mysticism, there was a definite, an appalling dogma. Though Lincoln did not carry the weight of Cromwell's dogma, perhaps the essential thing was the same in both—the overwhelming, encompassing sense that, God being just and our Father, human suffering must somehow be the consequence of our human sins. Endow Cromwell with Lincoln's power of expression, and we can imagine him in one of his grand moments writing that piece of superb humility, the Fast Day Proclamation. Again, was it superstition, was it premonition, that created in Lincoln, as he faced toward Washington, a personal unhappiness? No recollection of Lincoln is more singular than one preserved by his law partner with regard to this period of eclipse. He tells of Lincoln's insistence that their sign should continue to hang over the office door; of his sad eagerness to have everyone understand that his departure was not final; of his reiteration that some day he would come back, that his business would be resumed in the plain old office just as if nothing had happened.

Lincoln was so absolutely the reverse of the rhetorician that when he had nothing to say he could not cover up his emptiness with a lacquer of images. Never his the florid vacuousness of the popular orators of his day. When his vision deserted him, his style deserted him. It is confidently asserted that he never was able to press a law case unless he wholly believed in it. Strong evidence for the truth of the tradition is the obedience of his style to the same law. It behaved in this way, the eclipse being still upon him, when he was subjected to the misfortune of having to speak out of the shadow, in February, 1861, on his way to the inauguration. He could not escape this misfortune. The notions of the time required the President-elect to talk all the way from his home to the White House. This group of speeches forms an interlude in Lincoln's development so strange that the most psychological biographer might well hesitate to attack its problem. As statecraft the speeches were ruinously inopportune. Their matter was a fatuous assurance to the country that the crisis was not really acute. As literature, his utterances have little character. The force, the courage, the confident note of the second manner had left him. His partisans were appalled. One of the most sincere among them wrote angrily "Lincoln is a Simple Susan."

And then, lightning-like, both as statecraft and as literature, came the First Inaugural. Richard was himself again. He was much more, he was a new Richard. The final manner appeared in the First Inaugural. All the confident qualities of the second manner are there, and with them something else. Now, at last, reading him, we are conscious of beauty. Now we see what the second manner lacked. Keen, powerful, full of character, melodious, impressive, nevertheless it had not that sublimation of all these, and with that the power to awaken the imagination which, in argumentative prose, is beauty.

Lincoln had apparently passed through one of those indescribable inward experiences—always, it seems, accompanied by deep gloom—which in mystical natures so often precede a rebirth of the mind. Psychology has not yet analyzed and classified them. But history is familiar with a sufficient number to be sure of their reality. From Saul agonizing in his tent to Luther throwing his inkpot at the devil; from Cromwell wrestling with the Lord to Lincoln striving to be vocal when his mind was dumb—in a hundred instances there is the same range of phenomena, the same spiritual night, the same amazing dawn.

And now the most interesting of the literary questions concerning Lincoln presents itself. It is to be borne in mind that he was essentially non-rhetorical. He towers out of the literary murk of his day through his freedom from rhetoric. And yet, pernicious as it is, mere rhetoricity has its base in genuine artistic impulse. It is art perverted and made unreal, just as sentimentality is sentiment perverted and made unreal. And just as the vision of conduct which sentimentality perceives—and spoils—is an essential to noble living, so the vision of word-use which rhetoric perceives and spoils is essential to literature. Hitherto Lincoln had been ultra-sensitive to the spoiling done by rhetoricality. Had he been duly sensitive to the vision which the word-jobbers of his day had degraded to their own measure? It may be fairly doubted. But hereafter, in the literary richness of the final manner, no one can doubt the fulness and the range of his vision as an imaginative artificer in words. Had any new influence, purely literary entered into his life? One hesitates to say, and yet there is the following to consider. Lincoln submitted his First Inaugural to Seward. Several of Seward's criticisms he accepted. But Seward, never doubting that he was worth a dozen of the President in a literary way, did not confine himself to criticism. He graciously submitted a wholly new paragraph which Mr. Lincoln might, if he cared to, use as peroration. It read:

I close. We are not, we must not be, aliens or enemies, but fellow countrymen and brethren. Although passion has strained our bonds of affection too hardly, they must not, I am sure they will not, be broken. The mystic chords which, proceeding from so many battle-fields and so many patriotic graves, pass through all the hearts and all hearths in this broad continent of ours, will yet again harmonize in their ancient music when breathed upon by the guardian angel of the nation.

One of the most precious pages in the sealed story of Lincoln's inner life would contain his reflections as he pondered this paragraph. Deeply as he knew the hearts of men, here—in spite of its lack of weight—was something that hitherto he had not been able to use. The power of it in affecting men he must have understood. If it could be brought within his own instrument, assimilated to his own attitude, a new range would be given to his effectiveness. Was he capable of assimilating it? We do not know how he reasoned in this last artistic crisis; but we do know what he did. He made Seward's paragraph his own. Into the graceful but not masterly—the half-way rhetorical—words of Seward he infused his own quality. He reorganized their feeble pattern by means of his own incomparable sense of rhythm. The result was the concluding paragraph of the First Inaugural:

I am loath to close. We are not enemies, but friends. We must not be enemies. Though passion may have strained, it must not break our bonds of affection. The mystic chords of memory, stretching from every battlefield and every patriot grave to every living heart and hearthstone all over this broad land, will yet swell the chorus of the Union when again touched as surely they will be, by the better angels of our nature.

The final Lincoln, in the literary sense, had arrived. Though an ultra-delicate critic might find a subdivision of this final period in the year 1862, the point is minute and hardly worth making. During the four years remaining in his life, his style has always the same qualities: flexibility, directness, pregnancy, wealth. It is always applied art, never for an instant unfaithful to the business in hand. Never for an instant does it incrust the business,—as the rhetorician would do,—nor ever overlay it with decoration. At the same time it contrives always to compel the business to transact itself in an atmosphere that is the writer's own creation; an atmosphere in which great thoughts are enriched by golden lustres, while ordinary thoughts bear themselves as do poor souls transfigured, raised momentarily to a level with the great by a passionate vision of great things.

CHAPTER VII

Whitman

W ALT WHITMAN once declared his *Leaves of Grass* to
be "the most personal of all books ever published."

> This is no book;
> Who touches this, touches a man.

Thus he fits Hazlitt's description of Montaigne as one who
dared to set down as a writer what he thought as a man. This
being the claim of the volume, it becomes highly important to
determine the character of the author. Evidently Whitman
was not, in any conventional sense of the term, that "average
man" whose praises he sang, else even his novel form of expression would hardly have sufficed to keep his poetry so long a
time from the masses. He was a man and a writer who could
be hated as an impostor or adored as a Messiah but who was
in any case a challenge to discussion. Much light is thrown
on his character, of course, by the autobiographical parts of
his writings; but here it is frequently difficult to determine
which incidents belong to his outward and which to his inner,
or imaginative, life, so deftly do his vicarious mystical experiences blend with the sublimations of his own deeds, and so
carefully have many of those deeds been mystified or concealed. [1]

---

[1] For instance, a poem, *Once I Pass'd Through a Populous City*, taken by many
biographers to support the theory that Whitman had a romance with a lady of high
social standing during his 1848 visit to New Orleans, proves to have been addressed,
in the original draft of the poem, not to a lady but to a "rude and ignorant man";

Much remains for painstaking research to accomplish. This chapter attempts to set forth only the facts of his biography which are well established or establishable.

Born in the same year as Lowell, Whitman may be said to represent the roots and trunk of democracy, while Lowell may be likened to its flowers or fruits. Whitman, for his part, could hardly have been, or wished to be, a flower; it was not in his ancestry, his education, or his environment. Blending in his own nature the courage, the determination, and the uncompromising Puritan idealism of good, if somewhat decadent, English ancestry with the placid slowness,[1] self-esteem, stubbornness, and mysticism of better Dutch (and Quaker) ancestry, Walt[2] Whitman was born 31 May, 1819, at the hamlet of West Hills, a few miles south of Huntington, Long Island. His father, Walter Whitman, was a farmer and later a somewhat nomadic carpenter and moderately successful housebuilder, who, although, like the poet's excellent mother, he had even less education than their nine children were destined to have, was something of a free thinker. The Whitmans moved to Brooklyn about 1823–25,[3] but Walt, until he went to live in Washington during the Civil War, continued to be more or less under the wholesome influence of the country. Throughout childhood, youth, and earlier manhood he returned to spend summers, falls, or even whole years at various parts of the Island, either as a healthy roamer enjoying all he saw, or as a school-teacher, or as the editor of a country paper, or as a poet reading Dante in an old wood and Shakespeare, Æschylus, and Homer within sound of the lonely sea, and mewing his strength for the bold flights of his

---

on the other hand, the poem *Out of the Rolling Ocean, the Crowd*, to which no biographer has attached particular personal significance, can be shown to have been addressed, about 1864, to a married woman with whom Whitman was in love and with whom he maintained for a time a correspondence notwithstanding the jealous objections of her husband.

[1] This description does not allow for a high temper, displayed on occasion, which Whitman seems to have inherited from his father.

[2] Shortened from Walter to distinguish the son from his father, but not used in connection with his published writings until 1855.

[3] The exact date is uncertain. Whitman gives 1822–3 once, 1823 twice, 1824 twice, and 1825 once; the earliest record in the directory of the city (Spooner) is 1825. At any rate Whitman was probably accurate in his statement that he was "still in frocks."

fancy. Perhaps it was a certain disadvantage that while he was thus "absorbing" and learning to champion the common people, the "powerful uneducated persons," among whom he moved on equal terms though not as an equal, he was little thrown, in any influential way, among people of refinement or taste. In his old age nobility and common humanity jostled each other in his hospitable little parlour—or kitchen; but during his youth the breadth of his view and the democracy of his sympathy were somewhat limited, not so much in theory as in fact, by the conditions that surrounded him. At the same time his native "egotism," as he frankly calls what Emerson would probably have softened to "self-reliance" had it been a trifle less arrogant, was being abnormally developed, even for a genius, by conditions little fitted to correct it. Nevertheless, he thus early learned lessons from nature and from human nature which were as indispensable to the inspiring and shaping of his liberating art and his democratic philosophy as was his outdoor life in developing his remarkably sensitive and healthy physical constitution.

Whitman's youth in Brooklyn, though full of interest, was uneventful. As a child of six he was flattered by Lafayette's chancing to lay his hands on him during a visit to the city in 1825. He attended the public school for a few years, impressing his teacher, Benjamin Buel Halleck, only with his good nature, his clumsiness, and his poverty of special promise. He ran with the boys of the street and was familiar with the city and its environs, especially with Fulton Ferry, whose slip was not far from his home. Not Irving, not Charles Lamb was more intimately or passionately fond of city life, with its opportunities for human contact and for varied sights, than was Whitman, both as boy and man. When about eleven years old he left school to become an office-boy, first to a lawyer and then to a doctor, the former of whom kindly afforded him opportunities for reading such books as the *Arabian Nights* and the poetry and romances of Scott. At twelve he was learning to set type, in a building once used as Washington's headquarters, under the instruction of a veteran printer who had many tales to tell of Revolutionary heroism. Next he went to set type for a few dollars a week on Aldin Spooner's *Star*. He had already felt the satisfaction of authorship when "sentimental bits" had appeared from his pen in the newspapers. Later he became a compositor on unknown journals in New York.

In May, 1836, Whitman went down to his father's farm at Hempstead, and then began a wandering career as a well-liked but not altogether successful country school-teacher. He taught somewhat after the fashion of the transcendentalists, substituting moral suasion for the ferule, and "boarding round" in at least seven different districts in Queens and Suffolk counties, but seldom remaining more than a few months at any one school. His mind was but half on his work, and after two years of teaching he sought (June, 1838), a more congenial occupation in starting a village newspaper, *The Long Islander*, at Huntington. On this he did all the work, even to delivering the papers on horseback; but he did it so irregularly that in less than a year his financial backers entrusted the little sheet to more punctual hands. Again teaching had to be resorted to. When living at Jamaica (1839–41) Whitman spent some of his time, apparently after school hours, in learning the printing business in the office of James J. Brenton's *Long Island Democrat*, to the pages of which he contributed a considerable number of sketches and essays replete with juvenile philosophy, as well as a number of patriotic and sentimental poems in conventional measures. The poet's tendency to dream—to loaf and invite his soul—to the neglect of more earthly duties, a tendency that was to become a tradition wherever he thereafter worked, had already marked him as an unusual person. He was even then dreaming of composing a ponderous and prophetic book to teach men, among other things, the danger of riches. The Quaker's attitude toward truth and the mystic's attitude toward nature were already discernible in his writings. But his life was unhappy, full of irresolution and unrest, and frequently given to a morbid brooding on death, while his enormous capacity for sentimental friendship, equalled only by his capacity for taking delight in external nature, had already taught him to sing of unreturned affection, and drove him, no doubt, to take refuge, like Narcissus, in self-admiration. Yet he took part in the sports and merry-makings of the village and was interested in the political campaigns of the day, himself attaining some prominence as a stump speaker in Queens County and even in New York City.

Then, in the summer of 1841, he definitely and finally threw in his lot with the city, and the second important period of his development began. Heretofore the highly sensitive youth had been almost ladylike in his sentiments, often morbid in his contrary moods, but puritanically strict in word and deed. At twenty-two his passionate nature demanded a sort of reaction. He "sounded all experiences of life, with all their passions, pleasures, and abandonments,"[1] and became, in another sphere of indulgence, something of a dandy. He was developing his personality meanwhile, and he was learning to write.

Whitman's early pieces written in New York reflect the wave of sentimentality which was, in the forties, sweeping over the country, and display, along with their humanitarian feeling, a fondness for melodramatic extravagance which caused him later to wish them all "quietly dropp'd in oblivion." He was a reformer pleading for the abolition of intemperance (including the use of tobacco, tea, and coffee), of capital punishment, and of slavery; and urging, as the constructive side of his reform, the need of a native American drama, opera, and literature. His interest in the theatre and the opera was a vital one, the constant satisfaction of which was made possible by his having a pressman's pass. Here he received many hints for his declamatory and rhythmical style of verse. Altogether more than a score of tales, sketches, essays, and poems have been found which belong to this period. To these must be added a crude and hasty dime novelette, *Franklin Evans*,[2] addressed, in the cause of temperance, not to the "critics" but to "THE PEOPLE," and evidently written to order. In this period Whitman was connected with some of the best city magazines and newspapers as contributor, compositor, or editor. The most important position that he held was that of editor of *The Daily*

[1] John Burroughs, in *Notes on Walt Whitman as Poet and Person*, 1867, p. 81. The substance, if not the phrasing, of this indefinite though suggestive passage was supplied by Whitman himself.

[2] This was republished, in compressed form, under the caption *Fortunes of a Country Boy*, by J. R. S. in *The Brooklyn Eagle* (November, 1846) as an "original novel." *Death in the School Room*, *The Child's Champion*, *Little Jane*, *The Death of Wind-Foot*, and a few poems were similarly twice published by Whitman, in the lax fashion of the day.

[and *Weekly*] *Brooklyn Eagle*, a connection which extended from February, 1846, to January, 1848, when a "row with the boss," on account of Whitman's unreliability, and with "the party," on account of his progressive Barnburner politics, made it necessary for him to shift for a new position. This was readily found on *The Daily Crescent*, a paper about to be launched in New Orleans.

The trip which, with his favourite brother Jeff, Whitman made in the spring of 1848 by rail, stage, and Mississippi steamboat to New Orleans, his residence in that city for three months, and his return by way of the Mississippi and the Great Lakes[1] were rather less important than has commonly been supposed. It is doubtful whether the experience brought into his life a great but secret romance,[2] and it appears certain that he was not by it first made conscious of his mission as a poetic prophet. But the journey did give him a new and permanent respect for the undeveloped possibilities of his country, especially in the South and West, and it gave him opportunities for the study of the French and Spanish elements in New Orleans; while his observation of the South's "peculiar institution" caused him to remain, though a radical Free-Soiler, one careful not to be classed with the Abolitionists. But if this journey was of only measurable importance, perhaps others were of greater; for, though details are almost entirely unknown, it is practically certain that he made still other visits to the South.[3]

Notwithstanding the attractiveness that the new atmosphere had for all that was Southern in Whitman's temperament, he soon haughtily resigned his position, because of a

---

[1] Whitman's fullest and best account of the trip south was printed in the early numbers of the *Crescent*. This was not preserved in his collected prose editions, but a considerable portion of it was reprinted in *The Yale Review*, September, 1915.

[2] Whitman never married. In old age he confided to John Addington Symonds the information that, though unmarried, he had had six children, from intimate relations with whom he had been prevented by circumstances "connected with their fortune and benefit." For a fuller discussion of this confession and the questions arising out of it than is here possible the reader is referred to the biographies by Binns, Perry, Edward Carpenter, Bazalgette, De Sélincourt, and Traubel.

[3] Several lines of evidence point to this conclusion. Here it will be sufficient to refer to Whitman's autobiographical note published in *The Critic*, 28 February, 1885, over the pseudonym "George Selwyn."

difference with his employers, and left for home 27 May. Almost immediately after his arrival he was engaged by Judge Samuel E. Johnson to edit (and nominally to own) a new Free-Soil paper, the weekly[1] *Brooklyn Freeman*, as the organ of those Democrats with whom Whitman, but not the party leaders behind the *Eagle*, had sympathized the year before. The new paper appeared 9 September, but it had the hard fortune to be burnt out, with no insurance, in a great conflagration that swept the city that very night. But the *Freeman* was revived in November, and, though a small and apparently a very outspoken sheet, it attained a large circulation. The nature of the political warfare in those days of personal invective may be suggested by Whitman's valedictory, published when, without explanation, he resigned the paper, 11 September, 1849, into the hands of those who would compromise, as he would not, with his political opponents:

To those who have been my friends, I take occasion to proffer the warmest thanks of a grateful heart. My enemies—and old hunkers generally—I disdain and defy the same as ever.

Of the next six years of Whitman's life comparatively little is known. He is said to have been connected with certain newspapers,[2] to have run a book-store and printing establishment, and to have assisted his aging father, now suffering from paralysis, in building small houses for sale. He had here an opportunity for money-making which, to the disappointment of the family, he allowed to pass unimproved. What is more important, he was growing rapidly in his inner life, as he attended lectures, read miscellaneous magazine articles, Shakespeare, Epictetus, the Hebrew and the Hindoo bibles, and Emerson, and loafed on the shores of Coney Island, timing the new poetry he was composing to the rhythmic beat of the sea. Somewhere in this period probably belongs the mystical experience, described in the poem *Song of Myself*, Section 5,

[1] Changed to a daily in April, 1849.
[2] An article in the Springfield *Republican*, 28 March, 1892, states that Whitman helped to edit Levi D. Slamm's *Plebeian;* and a letter from Whitman's friend, T. H. Rome, the first printer of the *Leaves of Grass*, to Wm. E. Benjamin (September, 1898) mentions the fact that after his return from New Orleans Whitman conducted for a short time an advertising sheet called *The Salesman.* See also Hearne's city directory for 1851 and 1852.

which clarified his vision "of the world as love" and fused his purposes in life, and which some biographers, attaching to it more significance than did Whitman himself and forgetting that he had other such experiences, are inclined to consider the most important fact in his biography. At any rate, the book of which he had dreamed since adolescence and of which he had as early as 1847[1] written many passages was now, in 1854–5, written and rewritten, and printed in Brooklyn, without a publisher, in July, 1855.

The purpose of the author in writing this unique volume may be stated in his own comprehensive words, written in 1876:

I dwelt on Birth and Life, clothing my ideas in pictures, days, transactions of my time, to give them positive place, identity—saturating them with the vehemence of pride and audacity of freedom necessary to loosen the mind of still-to-be-form'd America from the folds, the superstitions, and all the long, tenacious and stifling anti-democratic authorities of Asiatic and European past—my enclosing purport being to express, above all artificial regulation and aid, the eternal Bodily Character of One's-Self.

The plan for his poetic life-work was to have been completed, he tells us in the Preface to the 1876 edition, by composing

a further, equally needed volume, based on those convictions of perpetuity and conservation which, enveloping all precedents, make the unseen soul govern absolutely at last.

The perfecting of this latter work, dealing with the soul and immortality, had proved beyond his powers and failing health, but a fair idea of what it meant to set forth is to be found, no doubt, in *The Two Rivulets* (1876).

If Emerson's *American Scholar* address was the intellectual declaration of American independence, this first edition of *Leaves of Grass*, though only a thin imperial octavo of ninety-five pages with a hastily written but vigorous and far-sighted explanatory preface, was the first gun in a major campaign of the war that was to win that

---

[1] A Whitman manuscript notebook in the possession of Thomas B. Harned, one of the poet's friends and literary executors, preserves these earliest known specimens of modern free verse. They have recently been published by the present writer in *The Uncollected Poetry and Prose of Walt Whitman* (1921).

independence. Of the form taken by so audacious a message space is wanting for accurate description. It may be said, however, that, denying to itself rhyme, regular metre, stanza forms, literary allusions, and "stock 'poetical' touches" in general, it frequently achieved, nevertheless, a deep and satisfying rhythm of its own—sometimes pregnant gnomic utterances, sometimes a chant or recitative, occasionally a burst of pure lyricism. Just where, if anywhere, Whitman found the hint for this flexible prose-poetic form critics have not agreed. Perhaps Biblical prosody, *Ossian*, the blank verse of Shakespeare and Bryant, the writings of Blake, the prose of Carlyle and Emerson, and his own impassioned declamation all assisted; but full allowance must be made for the unquestioned originality of his own genius, working slowly but courageously for the fuller liberation of song. [1]

The book, expecting opposition, was met by almost complete disregard. Except for a few copies which found their way to England and were later to secure for Whitman ardent disciples and his first English editor, William Michael Rossetti, there was practically no sale. Most of the reviews in the periodicals that noticed the book at all were as scandalized as had been anticipated; but a highly congratulatory letter from Emerson, who evidently recognized in Whitman the disciple he then professed to be, compensated for all neglect or abuse from other quarters, and a sentence from it was put to good, if indelicate, use as advertising on the back of the second edition (1856), a volume much larger than the first and more open to criticism because of its attempt to combat prudery in America by a naturalistic but fragmentary treatment of the facts of sex. Of this patent and confessed indebtedness to

---

[1] In one of the anonymous reviews which Whitman saw fit to write, in 1855, of his own first edition, he disclaims any model: "The style of these poems, therefore, is simply their own style, just born and red. Nature may have given the hint to the author of 'Leaves of Grass,' but there exists no book or fragment of a book which can have given the hint to them." *In Re Walt Whitman*, p. 16.

The first poem known to have been published in this measure was *Blood-Money*, which appeared in Horace Greeley's *Tribune* (Supplement), 22 March, 1850. But *Isle of La Belle Rivière*, published in the Cincinnati *Post*, 30 April, 1892, was written, in what is now called imagist verse, at the age of thirty (1849–50), while *New Year's Day, 1848*, written in an album just before Whitman's departure for New Orleans, shows a tendency to break away from conventional forms. By far more important are the Harned manuscript notebook specimens already mentioned.

Emerson, who had brought the simmering pot of Whitman's literary and patriotic ambition to a boil, Whitman had no cause to feel ashamed; for though lacking Emerson's sanity and mature idealism, he had a greater sympathetic, active, and emotional equipment than had the Concord sage. If Whitman was, as he said, "a child, very old," Emerson was a man, very young. It was almost as if the older champion of individuality had meditated the philosophy by which the younger was to live; but whereas the Emersonian gospel, addressing itself to the idealism of its readers, "breeds the giant which destroys itself," Whitmanism, appealing strongly to the religious sentiment, has already had the ironical fate of developing something not unlike a cult, both at home and in other countries.

Of course such a book failed to bring in royalties, and Whitman again fell back on the drudgery of editing a newspaper, in this instance the bantling *Daily Times* (Brooklyn). Just when this editorship began (1856 or 1857) is not easily determined, but it ended probably in the early part of 1859, after the editor had repeatedly rebuked certain church officials for the, as he thought, unfair treatment they had accorded to one Judge Culver, then the defendant in an ecclesiastical trial. At odd times Whitman wrote the new poems, including that incomparable lyric, *Out of the Cradle Endlessly Rocking*, which appeared now and then in the pages of the Bohemian *Saturday Press*, and the many others which were to be included in the 1860 edition of the *Leaves*. The country was full of lecturers in 1858, and Whitman planned to become one, both to support himself and to supplement the *Leaves*, which could hardly as yet have been called a success. But though he disciplined himself in a style of oratory only less novel than that of his poetry, writing "barrels of lectures" on religion, democracy, language, æsthetics, and politics, and though the desire thus to present his message in a more personal fashion than any sort of authorship, even his own, could afford, persisted throughout life, only a few memorial addresses—such as the tribute to Lincoln—and a few public readings of his own poems written for college commencements or other special occasions ever came of it.

Meanwhile Whitman was widening the circle of his acquaintance. Emerson not only called on him frequently when in the city but sent Alcott, Moncure Conway, and Thoreau to

do likewise.   Lord Houghton also came, and Bryant crossed
the river to share with him long walks into the country.   These
were the days of Whitman's Bohemianism.   A negligent,
open-throated attire and great soft hat that one might associate
with a carpenter or a sailor he insisted on wearing, Richter-like,
wherever he went.   In the earlier years of his journalism he had
worn a high hat, cane, and boutonnière; now the dandy had
given place to a man dressed in a habit more in keeping with
his new rôle as the national bard of democracy *en masse*.   The
affectations in his dress were, however, of less importance than
the inner character of the man.   And that character was one
of great human sympathy and magnetism, possessing a charm
which those who felt it most were least able to explain.   He
spent, as from childhood he had done, much time among the
people—boatmen, pilots, omnibus drivers, mechanics, fishermen
—going anywhere to "feed his hunger for faces."   He visited
prisons, attended the sick in hospitals, drove all one winter
the stage of a disabled driver, and mingled as a meditative
observer among the liberal-minded and light-hearted Bohe-
mians at Pfaff's restaurant.   In 1860 he went to Boston and
published, through Thayer and Eldridge, his third edition, full
of the echoes of this life, in which he had not always been a
mere observer.   Until the war drove its publishers to the wall,
the book had a fair sale.   The poems of two new groups—
Enfans d'Adam, celebrating the love, usually physiological,
between the sexes, and *Calamus*, celebrating that "adhesive-
ness" or "manly attachment" which Whitman then considered
the true cement of a democracy—have in the past provoked
much severe criticism and indignant defence, and the former
were the occasion, at various times, of a threatened official
prosecution, of a temporary exclusion of the book from the
mails, and of the author's being dismissed from a government
clerkship.   Emerson had urged Whitman to be more tactful
and worldly-wise, but the latter's inner conviction that he was
right and his stubborn determination to go ahead in the chosen
course blinded him to the value of tact and condemned him to
suffer from a reputation that he did not really deserve.   Whatever may be the true interpretation of these poems, one finds it
difficult to understand either the character or the writings of
Whitman unless one's eye is kept on the chronology of his pub-

lications, a feat which his method of grouping has rendered rather difficult; for he was a growth, as his poems were, in which a heroic and loving soul gradually freed itself from the passions of a very human and earthly body. His reaction from the asceticism of his adolescence was strong, tumultuous, almost tragic, but it was only a reaction; and when the war had passed over him with its purification and its pain, and when he had suffered severely in his personal affections, he sang more and more of the soul.

Whitman's optimistic faith in democracy was put to the severest possible test by the outbreak of the Civil War. But he did not come into personal touch with its heroic and pathetic sides until, in December, 1862, he went down to the front at Fredericksburg to look after his younger brother, an officer in a volunteer regiment, who had received a slight wound in battle. Shortly after the outbreak of hostilities Whitman had begun writing (June, 1861) for the weekly *Brooklyn Standard* a serial history of the city, entitled *Brooklyniana*, based on his own reminiscences, his conversations with older citizens, and his rather desultory historical reading. He had likewise been composing a few of the vivid war poems in *Drum-Taps*. But as the war became more serious he suspended this writing and took a loitering trip through many of his old haunts on Long Island, fishing, sailing, meeting people in the unceremonious manner of the country, and doubtless pondering the gloomy problems of the war. The early Whitman, so inadequately reported in the biographies, was preparing to give place to the well-known serious and noble Whitman of the Washington hospitals; and this leisurely visit was, one chooses to think, a farewell to the light-hearted irresponsibility of his protracted youth. Returning to Brooklyn in the fall, he took up the *Brooklyniana* again and occupied himself with it almost until the accident to George Whitman called him to the Virginia battle-field.

Thence he casually drifted into the finest employment of his life, that of caring for sick and wounded soldiers on the field and, especially, in the many military hospitals in and about Washington. He lived frugally, supporting himself for a time by doing copying[1] and by contributing wonderfully vivid sketches of his

---

[1] It is probable that Whitman had been reduced to the necessity of doing copying before, for the Brooklyn city directory (Lain) for 1860 gives "Walt Whitman, copyist."

experiences to the Brooklyn *Eagle* and *Union* and the New York *Times*.[1] To supply the little comforts and necessities of the hundred thousand soldiers, Northern and Southern, to whom, as he estimated, he ministered courage and cheer, he privately raised several thousand dollars from friends and correspondents in the North. When he obtained a salaried position in 1865, a generous portion of his earnings went into the same fund. But chiefly he gave himself, in undisguised affection. The full tenderness, almost motherliness, of this large-hearted, self-sacrificing man can be fully understood only in the modest but realistic account of his daily activities preserved in the letters written to his mother at the time and in the hospital-notebook jottings printed in *Specimen Days*. It would be a questionable service to Whitman to affirm that these three years of slow martyrdom sanctified the whole of his life; but it is literally true that the deepest and best instincts in him never before had found such full and beautiful expression. Partly, at least, as a result of his hospital service his magnificent health was lost, and the last twenty years of his life were those of a paralytic cripple.

Whitman's poetic power was still at its height. *Drum-Taps*, —the poetic complement to *Specimen Days* and *The Wound-Dresser*,—a booklet charged with the pathos and the spirituality of the war, was published in 1865, with the profoundly moving dirge for the martyred Lincoln. In *Democratic Vistas* (1871) he made use of prose, though with unequal success.

This period was also important because of the friendships that it made or fostered. Perhaps the most important was that with William Douglas O'Connor. When, in 1865, Whitman had been employed for several months in the Interior Department under Secretary Harlan, the latter, on learning that he was the author of *Leaves of Grass*, had him summarily dismissed; then O'Connor came to his friend's defence in a brilliant and passionate, though ill-advised, polemic, *The Good Gray Poet*, the title of which gave the bard a fit and enduring sobriquet. The advertising value of such a polemic, or of such an incident, though it was rated highly by Whitman and by some of his friends, may now be questioned. Thanks to such

[1] Most of these letters were reprinted in *Specimen Days* or in *The Wound-Dresser*.

staunch friends, however, Whitman was soon settled, for the eight following years, in a comfortable clerkship in the Attorney-General's Department.   Another close friend and enthusiastic disciple then and later was John Burroughs, who published in 1867 the first biographical and critical study of the poet.   An attachment more similar to those of the New York days was Whitman's singular friendship for Pete Doyle, an un-schooled young Confederate soldier, now a street-car conductor, with whom, notwithstanding the disparity in their ages and in-terests, the poet spent much of his leisure time.   To him Whit-man wrote the letters which were, after his death, published by one of his literary executors under the appropriate title *Calamus*. But this comfortable and congenial life was destined to a sud-den end.   Just when Whitman was beginning to make literary friends abroad—Rudolf Schmidt in Denmark, Freiligrath in Ger-many, Madame Blanc in France, Edward Dowden in Ireland, and in England William Rossetti, Swinburne,[1] Robert Bu-chanan, Roden Noel, John Addington Symonds, Tennyson, and Anne Gilchrist—and when he was beginning to become some-what favourably known abroad through Rossetti's expurgated selection, *Poems by Walt Whitman* (1868), and through frag-mentary translations in Continental countries, an attack of paralysis (January, 1873) compelled him first to suspend and finally to give up his clerical work.   Taking his savings, enough to tide him over the first few years of invalidism, he went to live with his brother, Colonel George Whitman, in Camden, New Jersey.   A leisurely trip to Colorado in 1879, a longer one to Canada in the following year, and various briefer visits and lecture journeys—now to New York, now to visit his friend Bur-roughs at his home on the Hudson, now to his own Long Island birthplace, but oftenest to recuperate and to write charming nature descriptions at his retreat on Timber Creek—except for these furloughs Whitman was to spend the remainder of his days, and to be buried, in Camden.   In March, 1884, he bought a little house (328 Mickle Street, now 330) with the proceeds from the very successful Philadelphia edition of the *Leaves* in 1882.

This period, the final act of Whitman's unique life, was natur-

---

[1] Swinburne, who had in *Songs before Sunrise* hailed Whitman as a new force in literature, considerably retracted his praise in later publications.

ally not a climax of achievement, though it was a severe test of his patience and optimism, a test which, on the whole, he stood with unassuming courage. He sent forth occasional contributions to various American and British magazines and newspapers, besides new editions of his works. The most notable of these latter was the autographed Centennial or Author's Edition in two volumes of prose and verse (1876), designed to be sold in England, his best market, in order to relieve the straitened circumstances of the author, who was then "paralyzed . . . poor . . . expecting death," and who had been fleeced by his New York publishers; *Specimen Days and Collect* (1882–3), a "diary of an invalid," which contains some of Whitman's most characteristic prose and is a storehouse of autobiographical data; and *November Boughs* (1888), containing reprints of short poems that Whitman had been writing regularly for the New York *Herald* and of miscellaneous prose essays that had appeared elsewhere, the most significant of these being *A Backward Glance O'er Travel'd Roads*.

New friends were made, as faithful as the old. One was Dr. Richard Maurice Bucke, of Canada, who, like Burroughs, hailed the *Leaves of Grass* as "the bible of democracy" and wrote (1883) the first comprehensive biography of its author, to set him forth as a mystical saviour of the modern world. Another was Thomas B. Harned, in whose hospitable home the poet met, during these later years, not a few American and foreign notables. A third was Horace Traubel, who until Whitman's death was his daily visitor, who, without pay, assisted him in his dealings with printers and publishers, and who has for some years been publishing a minute diary of his talks with the poet during 1888–92. These three friends became, by Whitman's will, his literary excutors. Space is wanting to mention even the most prominent of that host of other visitors, American and foreign, who made Camden the object of their pilgrimages, some with a selfish desire to secure the poet's bold autograph, others with a reverent wish to pay homage to a liberator of the soul. One of the most sincere and unreserved of these tributes was that proffered by Mrs. Anne Gilchrist, the English author (then a widow), who through his poetry came to love the man[1] and who

---

[1] The love-letters of Anne Gilchrist and Walt Whitman have been edited and published by Thomas B. Harned.

later with her children spent two years (1876–1878) in Philadelphia in order to be near him. Assistance of a substantial nature from abroad, due in part to the efforts of Mrs. Gilchrist, who had been the first woman to defend the *Children of Adam* poems in print, together with similar if somewhat later help from a growing number of friends and readers in America, lightened the burdens of Whitman's last years, affording him comforts that would otherwise have been denied him and giving him hope that the tide of disapproval and misunderstanding which he had been breasting for half a lifetime was beginning at last to turn. When a complication of maladies finally resulted in his death, 26 March, 1892, he had "positively appeared," a prophet and a poet not without honour even in his own country. He was buried, with unique but impressive ceremony, beside a number of near relatives, in a massive and costly tomb which he had built for the purpose the preceding year. Most of his property, valued at a few thousand dollars, was left for the support of an imbecile brother, to care for whom Whitman had for many years saved money from his own small income.

The influence of Whitman has in the past taken three directions. Those of his readers who, like himself, attach most significance to the revolutionary and the religious elements in his writings have naturally been somewhat indifferent as to whether a place could be found for Whitman among the recognized literary coteries. To them he has been a seer profound enough and a lover sincere enough to render ordinary literary criticism an impertinence—unless such criticism would content itself with mere exegesis. On the other hand a growing number of readers have seen in Whitman—quite aside from a personality which, for all its philosophical breadth and its friendly sweetness, was hampered by an occasionally repellent sentimental egotism and a marked deficiency in taste—a genuine artist and a true poet. All manner of liberal political, sociological, and religious movements have been fathered on Whitman the seer and prophet; while Whitman the poet has become the legitimate founder of the various forms of modern free verse. Criticism that confounds this twofold claim and this twofold appeal of Whitman's writings is destined to make little progress, as is also that criticism which considers the two methods of approach to be necessarily exclusive. Still a third class of readers, uninterested in poets or prophets, as such, have gone to Whitman for the refreshing presence of a man and a writer who was entirely himself and who loved nature and his fellow men.

16

CHAPTER VIII

The New Nation

1. MARK TWAIN

SAMUEL LANGHORNE CLEMENS, more widely known as Mark Twain, was of the "bully breed" which Whitman had prophesied. Writing outside "the genteel tradition," he avowedly sought to please the masses, and he was elected to his high place in American literature by a tremendous popular vote, which was justified even in the opinion of severe critics by his exhibition of a masterpiece or so not unworthy of Le Sage or Cervantes. Time will diminish his bulk as it must that of every author of twenty-five volumes; but the great public which discovered him still cherishes most of his books; and his works, his character, and his career have now, and will continue to have, in addition to their strictly literary significance, a large illustrative value, which has been happily emphasized by Albert Bigelow Paine's admirable biography and collection of letters. Mark Twain is one of our great representative men. He is a fulfilled promise of American life. He proves the virtues of the land and the society in which he was born and fostered. He incarnates the spirit of an epoch of American history when the nation, territorially and spiritually enlarged, entered lustily upon new adventures. In the retrospect he looms for us with Whitman and Lincoln, recognizably his countrymen, out of the shadows of the Civil War, an unmistakable native son of an eager, westward-moving people—unconventional, self-reliant, mirthful, profane, realistic, cynical, boisterous, popular, tender-hearted, touched with chivalry, and permeated to the marrow of his bones with the sentiment of democratic society and with loyalty to American institutions.

By his birth at Florida, Missouri, 30 November, 1835, he was a Middle-Westerner; but by his inheritance from the restless, sanguine, unprosperous Virginian, his father, who had drifted with his family and slaves through Kentucky and Tennessee, he was a bit of a Southerner and still more of a migrant and a seeker of fortune. His boyhood he spent in the indolent semi-Southern town of Hannibal, Missouri, which, as he fondly represents it, slept for the most part like a cat in the sun, but stretched and rubbed its eyes when the Mississippi steamboats called, teasing his imagination with hints of the unexplored reaches of the river. When in 1847 his father died in poverty brightened by visions of wealth from the sale of his land in Tennessee, the son was glad to drop his lessons and go to work in the office of the Hannibal *Journal*. There, mainly under his visionary brother Orion, he served as printer and assistant editor for the next six years, and in verse and satirical skits made the first trials of his humour. In 1853, having promised his mother with hand on the Testament "not to throw a card or drink a drop of liquor," he set out on an excursion into the world, and worked his way for three or four years as printer in St. Louis, New York, Philadelphia, Keokuk, and Cincinnati.

Through the winter of 1856–7 he pleased himself with a project for making his fortune by collecting cocoa at the headwaters of the Amazon; and in the spring of 1857 he actually took passage on the *Paul Jones* for New Orleans. But falling into conversation with the pilot, Horace Bixby, he engaged himself with characteristic impulsiveness as an apprentice to that exacting, admired, and, as it then seemed to him, magnificently salaried king of the river. In return for five hundred dollars payable out of his first wages Bixby undertook to teach him the Mississippi from New Orleans to St. Louis so that he should have it "by heart." He mastered his twelve hundred miles of shifting current, and became a licensed pilot. In the process he acquired without the slightest consciousness of its uses his richest store of literary material.

"In that brief, sharp schooling," he wrote many years later, "I got personally and familiarly acquainted with all the different types of human nature that are to be found in fiction, biography, or history. When I find a well-drawn character in fiction or biography, I generally take a warm personal interest in him, for the reason that I have known him before—met him on the river."

This chapter of his experience was ended abruptly by the outbreak of the Civil War and the closing of the river. His brief and inglorious part in the ensuing conflict he has described, with decorations, in his *Private History of a Campaign that Failed*, a little work which indicates that he rushed to the aid of the Confederacy without much conviction, and that two weeks later he rushed away with still less regret. Eventually, it should be remarked, General Grant became his greatest living hero, and his attitude towards slavery became as passionately Northern as that of Mrs. Stowe.

Meanwhile he went West. On 26 July, 1861, he was sitting on the mail-bags behind the six galloping horses of the overland stage headed for Carson City, Nevada, as assistant to his brother Orion, who through the good offices of a friend in Lincoln's cabinet had been appointed Territorial secretary. On his arrival, finding himself without salary or duties, he explored the mining camps and caught the prevailing passion for huge quick wealth. First he bought "wild-cat" stock; then he located a vast timber claim on Lake Tahoe; then he tried quartz mining in the silver regions; prospected for gold in the placer country; and, in daily expectation of striking it fabulously rich, sank his brother's salary in the most promising "leads."

That his claims did not "pan out" well is clear from his accepting in 1862 a position as local reporter for the Virginia City *Enterprise* at twenty-five dollars a week, having commended himself to the editor by a series of letters signed "Josh." Thus began his literary career. In reporting for this paper the sessions of the Legislature at Carson City he first employed the signature "Mark Twain," a name previously used by a pilot-correspondent of the New Orleans *Picayune* but ultimately commemorating the leadsman's cry on the Mississippi. His effervescent spirits, excited by the stirring and heroically convivial life of a community of pioneers, found easy outlet in the robust humour and slashing satire of frontier journalism. In 1863 Artemus Ward spent three glorious weeks revelling with the newspaper men in Virginia City, recognized the talent of Mark Twain, and encouraged him to send his name eastward with a contribution to the New York Sunday *Mercury*. A duel occasioned by some journalistic vivacities resulted in his migration in 1864 to San Francisco, where in 1864 and 1865 he wrote for *The Morning Call, The Golden Era*, and *The Californian;* and fraternized with the brilliant young coterie of which Bret Harte was recognized as the most conspicuous light. In a pocket-hunting excursion in January, 1865, he picked up a very few nuggets and the nucleus for the story of *Jim Smiley and his Jumping Frog*, which appeared in the New York *Saturday Press* in November and swiftly attained wide celebrity. In the following spring he visited the Sandwich Islands on a commission from the Sacramento *Union*, called upon his first king, explored the crater of Kilauea, struck up a friendship with the American ministers to China and Japan, and made a great "scoop" by interviewing a group of shipwrecked sailors in the hospital at Honolulu. Later he wrote up the story for *Harper's Magazine;* his appearance there in 1866 he calls his *début* as a literary person.

Returning to San Francisco, he made his first appearance as a humorous lecturer in a discourse on the Sandwich Islands, delivered with his sober, inimitable, irresistible drawl to a crowded and applausive house on the evening of 2 October, 1866. From this point his main course was determined. Realizing that he had a substantial literary capital, he set out to invest it so that it would in every sense of the word yield the largest returns obtainable. To the enterprise of purveying literary entertainment he, first in America, applied the wide-ranging vision and versatile talents of our modern men of action and captains of industry: collecting his "raw material," distributing it around the world from the lecture platform, sending it to the daily press, reworking it into book form, inventing his own type-setting machinery, and controlling his own printing, publishing, and selling agencies. He did not foresee this all in 1866; but it must have begun to dawn upon him as a great possibility.

By repeating his Sandwich Islands lecture widely in California and Nevada he provided himself with means to travel, and revisited his home, returning by way of Panama and New York. In May, 1867, he published his first book, *The Celebrated Jumping Frog of Calaveras County, and Other Sketches*, and lectured in Cooper Institute. Then on 8 June he sailed on the *Quaker City* for a five months' excursion through the Mediterranean to the Holy Land, first reported in letters to *The Alta-California* and the New York *Tribune*, and immortalized by his book *Innocents Abroad*. On 2 February, 1870, he married his most sympathetic reader and severest censor, Olivia Langdon of Elmira, New York, a sister of one of the *Quaker City* pilgrims who had shown him her photograph in the Bay of Smyrna. After a brief unprofitable attempt to edit a newspaper in Buffalo, he moved in 1871 to Hartford, Connecticut, and in 1874 built there the home in which he lived for the next seventeen years experiencing, among many diversities of outer fortune, the high adventures in the history of his genius. It was there, or during this period, that he wrote his greatest books and reached the full maturity of his humour and dramatic energy.

He formed a close association with his neighbour Charles Dudley Warner; was taken under the editorial wing of William Dean Howells and into his intimate friendship; contributed to *The Atlantic Monthly, Harper's Magazine*, and *The North American Review;* and ultimately made some progress with such festive New Englanders as O. W. Holmes, F. J. Child, and T. B. Aldrich; but his head was white before he became as much of a lion in Boston and New York as he had been in Carson City and San Francisco. At various times he made extended sojourns in England, Italy, France, Germany, and Austria, particularly in his later years in seasons of pecuniary retrenchment. He reaped a fortune by contracting for the publication of Grant's *Memoirs* and his royalties were steadily large; but bad ventures in his publishing business, his somewhat lavish style of living, and his unperfected type-setting machine, in which he sank $200,000, pushed him finally into bankruptcy. He had extended his reputation in 1873 by lecturing for two months in London; he made a big reading tour with G. W. Cable in 1884–5; and in 1895, at the age of sixty, disdaining the advantages of bankruptcy, he set out on a lecturing tour of the world which took on something of the aspect of a royal progress and ended in the triumphant discharge of all his obligations. Then he collected another fortune and built himself his mansion Stormfield in Redding, Connecticut.

In his last years he spent a good deal of time in New York and Washington, and a variety of causes kept him pretty steadily in the public eye as a figure of national interest: his valiant assumption of his debts, his great tour, his growing habit of commenting on public affairs, the publication of sections of his autobiography, his domestic bereavements, and the foreign tributes and honours which gradually assured his somewhat incredulous countrymen that he was a great man of letters. His first academic recognition had come from Yale University, which created him Master of Arts in 1888; in 1901 Yale and in 1902 the University of Missouri conferred upon him the degree of Doctor of Letters; but the crowning academic glory fell in 1907 when the University of Oxford called him across the sea and robed him in scarlet and made him Doctor of Literature, amid, as he noted, "a very satisfactory hurrah" from the audience. On his return from a trip to the Bermudas he died 21 April, 1910.

Mark Twain's literary independence is generally conceded. Except for a certain flavour of Dickens in *The Gilded Age* there is hardly an indication of any important relationship between him and modern writers. He was a lover of the elemental in the midst of the refinements of an English and an American Victorian Age. "I can't stand George Eliot and Hawthorne and those people," he said. "And as for 'The Bostonians,' I would rather be damned to John Bunyan's heaven than read that." Modern fiction generally impressed him as namby-pamby and artificial. Jane Austen was his pet abhorrence, but he also detested Scott, primarily for his Toryism, and he poked fun at, Cooper for his inaccuracies. His taste for books was eminently masculine. The literary nourishment of his style he appears to have found chiefly in history, travel, biography, and such works of imagination as one puts on a "five-foot shelf" —Shakespeare and the Bible, Suetonius's *Lives of The Cæsars*, Malory, Cellini, *Don Quixote*, *Gil Blas*, the *Memoirs of Casanova*, Lecky's *History of Civilization*, and Carlyle's *French Revolution*.

In his prose as in the verse of Whitman there is an appearance of free improvisation concealing a more or less novel and deliberate art. "So far as I know," wrote W. D. Howells in 1901, "Mr. Clemens is the first writer to use in extended writing the fashion we all use in thinking, and to set down the thing that comes into his mind without fear or favour of the thing that went before, or the thing that may be about to follow." Beside this assertion of a spontaneity approaching artlessness let us put Professor Matthews's caution: "His colloquial ease should not hide from us his mastery of all the devices of rhetoric." In a letter to Aldrich he acknowledges great indebtedness to Bret Harte, "who trimmed and trained and schooled me patiently until he changed me from an awkward utterer of coarse grotesquenesses to a writer of paragraphs and chapters that have found a certain favour in the eyes of even some of the very decentest people in the land." Finally, let the reader who doubts whether he was conscious of his own art read carefully his little article, *How to Tell a Story*, beginning: "I do not claim that I can tell a story as it ought to be told. I only claim to know how a story ought to be told, for I have been almost daily in the company of the most expert story-tellers for many years." The art which he had learned of such American masters of oral rhetoric as Artemus Ward, John Phoenix, and J. H. Riley he tested and developed in print and by word of mouth with constant reference to its immediate effect upon a large audience. Those principles the observance of which he found essential to holding and entertaining his public he adopted and followed; but literary "laws" which proved irrelevant to his business as entertainer of the masses he disregarded at pleasure as negligible or out of place in a democratic Æsthetic. Howells calls him "the Lincoln of our literature"; and with that hint we may add that Mark Twain's power and limitations are alike related to his magnanimous ambition to beguile all the people all the time.

Let us begin our illustration of his literary character with a review of his five great books of travel. Against every one of them the charge might be brought that it is ill-composed: the chapters follow a certain chronological and geographical order; but the paragraphs frequently seem to owe their juxtaposition to the most casual association of ideas. This license, however, is the law and studied practice of his humour. "To bring incongruities and absurdities together in a wandering and sometimes purposeless way, and seem innocently unaware that they are absurdities, is the basis," he declares, "of the American art." He is speaking here specifically of the humorous story; but obviously he applies the same principle to the book of travel, which, as he conceives it, is a joyous miscellany. It is a miscellany but with ingredients preconsidered and formulable. He is as inflexible as Aristotle on the importance of choosing a great subject. He holds with the classicists that the proper study of mankind is man. He traverses in each book territory of world-wide interest. He describes what meets his eye with rapid, vivid, unconventional eloquence. He sketches the historical background in a highly personal fashion and gives to his interlarded legends an individual twist. While he imparts a good quantity of information, useful and diverting, he keeps the thread of his personal adventures spinning, rhapsodizes for a page, then clowns it for another, or introduces an elaborate burlesque on the enthusiasm of previous travellers. It is a prepared concoction.

The Innocents Abroad justified the formula on which it was constructed by selling nearly a hundred thousand copies at three dollars and a half apiece within the first three years. Its initial success was due partly to its novelty and partly to the wide interest which the excursion itself had excited. Both these advantages it has now relinquished, yet, as his biographer tells us, it remains the most popular of all Mark Twain's travel books, and still "outsells every other book in its particular field." Time has not reduced the rich variety of its famous topics, though time has somewhat altered the nature of curiosity with regard to the conduct of the pilgrims; but even though their type of tourist were now quite extinct one might still gratify the historical sense by acquaintance with a representative group of Americans on a tremendous picnic with spirits high in rebound from the long depression of the Civil War. One hears in the book the rollicking voice of the ex-pilot, ex-miner, the joyously insolent Western American, emancipated from all terror of the minor or Sunday-school vices, fortified by certain tolerant democratic standards of his own, well acquainted with the great American cities, equipped with ideas of natural beauty and sublimity acquired on the Mississippi, the Great Plains, the Rockies, the Pacific, the Sandwich Islands, setting out to see with his own unawed eyes how much truth there is in the reported wonders of the "little old world." Mark Twain describes Europe and the East for men, roughly speaking, like himself.   He does not undertake to tell them how they ought to look at objects of interest, but quite resolutely how these objects of interest strike a thoroughly honest Western-American eye.   He is obliged to report that the barbers, billiard tables, and hotel accommodations of Paris are inferior; that the paintings of the Old Masters are often in a bad state of repair and, at best, betray to a democrat a nauseous adulation of princely patrons; that the French grisettes wear mustaches; that Vesuvius and Lake Como are nothing to Kilauea and Lake Tahoe; that priest-ridden Italy is a "museum of magnificence and misery"; and that under close inspection the glamour of the Holy Land gives way to vivid impressions of fleas, beggars, hungry dogs, sandy wastes, and the odours of camels.   But this young traveller with so much of the iconoclastic Don Juan in him has also a strain of Childe Harold.   For him as for Byron the deepest charm of the old world is the charm of desolation and decay, felt when the dingy palaces of Venetian doges or the ruined marbles of Athens are bathed in the moonlight.   And he like Byron gains many an effect of his violent humour by the abruptness of his transitions from the sublime to the ridiculous or *vice versa*.   He interprets, for example, with noble gravity the face of the Sphinx:

After years of waiting, it was before me at last.   The great face was so sad, so earnest, so longing, so patient.   There was a dignity not of earth in its mien, and in its countenance a benignity such as never anything human wore.   It was stone, but it seemed sentient. If ever image of stone thought, it was thinking. . . .   All who know what pathos there is in memories of days that are accomplished and faces that have vanished—albeit only a trifling score of years gone by—will have some appreciation of the pathos that dwells in those grave eyes that look so steadfastly back upon the things they knew before History was born—before Tradition had being—things that were, and forms that moved, in a vague era which even Poetry and Romance scarce know of—and passed one by one away and left the stony dreamer solitary in the midst of a strange new age, and uncomprehended scenes.

But one turns the page and comes upon the engineer who feeds his locomotive with mummies, occasionally calling out pettishly, "D—n these plebeians, they don't burn worth a cent—pass out a king."

In *Roughing It* (1872) he chose a subject doubtless less interesting to some good people of the Atlantic seaboard than a European tour—the narrative of his journey across the plains to Carson City, and his life and adventures in Nevada, California, and the Sandwich Islands. Various critics, however, have preferred it to *Innocents Abroad* as a truer book; and in a sense the preference is justifiable. As literal history, to be sure, or as autobiography, it is untrustworthy. Mark Twain follows his own advice to Rudyard Kipling: "Young man, first get your facts; then distort them as you please." He distorts the facts in *Roughing It*, and vitalizes them by a poetical enlargement and interpretation thoroughly characteristic of native Western humour. In painting frontier manners, no longer an outsider, as he was in Europe, he abandons the attitude of one exposing illusions, and seeks to exhibit the West under the glamour of imagination. His coyote, turning with a smile upon the pursuing hound and vanishing with a "rushing sound, and the sudden splitting of a long crack in the atmosphere"— his coyote is a beast of fable; so is his jackrabbit; so is his broncho; so is his Brigham Young. On all his pioneers, his stage-drivers, his miners, his desperadoes, his boon-companions he has breathed with a heroizing emotion recollected in literary tranquillity. In the clear light of the vanished El Dorado of his youth they and their mountains and forests loom for him larger than common nature, more passionate, more picturesque.

A Tramp Abroad (1880) sprang from no such fund of delightful experience and mellow recollection but from an expedition to Europe deliberately undertaken in order to escape from the growing harassment of business responsibilities and to collect material for a book. Before he could work himself into a satisfactory writing mood he found it necessary to invent a new humorous attitude and literary character. His new invention has three parts. In the first place, he announces himself an enthusiastic and intrepid pedestrian but actually presents himself as a languid and timorous person travelling luxuriously with agent and courier by railway, steamboat, carriage, raft, or by any means to avoid the use of his legs. Secondly, he professes himself a devoted student of art and decorates his pages with infantile sketches. Finally, he assumes the air of a philologist seriously studying the German language. The first of these devices he handles in many places ingeniously and pleasantly, presenting an amusing satire on the indolent middle-aged tourist who climbs his Alps by telescope and gets his thrills on his hotel veranda out of the books of Edward Whymper; but in the elaborate burlesque ascent of the Riffleberg the humour becomes crudely farcical and tiresome. His drawings are not very expressive; and from their fewness it may be inferred that he discovered the fact. Some fellow philologists have found inexhaustible satisfaction in the German legends in German-English and in the appendices treating of "the awful German language" and the German newspaper—possibly also in the violent attack on Wagnerian opera. Other favourite passages of various qualities are those dealing with the grand affair between M. Gambetta and M. Fourtou, the sunrise on Mt. Riga, and the 47-mile hunt for a sock in Chapter XIII; but the humorous jewel of the collection is "Baker's Bluejay Yarn" in Chapter III—a trivial incident touched with imagination and related in a supremely delicious manner. The serious writing, as in the description of the Jungfrau and Heidelberg and the student duels, is so good that one wishes there were more of it.

For *Life on the Mississippi* (1883) Mark Twain drew again from the treasure of Western material which he had amassed before he became a professional humorist; and that distinguished connoisseur, the ex-Emperor William II of Germany, therein agreeing with the *portier* of the author's lodging in Berlin, informed the author that it was his favourite American book. More strictly speaking, it is the first twenty of the fifty-five chapters that do for the Mississippi Valley what *Roughing It* does for the Far West, namely, invest it with the charm of recollected experience and imaginative apprehension. The latter part of the book, which might have been called "The Mississippi Revisited," is the journalistic record of an excursion made with a stenographer in 1882; it contains interesting auto-biographical notes, admirable descriptive passages, a remarkable diatribe on Sir Walter Scott for perpetuating outworn chivalry in the South, an account of a meeting with G. W. Cable and Joel Chandler Harris in New Orleans, and miscellaneous yarns and information; but it is of distinctly secondary value.   Stead-ily throughout the first twenty chapters the writer is elate with his youthful memories of the drowsy towns by the river, the old barbaric raftsmen, the pride and power of the ancient race of pilots, and the high art and mystery of piloting those in-finitely various waters in the days before the war.   The moon-light, one of his characters fancies, was brighter before the war; and he himself, travelled now and acquainted with glory, has experienced, he believes, nothing so satisfying to his inmost sense as his life in that epical calling with its manly rigours, its robust hilarity, its deep, wholesome, unreflective happiness. The spirit that, years before, inspired Emerson's blandly ex-pressed desire to make Concord and Boston Bay as memorable as the storied places of Europe becomes in these pages clear, strong, resounding: it is the new national pride declaring the spiritual independence of America.   Not in peevish envy, with no anxiety about the ultimate answer, out of his knowledge and the depths of his conviction Mark Twain cries: "What are all the rivers of Damascus to the Father of Waters?"

The material for *Following the Equator* (1897) he collected under the strain of debt, ill health, and the fatigues of the im-mense lecture-tour undertaken in 1895.   In Australasia, to which the first half of the book is given, the people impress him as Englishmen democratized, that is to say, as Americans, and the cities and towns offer little noteworthy.   In order to exhibit novelties he is obliged to present the history of the early set-tlers, the aborigines, and the fauna; and as he gets up his facts by visits to museums and hasty digestion of Australasian liter-ature, his treatment strikes one as, for him, noticeably second-hand and uninspired.   He also introduces later a good deal of "lifted" material of a vivid sort in his account of the Sepoy Mutiny, Suttee, and the Thugs—and here we may note his taste for the collection of atrocious incident.   India, however, for which Kipling had sharpened his appetite, inspired him to the task of imparting his oppressed sense of her historic and scenic immensities, stricken with plagues, famines, ferocious beasts, superstitions, over-population, and swooning heat:

a haunting sense of the myriads of human lives that have blossomed, and withered, and perished here, repeating and repeating and repeating, century after century, and age after age, the barren and meaningless process; it is this sense that gives to this forlorn, uncomely land power to speak to the spirit and make friends with it; to speak to it with a voice bitter with satire, but eloquent with melancholy.

There are satirical and witty disquisitions on imperialistic morality apropos of Madagascar, the Jameson Raid, Cecil Rhodes, and the British dealings with the Boers. The barbarity of the civilized in contact with the so-called backward peoples excites his indignation, but history and travel show him its universality and quiet his sensibilities to a state of tolerant contempt for all unregenerate mankind: "Christian governments are as frank to-day, as open and above-board, in discussing projects for raiding each other's clothes-lines as ever they were before the Golden Rule came smiling into this inhospitable world and couldn't get a night's lodging anywhere."

Mark Twain's fiction, a large and highly diversified section of his total output, should be regarded as, hardly less than the travel books, the work of a humorist whose most characteristic form was a medley in divers keys. His critical champions used to allege that recognition of his sterling literary talent was delayed by his reputation as a creator of laughter. At the present time the danger is perhaps rather that some of his novels and tales will be unduly disparaged precisely because criticism has been persuaded to take them too seriously. With an instinct for an ingenious plot and unquestionable power of characterization within certain limits, Mark Twain sometimes lacked the ability and the patience and even the desire to carry a long piece of fiction through in the key on which he began. He would begin a story, for example, on the key of impressive realism, shift to commonplace melodrama, and end with roaring farce; and this amounts to saying that he did not himself steadily take his fiction writing seriously. He sometimes took it very lightly, like an improvising humorist; and the discords which affect the severely critical ear as blemishes probably struck his own ear as a joke. There is amusement in the most uneven of his novels if one relaxes to the point of reading it in the mixed moods in which it was written.

The most uneven of his novels is *The Gilded Age*, begun in collaboration with Charles Dudley Warner in February, 1873, on the spur of a dinner-table challenge, and finished in the following April. The authors were proud of their performance; and it has admirable points. The title is a masterly epigraph on the flushed, corrupt period of the Reconstruction. The stage is set as for the representation of "the great American novel," with scenes in New York, Philadelphia, Washington, St. Louis, and villages of New England and Tennessee. The plot is designed to bring typical Easterners and Westerners into diverting sentimental, financial, and political relations. There is a lively satirical play upon a wide range of clearly conceived characters and caricatures, exhibiting most of the elementary passions from love-making and fortune-hunting to bribing Congressmen and murder; and the sanguine, speculative Colonel Sellers, said to have been modelled on a relative of Mark Twain's but certainly also modelled on Orion Clemens and on Mark Twain himself, is an American rival to Micawber. The book bristles with interesting intentions and accomplishments; yet its total effect is a bewildering dissonance of moods and styles, which fills one with regret that Mark Twain did not cut loose from his literary partner and work out by himself the story of Obedstown, Tennessee, opened by him with a rich realistic flow in the first eleven chapters. With all its demerits on its head, the novel sold forty thousand copies within a couple of months after publication, and a play built around the character of Sellers was immensely successful on the stage. Later, in collaboration with Howells, Mark Twain made a second Sellers play showing the hero aspiring to an English earldom; and this he worked over into *The American Claimant* (1891), a generally farcical romance streaked with admirable realistic passages. One may mention here also, as springing perhaps from experience not utterly remote from that of Sellers, Clemens's exhibition of the effect upon character produced by expectation of unearned wealth in two capital short stories: *The Man that Corrupted Hadleyburg* (1899) and *The $30,000 Bequest* (1904).

Tom Sawyer, his second extended effort in fiction and his first masterpiece, he began as a play in 1872 and published in its present form in 1876.   The long incubation contributed to its unsurpassed unity of tone.   But the decisive fact is that his irresponsible and frequently extravagant fancy is here held in check by a serious artistic purpose, namely, to make an essentially faithful representation of the life of a real boy intimately known to him by memory and by introspection and by those deductions of the imaginative faculty which start from a solid basis of actuality.   His own boyhood, we may believe, and that of his companions in Hannibal, lives in this intensely vital narrative.   It is significant of his unwonted austerity in the composition that he wrote to Howells on its completion: "It is not a boy's book at all.   It will only be read by adults. It is only written for adults."   He had some justification for feeling that his newly finished manuscript broke a long taboo. He had taken a hero who was neither a model of youthful virtues nor a horrible example but was distinguished chiefly by pluck, imagination, and vanity, and had made him leader of a group of average little Missouri rascals running loose in an ordinary small river town and displaying, among other spontaneous impulses, all the "natural cussedness" of boyhood.   Furthermore he had made a central incident of a rather horrid murder.   Remembering the juvenile fiction of the Sunday-school library, he suspected that the story of these fighting, fibbing, pilfering, smoking, swearing scapegraces was not for young people.   But Howells, after reading about Aunt Polly, the whitewashing of the fenee, Tom's schoolboy love, Huck and the wart-cure, and the pirates' island, ordered the profanity deleted, and declared it the best boy story ever written; and that was near the truth.   In the two sequels *Tom Sawyer Abroad* (1894) and *Tom Sawyer, Detective* (1896), the plots are rather flimsy contrivances of the humorous fancy, but the stories are partly redeemed by the established reality of the actors and the raciness of the narrative which comes from the mouth of Huck Finn, a personage whom Mark Twain had taken over directly from his recollections of Hannibal.

The Prince and the Pauper (1881), a first venture in historical romance, was deliberately written for children and tested in the process of composition on the author's daughters.   The plot, suggested by Charlotte M. Yonge's *The Prince and the Page*, is fascinating to the youthful imagination; and the notion underlying it is to the older reader the most characteristic element in the book. The exchange of clothes and stations effected by Tom Canty and Prince Edward, later Edward VI, provided for the prince opportunities for feeling the common lot which the democratic author would gladly have given to all the monarchs of Europe. Occasionally writing over the heads of his audience, he utilizes the situation to express his inveterate sense of the evil of monarchical institutions and in particular his peculiarly flaming indignation at obsolete English penal laws. Humorous situations, sometimes tragically humorous, are abundant; but neither in the simple and vigorous prose of the narrative nor in the archaic style of the dialogue does one find at full strength the idiom and the first-hand observation for which one values *Tom Sawyer*. *The Prince and the Pauper* is a distinguished book in the class to which *Little Lord Fauntleroy* was added in 1886; but it is overshadowed by Mark Twain's own work.

The Adventures of Huckleberry Finn (1884) overshadows it; but that is nothing. *Huckleberry Finn* exceeds even *Tom Sawyer* almost as clearly as *Tom Sawyer* exceeds *The Prince and the Pauper*. Mark Twain had conceived the tale in 1876 as a sequel to the story of Tom. In the course of its long gestation he had revisited the Mississippi Valley and had published his superb commemoration of his own early life on the river. He wrote his second masterpiece of Mississippi fiction with a desire to express what in *Tom Sawyer* he had hardly attempted, what, indeed, came slowly into his possession, his sense of the half-barbaric charm and the romantic possibilities in that grey wilderness of moving water and the rough men who trafficked on it. He had given power to the earlier story by the representation of characters and incidents which are typical of the whole of American boyhood in rural communities in many parts of the country. He gave power to *Huckleberry Finn* by a selection of unusual characters and extraordinary incidents which are inseparably related to and illustrative of their special environment. He shifted heroes, displacing quick-witted, imaginative Tom by the village drunkard's son, because Huck in his hard, nonchalant, adventurous adolescence is a more distinctive product of the frontier. He changed the narrator, letting Huck tell his own story, in order to invest the entire narrative in its native garb and colour. Huck perhaps exhibits now and then a little more humour and feeling for nature than a picaro is entitled to possess; but in the main his point of view is well maintained. His strange captivity in his father's cabin, the great flight down the river, the mysteries of fog and night and current, the colloquy on King Sollermun, the superbly incidental narrative of the Grangerford-Shepherdson feud, the appealing devotion and affectionateness of Nigger Jim, Huck's case of conscience,—all are stamped with the peculiar comment of Huck's earthy, callous, but not insensitive soul. The stuff and manner of the tale are unique, and it is as imperishably substantial as *Robinson Crusoe*, whether one admire it with Andrew Lang as "a nearly flawless gem of romance and humour" or with Professor Matthews as "a marvellously accurate portrayal of a whole civilization."

A *Connecticut Yankee in King Arthur's Court* (1889) is a work of humorous invention set in motion by G. W. Cable, who first brought Malory's *Morte d'Arthur* to Mark Twain's attention. For assignable reasons it has not had the universal admiration enjoyed by *Huckleberry Finn;* Andrew Lang, for example, could not bring himself to read it; yet one might plausibly argue that it represents Mark Twain more completely than any other single book on his list, and so may serve as a touchstone to distinguish those who care for the man from those who only care for some of his stories. It displays every variety of his style from the mock-heroic and shirt-sleeve journalese of the Yankee's familiar vein to the careful euphonies of his descriptions of English landscape and the Dantean mordancy of the chapter "In the Queen's Dungeons." It exhibits his humour in moods from the grimmest to the gayest, mingling scenes of pathos, terror, and excruciating cruelty with hilarious comic inventions and adventures, which prove their validity for the imagination by abiding in the memory: the sewing-machine worked by the bowing hermit, the mules blushing at the jokes of the pilgrims, the expedition with Alisande, the contests with Merlin, the expedition with King Arthur, Launcelot and the bicycle squad, and the annihilation of the chivalry of England. The hero is, despite the title, no mere Yankee but Mark Twain's "personal representative"—acquainted with the machine shops of New Haven but acquainted also with navigation on the Mississippi and with Western journalism and with the use of the lariat.   The moment that he enters "the holy gloom" of history he becomes, as Mark Twain became when he went to Europe, the representative of democratic America, preaching the gospel of commonsense and practical improvement and liberty and equality and free thought inherited from Franklin, Paine, Jefferson, and Ingersoll.   Those to whom Malory's romance is a sacred book may fairly complain that the exhibition of the Arthurian realm is a brutal and libellous travesty, attributing to the legendary period of Arthur horrors which belong to medieval Spain and Italy.   Mark Twain admits the charge.   He takes his horrors where he finds them.   His wide-sweeping satirical purpose requires a comprehensive display of human ignorance, folly, and iniquity.   He must vent the flame of indignation which swept through him whenever he fixed his attention on human history—indignation against removable dirt, ignorance, injustice, and cruelty.   As a radical American, he ascribed a great share of these evils to monarchy, aristocracy, and an established church, and he made his contemporary references pointed and painful to English sensibilities. *A Connecticut Yankee* is his *Don Quixote*, a sincere book, full of lifelong convictions earnestly held, a book charged with a rude iconoclastic humour, intended like the work of Cervantes to hasten the end of an obsolescent civilization.   Whether it will finally be judged a great book will depend in considerable measure on factors outside itself, particularly on the prosperity of western democratic sentiment in the world at large.   Since the War of the German Invasions there has been an increase of Quixotism in his sense, and what used to be considered his unnecessary rage at windmills now looks like prophetic tilting at giants.

The volume containing *Pudd'nhead Wilson* and *Those Extraordinary Twins*, published in 1894, one is predisposed to value because it is another specimen from the Mississippi "lead."   It adds, however, relatively so little that is distinctive to the record that one is tempted to use it as an unsurpassable illustration of haphazard method in composition.   The picture of a two-headed freak had given him the cue for a "howling farce." When he began to write, the contemplated short story swiftly expanded, and there developed unexpectedly under his hand serious characters and a tragic situation unrelated to the initiating impulse. After long study he extracted the "farce" by "Cæsarean operation," and appended it with amusing explanations to the "tragedy" which it had set in motion. *Pudd'nhead Wilson*, disfigured by vestiges of the farce in the incredible Italian twins, is, like *The Gilded Age*, a discordant medley with powerful character-drawing in Roxana and her half-breed son, and with a somewhat feebly indicated novelty in the philosophical detective Pudd'nhead.

The last certified claimant for a position in the front rank of the novels is *Joan of Arc* (1896), a romance containing as its core the ascertained facts concerning one of the most problematic figures in secular history, and as its important imaginative expansion Mark Twain's conception of her familiar charm and his pictures of the battles and scenes of state and trials through which she passed. As in the somewhat similar case of the supernatural powers of Jesus, of which he was certainly sceptical, he says nothing to raise a doubt of the Maid's divine assistance; he neither explained nor attempted to explain away Joan's mystery. Her character, her Voices, and her mission he presents throughout with an air of absolute reverence and indeed at times with almost breathless adoration. For the reader in whom illusion is not destroyed by constant involuntary attention to the line where fact meets fiction the total impression is doubtless both beautiful and deeply moving. In the last section, at least, which deals with the trial and martyrdom, the most impatient reader of historical romance can hardly escape the pang of actuality; he is too near the facts. Recognizing that the book was quite out of his customary vein, Mark Twain published it first anonymously; yet in 1908 he wrote: "I like the *Joan of Arc* best of all my books and it is the best; I know it perfectly well. And besides, it furnished me seven times the pleasure afforded me by any of the others; 12 years of preparation & 2 years of writing. The others needed no preparation, & got none." This much we must admit: we are glad to have *Joan of Arc* on the shelf beside *A Connecticut Yankee* to complete our conception of that versatile and representative American whom we call Mark Twain.

Without it, and its little companion-piece, *In Defence of Harriet Shelley* (1894), we should have a harder task to prove, against those that take him for a hard unsanctified philistine, his invincible chivalry and fineness in relation to womankind, feelings precious in a free society, and fostered, as we like to think, by a thoroughly established American tradition.

But if we value a book in proportion to its saturation with its author's most distinctive qualities and in proportion to its power, exerted or latent, to affect the general literary current, we shall hardly rate *Joan of Arc* among Mark Twain's most interesting or significant books. In its utterly reverent treatment of the traditional and the supernatural it impresses one as a counterpoise obviously unequal to the task of making a balance with the great burden of naturalistic and radically iconoclastic writing in the other scale.

Mark Twain counts as an influence because he is an innovator. The great notes of his innovation from *Innocents Abroad* to *A Connecticut Yankee* are: first, the disillusioned treatment of history; second, the fearless exploitation of "the natural man," or, the next thing to it, "the free-born American"; and, lastly, a certain strain of naturalistic pessimism. In the first class go the foreign-travel books, *The Prince and the Pauper*, and *A Connecticut Yankee;* and the impulse properly proceeding from them is imaginative satire. In the second class go *Roughing It, Tom Sawyer, Life on the Mississippi, Huckleberry Finn, Adam's Diary*, and *Eve's Diary;* and from such work has proceeded an observable impulse to the cultivation of the indigenous, the elemental, the primitive, and, perhaps, the brutal and the sensual. For the third class one can glean representative paragraphs only here and there among the writings published in Mark Twain's lifetime; but the posthumously published philosophical dialogue *What is Man?* (1905) and *The Mysterious Stranger* (1916), a romance, and some of the letters are steeped in a naturalistic melancholy and tinged with a philosophical bitterness of which American literature before Mark Twain showed hardly a trace. That strain seems likely to be influential too, and, unfortunately, not always in connection with the fine bravado of his American faith, which occasionally required an antidote to its natural insolence.

2. Howells

IN the days of Fenimore Cooper it seemed a difficult task to
naturalize romance in the United States, so accustomed
was the national imagination to think of fiction as belonging to more ancient regions and of the American soil as being
the home of facts, without glamour or mystery. Romancers
had to prepare the soil as well as find the seed. Within a
generation, however, their work had been done with such
thoroughness that the rise of realism in America was notably
slower than in Europe. Balzac and Thackeray had no American contemporaries. Our native realists all came later, in-
structed by the art of Turgenev and Tolstoy, Flaubert and
Zola. The interval was devoted to the cult of local colour, which
applied the amiable charm of Irving or the quaint raciness of
Dickens to all the nooks and corners of the country. For the
most part the local colour writers, followers of Bret Harte as a
rule, were incurably sentimental, optimistic, romantic. What
especially interested them, and their readers, was the signs of
the past in the Old South or in New England, or the vivid face
of adventure on the new frontier. They liked to portray curious characters and unusual incidents, and in most sections of
the country they resisted the importation of realistic doctrine
and practice.

It was perhaps a certain bareness in Middle Western life,
lacking both the longer memories of the Atlantic States and
the splendid golden expectations of California, that very
early established in the upper Mississippi valley the realistic
tradition which descends unbroken through the work of Eggleston, E. W. Howe, Hamlin Garland, and Edgar Lee Masters.

From the Middle West, too, came the principal exponent of native realism, in himself almost an entire literary movement, almost an academy. William Dean Howells was born at Martin's Ferry, Ohio, 1 March, 1837, the grandson of a Welsh Quaker and the son of a country printer and editor. Like his friend Mark Twain he saw little of schools and nothing of colleges, and like him he got his systematic literary training from enforced duties as a printer and journalist. But, unlike Mark Twain, he fell as naturally into the best classical traditions as Goldsmith or Irving, who, with Cervantes, earliest delighted him. In *My Literary Passions* Howells has delicately recorded the development of his taste. At first he desired to write verse, and devoted months to imitating Pope in a youthful fanaticism for regularity and exactness. From this worship he turned, at about sixteen, to Shakespeare particularly to the histories; then to Chaucer, admired for his sense of earth in human life; and to Dickens, whose magic, Howells saw, was rough. Macaulay taught him to like criticism and furnished him an early model of prose style. Thackeray, Longfellow, Tennyson followed in due course. Having taught himself some Latin and Greek and more French and Spanish, Howells took up German and came under the spell of Heine, who dominated him longer than any other author and who showed him once for all that the dialect and subjects of literature should be the dialect and facts of life.

Poems in the manner of Heine won Howells a place in the *Atlantic*, then the very zenith of his aspiration, and in 1860 he undertook the reverent pilgrimage to New England which he recounts with such winning grace in *Literary Friends and Acquaintance*. Already a journalist of promise, and something of a poet, he made friends wherever he went and was reconfirmed in his literary ambitions. At the outbreak of the Civil War appointed United States consul at Venice, married at Paris in 1862 to Miss Elinor G. Mead of Vermont, he spent four years of almost undisturbed leisure in studying Italian literature, notably Dante, as the great authoritative voice of an age, and Goldoni, whom Howells called "the first of the realists." In Italy, though he wrote poetry for the most part, he formed the habit of close, sympathetic, humorous observation and discovered the ripe, easy style which made him, beginning with

Venetian Life (1866) and *Italian Journeys* (1867), one of the happiest of our literary travellers. From such work he moved, by the avenue of journalism, only gradually to fiction. On his return to the United States in 1865 he became, first, editorial contributor to *The Nation* for a few months, and then assistant editor and editor of the *Atlantic* until 1881.

The literary notices which he wrote for the *Atlantic* during these years of preparation would show, had he written nothing else, how strong and steady was his drift toward his mature creed. Not alone by deliberate thought nor even by the stimulus of polemic was he carried forward, but rather by a natural process of growth which, more than an artistic matter, included his entire philosophy. From his childhood he had been intensely humane—sensitive and charitable. This humaneness now revealed itself as a passionate love for the truth of human life and a suspicion, a quiet scorn, of those romantic dreams and superstitious exaggerations by which less contented lovers of life try to enrich it or to escape it. "Ah! poor Real Life," he wrote in his first novel, "can I make others share the delight I find in thy foolish and insipid face?" Perhaps *Their Wedding Journey* (1871) ought hardly to be called a novel, but it is a valuable Howells document in its zeal for common actuality and in its method, so nearly that of his travel books. *A Chance Acquaintance* (1873), more strictly a novel, for the first time showed that Howells could not only report customs and sketch characters felicitously but could also organize a plot with delicate skill. A young Bostonian, passionately in love with an intelligent but unsophisticated inland girl, who returns his love, is so little able to overcome his ingrained provincial snobbishness that he steadily con-descends to her until in the end he suddenly sees, as she sees, that he has played an ignoble and vulgar part which con-vincingly separates them. Nothing could be more subtle than the turn by which their relative positions are reversed. The style of *A Chance Acquaintance*, while not more graceful than that of Howells's earlier books, is more assured and crisp. The central idea is clearly conceived and the outlines sharp without being in any way cruel or cynical. The descriptions are exquisite, the dialogue both natural and revealing, and over and through all is a lambent mirth, an undeceived kindliness of wisdom, which was to remain his essential quality.

In 1869 he had published a metrical novel, *No Love Lost,* and in 1871 a volume of *Suburban Sketches;* he continued to write criticism and later began to write farces; but an increasing share of his energy now went to novels. The study of the conflict between different manners or grades of sophistication, taken up at about the same time by Henry James, concerned Howells largely, and appears in *A Foregone Conclusion* (1875), *The Lady of the Aroostook* (1879), and *A Fearful Responsibility* (1881). Writing of spiritualism and Shakerism in *An Undiscovered Country* (1880), he made clear his suspicion of those types of otherworldliness. And in 1882, with the publication of *A Modern Instance,* Howells assumed his proper rank as the chief native American realist, generally accepted also as the principal critic of realism.

The superiority of this book to all that had gone before can less justly be said to lie in its firmer grasp of its materials, for Howells from the first was extraordinarily sure of grasp, than in its larger control of larger materials. It has a richer timbre, a graver, deeper tone. Marcia Gaylord, the most passionate of all his heroines, is of all of them the most clearly yet lovingly conceived and elaborated. In the career of her husband, Bartley J. Hubbard, Howells accomplishes the difficult feat of tracing a metamorphosis, the increase of selfishness and vanity, fed in this case by Marcia's very devotion, into monstrous growths of evil without a redeeming tincture even of boldness—mere contemptibility. The process seems as simple as arithmetic, but, like all genuine growth, it actually resists analysis. The winter scenes of the earlier chapters, faithful and vivid beyond any prose which had yet been written about New England, drawn with an eye intensely on the fact, have still the larger bearings of a criticism of American village life in general. The subsequent adventures of the Hubbards in Boston, though so intensely local in setting and incident, are applicable everywhere. Squire Gaylord's arraignment of his son-in-law in the Indiana courtroom vibrates with a passion seldom met in Howells; and Bartley's virtual offer of his former wife to his former friend belongs with the unforgettable, unforgivable basenesses in fiction. After these episodes, however, it must be owned that an anticlimax follows in Halleck's discovery that his New England conscience will now forever hold him from Marcia because he had loved her before she was free.

Between 1881, when Howells resigned from the *Atlantic*, and 1886, when he began to write for *Harper's*, he had some years of leisure, particularly signalized by the publication in 1884 of the novel which brought him to the height of his reputation as well as of his art. The theme of *The Rise of Silas Lapham* is the universal one, very dear in a republic, of the rising fortunes of a man who has no aid but virtue and capacity. Lapham, a country-bred, "self-made" Vermonter, appears when he has already achieved wealth, and finds himself drawn, involuntarily enough, into the more difficult task of adjusting himself and his family to the manners of fastidious Boston. A writer primarily satirical might have been contented to make game of the situation. Howells, keenly as he sets forth the conflict of standards, goes beyond satire to a depth of meaning which comes only from a profound understanding of the part which artificial distinctions play in human life and a mellow pity that such little things can have such large consequences of pain and error. The conflict, however, while constantly pervasive in the book, does not usurp the action; the Lapham family has serious concerns that might arise in any social stratum. Most intense and dramatic of these is the fact that the suitor of one daughter is believed by the whole family to be in love with the other until the very moment of his declaration. The distress into which they are thrown is presented with a degree of comprehension rare in any novel, and here matched with a common sense which rises to something half-inspired in Lapham's perception—reduced to words, however, by a friendly clergyman—that in such a case superfluous self-sacrifice would be morbid and that, since none is guilty, one had better suffer than three. A certain rightness and soundness of feeling, indeed, govern the entire narrative. As it proceeds, as Lapham falls into heavy business vicissitudes and finally to comparative poverty again, and yet all the time rises in spiritual worth, the record steadily grows in that dignity and significance which, according to Howells's creed is founded only on absolute truth.

Silas Lapham marked the culmination of Howells's art,

approached the next year in the exquisite interlude *Indian Summer*, gayly, lightly, sweetly, pungently narrating the loves of a man of forty, and not quite approached in *The Minister's Charge* (1887), which shows a homespun poet moving in the direction of comfortable prose. But Howells had not yet shaped his final philosophy, which grew up within him after he had left Boston for New York in 1886 and had established his connection with *Harper's Magazine*. Again, as from the *Atlantic* literary notices, light falls upon his growth from the monthly articles which he wrote for "The Editor's Study" between 1886 and 1891. Chiefly discussions of current books, concerned with poetry, history, biography nearly as much as with fiction, these essays remarkably encouraged the growth of realism in America, and most eloquently commended to native readers such Latin realists as Valera, Valdés, Galdós, and Verga, and the great Russians Turgenev, Dostoevsky, and Tolstoy. It will not do to say that these foreign realists moulded Howells, for his development, whatever his readiness to assimilate, was always from within outward, but it helps to distinguish between the Howells who lived before 1886 and the one who lived after that date, to say that the earlier man had one of his supreme literary passions for the art of Turgenev, and that the later Howells, knowing Tolstoy, had become impatient of even the most secret artifice. For Tolstoy was Howells's great passion. "As much as one merely human being can help another I believe," said Howells, "that he has helped me; he has not influenced me in æsthetics only, but in ethics, too, so that I can never again see life in the way I saw it before I knew him." Tolstoy's novels seemed to Howells as perfect as his doctrine. "To my thinking they transcend in truth, which is the highest beauty, all other works of fiction that have been written. . . . [He] has a method which not only seems without artifice, but is so."

This was some ten years after Howells had first read Tolstoy, ten years during which, in spite of Tolstoy's example, he had not at all reverted to the preacher but had published many merry farces and had begun to be sunnily reminiscent in *A Boy's Town* (1890) But though too much himself to be converted from his artistic practice, Howells had broadened his field and deepened his inquiries. *A Hazard of New Fortunes*

(1889), in which Basil and Isabel March, the bridal couple of *Their Wedding Journey*, now grown middle aged, give up Boston, as Howells had himself recently done, for a future in New York, is not content to point out merely the unfamiliar fashions of life which they meet but is full of conscience regarding certain evils of the modern social order.   Or rather, Howells had turned from the clash of those lighter manners which belong to Comedy and had set himself to discuss the deeper manners of the race which belong to morals and religion.   He wrote at a moment of hope:

We had passed through a period of strong emotioning in the direction of the humaner economics, if I may phrase it so; the rich seemed not so much to despise the poor, the poor did not so hopelessly repine.   The solution of the riddle of the painful earth through the dreams of Henry George, through the dreams of Edward Bellamy, through the dreams of all the generous visionaries of the past, seemed not impossibly far off.[1]

In this mood Howells's theme compelled him so much that the story moved forward almost without his conscious agency, "though," he carefully insists, "I should not like to intimate anything mystical in the fact." *A Hazard of New Fortunes* outdoes all Howells's novels in the conduct of different groups of characters, in the superb naturalness with which now one and now another rises to the surface of the narrative and then retreats without a trace of management.   New Englanders, New Yorkers, Southerners, Westerners, all appear in their true native colours, as do the most diverse ranks of society, and many professions, in their proper dress and gesture.   The episode of the street-car strike, brought in near the end, dramatizes the struggle which has been heretofore in the novel rather a shadow than a fact, but Howells, artist first then partisan, employs it almost wholly as a sort of focal point to which the attention of all his characters is drawn, with the result that, having already revealed themselves generally, they are more particularly revealed in their varying degrees of sympathy for the great injustice out of which class war arises. In this manner, without extravagant emphasis,

[1] Preface dated July, 1909.

Howells judges a generation at the same time that he portrays it in the best of all novels of New York.

Howells's Tolstoyanism appears still more frankly in his two Utopian tales, *A Traveller from Altruria* (1894) and *Through the Eye of the Needle* (1907), in which he compares America with the lovely land of Altruria, where all work is honourable and servants are unknown, where capital and interest are only memories, where equality is complete, and men and women, in the midst of beauty, lead lives that are just, temperate, and kind. The stern tones of Tolstoy Howells never learned, or at least never used, for he could not lose his habitual kindness, even when he spoke most firmly. It was kindness, not timidity, however, for though he held steadily to his art he did not keep silence before even the most popular injustices. He plead for the Chicago "anarchists" and he condemned the annexation of the Philippines in clear, strong tones; no good cause lacked the support of his voice. He was extraordinarily fecund. After 1892 he succeeded George William Curtis in "The Easy Chair" of *Harper's* and wrote monthly articles which, less exclusively literary than the "Editor's Study" pieces, carried on the same tradition. His most significant critical writings, chiefly concerned with the art he himself practiced, are found in *Criticism and Fiction* (1891), *Heroines of Fiction* (1901), and *Literature and Life* (1902). Reminiscences and travels assume a still larger place in his later work. After *A Boy's Town* came *My Literary Passions* (1895), and then *Literary Friends and Acquaintance* (1900), of accounts of the classic age of Boston and Cambridge easily the best. He revisited Europe and left records in *London Films* (1905), *Certain Delightful English Towns* (1906), *Roman Holidays* (1908), *Seven English Cities* (1909), *Familiar Spanish Travels* (1913), in which he occasionally drew his matter out thin but in which he was never for a page dull, or untruthful, or sour, after the ancient habit of travellers. *My Mark Twain* (1910) is incomparably the finest of all the interpretations of Howells's great friend, while *Years of My Youth* (1916), written when the author was nearly eighty, is the work of a master whom age had made wise and left strong. In 1909 he was chosen president of the American Academy, and six years later he received the National Institute's gold medal "for distinguished work in fiction." He died 11 May, 1920.

The Institute rightly judged that, important as Howells is as critic and memoir-writer, he must be considered first of all a novelist. His later books of fiction make up a long list. That he could produce such an array of fiction is sign enough that he had not been overpowered by humanitarianism; a better sign is the fact that these later novels are even kinder, gayer, mellower than the early ones. In them his investigation moves over a wide area, which includes the solid realism of *The Landlord at Lion's Head* (1897) and *The Kentons* (1902); the sombre study of a crime in *The Quality of Mercy* (1892); the keen statement of problems in *An Imperative Duty* (1892) and *The Son of Royal Langbrith* (1904); happier topics as in *Miss Bellard's Inspiration* (1905); and, very notably, subtle explorations of what is or what seems to be the supersensual world in *The Shadow of a Dream* (1890), *Questionable Shapes* (1903)—short stories, *Between the Dark and the Daylight* (1907)—short stories, and *The Leatherwood God* (1916), which last, the study of a frontier impostor who proclaims himself a god, best hints at Howells's views of the relation between the real world which he had so long explored and so lovingly portrayed and those vast spaces which appear to be beyond it for the futile tempting of religionists and romanticists.

Holding so firmly to his religion of reality, and with his varied powers, it is not perhaps to be wondered at that Howells produced in his fourscore books the most considerable transcript of American life yet made by one man. Nor, of course, should it be wondered at, that in spite of his doctrine of impersonality the world of America as he has set it down is full of his benignance and noble health, never illicit or savage and but rarely sordid. His natural gentleness and reserve, even more than the decorous traditions of the seventies and eighties, kept him from the violent frankness of, say, Zola, whose books Howells thought "indecent through the facts that they nakedly represent." What Howells invariably practiced was a kind of selective realism, choosing his material as a sage chooses his words, decently. Most of his stories end "happily," that is, in congenial marriages with good expectations. He did not mind employing one favoured situation—in which a humorous husband and a serious wife find themselves responsible for a young girl during her courtship— so often as to suggest a personal experience. Not without some complaint, he nevertheless not too rebelliously accepted the modern novelist's fate of writing largely for women, a sex which in Howells's world appears as often shallow and changeful and almost always quite unreasonable. Thus limited as to subjects by his temper and his times, he was likewise limited as to treatment. On every ground he preferred to make relatively little of impassioned or tragic moments, believing that the true bulk of life is to be represented by its commonplaces. "It will not do," he wrote, speaking of the ducal palace at Weimar, "to lift either houses or men far out of the average; they become spectacles, ceremonies; they cease to have charm, to have character, which belong to the levels of life, where alone there are ease and comfort, and human nature may be itself, with all the little delightful differences repressed in those who represent and typify."[1]   (The pendulum had swung far since the days when Cooper and Hawthorne repined over the democratic barrenness of American manners!)   No one has written more engaging commonplaces than Howells, though perhaps something like the century which has elapsed since the death of Jane Austen—Howells's ideal among English novelists—will have to pass before the historian can be sure that work artistically flawless may be kept alive, lacking malice or intensity, by ease and grace and charm, by kind wisdom and thoughtful mirth.

3. Henry James

HENRY JAMES was born an American and died an Englishman. He might never have formally transferred his allegiance had it not been for the War and our long delay in espousing the Allied cause. He became a British subject in July, 1915. The transfer had, however, been virtually made many decades earlier. Of the two ruling passions of James, one was surely his passion for "Europe." Of this infatuation the reader will find the most explicit record in his fragmentary book of reminiscences, *The Middle Years* (1917), record and whimsical apology which may well serve the needs of other Americans pleading indulgence for the same offence. James loved Europe, as do all "passionate pilgrims," for the thick-crowding literary and historical associations which made it seem more alive than the more bustling scene this side the water. Going to breakfast in London was an adventure,—being not, as at Harvard, merely one of the incidents of boarding, but a social function, calling up "the ghosts of Byron and Sheridan and Scott and Moore and Lockhart and Rogers and *tutti quanti*." In America, James had never so taken breakfast except once with a Boston lady frankly reminiscent of London, and once with Howells fresh from his Venetian post, and so "all in the Venetian manner." Everybody in Victorian London had, as he calls it, references—that is, associations, appeal to the historic imagination; and, as he humorously confesses, "a reference was then, to my mind, whether in a person or an object, the most becoming ornament possible." It was "with bated breath" that he approached the paintings of Titian in the old National Gallery; and when, in the presence of the Bacchus and Ariadne, he became aware,

at the same moment, of the auburn head and eager talk of
Swinburne, his cup for that day ran over. With the best of
introductions to the Rome of Story, the London of Lord
Houghton, the highest ambition of James was to establish
"connections" of his own with a world in which everything
so bristled with connections; and it is he who lets us know
with what joy he found himself, on the occasion of his first
visit to George Eliot, running for the doctor in her service,
since thereby "a relation had been dramatically determined."

But it is only in the light of his other ruling passion that
we can rightly understand the force of his passion for Europe.
Even more rooted was his love for art, the art of representation.
All his pilgriming in London and elsewhere was by way of
collecting a fund of material to draw upon "as soon as ever one
should seriously get to work." And is it surprising that he
should have been impressed with the greater eligibility of the
foreign material; that his impressions of New York and Boston
seemed to him "negative" or "thin" or "flat" beside the corresponding impressions of London? The old world was one
which had been lived in and had taken on the expressive character of places long associated with human use. It was not
simply the individual object of observation, but the "cross-ref-
erences"; or, again, the association of one object with another
and with the past, making up altogether a "composition."
Whatever person or setting caught his attention, it was always
because it "would fall into a picture or a scene." Of the
heroine of *The American*, a young French woman of rank, the
hero observed that she was "a kind of historical formation."
And along with his material, James found abroad a favourable
air in which to do his work. There he found those stimulating
contacts, there he could observe from within those movements
in the world of art, which were of such prime importance for his
own development. Lambert Strether, in *The Ambassadors*,
represents the deprivations of a man of letters, strikingly
suggestive in many ways of James himself, condemned to labour
in the provincial darkness of "Woollett Massachusetts."

In all this our American author seems identified with
anything but the American scene; and the case is not altered
when we consider his stories on the side of form. His form is
not American, nor his preoccupation with form. It is as

18

strictly international as that of Poe. James was a profound admirer of Hawthorne; but so was he an admirer of Balzac and of George Sand, and it is probably to later models than any of these that he owes whatever is most characteristic in his technique. There is at any rate nothing here drawn from American sources rather than from European; nothing which we can claim as our production.

Yet we have reasons for our claim upon him. This very passion for Europe, as he has exhibited it in himself and in so many of his creatures, this European "adventure" of Lambert Strether and Isabel Archer (of *The Portrait of a Lady*)—what more purely American product can be conceived? Even to the conscientiousness with which young James did his London sightseeing, mindful of his own feeble health, which threatened to cut it short, and above all mindful "that what he was doing, could he but put it through, would be intimately good for him!"

Altogether his theme turned out to be quite as much American character as European setting. We must not forget how predominantly his novels, and how frequently his short stories, have for their subject Americans,—Americans abroad, or even Americans at home seen in the light of foreign observation. In this connection the novels in particular may be divided into three groups, falling chronologically into three periods. In the first period, extending from *Roderick Hudson* to *The Bostonians*, 1875 to 1885, the leading characters are invariably Americans, though the scene is half the time abroad. In the second period, from *The Princess Casamassima* to *The Sacred Fount*, 1885 to 1901, the novels confine themselves rather strictly to English society. In the third period, from *The Wings of the Dove* to the novels left unfinished at the author's death, 1902 to 1917, James returned to his engrossing, and by far his most interesting, theme of Americans in Paris or Venice or London. Not a very original contribution to literature is the American scene itself—the New York of *Washington Square* (1881), the Boston of *The Europeans* (1878) and *The Bostonians;* and none of these novels was included by James in the New York Edition. His American settings are but palely conceived; and his figures do not find here the proper background to bring them out and set off their special character. But the crusading Americans—variegated types, comic and romantic—with the foreign settings in which they so perfectly find themselves, these make up a local province as distinct in colour and feature as those of Cable and Bret Harte, —a province quite as American, in its way, and for the artist quite as much of a *trouvaille*, or lucky strike.

These Americans abroad fall naturally into two classes. The first are treated in the mildly comic vein, as examples of American crudeness or simplicity. Such are the unhappy Ruck family of *The Pension Beaurepas*,—poor Mr. Ruck who had come abroad in hopes of regaining health and escaping financial worries, and his ladies whose interest in the old world is confined to the shops where money can be spent. Perhaps we might refer to this class Christopher Newman, the self-possessed and efficient American business man, hero of *The American* (1877); though in his case the comedy of character is by no means broad, and is strictly subordinate to the larger comedy of social contrast. In general, these people are treated not unkindly; and there is the one famous instance of *Daisy Miller*, in which the fresh little American girl is so tenderly handled as to set tears flowing—a most unusual proceeding with James. Generally the Americans emerge from the international comedy with the reader's esteem for sterling virtues not always exhibited by the more sophisticated Europeans. In the later group of stories in particular, the American character, presented with no hint of comic bias, actually shines with the lustre of a superior spiritual fineness. This is what Rebecca West has in mind in her somewhat impatient reference to James's characters as American old maids, or words to that effect.

And here we have the very heart of his Americanism, if we may make bold to call it that. There is something in James's estimate of spiritual values so fine, so immaterial, so indifferent to success or happiness or whatever merely practical issues, as to suggest nothing so much as the transcendentalism of Emerson, the otherworldliness of Hawthorne. There is here a psychology not of Scott or Thackeray, not even of George Eliot, still less of any conceivable Continental novelist; and one can hardly refer it to any but a New England origin and a date in New England's silver age.

William James, the novelist's grandfather, was an Irishman settled in Albany.   He was described in a New York newspaper of 1832 as "the Albany business man"; and he laboured so well at business that he left several millions to be divided among twelve heirs.   Otherwise the relatives of the novelist were quite innocent of practical affairs.   His father, Henry James, was a philosopher-clergyman, a friend of Emerson's, who carried with him everywhere the entire works of Swedenborg.   Henry James, Jr., was born 15 April, 1843, in New York; but he went to Europe as a babe in arms.   Two years later, still in long clothes and waggling his feet, he noted from the carriage window "a stately square surrounded with high-roofed houses and having in the centre a tall and glorious column"—the reader will recognize the Place Vendôme. From the earliest times, in New York and Albany, all his conceptions of culture had a transatlantic origin.   The caricatures of Gavarni, Nash's lithographs of *The Mansions of England*, the novels of Dickens read aloud in the family circle, —these fed his imagination.   He and his brothers went regularly to a New York bookseller for a boys' magazine published in London.   Even their sense of a "political order" was derived from Leech's drawings in *Punch*.   Their education was amazingly various and spasmodic,—better adapted, one might suppose, to the formation of novelists than of philosophers.   Dozens of private schools and tutors succeeded one another in bewildering rapidity in New York, not to speak of later instruction in Bonn and Geneva, in Paris and London, back and forth.

All this while the main occupation of the future novelist was the contemplative observation of character.   The world of Albany and New York was a world not of vulgar persons but of artistic "values."   Everyone was interesting as a "type": type of "personal France" or of French "adventuress" (referring to early governesses), type of orphan cousins, type of wild young man.   Cousin Henry was a kind of Mr. Dick, cousin Helen a kind of Miss Trotwood.   James's account in *A Small Boy and Others* shows him in those early days a mere vessel of impressions suitable to the uses of art.   All this was fostered by the kind of discipline, or no discipline, maintained by their metaphysical father.   For religion, the boys went to all the churches, and, we gather, in much the spirit in which they approached any other æsthetic experience. As for livelihood, or occupation, the father was always inclined to discourage any immediate decision upon that point, lest a young man might prematurely limit the development of his inner life. We are reminded how small a place is taken in the stories of James by what men do to earn a living. In America, it seemed, there were—apart from the unique case of Daniel Webster—but two possible destinies for a young man. Either he went into business or he went to the dogs. But the immediate family and connections of James were always aspiring to that more liberal foreign order in which was offered the third alternative of a person neither busy nor tipsy,—a cultivated and agreeable person of leisure.

In 1860 the family went to live in Newport, so that the older brother might work in the studio of William Morris Hunt; and Henry, who had earlier haunted the galleries of Paris with his brother, welcomed this occasion to frequent a place devoted to the making of pictures. In 1862, William being at Lawrence Scientific School, Henry entered the Harvard Law School; still noting, in boarding-house or lecture-room, personalities, chiaroscuro, *mise en scène*, more than the precedents of law. The Civil War was the one distinctly American fact which seems to have penetrated the consciousness of Henry James. While he was prevented by lameness from going to war himself, it was brought home to him, for one thing, by the participation of two of his brothers. But the war, like everything else, was followed by him, however breathlessly, as a spectacle rich in artistic values. In 1864 the family were living in Boston, and from 1866 they were definitely settled in Cambridge, William entering the Harvard Medical School in that year; and in these days the young author was forming excitingly important literary connections. One friendship dating from this time was that with E. L. Godkin, editor of the newly founded *Nation*. But most important no doubt was that with the Nortons of Shady Hill, who later introduced him to London society.

In 1870 died the person to whom James refers with the greatest personal affection, his cousin Mary Temple, the model for Milly Theale in *The Wings of the Dove*, as he tells us, and

also—as we guess—for Isabel Archer of *The Portrait of a Lady*
and more than one other of his loveliest American women.
Of her death he says "we felt it together as the end of our
youth." So far he brings the family record in his *Notes of a
Son and Brother* (1914). Meanwhile in 1869 occurred the
visit to London recorded in *The Middle Years*. To 1872
belongs a perhaps equally memorable visit to Italy. And
from that time forward until his death, 28 February, 1916,
he lived abroad; during the first years largely in Italy and
France ("inimitable France" and "incomparable Italy"), and
then, from about the year 1880, in the England of his adoption,—making his bachelor home in London or in the old
Cinque Port of Rye. But he continued almost to the end to
publish his novels and tales in the great American magazines,
so that his first appeal was generally to the public here.

Evidences of the honour in which he was held in England
were the Order of Merit conferred upon him at New Year's,
1916; and his portrait by Sargent, undertaken on the occasion
of his seventieth birthday, at the invitation of some two hundred and fifty English friends. At the outbreak of the War,
none was more enthusiastic for the cause of the Allies, which
was associated with everything he held most precious. His
feeling for England at this time, on looking out across the
channel from his Sussex home, is described in what is perhaps
his latest piece of writing, *Within the Rim*, published in the
Fortnightly Review in August, 1917. It has been said that his
mortal illness was provoked by the vigour with which he took
up the work of relief for suffering Belgium and France.

James began his literary career as an anonymous contributor of reviews to *The North American Review* and *The Nation;*
and such reviews and literary news-letters he continued to
write for many years. Only a small part of his critical writing
has appeared in book form; and it still remains for the curious
to trace the development of his literary theory from the
beginning. His books of fiction were frequently supplemented,
too, with books of impressions, in which he might commune
at length with the spirit of places,—English, French, American,
Italian. He also wrote many plays, a few of which made
brief appearances on the London stage. But they were

"talky" and untheatrical; and he succeeded neither in purging the theatre of the commercialism he deprecated nor even in taking the public fancy himself. His first attempts at fiction were printed in *The Atlantic Monthly* and *The Galaxy;* but he hardly emerges as an author of account before the appearance of *The Passionate Pilgrim* in 1871. His first important novel was *Roderick Hudson*, published in *The Atlantic* in 1875. His first and only approach to popularity, whether in long or short story, was made by *Daisy Miller* in 1878. The New York Edition of his novels and tales, published during the years 1907 to 1909, is of the greatest interest because of the extended discussion of his own work and the account of his imaginative processes found in the Prefaces. It is, however, very far from being a complete collection even of his works of fiction. It is simply the choice made by James at that late date, and according to his taste as it had then developed, of such of his stories as he wished to be known by. It remains to be seen how far posterity will submit to his judgment in the matter.

The threefold grouping of his novels already suggested was in connection with the treatment of American themes. In reference to form and method a more illuminating division would be one of two periods: first, *Roderick Hudson* to *The Tragic Muse*, 1875–1890; and second, *The Spoils of Poynton* to *The Sense of the Past*, 1896–1917.

In the novels of the first group, he includes, in general, more material than in the later ones, more incident, a greater number of characters, a more extended period of time; and he treats his material in the larger, more open, more lively manner of the main English tradition. He also chooses, in the earlier period, what may be considered more ambitious themes in the matter of psychology. In *Roderick Hudson*, for example, he undertakes to trace the degeneration of a man of genius, a young American sculptor, when given the freedom of the artistic life in Rome. This evolutionary—or revolutionary— process of character, suggestive of George Eliot, is a "larger order" than he would ever have taken on in the later period. In *The Tragic Muse* he reverts to the theme of the artistic tempera- ment—this time in disagreement with the world of affairs; and he develops it by means of two great interrelated stories, one dealing with an actress, one with a painter. In the later

years he would not have undertaken thus to tell two stories at
the same time; and perhaps the artistic temperament itself
would have seemed to him too ambitious a theme.   In the
earlier period, again, we find him sometimes treating subjects
touching on political or the more practical social problems,
though indeed his interest was never primarily in the problems.
The Bostonians is a somewhat satirical study, at one and the
same time, of the Boston character and of feminism; while in
The Princess Casamassima the leading persons are revolutionary socialists, and political murder lurks in the background.
Probably the best, as well as the best liked, of the earlier
novels is *The Portrait of a Lady* (1881), which records at
length the European initiation of a generous-souled American
girl.

In the course of six years between the first and second
periods no novel of James was published; but during that
interim came the culmination of his long activity as a short-
story writer. It was his tendency always to subordinate incident
to character, to subordinate character as such to situation—or
the relations among the characters; and in situation or character, to prefer something rather out of the ordinary, some aspect
or type not too obviously interesting but calling for insight and
subtlety in the interpretation.   Good examples, in the short
story, of this predilection are *The Pupil*, *The Real Thing*, and
The Altar of the Dead, all appearing in the early nineties; and
a little later, *The Beldonald Holbein* and *The Turn of the Screw*,
most haunting of ghost stories.   In *The Beldonald Holbein*
the beautiful great lady has chosen for her companion a
supposedly unattractive middle-aged American woman, who
will admirably serve as a foil to her beauty.   But certain
painters of her acquaintance having discovered that the foil is
herself remarkably "beautiful"—that is, distinguished, significant of feature, a subject worthy of Holbein—it becomes
necessary to send her back home and get another companion
with less character engraved upon her countenance.   How one
of the artists gets his revenge by painting Lady Beldonald
in all the splendour of her mediocrity is not the point of interest;
the point of interest is the fine discrimination shown by artist
—and author, and reader—in evidence of their superior good
taste.

Each tale of James is thus an "initiation" into some social or artistic or spiritual value not obvious to the vulgar. And each tale is a quiet picture, a social study, rather than the smart anecdote prescribed by our doctors of the "short-story." James is not rigorous in his limitation of the short story to the magazine length; so that his tales are as likely to take the form of the more leisurely *nouvelle* as of the brief and sketchy *conte*. And so it was not surprising to find a tale intended originally for a magazine short story enlarging itself by insensible degrees into what is practically a novel. Such was the case with *The Spoils of Poynton*, one of his finest stories, which has the length of a novel, together with the restricted subject-matter, the continuity, and economy of the short story.

But these traits, it is clear, had already grown to be James's ideals for a narrative of whatever length. They were the ideals of many of the foreign novelists whose personal influence had swayed him in Paris; and to a considerable extent those of George Eliot, whose influence upon him must have been mediate, working through her French imitators, as well as emanating directly from her own work. More and more, serious novelists were denying themselves the breezy and picturesque variety of materials, the broad free stroke, of the old masters, in favour of a dramatic limitation, a dramatic closeness of weave, a scientific minuteness of detail, an intimate psychological notation, and a pictorial (as distinguished from picturesque) consistency of tone,—all of which we find in their extremest development in the later novels of James. This is what makes the international character of his art. Note should be taken, of course, of a certain fussiness and long-windedness, as well as a certain tendency to the abstract, which are partly to be set down to the score of personal idiosyncrasy. But in general he is clearly following the ideals of George Eliot, of Flaubert, of Turgenev. Perhaps too we should admit the suggestion of F. M. Hueffer, who would trace back the lineage of James, through Stendhal and other French writers, ultimately to Richardson, the early master of the technique of manifold fine strokes, of the close and sentimental study of souls.

Along with *The Spoils of Poynton* may be mentioned,

among the later novels, *The Sacred Fount* (1901) and *What Maisie Knew* (1897) as partaking somewhat of the nature of long short stories. *What Maisie Knew* is, by the way, in a class by itself, not merely for reasons of technique too special to be considered here, but also by reason of the great charm of the little girl,—so naïve, so earnest, so much a lady and so much a girl, whose experience of evil is the subject of the story.

For the full-fledged novels of the later period, it will suffice to state briefly the themes of *The Awkward Age* (1899) and *The Golden Bowl* (1904)—without prejudice, however, to the special claims of *The Ambassadors*, the novel considered by James himself to be his most perfect work of art. *The Awkward Age* is concerned with the adjustment called for in a certain London circle by the emergence of the *jeune fille* and the consideration due her innocence of the world. The adjustments prove to be very extensive, but almost wholly subjective, and leaving things very much where they were before so far as any outward signs go. The book is almost literally all talk,—the talk of people the most "civilized" and "modern," people the most shy of "vulgarity," who have ever been put in a book. It is a fascinating performance—for those who have the patience to read it. *The Golden Bowl* is a study of a theme not unlike that of *The Portrait of a Lady*. It is the story of an American girl who marries an Italian prince, and the strategy by which she wins his loyal affection. The time covered is much shorter than that in the *Portrait*, the important characters only about half as many, the amount of action much smaller: and there is little change of scene as compared with the earlier novel. The length of the book is about the same; and the space saved by these various economies is devoted to the leisurely development of a single situation as it shaped itself gradually in the minds of those participating, the steady deepening of a sense of mystery and misgiving, the tightening of emotional tension, to a degree that means great drama for all readers for whom it does not mean a very dull book.

For many readers it certainly means a very dull book. In this recipe for a story almost everything has been discarded which was the staple of the earlier English novel, even of George Eliot,—exciting incident, dramatic situation, highly-coloured character and dialogue, humour, philosophy, social comment. Indeed, we may almost say the story itself has been thrown out with the rest. For in the later novels and tales of James there is not so much a story told as a *situation revealed;* revealed to the characters and so to us; and the process of gradual revelation, the calculated "release" of one item after another—that is the plot. It is as if we were present at the painting of a picture by a distinguished artist, as if we were invited to follow the successive strokes by which this or that detail of his conception was made to bloom upon the canvas; and when the last bit of oil had been applied, he should turn to us and say "Now you have heard Sordello's story told." Some of us would be satisfied with the excitement of having assisted at such a function, considering also the picture which had thus come into being. Others,—and it is human nature, no doubt,—would exclaim in vexed bewilderment "But *I* have heard no *story* told!"

The stories of James tend to be records of seeing rather than of doing. The characters are more like patients than agents; their business seems to be to register impressions; to receive illumination rather than to make up their minds and set about deeds. But this is a way of conceiving our human business by no means confined to these novels; is it not more or less characteristic of the whole period in which James wrote? One passes by insensible degrees from the world of Renan to that of Pater and Swinburne, and thence to that of Oscar Wilde and of writers yet living, in whom the cult of impressions has been carried to lengths yet more extreme.

Among all these names the most significant here seems to be that of Walter Pater, whose style and tone of writing—corresponding to his intellectual quality and bias—more nearly anticipate the style of James than do those of any other writer, English or French. It does not matter that Pater's subject is the art of the past and James's the life of the present. No two writers were ever more concerned with mere "impressions," and impressions mean for them discriminations, intimate impressions, subtle and finely sympathetic interpretations. None ever found it necessary, in order to render the special quality of their impressions, to try them in so many different lights, to accompany their statements with so many qualifications and reservations: impulses giving rise to sentences more curiously complex and of longer breath than were ever penned by writers of like pith and moment.   They were both of them averse to that raising of the voice, that vehement or emphatic manner, characteristic of the earlier Victorians and supposed to be associated with strong feelings and firm principles.   These reasonable and well-bred writers, if they ever had strong feelings or firm principles, could be trusted to dissimulate them under a tone of quiet urbanity.   They abhorred abrupt transitions and violent attitudes.   They proceed ever in their discourse smoothly and without marked inflection, softly, as among tea-tables, or like persons with weak hearts who must guard themselves against excitement.   There is a kind of hieratic gentleness and fastidiousness,—and yet withal a hint of breath-less awe, of restrained enthusiasm,—in the manner in which they celebrate the mysteries of their religion of culture, their religion of art.

This, we say of James, is anything but American, indige-nous; this is the *Zeitgeist;* this is the spirit of England in the "æsthetic nineties" reacting against the spirit of England in the time of Carlyle.   But then we think of the "passionate pilgrimage" of Isabel Archer and the others; we think of James's *Middle Years;* we think, it may be, of ourselves and eastward prostrations of our own.   And we realize that what the romancer has conjured up is a world not strange to our experience.   His genius is not the less American for present-ing us, before all things, this vision of a bride rushing into the arms of her bridegroom: vision of the mystic marriage (shall we say?) of new-world faith and old-world culture.

4. Lanier

THE conditions of Reconstruction were inimical to the production of literature. The life of the South, always sluggish, now became stagnant. A country of farms and plantations, there were in it few large cities to foster an intellectual life. The large planters whose travel and experience in government and statesmanship rendered them natural leaders were downcast by the sudden destruction of their wealth in slaves and soil. The poor whites lived too close to mother earth, and were too densely ignorant to furnish a public for literary activity. The isolation of the whole South was heart-sickening. Newspapers were few and ill-informed. Schools and colleges were few and far between. Even the will to attend them had to be fostered with great care. In short, literature in the section was impossible except for those with an unquenchable longing for expression. Nevertheless, in these devastated regions here and there existed persons with just such unquenchable longings, and they increased in number as the economic conditions of the South improved and despondency gradually waned. Southern orators lifted up voices that grew more and more hopeful. Northern periodicals and Northern publishers were hospitable, were even eager to give the South a hearing. The old rhetoric gave way to a less turgid idiom. Recrimination and defiance went out of date. Within a generation the sting of defeat was succeeded in many quarters by a new national spirit and a new allegiance to a common flag.

The most salient figure in this change, in fact the most distinguished man of letters of the New South, is Sidney Lanier, who was admirably endowed with a double gift—music and poetry. He was born in Macon, Georgia, 3 February, 1846.

His father was a lawyer of undistinguished abilities but of cultured and literary tastes. His mother was devotedly religious, and reared her family in the strict Presbyterian faith. His grandfather's hotel, the Lanier House, was the centre of a cordial, hospitable social life. The city of Macon, a prosperous commercial centre, counted among its citizens many wealthy plantation owners but few who aspired to higher education or intellectual achievement. Even his father's literary interests seem to have been confined to Shakespeare and Addison and Sir Walter Scott—to the items of that self-sufficient culture which reigned everywhere in the South before the Civil War.

Although Scott and Froissart fired Lanier's young mind with ideals of chivalry, the thing which set him apart from the Macon school boys was his remarkable musical ability. At seven he had made himself a reed flageolet, and on receiving a flute at Christmas he soon organized quartets and bands among his playfellows. Indeed, it was because of his leadership in serenading parties at Oglethorpe, which he had entered shortly before his fifteenth birthday, that his father brought him home to spend a year in the Macon post office. When he returned to Oglethorpe as a junior he began to play the violin with such effect that he would at times lose consciousness for hours. His father, fearing this stimulation, induced him to return to the flute and discouraged him as much as possible from devotion to music. The result is seen in the boy's journal:

The prime inclination—that is, natural bent (which I have checked, though) of my nature is to music, and for that I have the greatest talent; indeed, not boasting, for God gave it me, I have an extraordinary musical talent, and feel it within me plainly that I could rise as high as any composer. But I cannot bring myself to believe that I was intended for a musician, because it seems so small a business in comparison with other things which, it seems to me, I might do.

His later life seems to bear out the assumption that America, by his father's solicitude and the social pressure of Southern opinion at the time, was deprived of another distinguished name in music.

The life at Oglethorpe was a period of intellectual advance for Lanier. The major influence was exerted by James Woodrow of the department of science, who took the boy on long rambles, or on long drives, when the two of them would talk about everything either of them was interested in. Woodrow thought so much of Lanier that he secured for him an appointment as tutor. Better still, he gave the future poet a zest for science that remained with him to the end, and a vision of the intellectual life which shaped his aspirations and his future conduct. Giving up music as a possible career, Lanier resolved to spend two years in Heidelberg and to return to a professorship in some American college.

Then came the cataclysm of Civil War, and with it for Lanier a period of storm and stress that tossed him this way and that for a dozen years. At the outbreak he was enthusiastic at the prospect of a South more wealthy than history had yet seen. Macon, he thought, was to become a great art centre whose streets were to be lined with marble statues like unto Athens of old. At the close of the college year he, like nearly all the other teachers and the students of Oglethorpe, enlisted for service. The war itself was not an unmixed evil to Lanier. Although he saw some exciting service as a signalman along the James River, he was for three years allowed ample time for study and for cherishing that passion for the very highest which grew with his years. He now began to contemplate a literary life as his vocation. To his father he wrote in 1864, "Gradually I find that my whole soul is merging itself into this business of writing, and especially of writing poetry." He began his novel, *Tiger Lilies*, and sent several poems to his father for criticism. In 1864, however, he was transferred to Wilmington, North Carolina, where he served as signal officer on the blockade runners. In November he was captured in the Gulf Stream and sent to Point Lookout Prison in Maryland. There he continued to play the flute, which won him the friendship of Tabb. He busied himself with German poetry, but the prison conditions were so loathsome as to induce a breakdown in health. He came out emaciated to a skeleton, and when he finally reached Macon in March he fell ill and lingered near death for two months. Thereafter his life was an unavailing search for health.

The fact that members of his family "who used to roll in wealth are, everyday, with their own hands ploughing the little patch of ground which the war has left them, while their wives do the cooking and washing," did not disturb him. What he felt most keenly was the intellectual stagnation of the South. Already in 1866 he was, with characteristic breadth and lack of prejudice, writing thus to a Northern friend:

You are all so alive up there, and we are all so dead down here! I begin to have serious thoughts of emigrating to your country, so that I may live a little. There is not enough attrition of mind on mind here to bring out any sparks from a man.

Even among these untoward surroundings he continued to foster his literary ambitions. In another letter he continues:

We have no newspapers here with circulation enough to excite our ambition, and, of course, the Northern papers are beyond our reach. Our literary life, too, is a lonely and somewhat cheerless one; for beyond our father, a man of considerable literary acquirements and exquisite taste, we have not been able to find a single individual who sympathized in such pursuits enough to warrant showing him our little productions—so scarce is "general cultivation" here.

I am thirsty to know what is going on in the great art world up there; you have no idea how benighted we all are. I have only recently begun to get into the doings of literary men through "The Round Table" which I have just commenced taking.

That journal not only satisfied his thirst for the doings of the great world but helped to foster the national spirit which he was to voice more clearly than other poets of his section, and to fire his own ambition for a literary career. Several of his earlier poems appeared in its pages.

To the same inspiration may be traced his visit to New York in 1867 to find a publisher for *Tiger Lilies*. Possibly it was the reputation he gained from its publication which caused him to marry in the face of the precarious future. The setting up of the state governments under the Reconstruction Act of 1867 made the prospect for him, as for hundreds of others, even darker and more discouraging. Despairing of earning a living by his pen, and seeing that Southern colleges were so poor as "to hold out absolutely no inducement in the way of support to a professor," he yielded in January, 1869, to his father's solicitation and betook himself to the study of law.

The work in the law office kept him very busy. He did indeed write a few humorous dialect poems, published in various local papers, but in general his resignation was that expressed in a letter to Paul Hamilton Hayne in 1870:

> I've not put pen to paper, in the literary way, for a long time. How I thirst to do so, how I long to sing a thousand various songs that oppress me, unsung,—is inexpressible. Yet, the mere work that brings bread gives me no time. I know not, after all, if this is a sorrowful thing. Nobody likes my poems, except two or three friends,—who are themselves poets, and can supply themselves!

But music regained its ascendancy over him. Letters to his wife written in 1869, 1870, and 1871, on visits to New York, reveal the intensity of his pleasure in a violin solo, or the singing of Nilsson, or Theodore Thomas's orchestra, where he plunged into an amber sea of music and came away from what he felt might have been heaven.

The turning point of his life came in San Antonio, Texas, whither he went in the winter of 1872–3 for his health. He filled in part of his time there with literary projects, but the inspiration of his stay was found in a group of German musicians, who received "amid a storm of applause" his flute-playing before the *Maennerchor*. In February, 1873, he played before "a very elegant-looking company of ladies and gentlemen." He reported:

> I had not played three seconds before a profound silence reigned among the people. . . . When I allowed the last note to die, a simultaneous cry of pleasure broke forth from men and women that almost amounted to a shout, and I stood and received the congratulations that thereupon came in, so wrought up by my own playing with (hidden) thoughts, that I could but smile mechanically, and make stereotyped returns to the pleasant sayings, what time my heart worked falteringly, like a mouth that is about to cry.

Two weeks later he wrote:

I have writ the most beautiful piece "Field-larks and Black-birds," wherein I have mirrored Mr. Field-lark's pretty eloquence so that I doubt he would know the difference betwixt the flute and his own voice.

In the summer he confessed to Hayne:

Are you, by the way, a musician? Strange, that I have never before asked this question,—when so much of my own life consists of music. I don't know that I've ever told you, that whatever turn I have for art is purely musical; poetry being, with me, a mere tangent into which I shoot sometimes. I could play passably on several instruments before I could write legibly; and since then, the very deepest of my life has been filled with music, which I have studied and cultivated far more than poetry.

Inspired with this new faith, he again repaired to New York, this time determined to settle his future. He revelled in the musical associations which he quickly formed. By November he had been engaged by Asger Hamerik for the position of first flute in the new Peabody Orchestra forming in Baltimore. On 29 November he wrote his declaration of independence to his father:

Why should I, nay, how *can* I, settle myself down to be a third-rate struggling lawyer for the balance of my little life as long as there is a certainty almost absolute that I can do some other thing so much better. Several persons, from whose judgment there can be no appeal, have told me, for instance, that I am the greatest flute-player in the world; and several others, of equally authoritative judgment, have given me an almost equal encouragement to work with my pen. . . . My dear father, think how for twenty years, through poverty, through pain, through weariness, through sickness, through the uncongenial atmosphere of a farcical college and of a bare army and then of an exacting business life, through all the discouragements of being wholly unacquainted with literary people and literary ways—I say, think how, in spite of all these depressing circumstances, and of a thousand more which I could enumerate, those two figures of music and poetry have steadily kept in my heart so that I could not banish them. Does it not seem to you as to me, that I begin to have a right to enroll myself among the devotees of those two sublime arts, after having followed them so long and so humbly, and through so much bitterness.

Thus he entered upon the third and final period of his life, one of feverish activity. During the winter succeeding his great resolution he grew rapidly in the intellectual grasp of music. He had the soul of an artist, and gradually acquired the technical skill to bring the most out of his instrument. Still the strength of his renderings always resided in the emotion he imparted. His conductor testifies:

His conception of music was not reached by any analytical study of note by note, was intuitive, spontaneous; like a woman's reason: he felt it so, because he felt it so, and his delicate perception required no more logical form of reasoning. His playing appealed to the musically learned and unlearned—for he would mesmerize the listener; but the artist felt in his performance the superiority of the momentary living inspiration to all the rules and shifts of mere technical scholarship.

The next year he still yearned for a musical career. He told Dr. Leopold Damrosch, then conductor of the Philharmonic Society of New York, that music "is not a matter of mere preference, it is a spiritual necessity. I must be a musician, I cannot help it." But the conference with Damrosch impressed Lanier with the great handicap he suffered in lack of thorough technical training. Though he continued to gain intense joy from music, literature more and more occupied his thoughts and monopolized his time.

In February, 1875, *Corn*, which he had conceived the preceding summer and had rewritten during the winter, appeared in *Lippincott's Magazine*. It was one of the earliest Southern poems to receive publication in a Northern periodical. Notable, too, is the fact that the verses are not an effort to escape into some dreamland but the presentation of a widespread problem of Georgia agriculture.

Corn attracted favourable attention, notably from Gibson Peacock, editor of the Philadelphia *Evening Bulletin*. Within a month Lanier was at work on a second ambitious poem, *The Symphony*, which appeared in June, and which brought him the friendship of Bayard Taylor. The firm of Lippincott was able to fill Lanier's time with hackwork. The whole summer was spent in preparing "a sort of spiritualized guide-book" to Florida. Yet he was happy. He wrote of himself as one

who, after many days and nights of tribulation and bloody sweat, has finally emerged from all doubt into the quiet and yet joyful activity of one who knows exactly what his *Great Passion* is and what his God desires him to do. As for me, life has resolved simply into a time during which I must get upon paper as many as possible of the poems with which my heart is stuffed like a schoolboy's pocket.

When at the instance of Bayard Taylor he was appointed to write the cantata for the Centennial Exposition to be held in Philadelphia, he was jubilant. His patriotic fervour produced also *The Psalm of the West.* A place among American poets he challenged by bringing out a slender volume of poems late in the same year.

Because of a severe illness he was ordered South for the winter of 1876–7, but there he continued to throw off "a sort of spray of little songs" and to hope for "that repose which ought to fill the artist's firmament while he is creating."

The four remaining years of his life were spent in an unavailing search for that repose. He endeavoured to make sure where next week's dinners were coming from before carrying out his ambitions for creative work. He continued his connection with the Peabody Orchestra, but his chief endeavour turned him aside, this time into the field of scholarship. He wandered about in Old and Middle English, and ranged far in the Elizabethan period. These enthusiastic studies resulted in lectures at the Peabody Institute, and in 1879 in his appointment as lecturer in Johns Hopkins University. *The Science of English Verse* and *The English Novel* are the products of those two years, besides some books for boys and many poems. But consumption had made such advances that it was feared that he would not live to complete his last series of lectures. Indeed, those who listened to him momentarily feared that he would not survive to the end of the hour. In May, 1881, he was taken to the mountains of North Carolina, where he died 7 September.

What shall be said of the product of this eager and varied effort? Shall we lament the incompleteness and immaturity of a life fourteen years longer than Keats's and ten years longer than Shelley's? Shall we bemoan the constant battle with disease, which yet left to Stevenson the energy for an exquisitely wrought style? Shall we bewail the hard necessity of winning his daily bread in a land devastated by civil war and depressed by corrupt government, and the consequent removal to a more congenial and invigorating clime far from friends and family? Or shall we endeavour merely to disengage the essential characteristics and achievements of this troublous activity, so that his contribution to our American heritage may stand out clear?

He did, of course, engage in too much hackwork for his own good or his reputation. Yet so exuberant was his activity that he dispatched all of these tasks with zest. His "sort of spiritualized guide-book" to Florida contains many descriptions over which he must have lingered and which bear witness to a quick eye and a rich humour. He puts into the whole book, too, much of himself, his love of music, his over-refining intellect, his relish of local tradition. His boys' books, the Froissart and King Arthur and the rest, reveal even more of the man. He had from early youth cherished a recurring interest in the deeds and heroes of chivalry. They answered to an innate knightliness of spirit which was fostered by his Southern up-bringing. He would pick up the volume as it came fresh from the printers, familiar though it was by reason of the preparation and the proof-reading, and con page after page with pure delight. In his introductions he never learned to address his young readers, but through the mature style gleams his absorption in this fresh new world of romance.

The same personal reaction appears in his critical writings. The zeal with which he pursued these researches during the last years of his life astonishes one who remembers the meagre initiation he had received at college into the methods of scholarship. The attainments, too, of those few years are considerable. He read with an assiduity that helped to shorten his days and with a whole-souled enthusiasm and moral earnestness that lent to his utterances much of the fluency and high seriousness of Ruskin. But even greater than Ruskin's is his tendency to wander. He did not keep the goal in view.

He did not sift and arrange and clarify with a dominant impression in mind. He sauntered along the broad highway, frequently wandering off into the leafy woods and lingering there intent on the strange foliage. Consequently his critical writings are an amazing collection of individual vagaries and intuitive insights. *Shakespeare and his Forerunners* contains such surprising pronouncements as that Drummond of Hawthornden is "one of the chief glories of the English tongue." Yet he could often divine an essential quality, as in his remark on Chaucer's works as "full of cunning hints and twinkle-eyed suggestions which peep between the lines like the comely faces of country children between the fence-bars as one rides by."

The same want of the perspective and balance that come from broad and profound knowledge characterizes his lectures on *The English Novel*. His effort to trace the conception of personality from the time of the Greeks was a perilous undertaking for one who knew so little of Greek life and was so little acquainted with the sociological implications of any such investigation. The limitations of his upbringing also militated against success. The strict Presbyterian training of his childhood as well as an inherent moral bias conspired to give him a strongly ethical view of literature:

Indeed, we may say that he who has not yet perceived how artistic beauty and moral beauty are convergent lines which run back into a common ideal origin, and who is therefore not afire with moral beauty just as with artistic beauty; that he, in short, who has not come to that state of quiet and eternal frenzy in which the beauty of holiness and the holiness of beauty mean one thing, burn as one fire, shine as one light within him, he is not the great artist.

Consequently he fervently wished that the novels of Fielding and Richardson might be "blotted from the face of the earth." Consequently, too, "in some particulars *Silas Marner* is the most remarkable novel in our language," and its author the greatest of English novelists. The preachments in which he again reminds one of Ruskin are the most interesting portions, because in them the man Lanier shines out and his cherished and innate convictions lie bare.

The most valuable critical work of Lanier is undoubtedly

his *Science of English Verse*. For the consideration of the structure of English verse he was peculiarly well prepared. His own unusually sensitive organism enabled him to respond very delicately to musical effects in verse. Besides, the early impulse to science given by Professor Woodrow in that "farcical college" of his boyhood stimulated him to an investigation of the physics of sound and to a desire for reducing to law the apparent chaos of English versification. The result was pioneer work which appealed to many as the most sensible treatment of the subject which had then appeared. What differentiates this treatment from preceding ones is the insistence that the laws of music and verse are identical, that every foot represents a mathematically equal time interval. Length of interval, and not accent, is therefore the determining element in prosody. The valuable feature of this theory is that it emphasizes the relation of music and poetry and the fundamental importance of rhythm in poetry. Its unfortunate feature is that it insists too strongly on law. No such mathematical relation exists. Accent normally appears at equal time intervals and an accented syllable tends to acquire length. But Lanier wrote long before the psychological investigation of rhythm had begun. He therefore could not see the impossibility of trying to reduce to one rule all the innumerable individual senses of rhythm. Not only no two poets but no two readers would exactly coincide in their sense of rhythm. Lanier was on the right road. He merely made the mistake of taking his own sense of rhythm for a universal law.

Of his other prose writings the letters are the most important. They reveal the man with unusual fullness—the pulsating sea of emotion in which he lived, his exuberance, his passionate love of music, his wavering literary ambition, his buoyancy and humour and occasional despondency, together with his intellectual interests and preferences. Few letters written in America are more interesting. Yet on first dipping into them one is repelled by the same qualities which frequently give one pause in his other writings. The style seems highly artificial, fanciful in its imagery, strained and rhetorical in its phrasing, bookish and precious in its diction. Even in his last years he was rarely simple and direct, for he had from boyhood so steeped himself in the older writers of our tongue, Shakespeare in particular, that a plain and natural way of putting things would have seemed to him insipid, inane, and inartistic. The literary glamour which he casts over his writings, which draws attention from the thought itself to some supposed felicity of expression, never entirely left him. Yet some of his later books, particularly where he is pouring forth his convictions on music, literature, and life, possess all the fluency of the Old South, without ceasing to be strong, luminous, and eloquent.

These shortcomings have been explained away on the ground that his prose is the prose of a poet. Certainly it is as a poet that he jumps to the front rank among Southern writers. The single volume of his verse, gathered with loving care by his wife three years after his death, is paramount among his writings. Upon that corner-stone must be reared whatever reputation he may attain in American letters. Yet his poetry too suffers from defects similar to those in his prose. His verse in general betrays a lack of spontaneity without obtaining that finish, that technical polish, that wedding of word and thought which Tabb achieved. There are, to be sure, moments of fine phrasing, intermittent flashes from the heaven of song:

> Music is love in search of a word

or

> For when God frowns, 'tis then ye shine.

But the general impression is of an elaborated verse, not a gush of words from the heart. Indeed, it seems to have been Lanier's practice to write out the ideas of his poems in prose before turning them into verse. Not many of his poems sang themselves over in his soul before he committed them to paper. He was, on the other hand, forever haunted by ideas for poems. As an obscure lawyer in Georgia he complained to Paul Hamilton Hayne of the "thousand various songs that oppress me, unsung." Even after he had won the ear of the nation, he wrote to Gibson Peacock:

I'm taken with a poem pretty nearly every day, and have to content myself with making a note of its train of thought on the back of whatever letter is in my pocket. I don't write it out because I find my poetry now wholly unsatisfactory.

Sometimes a poem, like *The Symphony*, would shake him like a James River ague until he had finished it. Sometimes he would revise patiently, as in *Corn*. In general it is true that he did not work in that calm serenity which might have brought him closer to perfection of form. There is one blemish, however, that no amount of revision would have eliminated. His exuberant fancy betrayed him into conceits as far fetched as ever disfigured Donne or Crashaw or Tabb. An ox in a clover field becomes "the Course-of-Things," and the rising sun is "the Build-fire Bee." He did not see the grotesqueness of such comparisons, but cultivated them as original adornments to his verse.

Some of the dissatisfaction with the form of his verse is due to his theory that the principles of music and of metrics are identical. His sense of rhythm did not allow sufficient emphasis for accent as marking the equal intervals of time. But he was, naturally, enamoured of his own theory and felt happier when he put it into practice. Of *Special Pleading*, composed in 1875, he wrote: "I have allowed myself to treat words, similes, and metres with such freedom as I desired. The result convinces me I can do so safely." Thereafter he developed his own peculiar style more courageously, sometimes with beautiful effect, but often with the resulting impression of a straining for form. In *Sunrise*, for example, there is a passage descriptive of approaching dawn, beginning,

> Oh, what if a sound should be made!

which is unsurpassed in American poetry for its rendering of the ecstasy in the poet's heart. Yet only a few lines above this marvellous description is a section beginning,

> Ye lispers, whisperers, singers in storms

which illustrates how far his attention wandered from the thought in his elaboration of form, how he forgot that words are primarily symbolic, and that beauty of verse depends on poetic and beautiful thoughts.

Indeed, it must be confessed that Lanier's thought is liable on analysis to be found commonplace and prosaic. This quality is partly due to a didacticism that issued from an un-

swerving devotion to the ideal.   From his youth he cherished
a longing for the very highest.   How amid the uninspiring
surroundings of his boyhood he should have developed this
allegiance to the "sweet, living lands of Art" is another of those
mysteries with which the history of literature abounds.   Yet
there is no mystery about the moral purpose which led him to
employ poetry to combat intolerance, brutality, and commercialism.   It was bred into him at his mother's knee.   There
is no cynicism in his verse.   There is a very strong religious
strain.   Not only does he curiously eschew all mythological
allusions as being pagan in spirit, but he expresses a deeply
religious view of life in many poems, as in *The Crystal* and that
quaint but unsurpassed *Ballad of Trees and the Master*.

His idealism is also revealed in his eager intellectual interests.   Here too he triumphed over his untoward surroundings,
as the brief sketch of his life has indicated.   Pathetic witness
to this inherent bent is found in a letter to Bayard Taylor:

I could never describe to you what a mere drought and famine
my life has been, as regards that multitude of matters which I
fancy one absorbs when one is in an atmosphere of art, or when one
is in conversational relationship with men of letters, with travellers,
with persons who have either seen, or written, or done large things.
Perhaps you know that, with us of the younger generation in the
South since the war, pretty much the whole of life has been merely
not dying.

Such complaints did not remain topics of conversation or
correspondence.   He sought in poetry no refuge from the hard
conditions of life.   Rather is he one of the leaders of the New
South because he grasped at the intellectual and social problems
of the time.   He dealt with the necessity of planting corn for
cotton, with the nascent oppression of labour by capital, with
the mission of music and art.   His reading of Emerson in the
winter of 1876–7 revived an earlier penchant for metaphysics
and led to such poems as *A Florida Sunday* and *Individuality*.
If these abstruse problems are not handled with power, they at
least do honour to the author's lofty purpose and sincerity of
execution.

It must be conceded, too, that the profound and abiding
interests of his life—love and nature—are peculiarly Southern

in their colouring and substance. It is characteristic that love
is for him not that fleshly passion which has thrilled and burned
in verse since Sappho. It is a kneeling adoration, an ideal
emotion, the only love which one of his purity of life would
avow. He has been well called the Sir Galahad of American
literature. *My Springs* shows how deep and sincere was the
inspiration he received from his dearest partner in misfortune
and ill-health. But there was mingled with the personal devotion to one woman a chivalric devotion to women which came
partly from the Southern ideals of his day. There is in his
poetry no better expression of this than in *The Symphony*.

Nature was to him almost equally dear, and even more
Southern in its appeal. He found nothing within to answer
to the wild and rugged majesty of the mountains. He felt no
expansion of the soul in viewing the limitless plains of Texas.
The broad sand-flats of Florida roused only a longing for the
Georgia hills. Indeed, the only scene which called forth a love
of broad, free places was the long and often viewed marshes at
Brunswick, Georgia, which will go down in American literature
in the eloquent and musical *Marshes of Glynn*. It remains
true, however, that his love for nature was a delicate and
passionate love, the love of an attentive and scrupulous observer of leaves and plants and the thousand minute details of
the summer woods. So personal was the solace and uplifting
of nature that he addressed her various forms with terms of
endearment, more warm than Tabb, yet precisely like St.
Francis of Assisi. He sings of the "fair cousin Cloud," the
"friendly, sisterly, sweetheart leaves." Of himself it was
true that,

> With hands agrope he felt smooth nature's grace,
> Drew her to breast and kissed her sweetheart face.

The Southern aspect of nature lives again in his verse.

Though his abiding interests were Southern, he was not
narrowly Southern in his outlook. On the contrary, it has
already been indicated that much of Lanier's distinction
among Reconstruction poets lies not only in his interest in the
problems of his own time but likewise his sympathy and
comprehension in voicing the new idea of nationality. The

freedom from prejudice which led him to resume relations with a Northern friend at the close of the war, fitted him to sing the meditations of Columbia at the Philadelphia Centennial in 1876. There was nothing mean or narrow in his make-up. The breadth of his own soul and the exalted purpose of his life responded quickly to the new outlook before the nation. He leaped far ahead of his section in grasping and appropriating what he might of the new quickening spirit, but he was largely influential, with Lamar and Grady, in bringing the South to share in that quickening influence. He likewise revealed to the North, even before Grady, the possibilities of the recently vanquished section, and thereby hastened that spiritual *rapprochement* which went on steadily increasing to the end of the century. If Lanier had only had for poetic expression that genius which he apparently possessed for music, what position might he not have attained? With what full-throated ease then would the South at the Reconstruction period have sung out its inmost heart!

5. Harris

APART from its purely literary significance, *Uncle Remus: his Songs and his Sayings* makes a threefold claim upon our interest. (1) In the character of Uncle Remus the author has done more than add a new figure to literature; he has typified a race and thus perpetuated a vanishing civilization. (2) In the stories told by Uncle Remus the author has brought the folk-tales of the negro into literature and thus laid the foundation for the scientific study of negro folk-lore. His work has, therefore, a purely historical and ethnological value not possessed in equal degree by any other volume of American short stories. (3) In the language spoken by Uncle Remus the author has reproduced a dialect so accurately and so adequately that each story is worth studying as marking a stage in the development of primitive English.

The life of Joel Chandler Harris was comparatively uneventful though it was an ideal preparation for the work that he was to do. He was born in Eatonton, Putnam County, Georgia, 9 December, 1848,—a date now celebrated annually in all Georgia schools. It is a remarkable fact that the middle counties of Georgia have produced the most representative humorists of the South. Middle Georgia was also before the war the most democratic part of the slaveholding states, a circumstance not without its influence upon the development of Harris's genius.

"The sons of the richest men," he tells us, "were put in the fields to work side by side with the negroes, and were thus taught to understand the importance of individual effort that leads to personal independence. It thus happened that there was a cordial, and even an affectionate, understanding between the slaves and their owners, that perhaps had no parallel elsewhere. The poorer whites had no reason to hold their heads down because they had to work for their living. The richest slave owners did not feel themselves above those who had few negroes or none. When a man called his neighbour 'Colonel,' or 'Judge,' it was to show his respect, nothing more. For the rest, the humblest held their heads as high as the richest, and were as quick, perhaps quicker, in a quarrel."

Young Harris owed little to the schools but much to a country printing office and to a large library in which it was his privilege to browse at will. At the age of twelve he read one morning the announcement that a new newspaper, *The Countryman*, was to be started a few miles from Eatonton. The editor, Joseph Addison Turner, the owner of a large plantation and many slaves, was a man of sound but old-fashioned literary taste and wished his paper to be modelled after *The Spectator* of Addison and Steele. This announcement kindled the ambition of young Harris, who was already familiar with the best literature of Queen Anne's time and to whom the very name *Spectator* recalled days and nights of indescribable delight. He applied at once for the vacant position of office boy, received a favourable answer, and devoted the rest of his life to journalism in his native State. The duties of his new position were not onerous, and he found time, or took time, to hunt foxes, coons, opossums, and rabbits whenever he wished, and to make himself familiar with every nook and corner of the surrounding country.

It was in these early years that Harris laid the foundation for his future work. There was not a negro myth or legend in which he was not interested; there was not a negro custom or peculiarity that he did not know; and there was not a sound or idiom of the negro language that he could not reproduce.

"No man who has ever written," says Thomas Nelson Page, "has known one-tenth part about the negro that Mr. Harris knows, and for those who hereafter shall wish to find not merely the words but the real language of the negro of that section and the habits of mind of all American negroes of the old time, his works will prove the best thesaurus."

In addition to his interest in the life about him Harris soon came to have an equal interest in Turner's large library. Among his favourite books were the writings of Sir Thomas Browne, the essays of Addison and Steele, and later the Bible and Shakespeare. His best loved writer, however, from first to last, and the one whose genius was most like his own, was Goldsmith.

"The only way to describe my experience with *The Vicar of Wakefield*," he said in his later years, "is to acknowledge that I am a crank. It touches me more deeply, it gives me the 'all-overs' more severely than all others. Its simplicity, its air of extreme wonderment, have touched and continue to touch me deeply."

Among the writers of New England Harris seems to have cared least for Emerson and most for Lowell.

"Culture," he once wrote, "is a very fine thing, indeed, but it is never of much account either in life or in literature, unless it is used as a cat uses a mouse, as a source of mirth and luxury. It is at its finest in this country when it is grafted on the sturdiness that has made the nation what it is, and when it is fortified by the strong common sense that has developed and preserved the republic. This is culture with a definite aim and purpose . . . and we feel the ardent spirit of it in pretty much everything Mr. Lowell has written."

In the march through Georgia, General Sherman's army devastated the Turner plantation, and *The Countryman* was of course discontinued. After various experiences with different newspapers Harris joined the staff of *The Atlanta Constitution* in 1876. At this time he was known chiefly as an essayist and poet, but he began almost immediately to publish some of the plantation legends that he had heard from the lips of the negroes before and during the war. The first volume of these stories, *Uncle Remus: his Songs and his Sayings, the Folk-Lore of the Old Plantation*, was published in 1880. It contained thirty-four plantation legends or negro folk-tales, a few plantation proverbs, nine negro songs, a story of the war, and twenty-one sayings or opinions of Uncle Remus, all supposed to be sung or narrated by Uncle Remus himself. In 1883 appeared

Nights with Uncle Remus: Myths and Legends of the Old Planta-tion. This contained sixty-nine new legends and was prefaced by an interesting Introduction. Among the new legends were a few told by Daddy Jack, a representative of the dialect spoken on the coastal rice plantations of South Carolina and Georgia. These two volumes represent the author's best work in the domain of negro dialect and folk-lore, and were accorded instant recognition as opening a new and deeply interesting field both to literature and ethnology. Among the later works that continue the Uncle Remus tradition may be mentioned *Uncle Remus and his Friends* (1892), *Mr. Rabbit at Home* (1895), *The Tar-Baby Story and Other Rhymes of Uncle Remus* (1904), *Told by Uncle Remus* (1905), *Uncle Remus and Brer Rabbit* (1907), and *Uncle Remus and the Little Boy* (1910). There were also numerous stories of the War and of the Reconstruction period.

A year before his death Harris founded *Uncle Remus's Magazine*, which survived him only a few years. Immediately after his death in 1908 the Uncle Remus Memorial Association was formed, the purpose of which was to purchase the home of the writer of the Uncle Remus stories, near Atlanta, and to convert it into a suitable memorial. This has now been done.

It must be borne in mind that Harris came at a time when the interest in the negro was at its height. His value as literary material had been realized in part, but no satisfactory portrait of him had been drawn. The war, too, with its attendant saturnalia of Reconstruction, was over, and the negro was try-ing to fit himself into a new political and industrial régime. It is true also that Uncle Remus has characteristics very different from those with which the negro had hitherto been represented in literature. The character of Uncle Remus is noteworthy not only because it represents both a type and an individual, but because the type is now nearly extinct. Before the war every large plantation or group of plantations had its Uncle Remus; today he lingers here and there in a few villages of the South, but is regarded more as a curiosity, a specimen, a relic of the past than as a part of the present.

As portrayed by Harris, Uncle Remus sums up the past and dimly hints the future. The character was modelled in part after that of an old negro, Uncle George Terrell, whom Harris had learned to know intimately on the Turner plantation. The Uncle Remus of the stories is eighty years old, but still moves and speaks with the vigour of youth.

He had always exercised authority over his fellow-servants. He had been the captain of the corn-pile, the stoutest at the log-rolling, the swiftest with the hoe, the neatest with the plough, and the plantation hands still looked upon him as their leader.[1]

His life spanned three distinct and widely divergent periods; he had looked out upon three worlds—the South before the war, the South during the war, and the South after the war. He is tenderly cared for by his former owners, "Mars John" and "Miss Sally"; he has his own little patch of ground around his cabin; and he is devotedly attached to Miss Sally's "little boy." In spite of their difference in years, the child and the old man have one point in common: they both look out upon the world with eager, wide-eyed interest. Uncle Remus expresses their common point of view in a conversation with Brer Ab. Brer Ab had been telling Uncle Remus of some of the miraculous things seen by a coloured woman in a trance:

"She say she meet er angel in de road, and he pinted straight ter de mornin' star, and tell her fer ter prepar'. Hit look mighty cu'us, Brer Remus." "Cum down ter dat, Brer Ab," said Uncle Remus, wiping his spectacles carefully, and readjusting them—"cum down ter dat, an' dey ain't nuffin' dat ain't cu'us."[2]

Acting on this Aristotelian maxim, Uncle Remus explains to the little boy the mysteries of animal life, especially as they embody themselves in the character of the rabbit and the fox. The humour is entirely unconscious. It is not that of the Uebermensch, for the humour of the Uebermensch springs from the consciousness of intellectual power, and is, moreover, direct, cynical, self-assertive, masterful. The humour of Uncle Remus represents the world of the Underman; it has no reasoned philosophy but springs from the universal desire to correlate the unknown with the known and to explain the most

[1] *Nights with Uncle Remus*, p. 400.
[2] *Uncle Remus: his Songs and his Sayings*, p. 212.

20

mysterious things by reference to the most obvious.   If the rabbit lost his long tail on a certain historic occasion, then all the rabbits since born will have short tails.   In fact, Uncle Remus's philosophy is perfectly consistent in one thing: all physical characteristics, whether native or acquired, find their explanation not in past conditions but in past events.   The slow influence of environment yields place to a prompt and obliging heredity.

After all, however, the language of Uncle Remus is more interesting than his philosophy.   In the picturesqueness of his phrases, in the unexpectedness of his comparisons, in the variety of his figures of speech, in the perfect harmony between the thing said and the way of saying it, the reader finds not only a keen æsthetic delight but even an intellectual satisfaction.   It is probable that Uncle Remus's vocabulary would be found, on investigation, to be narrowly limited.   If so, he is a striking evidence of the varied effects that can be produced with but few words provided these words have been thoroughly assimilated.   He leaves the impression not of weakness but of strength, not of contractedness but of freedom.   What he says has not only been thought through but seen through and felt through.

It is only after repeated readings that one realizes how completely the character of Uncle Remus is revealed, or rather how completely he is made to reveal himself.   There are not many subjects within his range, or beyond it, on which he has not somewhere registered an interesting opinion.   If animals are his specialty, he is none the less willing to comment on negroes before and after the war, his favourite dishes, revivals, courtship, Christmas, witches, and religion.   These are some of the elemental things about which his thoughts play and through which we come at last to know him and to revere him.   Nowhere in American literature has an author succeeded better in harmonizing a typical character with an individual character than has been done in the character of Uncle Remus.   What James Fenimore Cooper did for the Indian, Harris has in fact done for the negro.   Just as Chingachgook is the last of the Mohicans, so Uncle Remus is the last of the old-time negroes. In literature he is also the first.

But Uncle Remus is interesting not merely in himself but also for the folk-tales of which he is the mouthpiece. These tales mark indeed the beginning of the scientific study of negro folk-lore in America. The author had, however, no ethnological purpose in publishing the Uncle Remus stories, and was greatly surprised to learn afterwards that variants of some of his tales had been found among the Indians of North and South America, and in the native literature of India and Siam. Variants of the Tar-Baby story, for example, have been found among the Natchez, Creek, and Yuchi Indians[1]; among the West Indian islanders[2]; in Brazil[3]; in Cape Colony[4]; among the Bushmen of South Africa[5]; along the lower Congo[6]; in West Central Africa[7]; among the Hottentots[8]; and among the Jatakas or "Birth-Stories" of Buddha.[9]

As to the accuracy with which the Uncle Remus stories are reproduced, the author speaks as follows:[10]

With respect to the folk-lore series, my purpose has been to preserve the legends themselves in their original simplicity, and to wed them permanently to the quaint dialect—if, indeed it can be called a dialect—through the medium of which they have become a part of the domestic history of every Southern family; and I have endeavored to give the whole a genuine flavor of the old plantation. Each legend has its variants, but in every instance I have retained that particular version which seemed to me to be the most characteristic, and have given it without embellishment and without exaggeration.

The animals that figure in these stories are, in addition to the fox and the rabbit, the opossum, the cow, the bull, the terrapin, the turtle, the wolf, the frog, the bear, the lion, the

[1] *Journal of American Folk-Lore*, July–Sept., 1913, p. 194.
[2] Andrew Lang's *At the Sign of the Ship* (*Longman's Magazine*, Feb., 1889).
[3] Romero's *Contos do Brazil*.
[4] *South African Folk-Lore Journal*, vol. I.
[5] James A. Honey's *South African Folk-Tales* (1910), p. 79.
[6] *The Sun*, New York, 17 March, 1912.
[7] *The Times*, New York, 24 Aug., 1913.
[8] Toni von Held's *Märchen und Sagen der afrikanischen Neger* (Jena, 1904), p. 72.
[9] *Indian Fairy Tales*, selected and edited by Joseph Jacobs (1910), p. 251.
[10] *Uncle Remus: his Songs and his Sayings*, Introduction, p. 3.

tiger, the pig, the billy goat, the deer, the alligator, the snake, the wildcat, the ram, the mink, the weasel, and the dog; among their feathered friends are the buzzard, the partridge, the guinea-fowl, the hawk, the sparrow, the chicken, and the goose. Why the rabbit should be the hero rather than the fox has been differently explained. Harris's own view seems, however, most in accord with the facts:

> The story of the rabbit and the fox, as told by the Southern negroes . . . seems to me to be to a certain extent allegorical, albeit such an interpretation may be unreasonable. At least it is a fable thoroughly characteristic of the negro; and it needs no scientific investigation to show why he selects as his hero the weakest and most harmless of all animals, and brings him out victorious in contests with the bear, the wolf, and the fox. It is not virtue that triumphs, but helplessness; it is not malice but mischievousness.

The origin of these tales is still in a measure unsettled, and there is urgent need of more scientific investigation of them. For a while it was thought that the negroes learned these stories from the Indians. It is at least certain that many of the Uncle Remus stories are current among the Indians of North and South America. It is equally certain that more is known of Indian folk-lore than of negro folk-lore. The present status of the question is overwhelmingly in favour of an African origin. The negro slaves, in other words, brought these stories with them from Africa to Brazil and the United States. The Indians in both countries learned them from the negroes.

Of the negro dialect in general as spoken in the United States today, there are four varieties:

(1) The dialect of Virginia, especially of Eastern or Tidewater Virginia. It is best represented in the works of Thomas Nelson Page. Broad *a* is retained in this dialect and there is a vanishing *y* sound (as in *few*) heard after *c* and *g* when broad *a* follows: *larst* (*last*), *farst* (*fast*), *grahss* (*grass*), *pahsture* (*pasture*), *chahmber* (*chamber*), *pahf* (*path*), *cyarn'* (*can't*), *kyars* (*cars*), *gyardin* (*garden*). Broad *a* is also heard in *cyar* (*carry*) and *dyah* (*there*). Such forms as *gyardin, seegyar, kyards, kyarvin' knife* are also used by Uncle Remus, but they are evidences of

Virginia influence.   Uncle Remus himself says, though he had dropped the broad *a*, that he "come from Ferginny."

(2)   The dialect of the Sea Islands of the South Atlantic States, known as the Gullah (or Gulla) dialect.   The name is probably derived from Angola, as many of the rice-field negroes of South Carolina and Georgia are known to have come from the west coast of Africa.   This diminishing dialect is spoken on the rice plantations of coastal South Carolina and Georgia as the Uncle Remus dialect is spoken on the cotton and tobacco plantations farther inland.   Gullah diverges widely from English and in its most primitive state is, as Harris says, "merely a confused and untranslatable mixture of English and African words."   Though it was used in a diluted form here and there by Poe and Simms and though Harris employs it for some of the stories in his *Nights with Uncle Remus*, it can hardly be said to have found a place in literature.   It has given us, however, the only pure African word still current in negro speech, the word *buckra*, meaning *boss* or *overseer*.   *Tote*, meaning *to carry*, which long claimed a place beside *buckra*, has been found in American writings of so early a date as to preclude the theory of African origin.

(3)   The dialect spoken by the Creole negroes of Louisiana. This dialect is of course not English but French, and is best represented, though sparingly, in the works of George W. Cable. Its musical quality and the extent to which elision and contraction have been carried may be seen in the following love song of the Creole negro Bras-Coupé, one of the characters in Cable's *Grandissimes*.   An interlinear translation is added:

En haut la montagne, zami,
On the mountain chain, my friends,
Mo pé coupé canne, zami,
I've been cutting cane, my friends,
Pou' fé i'a' zen', zami,
Money for to gain, my friends,
Pou' mo baille Palmyre.
For my fair Palmyre.
Ah! Palmyre, Palmyre, mo c'ere,
Ah! Palmyre, Palmyre, my dear,

Mo l'aimé 'ou—mo l'aimé 'ou.
I love you—I love you.

(4)   The Uncle Remus dialect, or the dialect spoken by the negroes in the great inland sections of the South and South-west. Though there have been changes in vocabulary and a decline in vigour and picturesqueness of expression, due to the influence of negro schools and to the passing of the old plantation life, this is the dialect still spoken by the majority of the older negroes in the country districts of the South, especially of the far South.   The characteristics of this dialect consist wholly in adaptation of existing English words and endings, not in the introduction of new words or new endings.   The plurals of all nouns tend to become regular.   Thus Uncle Remus says *foots* (*feet*), *toofies* (*teeth*), and *gooses* (*geese*), though the old plural *year* is retained.   The relative pronoun *who* is not used, its place being taken by *which* (or *w'ich*), *what* (or *w'at*), *dat*, and the more interesting *which he* and *which dey*, corresponding to Chaucer's *that he* and *that they*.   Thus: "She holler so loud dat Brer Rabbit, *which he* wuz gwine by, got de idee dat she wuz callin' him."

Another interesting characteristic of the Uncle Remus speech is found in the present tense of verbs.   Uncle Remus does not say, for example, *I make, you make, he makes, we make, you make, they make*, but *I makes, you makes, he makes, we makes, you makes, dey makes*.   Negro dialect, like the dialect of all illiterate peoples, is an ear dialect.   The eye has nothing to do with it.   The law of analogy, therefore, which is nothing more than the rule of the majority, has unfettered operation. The illiterate man, whether black or white, hearing the third person singular with its invariable *s*-ending far more frequently than he hears any other form of the present tense, makes it his norm and uses it for all forms of both numbers.   The same is true of the verb *to be*, though *is* has not in the language of Uncle Remus entirely succeeded in dispossessing *am* and *are*.

CHAPTER IX

The Short Story

THE period between the Civil War in America and the outbreak of the Great War in Europe in 1914 may be termed in the history of prose fiction the Era of the Short Story. Everywhere, in France, in Russia, in England, in America, more and more the impressionistic prose tale, the *conte*—short, effective, a single blow, a moment of atmosphere, a glimpse at a climactic instant—came, especially in the magazines, to dominate fictional literature. Formless at first, often overloaded with mawkishness, with essay effects, with moralizing purpose, and dominating background, it grew constantly in proportion and restraint and artistic finish until it was hailed as a new *genre*, a peculiar product of nineteenth century conditions, one especially adapted to the American temperament and the American *kultur*.

That the prose story was no innovation peculiar to later literature, is an axiom that must precede every discussion of it. It is as old as the race; it has cropped out abundantly in every literature and every period. That it has taken widely differing forms during its long history is also axiomatic. Every generation and every race has had its own ideals in the matter, has set its own fashions. One needs remember only *The Book of Ruth, The Thousand and one Nights*, the Elizabethan novella, the Sir Roger de Coverley papers, Johnson's *Rambler*, Hannah More's moral tales, and the morbid romance of the early nineteenth-century annuals. The modern short story is only the latest fashion in story telling—short fiction *à la mode*.

In America the evolution of the form may be traced through at least four stages. It began with the eighteenth-century tale of the Hannah More type, colourless, formless, undramatic, "subservient," to use a contemporary phrase, "only to the interest of virtue"—a form peculiarly adapted to flourish in the Puritanic atmosphere of the new nation. Such stories as *Chariessa, or a Pattern for the Sex* and *The Danger of Sporting with Innocent Credulity*, both from Carey's *Columbian Magazine* established in 1786, satisfied the American reading public for half a century.

Then came the work of Washington Irving[1]—the blending of the moral tale with the Addisonian essay, especially in its Sir Roger de Coverley phase. The evolution was a peculiar one, a natural result of that isolation of early America which belated all its art forms and kept it always a full generation behind the literary fashions of London. Irving's early enthusiasms came from the shelves of the paternal library rather than from the book stalls of the vital centres where flowed the current literature of the day. To the impressionable youth Addison and Steele and Goldsmith were as fresh and new as they had been to their first readers. The result appears in his first publication, *Salmagundi*, a youthful *Spectator*, and later in his first serious work, *The Sketch Book*, another essay periodical since it was issued in monthly numbers—a latter-day *Bee*. Never did he outgrow this formative influence: always he was of the eighteenth century, an essayist, a moralist, a sketcher of manners, an antiquarian with a reverence for the past, a sentimentalist. His sketchy moral essays and his studies of manners and character grew naturally into expository stories, illustrations, narratives of a traveller set in an atmosphere attractive to the untravelled American of the time, all imagination and longing. He added to the moral tale of his day characterization, humour, atmosphere, literary charm, but he added no element of constructive art. He lacked the dramatic; he overloaded his tales with descriptions and essay material; and he ended them feebly. His stories, even the classic *Rip Van Winkle*, are elaborations with pictorial intent rather than dramas with culminative movement and sharp outlines. They are essays rather than short stories.

Irving advanced the short story more by his influence than by his art. The popularity of *The Sketch Book* and the others that followed it, the tremendous fact of their author's European

[1] See also Chap. II.

fame, the alluring pictures of lands across the sea, the romantic atmosphere, the vagueness and the wonder of it, laid hold mightily upon the imagination of America. They came just in time to capture the young group of writers that was to rule the mid-century. The twenties and the thirties in America were dominated by *The Sketch Book*. All at once came an outburst of Irvingesque sketches and tales. That the unit of measure in American fiction is a short one is to be accounted for in a very great degree by the tremendous influence of Irving in its early formative period, **and indeed** to a date later than is commonly realized.

For the new form there sprang up in the twenties a new vehicle, the annual. For two decades the book-stands were loaded with flamboyantly bound gift books—*The Token, The Talisman, The Pearl, The Amaranth,* and the others, elaborate *Sketch Books* varied soon by echoes from the new romanticism of Europe. Never before such a gushing of sentiment, of mawkish pathos, of crude terror effects, and vague Germanic mysticism. From out of it all but a single figure has survived, the sombre Hawthorne[1] who was genius enough to turn even the stuff of the annuals into a form that was to persist and dominate. Hawthorne added soul to the short story and made it a form that could be taken seriously even by those who had contended that it was inferior to the longer forms of fiction. He centred his effort about a single situation and gave to the whole tale unity of impression. Instead of elaboration of detail, suggestion; instead of picturings of external effects, subjective analysis and psychologic delineation of character. Hawthorne was the first to lift the short story into the higher realms of art.

The forties belong to Poe.[2] With him came for the first time the science of the short story, the treatment of it as a distinct art form with its own rules and its own fields. Laws the form was bound to have if it was to persist. As the century progressed and as modern science swept from men's minds the vague and the generalizing and the disorderly, there came

---

[1] See also Chap. IV. Here may be mentioned, however, one short story before Hawthorne which seems rather to anticipate him than to follow Irving, William Austin's tantalizing *Peter Rugg, the Missing Man,* of which the first part appeared in 1824.

[2] See also Chap. III.

necessarily the demand for more reality, for sharper outlines, for greater attention to logical order. The modern short story is but the fiction natural, and indeed inevitable, in a scientific age, and Poe was the first to perceive the new tendency and to formulate its laws.

In Poe's opinion the short story owed its vogue in America to the great number of literary magazines that sprang up during the mid years of the century. "The whole tendency of the age is magazineward," he wrote in the early forties. The quarterlies are

quite out of keeping with the rush of the age. We now demand the legal artillery of the intellect; we need the curt, the condensed, the pointed, the readily diffused—in place of the voluminous, the verbose, the detailed, the inaccessible. . . . It is a sign of the times—an indication of an era in which men are forced upon the curt, the condensed, the well digested, in place of the voluminous—in a word, upon journalism in lieu of dissertation.

Fiction, he contended, to be scientific must be brief, must yield a totality of impression at a single sitting. The writer must concentrate upon a single effect.

If his very initial sentence tend not to the outbringing of this effect, he has failed in his first step. In the whole composition there should be no word written of which the tendency, direct or indirect, is not to the one pre-established design.

As he wrote this, Poe was thinking of his own art more than of Hawthorne's. He had been a magazinist all his life, and he had learned to view the tale from the standpoint of the editor. He who has but a brief space at his command in which to make his impression, must condense, must plan, must study his every word and phrase. All of his stories are single strokes, swift moments of emotion, Defoe-like massings of details with exactness of diction, skilful openings, harrowing closes.

More than this we may not say. He did not work in the deeps of the human heart like Hawthorne; he was an artist and only an artist, and even in his art he did not advance further than to formulate the best short story technique of his day. His tales are not to be classified at all with the products of later art. They lack sharpness of outline, *finesse*, and that sense of reality which makes of a tale an actual piece of human life. His creations are *tours de force;* they reflect no earthly soil, they are weak in characterization, and their dialogue—as witness the conversation of the negroes in *The Gold Bug*—is wooden and lifeless. Poe was a critic, keenly observant of the tendencies of his day, sensitive to literary values, scientific, with powers of analysis that amounted to genius. He was not the creator of the short story; he was the first to feel the new demand of his age and to forecast the new art and formulate its laws.

In the realm of the short story Poe was a prophet, peering into the next age, rather than a leader of his own time. Until later years his influence was small. He had applied his new art to the old sensational material of the thirties—old wine in new bottles. The annuals and all they stood for were passing rapidly. *Putnam's Magazine* noted in February, 1853, the great change that had come over the literature for the holiday period.

It used to be the custom to issue when Christmas approached an almost endless variety of "Gifts," "Remembrances," "Gems," "Tokens," "Wreathes," "Irises," "Albums," &c, with very bad mezzotint engravings and worse letter-press,—ephemeral works, destined to perish in a few weeks; but that custom appears to be rapidly passing away.

The decline of the old type of story explains why Hawthorne turned to the production of long romances. The age of the Hawthornesque short story had passed. With the fifties had come a new atmosphere. To realize it one has but to read for a time in *Godey's Lady's Book* and *Graham's Magazine* and the annuals and then to turn to *Harper's Magazine*, established in 1850, *Putnam's Magazine*, in 1853, and *The Atlantic Monthly*, in 1857.

In England it was the period of Dickens and Thackeray and Reade and George Eliot, the golden age of the later novel. American magazines like *Harper's* were publishing serial after serial by British pens, yet the demand for short fiction increased rather than declined. During its first year *The Atlantic Monthly* published upward of thirty-three short stories by twenty-three different authors, or an average of

almost three in every number.   It was no longer fiction of the
earlier type.   A new demand had come to the short story
writer; in the "Introductory" to the first volume of *Putnam's
Magazine* the editor announced that American writers and
American themes were to predominate, adding that "local
reality is a point of utmost importance."   In the first volume
of the *Atlantic*, Emerson struck the new note: "How far
off from life and manners and motives the novel still is.   Life
lies about us dumb"; and in the same volume a reviewer of
George Eliot notes "the decline of the ideal hero and heroine."
"The public is learning that men and women are better than
heroes and heroines."   By 1861 a writer like Rebecca Harding
Davis could open her grim short story, *Life in the Iron Mills*,
with a note like this;

I want you to hide your disgust, take no heed to your clean
clothes, and come right down with me,—here into the thickest of
the fog and mud and effluvia.   I want you to hear this story.
There is a secret down here, in this nightmare fog, that has lain
dumb for centuries: I want to make it a real thing for you.

The fifties and sixties in America stand for the dawning of
definiteness, of localized reality, of a feeling left on the reader
of actuality and truth to human life.

The first significant figure of the transition was Rose
Terry (1827–92), later better known as Rose Terry Cooke,
who has the distinction of having contributed seven short
stories to the first eight numbers of the *Atlantic*.   Born in
Connecticut—the heart of New England, a school teacher
with experience in country districts, she wrote with knowledge
and conviction of the area of life that she knew.   In her long
series of stories beginning in the forties with unlocalized romantic tales in *Graham's* and extending throughout the transition period into the seventies and eighties, and ending with a
final collection as late as 1891, one may trace every phase of
the American short story in half a century.   Her early *Atlantic*
narratives lean decidedly in the direction of the *Young Ladies'
Repository* type of fiction, sentimental, leisurely, moralizing,
and yet even in the poorest of them there is a sense of actuality
that was new in American short fiction.   They were not romances; they were homely fragments of New England rural

life. The heroine may be introduced in this unromantic fashion:
"Mrs. Griswold was paring apples and Lizzie straining squash."
Here for the first time we may find dialect that rings true, and,
moreover, here for the first time are sprightliness and rollicking
humour, varied at times with tragedy and true pathos. As
one traces her work from *Atlantic* to *Atlantic*, a gradual increase
in power impresses one until after her declaration of independence at the opening of *Miss Lucinda* (August, 1861)—"I
offer you no tragedy in high life, no sentimental history of
fashion and wealth, but only a little story about a woman who
could not be a heroine"—it is felt that she has found herself
and that with her later work like *Odd Miss Todd*, *Freedom
Wheeler's Controversy with Providence*, *The Deacon's Week*,
and last of all and in many ways her best, *The Town and Country
Mouse*, the final story in her collection *Huckleberries*, she has
passed into the new period and taken a secure place with the
small group of masters of the short story. Unlike Harriet
Prescott Spofford, whose gorgeous *In a Cellar* and *The Amber
Gods* fluttered for a time the readers of the early sixties, she
was able to heed the voice of the new period and to grow and
outgrow, and it was this power that made her the pioneer
and the leader not only of the group of depicters of New England life, but of the whole later school of makers of localized
short fiction realistically rendered.

Rose Terry came gradually, an evolution, without noise or
sensation; not so Fitz-James O'Brien (1828–62), who, after his
The Diamond Lens (January, 1858), was hailed loudly as a new
Poe. O'Brien's career in America was meteoric. He appeared
unheralded, in 1852, an adventurer who had been educated in
Dublin University, and who had squandered a rich patrimony
in London. For ten years he lived in the Bohemian circles of
New York, writing impetuously, when the mood was upon
him, temperamental, Celtic-souled material which he published
here and there in the magazines—*Harper's*, *Putnam's*, the
Atlantic, until, enlisting in one of the first regiments of volun-
teers, he fell in one of the earliest skirmishes of the Civil War.
His short stories *What Was It?* and *The Wondersmith* have
undoubted power, but they are not to be compared with the
best work of Hawthorne and Poe. What O'Brien might have
done had he lived into the next period of the short story it is

idle to conjecture. As it is, he must be regarded only as an
episode, a passing sensation, and he might be dismissed unmentioned but for the fact that he was an undoubted influence
in the period of transition. To the art and the impressionism
of Poe he added the new element of actuality. His shuddery
tale *What Was It?* is laid in a New York boarding-house
with convincingness. Even his Hawthorne-like fantasia *The
Wondersmith* has as a background a New York slum street
drawn with all the pitiless realism of a Zola. O'Brien added
the sense of actuality to Poe's unlocalized romance, but his
influence was not large.

Another figure in the transition was Edward Everett Hale
(1822–1909), whose *The Man without a Country*, first published in 1863, has been accepted generally as an American
classic. Little else that he has written, and he wrote much in
many fields, gives promise of surviving, and the reasons why
this should survive are not immediately evident. As a short
story it would seem to have almost fatal defects. It may be
used as an example of mid-century diffuseness, its moralizing
intent is only thinly veiled, it is episodic, and it does not culminate. Undoubtedly its timeliness—it is a document in the
history of the war—and its genuine atmosphere of patriotism
account partly for its success, but there are more vital reasons.
It is really a work of art. With all its episodes it presents
but a single situation, and that situation at the close has been
so worked upon that it becomes to the reader a haunting
presence, never to be forgotten. Moreover, there is reality
to the story. Everything is in the concrete. The author
adds specific detail to detail with the skill of a Defoe until, in
spite of its manifest impossibility, the tale becomes alive, a
piece of actual history, a human document. Few modern
writers have surpassed Hale in what may be called the art of
verisimilitude. He was the precursor of Stockton. A story
like *My Double and how he Undid me* is manifestly a *tour de
force*, yet one is in danger of gravely accepting it as a fact.
Hale added to the short story not alone the sense of reality;
he added plausibility as well.

With Henry James[1] the period of transition came to an
end. From 1865, when he published his first story, until 1875,

[1] See also Chap. VIII.

the date of *Roderick Hudson*, he devoted himself to short fiction, contributing fourteen stories to the *Atlantic* alone, and he brought to his work not only the best art America had evolved, but the best of England and France as well. He was a scientist, an observer, a tabulator, as cool and accurate as even his brother William James, the psychologist. Unlike O'Brien and the others, he threw away completely the machinery of the mid-century tale—not without regret it would appear from his *Romance of Certain Old Clothes* and other early tales—and sought only the uncoloured truth. The art of Poe, especially the French adaptations of that art, he retained, but he rejected all the rest of Poe's outfit. That he understood the full possibilities of the supernatural as short story material we know from his grim tale *The Turn of the Screw*, but the field was little to his taste. He was a naturalist rather than a supernaturalist, and his sensitive and fastidious soul could not endure the harsh and the horrible. In an early story, *My Friend Bingham* (1867), he wrote: "I am of a deep aversion to stories of a painful nature . . . the literature of horrors needs no extension." He rejected allegory and mystery and vague impressionism as unscientific. He condemned the tradition that "a serious story of manners shall close with the factitious happiness of a fairy tale." He was a scientist; his second paper in the *Atlantic* is a defence of George Eliot, scientist. To both of them the first requisite of fiction was the truth, the truth told directly, simply, concretely.

An age of science could no longer tolerate the unrelieved black and white of the earlier periods, but demanded shades, traces of white found even in the black. According to James, a short story was the analysis of a situation, the psychological phenomena of a group of men and women at an interesting moment. Given two, three, four different temperaments, bring them into a certain situation, and what would be the action and reaction? The story was a problem to be solved. Little was to be said *about* the characters: they were to reveal themselves, gradually, slowly as they do in actual life, by long continued dialogue, by little unconscious actions and reactions, by personal peculiarities in dress, manners, movement, revealed by a thousand subtle hints, descriptive touches, insinuations. Under such conditions the movement of the story must be slow: in some of his work there seems to be no story at all, only the analysis of a situation. The method requires space: James has stretched the length of the short story to its extreme. *The Aspern Papers*, the bare story of which could have been told in three pages, dragged through three magazine instalments. Twenty-eight of the one hundred and three stories in Henry James's final list are long enough to appear as volumes. Yet one may not doubt they are short stories: they are each of them the presentation of a single situation and they leave each of them a unity of impression.

James was the most consummate artist American literature has produced. He was fastidious by nature and by early training. He had studied his art in France as men study sculpture in Italy, and he had learned the French mastery of form. Nowhere in his writings may we find slovenly work. His opening and closing paragraphs are always models, his dialogue moves naturally and inevitably,—in all the story despite its length nothing too much,—and everywhere a brilliancy new in American fiction. He is seldom spontaneous; always is he the conscious artist; always is he intellectual; always is he working in the clay of actual life, a realist who never forgets his problem to soar into the uncharted and the unscientific realms of the metaphysical and the romantic.

The chief criticism of the short stories of James must concern their spirit rather than their form. The tendency of science has been to repudiate the spiritual. Romance with intuition in place of sense perception found at least the heart. With James the short story became an art form simply, cold and brilliant, a study of the surface of society, manners, endless phenomena jotted down in a note-book, human life from the standpoint of the laboratory and the test tube. Beyond the brilliant art of Henry James, the impressionistic study of situations from the standpoint of scientific truth, the American short story has never advanced. He gave distinctness to the form. Nevertheless, he is not a supreme master: that dominating factor in life that eludes scapel and test-tube he never found, and, neglecting it, he falls inevitably into second place as an interpreter of human life.

That James and others of his school, like T. B. Aldrich, for instance, and H. C. Bunner, could have directed the short story permanently into the channels that it has followed in France, is doubtful. The great success in the middle seventies of the anonymous *Saxe Holm's Stories*, with their mid-century sentiment and romantic atmosphere, would imply that America at heart was still what it was in the days of Hawthorne and the annuals. What might have happened had James and Howells and Aldrich had full control it is idle to speculate; what did happen was the sudden appearance of a short story that stampeded America and for two decades set the style in short fiction. Bret Harte's *The Luck of Roaring Camp*, whatever one may think of its merits, must be admitted to be the most influential short story ever written in America if it may be judged by its imitators.

Francis Bret Harte was born in 1839 at Albany, where his father, a scholar and an itinerant teacher of languages, happened at the time to be stationed. A youth of frail physique, he became a precocious reader, preferring a Hawthorne-like seclusion among books to playground activities among boys of his own age. From his childhood he was predisposed to literature; he dreamed over it, and he began to make poems even in his early school days. His removal to California at the age of fifteen, five years after the first gold rush, came from no initiative of his. To the delicate youth dreaming over his books it was an exile at the barbarous ends of the world. For a time he lived at his mother's home at Oakland—after a nine years' widowhood she had married again—and then half heartedly he began to support himself as a school teacher, as a private tutor, as a druggist's clerk, and later as a type-setter on a rural newspaper. There is little doubt that for a time he saw something of mining life during a visit to Humboldt County, but the experience was brief. He had no taste for the rough life of the border. The greater part of his seventeen years in California he spent in San Francisco, first as type-setter, then as editor in various newspaper and magazine establishments. He was a man of the city, a professional literary worker, a poet, and a dreamer over the work of the older poets and romancers.

Harte came to the short story by way of Irving. His first dream was to do for the lands of the Spanish missions what Irving had done for the highlands of the Hudson. As early as

1863 he had contributed to *The Atlantic Monthly* his *Legend of Monte del Diablo*, which, with half a dozen other pieces written during the same period, breathed the soul of *The Sketch Book*. Poe had affected him not at all, but he had read much in the French, and he had been from his boyhood a devotee of Dickens. When in 1868, therefore, he found himself editor of the new *Overland Monthly*, which was to be the *Atlantic Monthly* of the Pacific coast, it was not strange that he should have evolved for its second number a short story like *The Luck of Roaring Camp*. The time was ready for such a production, and the place was ready: it could have come only during the decade following the war, and, moreover, it could have come only from California.

The story was woven of four strands: first, there was the Dickens sentiment, melodrama, theatric presentation of lowly material; second, there was the French art that had been adapted from Poe—form, *finesse*, nothing too much; third, there was the unusualness of background, new skies, strange types, presented by one who seemingly had been a part of what he told, a voice of the new spirit of the age in America; and, finally, over it all there was a reminiscence of Irving, that impalpable atmosphere of romance which covers it with the soft haze of remembered things, of the far-off and the idealized. Only the third was new, the "local colour" we have come to call it, that touch of strangeness added to the picture by means of strongly picturesque characters and scenes hitherto unknown to the reader. A mere spice of novelty it was, a detail of stage setting wholly subsidiary to the vital elements of the tale, and yet it was largely this single element that gave *The Luck of Roaring Camp* its enormous vogue and that made its author —at least in America—the most influential writer of short stories in a generation.

And yet Harte was an effect rather than a cause. America was ready for local colour. He was the voice that started the avalanche that was bound to come sooner or later. The Civil War had liberated America from provincialism. It had done away with the boundaries of New England, of the South, of New York, of the West. The new emphasis was now upon the nation rather than upon the state or section. The first railroad across the continent was completed in 1868. Now everywhere were problems national in scope. The tremendous activities of the war were now transferred to the breaking of the great West, to the building of new cities and industries, and to the extending into every part of the continent of a network of communication. Books of travel like Bowles's *Across the Continent* and King's *The Great South* began to appear, and all at once the nation awoke to a realization of its own riches, of its own picturesque diversity. The long period of the settlement had bred individualism; it had covered America with little isolated areas as provincial as if they were the only settlements on the continent. The era following the war was an era of self-discovery. America was as full of new and interesting life and environment as even Europe, and for two decades and more American writers exploited the strange new riches of the land as the first wave of placer miners excitedly rifle the nugget pockets of a new-found bonanza. Eagerly the public read of the picturesque conditions that had evolved from the California rush of '49; it wondered at the new world that Mark Twain revealed in his *Jumping Frog of Calaveras County*, and that Cable opened in old Creole New Orleans, and at the grotesque Hoosier types revealed by Eggleston; it thrilled with astonishment at Charles Egbert Craddock's pictures of the dwellers in the Tennessee Mountains, and at Octave Thanet's revelations of life in the canebrakes of Arkansas; and it lingered over the Old South before the war as revealed by Johnston, and Harris, and Page.

Never was movement launched with more impetus. No sooner had *The Luck of Roaring Camp* reached the East than the foremost publishing house of Boston hailed it as a new classic. Its author immediately was offered ten thousand dollars a year to write for *The Atlantic Monthly*, and the progress of his train east as he came to accept his unprecedented commission was indicated by daily bulletins in the newspapers as if he were a royal personage on a tour of the land. When was short story ever so advertised before? No wonder that everybody at the earliest opportunity read it, and later, in 1870, bought the book of short stories to which it gave the title.

Harte's arrival in Boston marks the climax of his career. We need not follow him to Europe whither he afterwards went to spend the rest of his life, or read widely in his voluminous later product. The work in that first collection containing *The Luck of Roaring Camp* he never surpassed, though over and over for years he repeated its characters and backgrounds in stories of California life. If he is to endure it will be on account of the title story, or *Tennessee's Partner,* or *The Outcasts of Poker Flat.*

Like James, Harte was a conscious artist, a workman who had served a careful apprenticeship. His stories are models of condensation, his characters are as distinct and as striking as are those of Dickens, his climaxes are dramatic, and his closing effect is always impressively theatric. Sentiment he used with a free hand, but he kept it more within control than did the creator of Little Nell. Fiction with him, as with Poe, was a deliberate thing, to be written with the reader always in mind. His unit necessarily was short. He had no power to trace the growth of a soul or to record the steps of an evolution. His one attempt at a novel, *Gabriel Conroy*, was a failure. He could make a situation dramatic, he could make alive a climactic moment in a reckless career, but he was powerless to deal with the resultant effects from a complexity of motives and situations. What he added to the short story of his time, aside from the obvious local colour, was the dramatic element. His stories move, they culminate, they may be translated with little change into acting plays. Moreover, Harte was the first prominently to bring into the short story the element of paradox. It is the object of the theatrical always to move strongly the emotions, to keep interest taut by swift change and by unexpected turns. With Harte paradox became almost a mannerism. Everywhere anticlimax: in a desperado suddenly an outburst of Christlike self-sacrifice; from a mild youth with seraphic countenance a fiendish outburst; from a seeming clergyman, all in a moment, profanity.

The weakness of Harte was his lack of sincerity and of moral background. Unlike Cable and Page, he stood apart from his material, cold and unmoved, and sought not the truth but effect upon the reader. Every one of his extreme characters may have had somewhere a counterpart, and every separate incident, no matter how startling, may actually have happened at some time during the mining era, but the assembling of all this mass of exceptions and of isolated extremes into pictures that give the impression that they represent the ordinary course of life everywhere in California during a period is in reality a violation of the truth. The stories are unnatural: they have about them the atmosphere of the theatre. They are melodrama: they are compounded of the stage properties of the showman. Great as has been his influence, Harte cannot rank with the supreme masters of the short story. Lacking sincerity and sympathy and moral background, he becomes a picturesque incident rather than a permanent force.

After the enormous publicity given to Harte and the universal praise accorded his work both in America and in Europe, one might expect to find that a sudden change came over the spirit of American fiction. A change there was, indeed, but it was not sudden. One may leaf through whole volumes of such periodicals as *Harper's Magazine* and find no hint of the new vogue. Artists like James and Aldrich went on with their work as if *The Luck of Roaring Camp* had never been written. The writers who were to be influenced—that group which later was to be known as the "local colour school" —in 1870 were just beginning to find themselves, and they fell under the spell of Harte just as Longfellow and his circle in earlier days had fallen under the spell of Irving. It was not until the eighties and the early nineties that the tide which had begun in *The Overland Monthly* in 1868 came to its full.

Perhaps the most interesting transition during the period is that which may be traced in the work of Constance Fenimore Woolson (1838–94), a grandniece of Cooper, a native of New Hampshire, and a dweller successively by the Great Lakes, in the South, and in Italy, where she died. At the beginning of the seventies Miss Woolson was writing unlocalized poetic stories for *Harper's*, *A Merry Christmas*, *An October Idyl*, and the like, tales that might have come from the early period of Rose Terry Cooke. But soon one notes a change, a new sense of the value of background and of strongly individualized types for characters. By 1874 she was choosing the West for her materials. Her *Solomon* is a study of a unique character in an isolated German settlement on One-leg Creek which flows into the Tuscarawas River in Ohio, and her *Jeanette* and most of the other stories in *Castle Nowhere* (1875) deal with the primitive French habitants on Mackinac and the islands of Lake Superior. She had been reading Harte. Later, in the South, she was stirred by the desolation and the poverty wrought by the war, and now with her heart in her work she wrote the first post-bellum Southern short stories founded upon the contrast between what was and what had been. And still later in Italy she caught again the soul of a people and wrought it into the tales to be collected under the title *The Front Yard*. With each volume there had been an increase in definiteness, in picturesque characterization, in dramatic effect. She worked without dialect and she threw over her work the soft evening light, yet was she a realist, as Harte never was, and unlike him too she worked always with insight and sympathy. Stories like her *The Front Yard* are constructed of the materials of life itself. One cannot forget them.

A transition from another source is to be found in the stories of Sarah Orne Jewett (1849–1909), who also stands on the border line between the real and the romantic. She was affected not at all by Harte, but by Mrs. Stowe and Rose Terry Cooke. In her *Deephaven* (1877) she struck the new note of the decade, concreteness, geographical locality made so definite and so minutely real that it may be reckoned with as one of the characters in the story. Rose Terry Cooke had written of New England; Miss Jewett wrote of Deephaven, which was Berwick, Maine, her native town. Mrs. Stowe and Mrs. Cooke wrote of the New England flood tide; Miss Jewett wrote of the ebb, not despairingly like Miss Wilkins and the depressed realists, but reverently and gently. Over all her work is the hint of a glory departed, that Irving-like atmosphere which is the soul of romance. She delighted in decaying old seaports with their legends of other and better days, of old sea captains mellow and reminiscent, and of dear old ladies serene in spite of the buffets of time.

Her knowledge of her materials was intimate and thorough. All through her girlhood she had ridden much with her father, a country doctor, as he went his daily round among his patients. From him she learned the soul of the region, and she sympathized with it, and later she interpreted it in story after story based accurately upon what she knew. Unlike Mrs. Cooke, she came late enough to avoid the mid-century gush of sentiment. With her it became pathos, the pathos of sympathy and understanding; there is a grip of it in each one of her tales. One does not cry over a story like *A White Heron*, but one feels at the end of it like finding the sturdy little heroine and calling her a good girl. No art can go farther. Her delight was in the simple and the idyllic rather than in the dramatic. A story like *A Native of Winby* has very little of plot; but no tale was ever more worth the telling. It is a quivering bit of human life, a section of New England, a tale as true as a soul's record of yesterday.

There remains the element of style. She was one of the few creators of the short story after the seventies who put into her work anything like distinction. She was of the old school in this, of the school of Irving and Hawthorne and Poe. Indeed her style has often been likened to Hawthorne's, effortless, limpid, sun-clear in its flowing sentences, and softened and mellowed into a Sleepy-Hollow atmosphere—the perfect style, it would seem, for recording the fading glories of a charming old régime.

Her best stories are perhaps *Miss Tempy's Watchers*, *The Dulham Ladies*, *The Queen's Twin*, *A White Heron*, and *A Native of Winby*. Lightness of touch, humour, pathos, perfect naturalness—these are the points of her strength. She was a romanticist, equipped with a camera and a fountain pen.

To touch the seventies anywhere is to touch romance. Even Howells was not fully a realist until into the eighties. The new local colour work was not primarily realism. The new writers who now sprang up to portray local peculiarities in all parts of the land sought, even as Harte had done, to throw an idealized atmosphere over their pictures. One thinks of Mrs. Jackson and *Ramona* and of Eggleston and *The Hoosier Schoolmaster*, and, in the realm of the short story, of George W. Cable and Charles Egbert Craddock.

Cable was one of the discoveries of Edward King during his tour of the South for *Scribner's Monthly* in 1872. It was in New Orleans that he found him working as a humble clerk by day, and by night dreaming over a collection of reading matter as foreign to his work-day world as that which once had engaged another dreaming clerk, Charles Lamb. Among his enthusiasms were the old Spanish and French archives of the city; old relations of the priest-explorers; French novels—Hugo, Mérimée, About; English literature and American—Thackeray, Dickens, Poe, Irving. The composite of all this, plus a unique and evanescent quality which we call personality, was already finding form in sketches and stories which Cable was writing for himself and for the New Orleans papers. Some of his stories he showed to King, who advised him to send them to *Scribner's*. One of these, *'Sieur George*, was published the following year; others came at intervals. The young artist was not to be hurried; it was not for half a dozen years that enough had accumulated to make a volume. He had grown slowly upon the American consciousness, but the growth had been steady and sound. *Old Creole Days* (1879) was accepted at once as a masterpiece, and there has been no revulsion of feeling.

This collection, together with *Madame Delphine* the sum-total of his really distinctive short stories, owes its charm not alone to quaintness and strangeness of materials. It is as redolent of Cable as *The Luck of Roaring Camp* is of Harte. Cable's technique and his atmospheres may have been influenced by the French, but his style,—epigrammatic, Gallic in its swift shiftings and witty insinuations, daintily light, exquisitely pathetic at times, exotic always in its flavour of the old Creole city so strange to Northern readers,—all this is his own. No one has excelled him as a painter of dainty femininity, as a master of innuendo and suggestion, as a creator of exotic atmospheres. Whether his backgrounds are realistically true we do not ask, and whether his characters are actual types we do not care. They are true to the fundamentals of human life, they are alive, they satisfy, and they are presented ever with exquisite art. *Old Creole Days* stands unique, one of the undisputed masterpieces in the realm of the short story, American or foreign.

Two distinct schools ruled the short fiction of the seventies, that vital seed-time of a period: the school of unlocalized art, timeless and placeless, as Poe and Hawthorne had written it, and the new "local colour" school of Harte, which was going more and more to extremes. A few there were like Henry James who went on with their work utterly oblivious of the new demand for the violently localized. T. B. Aldrich was one. His little story *Marjorie Daw* was published in the *Atlantic* five years after Harte's sensational début. A trivial thing it was compared with such tragedies as *Tennessee's Partner* or *Madame Delphine*, an American humorous anecdote elaborately expanded, with a "point" at the end to be followed by laughter, yet its appearance marked a new stage in the history of the American short story. Tales already there had been that had held a sensation in the last sentence. *The Amber Gods* had ended with the startling words: "I must have died at ten minutes past one." But in *Marjorie Daw* the device was handled with a skill that made the story a model for later writers. After Aldrich, Stockton and Bunner and O. Henry and all their dexterous companions.

Aldrich brought a style to the short story as distinctive as Cable's, a certain patrician elegance, yet a naturalness and a simplicity that concealed everywhere its art, for art is the soul of it; every sentence, every word a studied contribution toward the final effect. There is no moral, no hidden meaning, no exotic background to be displayed, no chastening tragedy; it is a mere whimsicality light as air, a bit of American comedy. The laugh comes not from what is told but from the picture supplied by the reader's imagination. All of Aldrich's thin repertoire of short stories is of the same texture. He may be compared with no American writer. To find a counterpart of *Marjorie Daw* one must go to the French—to Daudet for its whimsical lightness of touch, and to Maupassant for its exquisite technique.

But the interest created by the appearance of *Marjorie Daw* was mild compared with that accorded to Frank R. Stockton's *The Lady or the Tiger?* (1884). Stockton (1834–1902) had not the technique of Aldrich nor his naturalness and ease. Certainly he had not his atmosphere of the *beau monde* and his grace of style, but in whimsicality and unexpectedness and in that subtle art that makes the obviously impossible seem perfectly plausible and commonplace, he surpassed not only him but Edward Everett Hale and all others. After Stockton and *The Lady or the Tiger?* it was realized even by the uncritical that short story writing had become a subtle art and that the master of its subtleties had his reader at his mercy.

The best of Stockton's short work is to be found in his *Negative Gravity, The Transferred Ghost, The Remarkable Wreck of the "Thomas Hyke,"* and *The Late Mrs. Null.* It is like nothing else in American literature: everywhere paradox presented with the utmost gravity, everywhere topsy-turviness and anticlimax and the grotesquely unexpected. There is little of substance in it all; it is *opéra bouffe*, amusing, delightful, ephemeral. Even now Stockton is remembered only for *The Lady or the Tiger?* and the present generation considers even that story clumsy work when compared with the creations of his successor, O. Henry.

Another who did much to advance the short story toward the mechanical perfection it had attained to at the close of the century was Henry Cuyler Bunner (1855–96), editor of *Puck* and creator of some of the most exquisite *vers de société* of the period. The title of one of his collections, *Made in France: French Tales with a U. S. Twist*, forms an introduction to his fiction. Not that he was an imitator; few have been more original or have put more of their own personality into their work. His genius was Gallic. Like Aldrich, he approached the short story from the fastidious standpoint of the lyric poet. With him, as with Aldrich, art was a matter of exquisite touches, of infinite compression, of almost imperceptible shadings. The lurid splashes and the heavy emphasis of the local colourists offended his sensitive taste: he would work with suggestion, with microscopic focussings, and always with dignity and elegance. He was more American than Henry James, more even than Aldrich. He chose always distinctively native subjects,—New York City was his favourite theme,—and his work had more depth of soul than Stockton's or Aldrich's. The story may be trivial, a mere expanded anecdote, yet it is sure to be so vitally treated that, like Maupassant's work, it grips and remains, and, what is more, it lifts and chastens or explains. It may be said with assurance that *Short Sixes* marks one of the high places which have been attained by the American short story, particularly when the art of the form is considered.

In the same group belongs Ambrose Bierce (1838–1914?), though in mere point of time he is to be counted with the California group of the early *Overland Monthly* days. A soldier of the Civil War, editor of the San Francisco *News Letter* in 1866, associate editor with the younger Tom Hood, of *London Fun* in 1872, author in London of the brilliant satirical fables *Cobwebs from an Empty Skull* in 1874, then in California again as editor of *The Argonaut* and *The Wasp*, and finally a resident of Washington, D. C., he was one of the most cosmopolitan of American writers. It was not until 1891 that his *Tales of Soldiers and Civilians*, later changed to *In the Midst of Life*, gave him a place with the short story writers, a very prominent place some critics would insist. Power undoubtedly he had, a certain scintillating brilliance, and a technique almost uncanny. His world was the world of Poe, timeless and placeless, ghastly often, chilling always and unnerving. At his best he was Poe returned after a half century equipped with the short story art of the new generation. Few have surpassed him in precision of diction, in reserve, in the use of subtle insinuation and of haunting climax. Some of his tales cling in one's soul like a memory of the morgue. His failure was his artificiality and his lack of sincerity and of truth to the facts of human life. Like Poe, he was a man of the intellect only, a craftsman of exquisite subtlety, an artist merely for the sake of his art.

With the eighties the short story came in America fully to its own. Up to 1884 it had generally been regarded as a magazine form, a rather trivial thing as compared with the stately novel. Hawthorne had abandoned the form early with the implication that he had used it as a prentice exercise. Harte no sooner had gained recognition than he began on *Gabriel Conroy*. Henry James, though it must be noted that it was after his long English residence, while revising his work declared that he had felt a sense of relief when he abandoned the frail craft of the short story where he ever had felt in danger of running ashore. Scarcely one of the later group of short story writers but sooner or later sought permanence in what, though they might not have confessed it, seemed to them the more permanent and dignified form of fiction.

Beginning in 1884, however, collections more and more began to dominate the output of fiction. Henry James in 1885 gathered up his scattered work of a decade and put it forth as *Stories Revived*. Others followed him, until seven years later the critic Copeland could devote an entire *Atlantic* article to the short-story collections of the year. The full triumph came in 1891, which produced this significant list of collections: *Elsket, and Other Stories*, Thomas Nelson Page; *Balaam and his Master*, Joel Chandler Harris; *Flute and Violin*, James Lane Allen; *Otto the Knight*, Octave Thanet (Alice French); *Main-Travelled Roads*, Hamlin Garland; *Gallegher, and Other Stories*, Richard Harding Davis; *Fourteen to One*, Elizabeth Stuart Phelps; *Huckleberries Gathered from New England Hills*, Rose Terry Cooke; *Iduna, and Other Stories*, George A. Hibbard; *Three Tales*, William Douglas O'Connor; *Uncle of an Angel*, Thomas A. Janvier; *Zadoc Pine, and Other Stories*, Bunner; *With My Friends*, Brander Matthews; *Rudder Grangers Abroad*, Stockton; *The Adventures of Three Worthies*, Clinton Ross.

1884 was the climactic year in the history of the short story inasmuch as it produced *The Lady or the Tiger?* and *In the Tennessee Mountains*, each one of them a literary sensation that advertised the form tremendously. No book since Harte's *The Luck of Roaring Camp* had been launched with such impetus as the latter of these. For six years the name of Charles Egbert Craddock had been appealing more and more to the national imagination because of a series in the *Atlantic* of strongly impressionistic studies of life in the Tennessee mountains. Now suddenly it came to light that the author was a woman, Miss Mary N. Murfree. The sensation in the *Atlantic* office spread everywhere and gave tremendous vogue not only to the book but to the type of short story that it represented. No one had gone quite so far before: the dialect was pressed to an extreme that made it almost unintelligible; grotesque localisms in manners and point of view were made central; and all was displayed before a curtain of mountains splashed with broad colours. The year was notable too because it produced Brander Matthews's *The Philosophy of the Short-story*, a magazine article later expanded into a volume, the first scientific handling of the art of the form since Poe's review of Hawthorne.

Realism, or more exactly, perhaps, naturalism, ruled the decade. From all sections of the country came now a tide of short fiction the chief characteristic of which was its fidelity to local conditions. The *Century* published Page's *Marse Chan*, a story entirely in negro dialect. Joel Chandler Harris[1] contributed his inimitable Uncle Remus studies of negro folklore and added to them short stories of the mountain "crackers." *Mingo and Other Sketches*, which appeared the same year as *In the Tennessee Mountains*, deals with the Craddock region and people but with surer hand. Harris was himself a native of Georgia hills, though he was by no means a "cracker," and he spoke with the sympathy and the knowledge of a native, not as an outside spectator and an exhibitor like Miss Murfree. The same may be said of Richard Malcolm Johnston (1822–98), whose *Dukesborough Tales*, dealing with rural life in the Georgia of his youth, first were given to Northern readers in 1883.

The evolution of Johnston's art is an interesting study. He was inspired not by Irving or by any of the Northerners, but by Longstreet, whose brutally realistic *Georgia Scenes* had appeared as early as 1835. In 1857 Johnston had written *The Goose Pond School* and had followed it with other realistic studies for *The Southern Magazine*. Later they were gathered for a Southern edition entitled *Georgia Sketches*, and still later, in 1871, he had reissued them in Baltimore as *Dukesborough Tales*. He, therefore, must be reckoned with Harte as a pioneer, though his work had few readers and no influence until it was again reissued by the Harpers in 1883. Even then, and afterwards when he had added new and more artistically handled material, he was not a highly significant figure. Studies of provincial Georgia life he could make, some of them bitingly true, but his range was small and his soundings, even within his narrow area, were not deep. He must be classified with the makers of sketches like Longstreet rather than with the short story writers of the period in which he first became known.

So completely was local colour the vogue of the eighties that the novelist was regarded as a kind of specialist who moved in a narrow field of his own and who was to be reprimanded if he stepped beyond its limits. The movement had three phases: first, the Irvingesque school that romanticized its material and threw over it a softened light,—Harte, Miss

[1] See also Chap. VIII.

Jewett, Cable, Page; second, the exhibitors of strange material objectively presented,—Charles Egbert Craddock, Octave Thanet, and the dialect recorders of the eighties; and third, the veritists of the nineties who told what they considered to be the unidealized truth concerning the life they knew,— Garland, Miss Wilkins, Frank Norris, and the rest. This third group approached its task scientifically, stated its doctrines with clearness,—as for example in Hamlin Garland's *Crumbling Idols*,—and then proceeded to work out its careful pictures with deliberate art. Garland's *Main-Travelled Roads*, stories of the settlement period of the Middle Border, have no golden light upon them. They tell the truth with brutal directness and they tell it with an art that convinces. They are not mere stories; they are living documents in the history of the West. So with the Maupassant-like pictures of later New England conditions by Mary E. Wilkins Freeman, in *A Humble Romance* (1887) and *A New England Nun* (1891). If the florid, sentimental school of the mid-century went to one extreme, she went to the other. Nowhere in English may one find more of repression, more pitiless studies of repressed lives, more bare searchings into the soul of a decadent social system. She wrote with conviction and a full heart of the life from which she herself had sprung, yet she held herself so firmly in control that her pictures are as sharp and cold as engravings on steel. Her fault is that she repeated a few formulas too frequently.

With the nineties came the full perfection of short story art. Within their limited field *A New England Nun* and *Main-Travelled Roads* may not be surpassed. In another area of the short story James Lane Allen's *Flute and Violin* stands by itself, and in still another such work as Margaretta Wade Deland's *Old Chester Tales*, Grace King's *Monsieur Motte*, and Alice Brown's *Meadow Grass*. No more exquisite work, however, may be found in the whole range of the local colour school than that in Kate Chopin's (1851–1904) *Bayou Folks* (1894). She was of Celtic blood and spontaneously a storyteller. She wrote with abandon, yet always it was with the restrained art that we have got into the habit of calling French. Such stories as *Désirée's Baby*, the final sentence of which grips one by the throat like a sudden hand out of the dark, and

Madame Célestin's Divorce, with its delicious humour and its glimpse into the feminine heart, are among the few unquestioned masterpieces of American short story art.

The local colour vogue during the period undoubtedly was an element toward the making of the American fictional unit short. He who would deal with the social régime of a provincial neighbourhood must of necessity be brief. There was no background of established manners in the corners of America, or in the centres, for that matter, sufficient to afford material for a Richardson or a Thackeray. Harte and Charles Egbert Craddock and most of the others attempted novels and failed. One may make a moving drama of the culminating moment in Mother Shipton's or Tennessee's life, but a complete novel written about either of them would be only a succession of picaresque adventures. The short story was peculiarly the vehicle for recording American life, so squalid, yet so glorious and moving, during the era when the country had no manners but only the rudiments of what were to become manners.

Beginning about 1898 with the early work of O. Henry and Jack London, there has come what may be called the last period in the history of the short story—the work of the present day. It is the period of magazines devoted wholly to short stories, of syndicates which handle little else, of text books and college courses on the art of the short story, and even of correspondence courses in which the art of making marketable stories may be learned through the mails. In America the short story seems to have become an obsession and in some respects a delusion.

The demand of the decade has been for "stories with a punch." The material must be out of the ordinary; it must not only breathe the breath of unfamiliar regions but it must give the impression that it is a bit of autobiography, or at least a section of life that has passed under the author's own eyes. The short story work of F. Hopkinson Smith (1838–1915) may be taken as an illustration. There is in it the breath of foreign parts, the sense of cosmopolitanism, breezy knowledge of the world. Everywhere alertness, wide-awakeness, efficiency, in an easy colloquial style of narrative that has about it a businesslike ring. His brilliant narratives in such a collection as *At Close Range* are the work of one who would have made a most efficient special reporter for a city daily. Here are modern instances in all parts of the world, engagingly told. He has been everywhere, he has seen everything, he has learned all the world's rituals and all its secrets. There is no leisurely approach, no sentimental colourings, no literary effects; they are life seen in flashes, a vivid fragment snipped from the moving film of human life.

It may be illustrated also by Jack London's (1876-1916) headlong art: strangeness always,—Alaska of the gold rush, the ultimate South Seas, the unknown recesses of the prize ring, the no-man's land of the hobo,—impressionistic studies in sensation. He was writing for money and for little else, and he studied his market like a broker. Earlier literature was aristocratic,—it was written for the refined few; the latest literature is democratic,—it is written for the mass, and the mass is uncritical and unrefined. Its demands are gross: sensation, movement, physical thrill. London gave the mass what it demanded, every sensation which the brutal underworld he knew had afforded him, and he sold his work well. Of the graces demanded in the earlier periods, finish, elegance of style, melody, elevation in tone, he knew nothing. He had immediacy—he told vivid stories of physical prowess in the world of the present moment; he had the note of authority—he wrote only of wild epic things of which he had himself been a large part; he had sensation—the appeal of crude physical horror, the strange and the unheard-of in hitherto unknown regions; and he had a barbaric style—a lurid wealth of adjectives, a melodramatic intensity, and a headlong rush of incident that sweeps the reader along as in a stampede. Force undoubtedly he had and freshness of material, but, lacking poise and moral background and beauty of style, he must be passed as an ephemeral sensation as regards all but a handful of his stories.

From the multitude of the later short story writers Richard Harding Davis (1864-1916), whose literary life, from the appearance of *Gallegher* in 1891 to his death, coincided almost exactly with the modern period in American literature, may be chosen as the typical figure. Reared in a literary home,— his mother was the author of *Life in the Iron Mills,*—educated at Lehigh University, trained in a city newspaper office until he became one of the most successful special correspondents of his generation, he was admirably fitted to give to the reading public—enormous now because of the universality of the public school and the newspaper and the popular magazine—what it most wanted. He had what Jack London lacked utterly, literary traditions, poise, a certain patrician touch, and an innate love of the romantic. What he might have become in an earlier and more literary era it is not hard to conjecture; what he did become was the result of the spirit of the age, for he became a·journalist, a recorder of the ephemeral moment for the ephemeral moment, a reporter with pen marvellously facile and ready, a literary craftsman who mastered every detail of his craft.

That Davis satisfied his generation goes without saying. A good newspaper man, he gave it what it desired, up-to-dateness, swift action, strangeness of setting presented with the authority of an eye-witness, and, moreover, a sprinkling of sentiment and mystery and romance. All of his work is brilliant, and there are parts that have the touch of distinction, but nowhere does it satisfy the supreme tests. He attempted too much, he skimmed over too much ground, he observed too much of the superficial and not enough of the real underlying heart of life. He was a facile sketcher of surfaces, a versatile entertainer, a craftsman rather than a critic of human life, an artist enamoured with his art rather than a creator who worked with the deeper materials of the human tragedy and comedy.

The period closes with the work of William Sydney Porter, better known as O. Henry (1862–1910), whose sudden rise and enormous popularity are one of the romances of the history of the short story. Only the bare facts of his biography need detain us: his Southern origin, his limited education, his sixteen years in Texas, his unfortunate experience as a bank clerk, his flight to South America, his return after a few months to serve a sentence in the Ohio State prison, and finally his last years in New York City—as picturesque a life as may be found in the annals of literature.

His short story career began almost by accident, the result of his enforced leisure in prison. His first story, *Whistling*

Dick's Christmas Stocking, redolent of Bret Harte, was published in *McClure's Magazine* in 1899. Following it irregularly, came a series of Western and South American tales, and then finally a most remarkable output of stories dealing with the human comedy and tragedy of New York City.

Nowhere is there anything just like them. In his best work—and his tales of the great metropolis are his best—he is unique. The soul of his art is unexpectedness. Humour at every turn there is, and sentiment and philosophy and surprise. One never may be sure of himself. The end is always a sensation. No foresight may predict it, and the sensation always is genuine. Whatever else O. Henry was, he was an artist, a master of plot and diction, a genuine humorist, and a philosopher. His weakness lay in the very nature of his art. He was an entertainer bent only on amusing and surprising his reader. Everywhere brilliancy, but too often is it joined to cheapness; art, yet art merging swiftly into caricature. Like Harte, he cannot be trusted. Both writers on the whole may be said to have lowered the standards of American literature, since both worked in the surface of life with theatric intent and always without moral background. O. Henry moves, but he never lifts. All is fortissimo; he slaps the reader on the back and laughs loudly as if he were in a bar-room. His characters, with few exceptions, are extremes, caricatures. Even his shop girls, in the limning of whom he did his best work, are not really individuals; rather are they types, symbols. His work was literary vaudeville, brilliant, highly amusing, and yet vaudeville.

On the whole the short story episode in American literary history has been a symptom not of strength but of weakness. "Short story writing is a young man's game," says H. G. Wells, and it may be added that it is also the natural device of the young nation just emerging from its adolescent period. To see life in true perspective, to know the truth in its breadth and depth, demands that we fix our attention not on fragments of life, on snatches of experience, on glimpses, swift impressions, but on wholes. America has not had the time to look steadily and long at any phase of the human play. All it has wanted has been momentary impressions artistically given, surface and sensations. It has been satisfied with cleverness rather than mastery, entertainment rather than instruction, with journalism rather than literature. What the coming period is to be it is not within the province of the historian to seek.

CHAPTER X

Historians and Scholars

1. PRESCOTT

WILLIAM HICKLING PRESCOTT (1796–1859) had all that a young Bostonian of a century ago could wish for, except health. He was handsome, with good and sound inheritance, cultivated surroundings, sympathetic and congenial parents and well-to-do family circumstances, and he was as well equipped for intellectual life as Harvard could make him. But ill-health and partial blindness, caused by an accident at college, barred the way to active life.

Thus it was, in 1821, seven years after graduation from college, that he decided to take up his pen as an occupation. First making a systematic study of rhetoric and diction, he read widely in English, French, and Italian literature, and then, through George Ticknor's interest in things Spanish, turned to that language. Once embarked, he sailed on in Spanish interests until his death. "What new and interesting topics may be admitted—not forced into—the reign of Ferdinand and Isabella?" he noted in 1825.

The whole sweep of events taking place on the Peninsula seems to have flashed before his vision: the constitutions of Castile and of Aragon, of the Moorish dynasties, the causes of their decay and dissolution, the Inquisition, the conquest of Granada, the discoveries in the unknown West, monarchical power *versus* aristocracy; and he saw their relation to the whole world. With his scene firmly set, he began a systematic course of international and legal history, in addition to a general survey of Spain, geographical, economical, ecclesiastical, and civil, especially with reference to fifteenth-century conditions. This necessitated the consultation of several hundred volumes in working days of about four hours each, with actual reading power of an hour a day at best, a few minutes or nothing, at worst. For a while he lingered at the threshold before plunging into Spanish details. He recurred to Montesquieu's *Esprit des lois*, to Voltaire, and to other philosophical considerations of history and human conditions; he heard governmental, theological, and chivalric works, many biographies and the classics, the last now in translation that they might be read aloud. By this time he had acquired a capacity of holding firmly in his mind the portions he saw he could use, while putting aside the non-essential.

The actual composition of *Ferdinand and Isabella* began in 1829, after eight years of preliminary reading. When it came to the form of his narrative, Prescott followed Mably as a guide, having read his *Étude de l'histoire* ten times. He would think out a chapter on the same structural plan as for a romance or a drama, letting the events develop towards some obvious point or conclusion. Everything pertinent to his subject, and accessible at that time, that could be taken out of Spain, was imported in original or in transcript and digested very slowly. Prescott worked his direct quotations into his text, as a rule, instead of giving excerpts thrown or jerked into the narrative. At the same time, his references are precise and accurate. When the book was finally done and submitted to the criticism of various friends, it excited only delighted approval and stimulating comments, encouraging the author to have 1250 copies printed at his own expense (1836–37). Such a success America had never before seen or heard of. The edition was exhausted in five weeks. Prescott was received at once into the international circle of authoritative scholarship. Hallam, Guizot, Milman, Sismondi, Thierry, were among those to give Prescott not condescending but cordial welcome as one of their own rank. Such an authority as C. P. Gooch states in 1913 that the work published in 1837 has not been superseded to this day.

Stimulated by the prompt recognition accorded to him, Prescott turned to his next venture, *The Conquest of Mexico*

(1844). It is characteristic of his methods that his first step towards beginning the narration in which one figure, Hernando Cortes, was to hold the centre of the stage, was the examination of certain celebrated biographical records of exploits—Voltaire's *Charles XII*, Livy's *Hannibal*, Irving's *Columbus*. The interest in the *Mexico* flags at the end. Where the glow of achievement is ahead of his hero, the narrative marches and carries the reader on. Or is it that Bernal Diaz carries the story triumphantly up to the Aztec city? That veteran soldier, unskilled in letters, moved to set down his recollections of the great events in which he had participated half a century back, because Gomara's official history gave Cortes undue, and his comrades insufficient, credit for the Conquest, was a delightful guide to follow. His untaught phrases are alive and Prescott makes them more so. While later judgment discounts some of the conquistadore's statements, it cannot deny the fact that it was these glowing descriptions that affected the European imagination of the sixteenth century. For the ultimate rating of the veracity of the complaisant adventurer archæology has brought its later contribution, and of that science Prescott was ignorant, as was the rest of the world when he wrote. Both *The Conquest of Mexico* and *The Conquest of Peru* (1847), which followed in regular course with much the same qualities as the *Mexico*, were important works in the development of American literature and the American attitude towards knowledge. Neither the reputation nor the libraries of New England could have spared them. Count d'Haussonville ranks the incomplete *Philip II* (1855), to which Prescott next turned, as his best work. That is a dictum hard to accept. The author's attitude towards his central figure may be called just, but there is a certain meagreness in the treatment.

Prescott has been called a great amateur in the historical field, and in one sense the term applies. Born only a year after Leopold Ranke, he missed the influence spread abroad, eventually far beyond German university circles, by the great German scholar. The very vocabulary now used had not come into being. Prescott made his own standards. Nor did he have the incidental training that has been the strength of many an historian. Not trained in the methods of the École des

Chartes, nor in the precise legal knowledge of jurisprudence, like Maitland, nor in active political service for his own state, nor in a school of philosophy, still less in the academic methods of research, Prescott simply assimilated language first and then events, and painted pictures of the past by a skilful union of the two. His style is a fine instrument of expression. His language plays him no tricks. He holds it in his own control, firmly, like a well-wrought, highly-tempered tool. His own temperament manifests itself very little in his writings. Nor is there any echo of contemporary politics in his treatment of the past. He was a Bostonian who hated strife and felt that agitation was disagreeable. Perhaps had Prescott survived the outbreak of the Civil War his sentiments would have changed. As it was, he passed from the scene before the outbreak, and thus is crystallized as a figure detached from strife, a non-partisan, hard-working yet leisurely historian, sheltered from the hard things of life, almost untouched by his generation, endowed with the best New England could give to a few of her sons, and with the type of New England conscience that led him to use the talents he had but which also permitted him to hold aloof from daily troubles.

2. Motley

JOHN LOTHROP MOTLEY (1814–77) was like Prescott in being a son of Massachusetts and born with a silver spoon of pure Boston metal in his mouth. But whereas Prescott was a prisoner within his own library, Motley had the stimulus of world contact, of hearing statesmen's voices, of activities of which Prescott was wholly ignorant. Motley's Harvard career was begun at the age of thirteen and completed at seventeen—an age young even for the time. His class work did not give him high rank—indeed, he was rusticated for negligence—but his personality was charming and his kind of cultivated human interest convincing. His facility in grasping the gist of a book was marvellous, but as it did not presage minute and accurate research, there was natural astonishment among his contemporaries over the industry evinced by his later work. Harvard was followed by two years of study at Göttingen and Berlin and of foreign travel. Perhaps the most interesting contribution to his training given by the Göttingen episode was his acquaintance and intimate association with Count Bismarck, the foundations of a life-long friendship. Later, Motley had the still rarer chance of glimpses at the inside happenings or intentions of Prussian politics. He saw a master mind in the making and in the doing. He worked hard, indeed, at law in both universities, but it was the glimpses of Europe and the human side of its life, both past and present, that were the really vital part of the educational results for the young American. Intellectual Germany was still palpitating with the influence of Goethe. Motley met scholars and learned what minute research could be. At the same time he retained an impressionistic attitude towards history. He always saw the past instinct with life.

When the wanderer returned to Boston he continued his preparation for law, but it never became his serious profession. Between the production of two novels, *Morton's Hope* (1839) and *Merry Mount* (1849), he had fresh experiences in the world of affairs. In 1841 he was appointed secretary to the legation at St. Petersburg and spent some months in the Russian capital. He served in the Massachusetts legislature for one term (1849). But now he began to show himself in another light than that of romancer or legislator. Before the publication of his half-historical *Merry Mount* he had selected the theme of the contest between the Netherlands and Spain for an extensive work, had been checked momentarily by the news of Prescott's projected *Philip II*, had been spurred on by the kindly words of the elder American, and had then devoted himself to going to the foundations of the story of the events. For nearly ten years he plodded on, at first in Boston and then in archives abroad, in Berlin, Dresden, The Hague, and Brussels. He bathed in local colour. In 1855 he had his three volumes ready for the printer. Like Prescott, Motley was obliged to take his own risks, and *The Rise of the Dutch Republic* (1855) was published at the author's expense. The sale of fifteen thousand copies in two years proved the fallibility of human judgment. The reviews were not as uniformly favourable as in Prescott's case. J. A. Froude, however, did full justice to the unknown American writer, though dissatisfied with Motley's estimate of Queen Elizabeth. All the eminent authorities on the period treated do just what Froude does. They like the way Motley has navigated the whole sea of difficulties but think he has lost his way on their private pools. In Holland and Belgium scholars received the book with pleasure as well as with profound surprise that any foreigner had cast his plummet down their deeps with so much assiduity. Motley could not complain of lack of appreciation in the Netherlands, and had reason to flatter himself that his work was a spur to the Netherlanders to look to their own dykes and consider carefully what was true among their writers of the sixteenth century and what needed to be winnowed.

Scarcely taking breath after the publication of this first great effort, the author plunged into the sequel and brought out two volumes of *The United Netherlands* in 1860. This time neither publisher nor public was shy. The English reviews were very favourable, on the whole; the American reviews had no reservations in their praise of both works. In Holland the second book received the same greeting as did the first, a greeting marked by pride and pleasure that a stranger had devoted so much of his life to their affairs, tempered by some careful and discriminating criticism. Fruin once more criticized Motley's failure to differentiate the values of his authorities and considered him often tempted to expand a phase simply because he had a rich store of material bearing upon it, but without due regard to the need of that phase in the narrative. That Motley's vivid imagination inspired him with interlinear visions, hardly substantiated by a strict construction of the text, was gently intimated by Fruin with one or two striking examples. Undoubtedly this is the same imagination that led the tourist to people the Rome before his eye with actors once within her walls.

The spring of 1861, momentous in the history of the United States, found Motley in London when news came of the outbreak of the Civil War. The London *Times* gave much space to comments on the terrible anachronism of war in general, and on the horror of seeing thirty million Anglo-Saxons slaying each other like the Indians whom they had displaced. After a little it declared that the spirit of George III had passed into Seward and that his reluctance to let the South go its own way was couched in language quite as tyrannical as that of the British monarch to his colonies when they desired "secession." Under the stimulus of these daily reiterations, Motley wrote two long letters on *The Causes of the Civil War*, to which the *Times* gave prominent space, and which were reprinted in New York within a few weeks. They were a plea for the sacredness of the Union as an organic, vitalized whole. The tariff, as an irritating cause of division, was discussed, while slavery was touched on very lightly. The Queen's Proclamation of Neutrality had already checked the press, and Motley's words were allowed to be worth noting, as coming from one already recognized as an historian of European reputation.

Shortly after this incident, Motley returned home, regretted that his forty-seven years disqualified him from enlisting without previous training, but was stirred to the depths of his being by the emotion of the summer months of 1861. Summoned to do other work for the republic, he accepted the mission to Austria, where, it was felt, the sentiment he had shown in his London letters might be serviceable. His office was no sinecure. In addition to the complications arising from the war, there were others connected with Maximilian's expedition to Mexico, in which he showed good judgment. But after the unexpected elevation of Andrew Johnson to the presidency in 1865, Motley took offence at an unjust accusation brought against him and resigned his post. The secretary of state would have taken no notice of a resignation offered under a momentary smart, but when Johnson said "Let him go," Seward did not try to stay his hand. The result was that Motley left Vienna with a very sharp wound to his self-respect.

Luckily for the ex-diplomat, the seventeenth century was waiting till he should be released from the claims of the nineteenth, and he plunged at once into the next period of his Netherland story. *The History of the United Netherlands* was concluded by two more volumes issued in 1868. A continuation centred about John of Barneveld was finally published in 1874. Motley returned from Vienna to Boston and was settled there at the time of Grant's first campaign, into which he entered with much interest. At the suggestion of Sumner, he was honoured by Grant with the appointment to the Court of St. James, the highest diplomatic post in his gift. That was pleasant after the Vienna incident. Unfortunately, Grant identified Motley with Sumner, and when a breach came between the president and the senator from Massachusetts, the former found a pretext to recall Motley, and again a secretary of state failed to protect the minister. The incident ended with added discomfiture for Motley. It is curious to note how his unpleasant experience colours the story of the relations between Maurice of Nassau and John of Barneveld. The inability of the soldier, acting as statesman, to understand the diplomat is dwelt on in a fashion to show that General Grant was in the historian's thoughts when he wrote of Count Maurice. Indeed, *John of Barneveld* is a reflection of autobiography almost as much as

Morton's Hope. Every point having to do with the ambitions of the individual province and the needs of the United Netherlands is coloured by the crisis through which the United States had just passed. In the Netherlands the book, having treated a period marked by the bitterest kind of theological disputes, brought down upon Motley's head a flood of pained criticism from the heirs to both sides of the controversy. At the same time, Dutch scholars paid warm tributes to the American's conscientious use of sources, though they might not accept his interpretation. In 1871 the Queen of the Netherlands offered him a house in the Dutch capital, where he spent part of the years when he was working at *John of Barneveld*.

What is the judgment of posterity upon the work into which Motley poured so much vigorous painstaking effort? This much can be said: he was first a brilliant searchlight, sweeping over an unknown field, and then an able draughtsman in describing the scene. Every new generation claims to have a light in its own hand which enables it to judge the past with greater accuracy than its predecessors. Scholars of today in Holland, Blok, Japikse, Colenbrander, all consider that the American failed to treat Netherland history on scientific lines. He did not understand Europe at large, he did not understand the Church. In his hands Philip II was treated too severely, as was Maurice in his conflict with Barneveld. There was a lack of perspective in his every estimate. Not only that, but in making one period so dominant, he dislocated the perspective of the whole history of the Netherlands. For the last thirty years scholars in Belgium as well as Holland have been working over the ground, bringing small dark places into sober light, shading down other points too highly illuminated. A fair result will be reached at last. But the great light was a pleasant and valuable thing.

3. Parkman

FRANCIS PARKMAN (1823–93) touched Prescott and Motley on one side by his interest in romantic themes, and on another side touched the more recent school of American historiography by his habits of elaborate research and his use of all accessible manuscript documents as well as of secondary material; but he was first of all an artist in expression, working in the field of history with such results as he could obtain, and yet working much as he might have done had he been a romancer of a very superior conscience.

Like Prescott, Parkman had the best of Boston's inheritance except health, and against the effects of that handicap he interposed a resolute spirit which enabled him to devote to his books the few hours he could snatch from a constant state of pain. From early life he had the desire to write the history of the New England border wars. During his college vacations he visited the scenes of these conflicts, and he read always widely in the books on that subject. In 1842 illness drove him to Italy to regain his health, and he there spent some time in a Passionist monastery, believing that he thus got some insight into the motives and spiritual processes of a type of mind which played a large part in the French civilization of the New World, though so alien to the English modes of religion among explorers and colonists. When Parkman graduated at Harvard in 1844 he knew the New England Indians thoroughly. Much of the next two years was spent in visiting the historic spots on the Pennsylvania border and in the region beyond. In 1846 he made a journey to the land of the Sioux, where he spent some weeks in the camps of a native tribe, studying the Indian in the savage state. His experiences were described in a series of letters in *The Knicker-bocker Magazine* and republished in his first book, *The California and Oregon Trail* (1849), still considered one of our best descriptions of Indian life.

Now prepared for his main task, Parkman took a striking incident of Indian history and wrote on it his *Conspiracy of Pontiac* (1851). In this book he placed much introductory matter on the Indians, together with a comprehensive review of the history of the French settlements before 1761, when the conspiracy of Pontiac began. From this large use of preliminary materials it would seem that he had not yet determined to undertake the series of volumes in which he later treated the same period. The *Pontiac* was well received and it was a good book from a young author. But it lacked conciseness and was overdrawn.

For several years after its publication Parkman suffered great physical pain, and he seemed about to lose the use of his eyes and limbs. But he never gave up his ambition or ceased to collect information about the Indians. In this interval he wrote *Vassall Morton* (1856), a novel which did not succeed. Turning back to history he revised his entire plan and outlined his *France and England in North America*. The series was limited to the period before the Pontiac war. It embraced the whole story of French colonization in North America from the Huguenot colonies of the sixteenth century to the fall of Quebec. The various parts appeared as follows: *The Pioneers of France in the New World* (1865); *The Jesuits in North America* (1867); *La Salle and the Discovery of the Great West* (1869); *The Old Régime in Canada* (1874); *Count Frontenac and New France under Louis XIV* (1877); *Montcalm and Wolfe* (2 vols., 1884); and *A Half Century of Conflict* (2 vols., 1892). He described the series as including "the whole course of the American conflict between France and England, or in other words, the history of the American forest; for this was the light in which I regarded it. My theme fascinated me, and I was haunted with wilderness images day and night." Parkman's purposes were wholly American. He loved the vast recesses of murmuring pines, with their tragedies, adventures, and earnest striving. Prescott and Motley might paint the gorgeous scenes of royal courts and Bancroft might interrupt his labours in writing the panegyric of democracy to play a complacent rôle as minister at Berlin, but Parkman never ceased to find his chief interest in the American forest and its denizens.

His avowed method of writing was "while scrupulously and rigorously adhering to the truth of facts, to animate them with the life of the past, and, so far as might be, clothe the skeleton with flesh. Faithfulness to the truth of history involves far more than research, however patient and scrupulous, into special facts. The narrator must seek to imbue himself with the life and spirit of the time." Few writers have achieved their ideal of expression as well as he. What Cooper did in the realm of fiction Parkman did with even better fidelity to nature in the realm of history. He never studied in the seminar school, but he understood its lessons instinctively and made them his own without loss of the best things in the old school—vigour, harmony, and colour. "With all its manifold instructiveness," says John Fiske, "his book is a narrative as entertaining as those of Macaulay or Froude. In judicial impartiality Parkman may be compared with Gardiner, and for accuracy of learning with Stubbs." In American literature he holds a singularly enviable place. Although he may be said to have created his own particular province of history, that concerned with the French in America, and though the field has since been often invaded by admirers and imitators, he still stands supreme in his department, the truest and most delightful of all who have touched those engaging matters.

4. Henry Adams

OF the three sons of Charles Francis Adams, grandsons of John Quincy Adams, who became historians, two of them, Charles Francis Adams, Jr., and Henry Adams (1838–1918), present a particularly interesting contrast. Both of them had the Puritan mind, so strong in their ancestry, as well as that independent Adams spirit which put the family, from John Adams to Henry, out of touch with the dominant thought of Boston. Turning to history, both of them became able critics of conventional views and won high respect from an age turning towards cosmopolitan ideals. The elder of the two, however, did not go all the way in revolt. New Englander he remained to the last. He loved Boston, although he rapped its knuckles at times, and he sought to reform its intellectual life. The younger clung to Boston for many years, giving himself to a phase of our history in which the town had a deep interest; but finally, having reached a stage of disillusionment, as he considered it, he broke local ties, turned toward the unanchored spaces of the remote past, and became a master in the realm of detached thinking.

The historical career of Henry Adams falls into two periods. One of them began with his return from London in 1868, where he had been private secretary to his father, then minister to Great Britain, and continued until 1892, when he turned his back on all he had been doing and began again what he termed his "education." The second extended from that change of purpose to his death. The editorship of *The North American Review* (1869–76) and an assistant-professorship in history at Harvard (1870–77) ushered in the first period. Teaching did not suit him and he resigned because he felt that his efforts were failures. His mind was too original to go through life in the routine of college instruction. He now turned to American history, producing by much industry in fourteen years the following books: *Documents Relating to New England Federalism* (1877), *Life of Albert Gallatin* (1879), *Writings of Albert Gallatin* (1879), *John Randolph* (1882), *History of the United States during the Administrations of Jefferson and Madison* (9 vols., 1889–91), and *Historical Essays* (1891). The best scholarship and excellent literary form characterize all these books. No better historical work has been done in this country. Yet the books were little read and the author became discouraged. He concluded that what he had been doing was without value to the world, since it was not noticed by the world. Of the two novels which he wrote during this period, the anonymous *Democracy* (1880) aroused much discussion by its mordant pictures of political corruption at Washington, but *Esther* (1884), which Adams persisted in publishing under a pseudonym and refused to allow to be advertised, fell upon a perfectly heedless world, though its discussion of current theological problems has genuine interest.

Then began the second period of his literary life. Settling down to a quiet life of study, and following his taste, he delved long and patiently in the Middle Ages. The result appeared in *Mont Saint Michel and Chartres* (1904, 1913), probably the best expression of the spirit of the Middle Ages yet published in the English language. It was followed by *Essays in Anglo-Saxon Law* (1905), *The Education of Henry Adams* (1906, 1918), *A Letter to American Teachers of History* (1910), and *Life of George Cabot* (1911). Two of these books, the *Mont Saint Michel* and the *Education*, deserve to rank among the best American books that have yet been written. The first is a model of literary construction and a fine illustration of how a skilled writer may use the history of a small piece of activity as a means of interpreting a great phase of human life. Through the *Education* runs a note of futility, not entirely counter-balanced by the brilliant character-sketching and wise observations upon the times. But the *Mont Saint Michel* redeems this fault. It shows us Henry Adams at his best, and under its charm we are prepared to overlook the aloofness which limited his interests while it depressed his spirits

In the *Education* Henry Adams defined history in these words: "To historians the single interest is the law of reaction between force and force—between mind and nature—the law of progress." He thus announced in his maturity his allegiance to the most modern concept of history. In his early historical writings he dealt with the relations of men with men, as Parkman, Lea, Mahan, and many others dealt. In his revised opinions he conceived that the story of man's progress as affected by natural forces was the true task of the historian. It is a concept to which the best modern thinkers have been slowly moving. Adams grasped it with the greatest boldness and in the *Mont Saint Michel* gave future historians an example of how to realize it in actual literature.

5. Ticknor

GEORGE TICKNOR was born in Boston in 1791. Having graduated from Dartmouth in 1807, he read Greek and Latin authors for three years with the rector of Trinity Church, Boston, a pupil of Samuel Parr. From 1810 Ticknor read law and in 1813 was admitted to the bar, but he gave up practice in a year. The country, he thought, "would never be without good lawyers," but would urgently need "scholars, teachers, and men of letters." From Madame de Staël's *De l'Allemagne* (1813) Ticknor had got an intimation of the intellectual mastery of the Germans; he elected therefore to study in Germany, and particularly at Göttingen.

Before going abroad, though, he must make the American grand tour to Washington and Virginia. During the winter of 1814–15 he travelled by slow stages and sometimes under difficulties as far as Richmond, everywhere supplied with introductions to and from eminent persons such as John Adams, President Madison, and Thomas Jefferson. He met, among others, Eli Whitney, Robert Lenox, John Randolph, and Charles Carroll of Carrollton; attended the Hartford Convention; saw the ruins of Washington, then recently burned by the British; and at Monticello got the news of their defeat at New Orleans. Already he was exhibiting the social gifts which later distinguished him—a power of holding substantial conversation when that was in order; a tact that kept him wisely and quizzically silent during an outburst of bad temper on the part of Adams, and in the presence of Jefferson's philosophical oddities; together with a cool sub-acid judgment in estimating and reporting such phenomena as these and the ways of men in general. He made an especially favourable impression upon

Jefferson, who twice—in 1818 and again in 1820—invited him to a chair at the University of Virginia.

In April, 1815, Ticknor sailed for Liverpool with Edward Everett and several other friends. At Liverpool and on the way to London he paid his respects to Roscoe and to Dr. Parr. In London he met Hallam, and various lesser scholars. At Göttingen Ticknor settled down to a monastic regimen of study, specializing in Greek. He met the Homeric Wolf, "coryphæus of German philologists," then on a visit to Göttingen; and, during an eight weeks' holiday trip across Germany, Gesenius and Goethe. For a full year he continued his classical studies without any notion that his field was to lie elsewhere. From Byron in London he had got hints for a tour in Greece, and he was preparing to make it, when late in 1816 Harvard offered him the College Professorship of the Belles Lettres and the Smith Professorship of the French and Spanish Languages and Literatures, then just established upon the death of its founder Abiel Smith. Accordingly Ticknor gave up his Greek tour, and after a few months in Göttingen began in the spring of 1817 an extensive course of travel and study in the Latin countries. In Paris he worked with great diligence at French and Italian. In Rome by November he studied Italian and archæology. Leaving Rome late in March of 1818, he made his way slowly to Spain via Italy and southern France. In Madrid he at once settled into his habitual studious ways. During the summer and autumn of 1818 he made several excursions and a considerable journey in Spain and Portugal; whence in November he went via England to Paris again. Here he privately studied Spanish literature, Portuguese, and Provençal. In London in January, 1819, he dropped study for awhile, and was taken up by the great Whigs—Lord Holland, Sir James Mackintosh, Richard Heber, Hookham Frere, Lord John Russell, and Sydney Smith. He visited the Marquis of Salisbury at Hatfield House and the Duke of Bedford at Woburn Abbey; again touched classical studies in a sojourn at Cambridge; and before February reached Edinburgh. Picking out, as was usual with him, a specialist to help him in his studies, he read Scotch poetry. Here he frequented the Tory circle of Mrs. Grant of Laggan, and made the acquaintance of

Scott, whom he visited at Abbotsford for a few days; proceeding thence to Southey at Keswick and to Wordsworth at Rydal Mount. At Hatton he saw old Dr. Parr once more, who condemned everything contemporary but gave Ticknor his blessing.

In London again, early in April, Ticknor went with Irving to the "damning of a play" and afterwards to the Lord Mayor's ball, which he also damns in a series of contemptuous remarks about the "City crowd." Though he had already disparaged Godwin as the "notorious William Godwin," he dined at his house; and then proceeded to disparage him further, together with the company he met there, including Hazlitt, Hunt, and Lamb. Ticknor was as much at home with the "big Whigs" as with the grand Tories, especially the great Tory of Abbotsford; *Whig Toriusve mihi nullo discrimine agetur*, he might have said; but he could not abide a Philistine or a Bohemian.

At the end of April, 1819, after a brief visit to Roscoe in Liverpool, he sailed for home, and reached Boston early in June, with an equipment far beyond that of any previous American student. His teaching at Harvard began in the same year and continued until he resigned in 1835. Like Everett's, it was so far in advance of his time and of the training his students brought to it that he founded no school of research and made no disciples in advanced scholarship. But he greatly improved elementary instruction in the modern languages, and could find sometimes (as in 1831) a class that would read Dante with him; he established for his own subjects a departmental system, with considerable freedom of election, and with promotion and grouping according to proficiency; and he went as far as the college authorities would allow in establishing an elective system within his own jurisdiction. These reforms being opposed, actively by some other members of the faculty, passively by President Kirkland, Ticknor felt, after sixteen years of service, that he had done all the missionary work that could reasonably be expected of him. He resigned his professorship, and made a second sojourn in Europe (1835–38), Longfellow having been chosen to be his successor.

This second residence in Europe Ticknor undertook not primarily as a student but as a ripe scholar; and although he had as yet produced no great work, he was everywhere received as one whose standing was assured. The acquaintances he formed or renewed are too numerous to be even catalogued in full. In England he saw a good deal of the scientific men. At Dresden he examined Ludwig Tieck's collection of Spanish books, and he joined the scholarly circle of Prince John of Saxony. In Berlin in the spring of 1836 Ticknor visited the church historian Neander, and saw Alexander von Humboldt frequently. In Vienna, in June, he examined the old Spanish books in the Imperial Library. After a summer in Switzerland and southern Germany, he moved towards Rome, which he reached in December, and in which he remained until May of 1837. He went north for the summer again, to Venice, Innsbruck, and Heidelberg, and to Paris for the winter, where he looked over the Spanish library of Ternaux-Compans and frequented the study of Augustin Thierry. By March, 1838, Ticknor was in England again, having long talks with Hallam. He once more visited Southey and Wordsworth at Keswick; was disappointed in the Spanish collection at the Bodleian; met at breakfast "a Mr. Ruskin," who had a most beautiful collection "of sketches, made by himself, from nature, on the Continent"; and heard Carlyle lecture.

Arriving at home in June, 1838, Ticknor settled down to research, to extensive correspondence with many friends, both European and American, to the collecting of Spanish books, and to the writing of his *History of Spanish Literature*, which was published in 1849 and was at once recognized as a work of international standing. He found time also to work hard for the Boston Public Library, of which he was a trustee; doing for it what his friends Buckminster and Cogswell had done respectively for the Athenæum and the Astor. Upon the third and last of his European tours, undertaken in 1856–57 for the sake of the library, he had little time for his own studies, but he was lionized—being now the author of a famous book—as never before, and moved in the most brilliant society. At home again from September, 1857, Ticknor took up once more his life of study and business, serving the library until 1866, revising the *History of Spanish Literature* for its third and its fourth editions, maintaining a voluminous correspondence, and, after the death of Prescott in 1859, writing his *Life* (1864). At this time, too, Ticknor resumed his active interest in Harvard. He died in 1871.

Ticknor's life, as recorded in his *Life, Letters and Journals*, is that of a great man of business, a great social talent, almost a *grand seigneur*, who stood before kings, or rather sat down with them,—and who was incidentally a scholar. It is necessary, in an account of his works, to distribute the emphasis in this way, partly because the *Life*, considered as one of them, depends decisively upon his social powers, which elicited characteristic attitudes and utterances from the persons he met, and partly because these powers gave a characteristic turn even to the *History of Spanish Literature*. The *Life*, a treasury of anecdote and portraiture, which it costs an effort not to quote, would, if well annotated, be found to be also a compendium of European history in its social and literary aspects during the first half of the nineteenth century. The English great houses, the Paris salons, the German courts and scholars, the international social complex at Rome and Florence—Ticknor saw more of these than any other American, and than any but a few of the most highly placed Europeans. His *Life* is, emphatically, good reading, and can only increase in interest with time.

His *History of Spanish Literature* has so impressed critics by its great reputation and by its great conception, scope, and bulk, that they have given it rather praise than appraisal. The claim made by the editors, in their preface to the fourth edition, represents the current opinion of its merits. "So far as the past is concerned, the history of Spanish literature need not be written anew, and the scholars who may hereafter labour in this field of letters will have little else to do than to continue the structure which Mr. Ticknor has reared." Now it is true that Ticknor is strong in his sense of fact, in his feeling for evidence, and in the sanity of his opinions. Very few indeed of his attributions need revision in the light even of the acutest later scholarship. His very comprehensive bibliography, universally praised by his critics, is a second consequence of his strength. He had probably handled and read more Spanish books than had anybody else in his time. His thoroughness extends also to a pretty full use of existing authorities, Spanish, German, French, and English. His combination of their results with those of his own bibliographical research constitutes his title to be considered a pioneer. Still, pioneer work is one thing; definitive work is another. In many fields of Spanish literature it was Ticknor's task actually to find and identify the works he describes. For such work—the primary dealings with raw material—his mind was well fitted. But the later regroupings and higher generalizations of the inductive process, the perception of broad differences, resemblances, connections, and tendencies, the framing of comprehensive concepts, and, in general, the freedom of movement in the conceptual world—these things require a mind set free from the pedestrian tasks to which Ticknor willingly committed himself, and another strength than the one he had. There were temperamental reasons, too, why Ticknor could never have made such a higher synthesis. He belongs essentially to the hard-headed group of American writers who, like Andrews Norton, stopped short of transcendentalism. Ticknor's German training had taught him what much of the British scholarship of his time sorely needed to learn—the need of the broadest possible basis in facts; from that point onward, however, his scholarship remained essentially British in its distrust of ideas. The *History of Spanish Literature* is much more like Warton's *History of English Poetry* and Hallam's *Middle Ages* than it is like anything German. More serious temperamental defects are still to be mentioned. The plain fact is that Ticknor did not possess certain of the indispensable organs of literary scholarship. He lacked *ordonnance;* he was blind to the French literature of the Middle Ages and of the Renaissance; and he wanted ear—especially for verse. His lack of the sense for sequence, arrangement, and emphatic or conspicuous position appears even in the unworkmanlike construction of many of his sentences, and in the misplacement of matter (especially in footnotes) just at the point where random association happened to make him think of it. In his references to French literature, which in the Middle Ages and the Renaissance was so closely connected with Spanish, he disparages Ronsard and misassigns him with the decadents; he has not a word about Du Bellay; and, almost incredibly, he seems not even to have known of the *Chanson de Roland.* His want of ear and want of the sense of arrangement make his history difficult reading. Only occasionally does it attain anything worthy of the name of style.

6. Whitney

THE greatest English-speaking student of general linguistics and of the science of language, William Dwight Whitney (1827–1894), was born at Northampton to a fine local and family tradition of manners, character, and scholarship. Having graduated in 1845 at Williams College, he later became an assistant to his brother Josiah, who in 1849 was conducting the United States survey of the Lake Superior region; and he wrote for the report of the expedition the chapter on botany. Meanwhile he had become interested in Sanskrit; he studied it in his leisure time during the survey, and immediately afterward went to Yale for graduate study in the Department of Philosophy and the Arts, which Professor Salisbury had been active in organizing (1846–48), and which was the first graduate school of genuine university rank in the United States.

From 1850 to 1853 Whitney studied in Berlin under Weber, Bopp, and Lepsius, and at Tübingen under Roth. Returning to the United States in 1853, he was next year appointed Salisbury's successor in the chair of Sanskrit, his duties including instruction in the modern languages. He was not released from undergraduate teaching until 1869, when Salisbury increased the endowment of Whitney's Yale professorship, and Whitney became "the only 'university professor' . . . in the whole country." He was now enabled to organize fully a graduate school of philology, which very soon attracted able students, among them Charles R. Lanman, Irving Manatt, Bernadotte Perrin, A. H. Edgren, and William Rainey Harper, who well represent the variety of interest arising from the studies which Whitney directed. From 1850 Whitney had been a member of the American Oriental Society, and he became successively its corresponding secretary, its librarian, and its president. From 1857 to 1885 more than half of the Society's *Journal* came from his busy pen. He was also one of the founders and was the first president of the American Philological Association.

Whitney produced a large volume of work, and left his mark upon many different departments of scholarship. His important achievements in his particular field of Indology can be truly evaluated only by Indologists. His first large work in Indian scholarship was his edition, with Roth, of the *Atharva-Veda-Sanhitā* (1855–56), and his very last was the translation of the same Veda, edited after his death by Charles R. Lanman (1905). Whitney edited in 1862 the *Atharva-Veda-Prātiçākhya* with a translation and notes, and in 1871 the *Taittirīya Prāti-çākhya*. "The Prātiçākhyas are the phonetico-grammatical treatises upon the texts of the Vedas, and are of prime importance for the establishment of the text. Their distinguishing feature is minutiæ of marvellous exactness, but presented in such a form that no one with aught less than a tropical Oriental contempt for the value of time can make anything out of them as they stand. Whitney not only out-Hindus the Hindu for minutiæ, but also, such is his command of form, actually recasts the whole so that it becomes a book of easy reference."[1] These intensive studies of the Hindu grammarians and of the Sanskrit texts gave Whitney the material for his great Sanskrit *Grammar* (1879), with its supplement, *The Roots, Verb-forms, and Primary Derivatives of the Sanskrit Language* (1885), which together form "the crowning achievement" of his work as a Sanskrit scholar. Whitney's book goes behind the Hindu grammarians and rests upon direct induction from the texts. Beginning thus with the phenomena, Whitney might not be too severely condemned if, like Ticknor in the *Spanish Literature*, he had failed to rise much above their merely factual level. But his induction is complete; there are none of those confused categories or obscure arrangements that betoken failure to reach illuminating concepts. Whitney has thus left for the use of students in Indo-European linguistics an organon that is not likely to be soon discarded.

[1] C. R. Lanman: *Memorial Address*, in Whitney Memorial Volume.

Whitney's works upon the general science of language—*Language and the Study of Language* (1867), *The Life and Growth of Language* (1875), etc., might perhaps never have been written if he "had not been driven to it by . . . the necessity of counteracting as far as possible the influence" of Max Müller's views. Against the idealism, transcendentalism, and logical fallacies of Müller, Whitney takes a distinctly common-sense and almost pragmatic view. Language is for him a human institution, an instrument made by man to meet human needs, and at no time beyond human control. It has to be acquired afresh by every speaker, for it is not a self-subsisting entity that can be transmitted through the body or the mind of race or individual. Whitney thus decisively ranges himself against all absolutist and determinist theories of the nature of language. Upon the origins of language, though he declined to commit himself, as feeling that the evidence warranted no positive assertion, he yet felt equally certain that the evidence did *not* warrant Müller's assertion of a multiple origin—languages springing up here, there, and everywhere upon the surface of the earth. The trend of Whitney's opinion, though he asserts nothing positively, is towards a single primal language.

As in Indology, so in general linguistics, Whitney left a school, represented in Germany by the so-called Jung-Grammatiker, who include Osthoff, Brugmann, Leskien, Fick, and Paul, and in the United States by Professor Hanns Oertel and other disciples. They emphasize the importance of analogy and of phonetic economy, as chief among the psychic factors that must be added to the physical in order to account fully for linguistic change. All Whitney's modes of thinking tended away from those integrations which take the investigator back towards undifferentiated origins, and worked forward among the differentiations that account for linguistic progress towards the present and the future. Whitney is much more interested in the processes of linguistic change than in the evidences of linguistic unity.

The forward look is equally characteristic of his work in orthography and lexicography, which assumed that neither in meaning nor in form is language to be dominated by its past. He consistently and lucidly favoured a reformed spelling, but here too his common sense and regard for present actualities controlled his doctrine, and he never made among the lay public any propaganda looking to the adoption of a phonetic system. In the same way, when he came to the making of *The Century Dictionary*, he conceived it as bound to offer, not a standard of "correctness" derived from classical periods in the past, but a compendium of the actual use and movement of the word throughout its history. Together with this kinetic conception both of the vocabulary and of the semantics of his *Dictionary*, Whitney gave the most minute attention to his etymologies and definitions. Among the editors of Webster's *Dictionary* in 1864, Whitney and Daniel Coit Gilman had had special charge of the revision of the definitions; for the *Century* Whitney obtained the assistance of his brother Josiah in defining the technological words, and the assistance of other experts in their special fields. The result was an extensive vocabulary intensively defined. The etymologies are brought up to the state of knowledge in 1891. The quotations (undated) illustrate rather than fully set forth the semantic history of the word; the *Century* in this respect is surpassed by the *Oxford Dictionary*, to which alone among English dictionaries it is in any respect second.

Whitney's own writing is a model of lucid exposition. It neither has nor needs adventitious ornament; it does not even need the play of humour to make his most technical essays readable. There are to be sure, flashes of a polemic wit, but what keeps the text alive and at work is the reader's sense that he is in powerful hands that bear him surely along. Whitney seems to divine that particular analysis of his material which will carry the reader cleanly through it. The ultimate impression left by his writings is that of a powerful intellect controlling enormous masses of fact and moving among them as their master. To be interesting, such power needs no play other than its own.

CHAPTER XI

Preachers and Philosophers

1. BEECHER

HENRY WARD BEECHER was born in the orthodox uplands of Litchfield, and of a strictly Calvinistic sire. Lyman Beecher had studied theology under Timothy Dwight at Yale; had occupied, after 1798, first the Presbyterian pulpit at Easthampton, Long Island, next the Congregational pulpit at Litchfield, and lastly that of the Hanover Street Church in Boston; until in 1832 he became President of the newly established Lane Theological Seminary in Cincinnati. He is best known, perhaps, for his *Six Sermons on Intemperance*, but he was a dogmatist as well as a moralist, staunchly supporting the Calvinism of his native tradition.

His son Henry, graduating at Amherst in 1834 in no doubt as to his vocation, at once entered the Lane Theological Seminary, and studied under his father and under Calvin Stowe, an Oriental scholar of real attainment, who in 1836 married Beecher's sister Harriet. Beecher served his apprenticeship in the pulpit at Lawrenceburg and Indianapolis, whence in 1847 he was called to the new Brooklyn congregation of Plymouth Church. The liberal movement of his thought paralleled his geographical wanderings from the region of orthodoxy, through the region of culture, to the practical West, and back to the metropolitan East. He had had his fill of dogmatic theology in youth, and never took much further interest in it. He became more and more a minister, looking rather to the needs of humanity than to the theory of divinity. In the West, under the stress of primitive conditions, he soon threw overboard a system of doctrines in which, he found, plain people were not interested; so that by the time he took the Brooklyn pulpit, which soon became a national platform, he was preaching straight at human nature, and touching it with a more and more liberating hand as he advanced in years.

From his *Seven Lectures to Young Men* (1844) to his *Evolution and Religion* (1885) he came a long way. The *Lectures* are addressed apparently not to young men in general, but to young employees—clerks, mechanics, salesmen, and apprentices. Hence their flavour of *Poor Richard* and the *Industrious Apprentice*. Guided to his audience by Franklin and Hogarth, Beecher combines allegory with vivid eighteenth-century realism; bigoted invective against the theatre and novels, with "characters": the Sluggard, the Busybody, the Dandy, the Pleasure-Loving Business Man, the Cynic, the Libertine. This antique literary material explains the excessively old-fashioned flavour of the book. Though Beecher grew immeasurably away from it, he seems never to have disavowed or changed it, and for fifty years it remained perhaps his most popular work.

To Beecher's Western period also belong short pieces which first appeared in an Indiana agricultural paper and were later (1859) reprinted as *Plain and Pleasant Talk about Fruit, Flowers and Farming*. Of no intrinsic literary importance, they are of interest as showing the sources of much of Beecher's imagery. He was always close to the soil, and he drew from natural phenomena some of his most effective "illustrations." The *Star Papers* (1855 and 1859) and the *Eyes and Ears* (1862), collections of short essays, are good reading even now. With naïveté and self-depreciation, Beecher records his impressions of his first tour in Europe, tells of holiday outings among the Connecticut hills and trout streams, and gives plainly and modestly his very sensible opinions upon such subjects as sudden conversion, mischievous self-examination, and total depravity. The latter doctrine he rejects, accepting the doctrine of men's sinfulness and the necessity of their atonement not because Adam fell but because sin is actual and present. With regard to conversion, he takes the empiricist view that only in rare cases does the inner clock strike twelve when men have found grace; they may have it, yet not have infallible evidence. Hence he deprecates excessive introspection and hesitation, and says "Go ahead." His reminiscences, too, of old Litchfield at a time when that lucky town held Miss Pierce's Female Seminary and the celebrated Law School of Judge Gould and Judge Tapping Reeve, are discursive essays of permanent interest. His story of how, having as a boy of thirteen visited the Charleston Navy Yard, he stole a cannon ball and went away with it in his hat, is as enjoyable as Franklin's apologues of *The Axe to Grind* and of *Paying too Dear for One's Whistle.* The *Essay on Apple Pie* is not *toto cælo* removed from the *Dissertation upon Roast Pig.* *Home Revisited,* the record of a few days in Indianapolis, recalls the first of his sermons which he considered a success because it was aimed at his hearers; and tells by the way of his awe of Jonathan Edwards. "I never could read . . . *Sinners in the Hands of an Angry God* . . . at one sitting. I think a person of moral sensibilities, alone at midnight, reading that awful discourse, would well nigh go crazy." Through many of these pieces there breathes a frank sensuous enjoyment of physical beauty, which passes easily into religious exaltation. Beecher revels in the form and colour of great painting, and in the sounds, sights, and colours of landscape; the pictures in the Louvre and the glories of a sunset are to him literally revelations. These volumes testify once more to the richness of his mental imagery, and to its decided growth in range and in culture after his removal to the East.

Meanwhile, during all the years from his first pulpit to the beginning of the Civil War, his opposition to slavery had been deepening. He never joined the Abolitionists, but untiringly opposed the extension of slavery, and during the decade from 1850 to 1860, in lectures and in contributions to periodicals, denounced the various compromises and outrages that led up to the conflict. *Freedom and War* (1863), a volume of spirited sermons and addresses from the Brooklyn pulpit, exhibits the growth of his opinions up to the moment when he began to advocate immediate abolition—a moment just before the Emancipation Proclamation itself.

In educating public opinion upon slavery, Beecher had been

unconsciously preparing his own armament for uses which he could not have guessed. While upon a vacation in England in the autumn of 1863 he was asked to speak on the war, and in the course of eleven days delivered almost impromptu, at Manchester, Glasglow, Edinburgh, Liverpool, and London, the series of addresses which gave him perhaps his greatest celebrity. Some of his audiences, notably those at Liverpool and Glasglow, were most tumultuous, and had actually to be conquered by the speaker. He conquered them, and won over the English middle class to sympathy with the Union cause. The determination of the British government to maintain strict neutrality is said to have been largely due to Beecher's effect upon public opinion. As literature, the addresses in England, though of course they bear the marks of their hasty composition and contested delivery, yet reveal the easy mastery of his material which Beecher had been storing up in his years of preparatory Writing and speaking. Their lucidity and humour are still delightful; they still throw off visibly the live sparks that were struck out in the original clash between the speaker and his hearers; they reproduce the time in its very form and pressure; and in their way, too, they are classics of argumentation, for Beecher realizes the essential Aristotelian form of rhetoric—the orator's persuasion of an audience confronting him. The history of slavery and of secession could hardly be read in a more interesting form.

In *Norwood, or Village Life in New England* (1868), advertised as "Mr. Beecher's only novel," Beecher attempted an excursion into imaginative literature, but failed for want of breath. He had no power of construction and very little power of characterization. The personages are lay figures moving through an action prescribed for them by the author, and speaking his language, not their own. The general woodenness of the book, and several delightful absurdities, lay it open to easy parody. So much allowed, *Norwood*, if taken not as a novel but as a series of sketches of New England types, descriptions of New England scenery, and discussions not too profound of topics in religion, politics, and æsthetics, has distinct merit. This is much the same merit that is exhibited, under much the same limitations, by Beecher's essays and sermons: though he had imagination, he had no architectonic.

Beneath the routine activities of the next twenty years—his regular sermons, the public addresses for which he was more and more in request, and his sentimental *Life of Jesus the Christ* (1871), Beecher was quietly conducting an earnest study of the evolutionary philosophy. From the very beginning of his acquaintance with the new way of thinking, he seems to have felt that it would be his latest and his last instrument for enfranchising the soul; and when he had accomplished his task of educating public opinion at home and abroad toward the abolition of slavery, he turned to this other task of spiritual emancipation. "If I had preached thirty years ago," he says in one of the sermons of his *Evolution and Religion* (1885), "what I preach now, it would have been a great mischief to you; but for thirty years I have been cautious, and have fed you as you could bear it."

Beecher did not, it would seem, understand the full power of the instrument he was employing, and as he was a man of images and not of ideas he never brought his own self-contradictions to a clear issue. In his prevailing mood he makes the assumption, which comes down to him from Platonism, natural religion, and Transcendentalism, that nature is a symbol of God and the moral order, is a continuing revelation of God, is sympathetic with humanity, and is parallel, analogous, and favourable to religion and morals. Often, however, he realizes to some extent, and frankly declares as far as he realizes it, the inevitable implication of the theory of natural selection, that nature is alien to the moral strivings of man, and is thoroughly unmoral if not immoral. When he is conscious of his self-contradiction at all, Beecher seems merely puzzled by it as by one mystery among many. It would of course be fatal to his work if that work were a philosophical system—which it is not.

Despite his indecision upon this central problem, really the problem of evil itself, Beecher succeeds in giving sight and freedom to souls weighed down and blinded by the old unhappy dogma of depravity. Without denying man's sinfulness, he reverses the whole prospect of humanity by simply declaring that it is not true that men were created innocent but fell and incurred a debt which they could never hope to pay; but rather that the human race began low down, has not come up very far, and has the opportunity for limitless development upward.

Beecher's close contact with his audience and the abundance of his imagery are the sources of his peculiar power. They keep his style homely and racy (Robert South he declared to have been his chief model), and hold his thought and feeling near to human needs. He deliberately cultivated both. He carried pocketfuls of gems, which he loved to turn over and examine; he haunted picture-galleries and jewellers' shops. Like Whitman, whom he is said to have influenced, he walked the streets, spent whole days among the docks and ferry boats, made himself familiar with all sorts of trades, and talked with all sorts of people. These sources of power were also at times sources of weakness. Beecher came to depend upon hearers rather than readers; his hand faltered when he felt himself out of contact with an audience; and as he could not bring himself to revise with any degree of care the reports of his oral discourse, the form in which much of it has come to us is distinctly sub-literary. His exuberance of imagery also upon occasion betrayed him into incongruity and bathos. Yet his writings as a whole produce a deepening impression of merit. Here was a large personality, all of a piece, singularly free from repressions, and with no closet for a skeleton to lurk in. Beecher's openness of soul—exhibiting frankly his delight in beautiful things and in human contacts—is perhaps his characteristic note, and together with the great historical interest of his work will probably go far to render it permanent.

2. Brooks

PHILLIPS BROOKS (1835–93)[1] was most fortunately constituted and placed to be a great preacher. Just about the time of his birth in Boston, his family gave up its pew in the Unitarian meeting-house and, as a compromise between its Unitarian and Congregational strands, took one in St. Paul's Episcopal Church, its freedom and strength becoming tinged with mystery and wrapped about indignified historicity. And when Phillips Brooks, after an unsuccessful experiment in teaching in the Boston Latin School, hesitatingly determined to be a minister, his mind seemed to rest in the solidarity of humanity, in the perpetual and abiding emotions, conceptions, and satisfactions which underlie all change. The strong conservatism, so often noted in college students, seemed to remain with him long after the undergraduate years and to be a constitutive element of his character.

With the great controversies of his times he was not unacquainted. He took the gradually prevailing view with regard to them all. He believed the great books of other religions to be "younger brothers" of the Bible. He travelled with sympathetic interest in India and Japan. "No mischief," he thought, "can begin to equal the mischief which must come from the obstinate dishonesty of men who refuse to recognize any of the new light which has been thrown upon the Bible." When Heber Newton was threatened with a trial for heresy because of his belief in the methods and some of the more radical conclusions of the higher criticism, Brooks invited

[1] The volume the writer of this chapter would recommend as an introduction to Brooks's writings is the fourth series of his sermons, entitled *Twenty Sermons*, published in 1886. The new edition (1910) is entitled *Visions and Tasks*.

him to preach in his pulpit.   He says remarkably little regarding the Darwinian controversy.   He had but a superficial acquaintance with science.   He finds his comfort in believing that "the orderliness of nature must make more certain the existence of an orderer," and suggests that "Christ's truth of the Father Life of God has the most intimate connection with Darwin's doctrine of development, which is simply the continual indwelling and action of creative power."   He added, however, but little to the controversies.   Save where, as in the problem of comparative religion, they came into close contact with his own gospel of the universal sonship of man to God, he was not fundamentally interested in them. His sympathetic sermon on Gamaliel, who left the upshot of controversies to God, is characteristic.   In the Theological Seminary at Alexandria he wrote in his student's notebook:

> Truth has laid her strong piers in the past Eternity and the Eternity to come and now she is bridging the interval with this life of ours. . . .   Controversies grow tame and tiresome to the mind which has looked on Truth. . . .   We walk the bridge of life. Can we not trust its safety on the two great resting-places of God's wisdom?

Phillips Brooks was habitually more aware of the background than of the foreground.   Occasionally, indeed, it was otherwise.   In his Philadelphia ministry he spoke out boldly, at the conclusion of the War, for negro suffrage.   In his later life the radical in him showed itself more conspicuously.   He rose in his place in the Church Congress to plead for the use of the Revised Version of the Bible in public worship, and in the Convention of 1886 he protested vigorously against the proposal to strike the words "Protestant Episcopal" from the title of his Church.   On his return from the Convention to Boston, he even went so far as to declare from the pulpit that if the name were changed, he did not see how any one could remain in the Church who, like himself, disbelieved in the doctrine of Apostolic Succession.   But in the main he lived above controversy.   He believed neither in "insisting on full requirements of doctrine nor on paring them down. . . .   The duty of such times as these is to go deeper into the spirituality of our

truths. . . . ɹesus let the shell stand as he found it, until
the new life within could burst it for itself." His rare biographer, A. V. G. Allen, makes this significant comment upon
a Thanksgiving sermon of his:

He offers no solution of the conflict between religion and science.
But it means something that in the disorder of thought and feeling,
so many men are fleeing to the study of orderly nature. He urges
his hearers to make much of the experiences of life which are perpetual, joy, sorrow, friendship, work, charity, relation with one's
brethren, for these are eternal.

For Brooks this was no evasion. It was digging below the
questions of the day to the eternal, unquestioned, proven
truths of human experience. It was losing one's self in humanity. He occasionally looked forward, and increasingly,
but he loved best to look from the present backward and upward. Just after his graduation from Harvard, we find this
in his notebook:

A spark of original thought . . . strengthens a man's feeling of
individuality, but weakens his sense of race. It is an inspiring,
ennobling, elevating, but not a social thing. But what a kindly
power, what a warm human family feeling clusters around the
thought which we find common to our mind and to some old mind
which was thinking away back in the twilight of time. . . . So
when we recognize a common impulse or rule of life . . . we must
feel humanity in its spirit, bearing witness with our spirits, that it
is the offspring of a common divinity.

His native conservatism lived through the awakening years
of the Seminary. We find these musings in his notebook:

Originality is a fine thing, but first have you the head to bear it?
. . . Our best and strongest thoughts, like men's earliest and
ruder homes, are found or hollowed in the old primæval rock. . . .
Not till our pride rebels against the architecture of these first homes
and we go out and build more stately houses of theory and speculation and discovery and science, do we begin to feel the feebleness
that is in us.

As this biographer keenly says: "Nowhere in these note-books does Brooks regard himself as a pioneer in search of new thought. . . . He does not test truth by individual experiences but by the larger experiences of humanity." He told the Yale theological students in his middle life that a part of the Christian assurance lies in the fact that the Christian message is "the identical message which has come down from the beginning." Part of his satisfaction in preaching lay in his confidence that he was in his proper communion. He rejoiced "in her strong historic spirit, her sense of union with the ages which have passed out of sight." The insignia of spiritual truth to him were largely antiquity and catholicity. He had profound faith in the people. He believed in prophets when they had been accepted by the people; that is, usually some ages after they have lived and died. Few prominent men have let their friends and the public decide in their crises more than Brooks—and in nearly every case against his own original instinct. He relied on the heart of humanity as the supreme judge. Out of this primitive conviction of his grew his one essential message, that every man who has ever lived is a son of God. Consequently when a great doctrine came before him which had the ages of experience behind it or upon it, the question he asked was not "Is it true?" but "Why is it true?" or "Wherein resides its truth?" So it was with the great pivotal doctrine of the divinity of Christ, or, as he preferred to call it, the Incarnation. He found its truth to reside in the fact that Christ had lived out the secret yearnings and possibilities of humanity; Christ was the prophecy of the Christ that was everywhere to be. On the great question of the miracles he was orthodox. He lived in a time when Biblical criticism in this country was in its earlier stages. He could honestly write to a German inquirer: "There is nothing in the results of modern scholarship which conflicts with the statements in the Apostles' and Nicene Creeds concerning the birth of Jesus." As Allen remarks, Brooks was in the habit of "sheathing his critical faculties where the people's faith was concerned." He used the Bible, therefore, pretty much as he found it, or rather he used what he found beneath it.

It was toward middle life, about the time that a fresh study of the Gospels found expression in the *Influence of Jesus* (1880), that his emphasis seemed to shift from historic Christianity to the personal Christ. Over and over he insisted on the centrality of Christ. "Not Christianity but Christ! Not a doctrine but a person! Christianity only for Christ! . . . Our religion is—Christ. To believe in Him is what? To say a Creed? To join a church? No, but to have a great, strong, divine Master, whom we perfectly love." And how perfectly he loved him and how Christ responded to the embraces of this man's love, a letter on the eve of his consecration to the bishopric shows:

These last years have a peace and fulness which there did not use to be. I do not think it is the mere quietness of advancing age. I am sure it is not indifference to anything which I used to care for. I am sure that it is a deeper knowledge and truer love of Christ. . . . I cannot tell you how personal this grows to me. He is here. He knows me and I know Him. It is no figure of speech. It is the reallest thing in the world. And every day makes it realler. And one wonders with delight what it will grow to as the years go on.

And yet, notwithstanding his anchorage in the past, he believed in a port ahead, for each individual primarily, but also for the race. Even his ecstatic and unreserved loyalty to the incarnate Christ did not serve as an iron door let down athwart the highway of progress. He intimated that his teaching regarding divorce was determined by temporary circumstances and that his scheme of punishments is not an essential factor of his religion. It is true, naturally, with his strong belief in immortality and in the individual's sonship to God, that he held that society is here for the sake of the individual and not the individual for the sake of society. But in the later years we find almost a new note in his writings. "Life may become too strong for literature," he says. "It may be the former methods and standards are not sufficient for the expression of the growing life, its new activities, its unexpected energies, its feverish problems. . . . A man must believe in the future more than he reverences the past." In a speech before the Boston Chamber of Commerce he is reported as having said that "the world was bound to press onward and find an escape from the things that terrified it, not by retreat but by a perpetual progress into the large calm that lay beyond." In the sermon which gives the title to his volume *The Light of the World* (1890),—wherein is succinctly set forth his gospel, "the essential possibility and richness of humanity and its essential belonging to divinity,"— we have these majestic words:

It is so hard for us to believe in the mystery of man. "Behold man is this," we say, shutting down some near gate which falls only just beyond, quite in sight of, what human nature already has attained. If man would go beyond that, he must be something else than man. And just then something breaks the gate away, and, lo far out beyond where we can see, stretches the mystery of man, the beautiful, the awful mystery of man. To him, to man, all lower lives have climbed, and, having come to him, have found a field where evolution may go on for ever.

Such passages are rare in his writings, for usually his gaze takes in the past with Christ resplendent in it and does not lose itself in the future; then gratitude gets the upper hand of struggle. He rarely preaches an entirely "social" sermon. In *The Christian City*, wherein he departs from his custom, he beseeches Londoners to take heart because the modern city is so Christian, though unconsciously. *The Giant with the Wounded Heel* is one of the finest and most characteristic of his sermons. He believes the giant, man, is constantly crushing the serpent, and he is content to see a pretty large wound in his heel.

This largeness and poise of view is the most distinctive characteristic of Phillips Brooks. It stamps him with the mark of intellect. Occasionally he seems to value the mind for itself and to ascribe to it standards of its own. "The ink of the learned is as precious as the blood of the martyrs." Once he admits, without catching himself, that the mind is "the noblest part of us." In the sermon where this admission is made, *The Mind's Love of God*, he declares: "You cannot know that one idea is necessarily true because it seems to help you, nor that another idea is false because it wounds and seems to hinder you. Your mind is your faculty for judging what is

true." But these are isolated sayings. Ordinarily he refuses to
think of the intellect as a thing apart from the entire man, and
he finds truth, as did his Master, inherent in life, a personal
quality, discovered, determined, and determinable by personal
ends. When he first began to think, Socrates was almost the
ideal figure. But later, Socrates seemed thin in comparison with Christ. "Socrates brings an argument to meet an
objection. Jesus always brings a nature to meet a nature; a
whole being which the truth has filled with strength to meet
another whole being, which error has filled with feebleness."
In his sermon on the death of Lincoln he discloses his inner
thought:

> A great many people have discussed very crudely whether
> Abraham Lincoln was an intellectual man or not, as if intellect
> were a thing, always of the same sort, which you could precipitate
> from the other constituents of a man's nature and weigh by itself.
> . . . The fact is that in all the simplest characters, the line between
> the mental and moral nature is always vague and indistinct. They
> run together, and in their best combination you are unable to dis-
> criminate, in the wisdom which is their result, how much is moral
> and how much is intellectual.

In his student days he confided to his notebook: "A fresh
thought may be spoiled by sheer admiration. It was given us
to work in and to live by. . . . It will give its blessing to us
only on its knees. From this point of view, thought is as holy a
thing as prayer, for both are worship." The best description,
perhaps, of his own mind is to be found in his enumeration of
the "intellectual characteristics which Christ's disciples gathered from their Master," namely: "A poetic conception of
the world we live in, a willing acceptance of mystery, an expectation of progress by development, an absence of fastidiousness that comes from a sense of the possibilities of all humanity,
and a perpetual enlargement of thought from the arbitrary into
the essential."

These peculiar intellectual characteristics, rooted in their
passionate reverence for humanity, for its ideals and its achievements, determine the place of Brooks among the great preachers
of the world. He is at his best when he preaches by indirec-

tion.   Enlargement is his effect.   A man sees his own time in relation to all time, discovers his greatness by the greatness of which he is a part.   Brooks's mission was not to advance the frontiers of knowledge, not even of spiritual knowledge, but rather to annex the cleared areas to the old domains.   His abiding preoccupation—fatal to the scientist, detrimental to the sociologist, fortunate for the fame and immediate influence of the preacher—was to hold the present, changing into the future, loyal to the past.   He was not the stuff of which martyrs are made, but his soul was of that vastness which kept the public from making martyrs of the truthful.   He seems to watch and bless rather than to urge forward.   His great service to his age was that of a mediator.   Standing himself as a trinitarian and a supernaturalist, rejoicing in the greenness of the historic pastures, he discovered at the base of his doctrines the same essential spiritual food which others sought on freer uplands and less confined stretches.   He ministered to orthodox and unorthodox alike beneath their differences.   He did much to keep spiritual evolution free from the bitterness and contempt of revolution.

3. Royce

UNLIKE most of America's distinguished philosophers, Josiah Royce (1855–1916) was not brought up in New England. He was born in a mining town in California and received his philosophic education in the university of his own state, at Johns Hopkins, and at Göttingen, where he studied under Lotze. Many diverse elements stimulated his subtle and acquisitive mind to philosophic reflection; the theistic evolutionism of the geologist Le Conte, the fine literary spirit of E. R. Sill, and his own reading of Mill and Spencer as well as of the great German philosophers, Kant, Schelling, Hegel, and Schopenhauer.

In 1882 he went to Harvard, where his prodigious learning, his keen and catholic appreciation of poetry, and the biblical eloquence with which he expressed a rich inner experience, at once made a profound impression. His singularly pure and loyal, though shy, spirit attracted a few strong friendships; but his life at Cambridge was in the main one of philosophic detachment. As a citizen of the great intellectual world, however, he closely followed its multitudinous events; and his successive books only partly reflected his unusually active and varied intellectual interests. In his earliest published papers he is inclined to follow Kant in denying the possibility of ultimate metaphysical solutions except by ethical postulates, but in his first book, *The Religious Aspect of Philosophy* (1885), he comes out as a full-fledged metaphysical idealist. This brilliant book at once made a profound impression, especially with the arguments that the very possibility of error cannot be formulated except in terms of an absolute truth or rational totality which requires an absolute knower. Like the parts of a sentence, all things find their condition and meaning in the final totality to which they belong. The world must thus be either through and through of the same nature as our mind, or else be utterly unknowable. But to affirm the unknowable is to involve one's self in contradictions. Royce delights in these sharp antitheses and the reduction of opposing arguments to contradictions.

In his next book, an unusually eloquent one entitled *The Spirit of Modern Philosophy* (1892), the element of will rather than knowledge receives the greater emphasis. The Berkeleian analysis of the world as composed of ideas is taken for granted, and the emphasis is rather on the nature of the World Mind or Logos. Following Schopenhauer, he points out that even in the idealistic view of the world there is an irrational element, namely, the brute existence of just this kind of world. The great and tragic fact of experience is the fact of effort and passionate toil which never finds complete satisfaction. This eternal frustration of our ideals or will is an essential part of spiritual life, and enriches it just as the shadows enrich the picture or certain discords bring about richer harmony. The Absolute himself suffers our daily crucifixion, but his triumphant spiritual nature asserts itself in us through that very suffering. This profoundly consoling argument, which both elevates us and sinks our individual sorrows in a great cosmic drama, is, of course, an expression of the historical Christian wisdom of the beatitude of suffering. But it offended the traditional individualism which finds its theologic and metaphysical expression in the doctrine of free will. If each individual is a part of the divine self, how can we censure the poor wretch who fails to live up to the proper standard?[1] It is significant of the unconventionality of Royce's thought that he never attached great importance to the question of blame or the free and intentional nature of sin. The evils uppermost in his mind are those resulting from ignorance, from the clumsiness of inexperience rather than from wilful misdeeds; and, unlike most American philosophers, he rightly saw that the religious conscience of mankind has always regarded sin as something which happens to us even against our will. Against the complacent belief of

[1] See Howison in *The Conception of God*, by Royce, Le Conte, Howison, and Mezes.

the comfortable that no one suffers or succeeds except through his own sins or virtues, Royce opposes the view of St. Paul that we are all members of each other's bodies and that "no man amongst us is wholly free from the consequences or from the degradation involved in the crimes of his less enlightened or less devoted neighbours, that the solidarity of mankind links the crimes of each to the sorrows of all."

For the elaboration of the social nature of our intellectual as well as of our moral concepts, Royce was largely indebted to suggestions from Peirce. In his earliest books we find no direct reference to Peirce. We can only conjecture that he owed to that man of genius the emphasis on the social nature of truth and the formulation of the ethical imperative: Live in the light of all possible consequences. But with the publication of the two volumes of *The World and the Individual* (1901), Royce's indebtedness to Peirce becomes explicit and steadily increases thereafter.

The main thesis of that book, the reconciliation of the existence of the Absolute Self with the genuine individuality of our particular selves, is effected by means of illustrations from the field of modern mathematics, especially by the use of the modern mathematical concept of the infinite as a collection of which a part may be similar to the whole. C. S. Peirce had done this before him in a remarkable article entitled *The Law of Mind*, in the second volume of *The Monist*. In generously acknowledging his obligation to Peirce, Royce rightly felt his fundamental idealistic position to be independent of that of Peirce; but it is noticeable that all Royce's references to the logic of mathematics are in full agreement with Peirce's view of the reality of abstract logical and mathematical universals, and it may well be questioned whether this can be harmonized with the nominalist or Berkeleian elements of Royce's idealism.

His subsequent work falls into two distinct groups, the mathematical-logical and the ethical-religious. Of the former group, his essay on logic in *The Encyclopædia of the Philosophical Sciences* is philosophically the most important. Logic is there presented not as primarily concerned with the laws of thought or even with methodology but after the manner of Peirce as the most general science of objective order. In this as in other of his mathematical-logical papers Royce still professes adherence to his idealism, but this adherence in no way affects any of the arguments which proceed on a perfectly realistic basis. In his religio-ethical works he follows Peirce even more, and the Mind or Spirit of the Community replaces the Absolute. In his last important book, *The Problem of Christianity* (1913), all the concepts of Pauline Christianity are interpreted in terms of a social psychology, the personality of Christ being entirely left out except as an embodiment of the spirit of the beloved community.

The World and the Individual is still, as regards sustained mastery of technical metaphysics, the nearest approach to a philosophic classic that America has as yet produced. Its publication was the high-water mark of the idealistic tide. Royce's previous monism had aroused the opposition of pluralistic idealists like George Howison and Thomas Davidson. But with the beginning of the twentieth century idealism itself became the object of organized attack by two movements known as pragmatism and naïf- or neo-realism. The former was due to the work of William James and John Dewey; the latter to the spread of renewed and serious interest in scientific philosophy, especially in the renaissance of mathematical philosophy best represented by Bertrand Russell. It is, however, an historic fact that Royce contributed very largely to the effective spread of these new philosophies, to pragmatism by his ethical (as opposed to intellectual) idealism and by his emphasis on the practical aspect of ideas, and to neo-realism by his teaching and writing on mathematical logic. His profound and loyal devotion to the ethical interests of mankind did not prevent him from regarding the question of human immortality as "one for reason in precisely the same sense in which the properties of prime numbers and the kinetic theory of gases are matters for exact investigation." In this way he continued to represent, against the growing tide of anti-intellectualism, the old faith in the dignity and potency of reason which is the corner-stone of humanistic liberalism.

4. William James

IN William James (1842–1910) we meet a personality of such large proportions and of such powerful appeal to contemporaneous sentiment that we may well doubt whether the time has yet come when his work can be adequately estimated. There are many who claim that he has transformed the very substance of philosophy by bringing it down from the cold, transcendental heights to men's business and bosoms. But whether that be so or not, the width and depth of his sympathies and the irresistible magic of his words have undoubtedly transformed the tone and manner of American philosophic writing. Outside of America also his influence has been impressive and is steadily increasing.

It is instructive to note at the outset the judgment of orthodox philosophers, boldly expressed by George Howison:

> Emerson and James were both great men of letters, great writers, yes, great thinkers, if you will, but they do not belong in the strict list of philosophers. Mastery in logic is the cardinal test of the true philosopher, and neither Emerson nor James possessed it. Both, on the contrary, did their best to discredit it. [1]

As a criticism this is hardly fair. James certainly elaborated definite doctrines as to the nature of mind, truth, and reality. In his *Radical Empiricism* and in *The Meaning of Truth* he even showed considerable dialectic skill. Moreover, it may well be maintained that he did not seek to discredit logic in general, but only the logic of "vicious intellectualism." Nevertheless, Howison's opinion is significant in calling attention to the distinction between philosophy as technique and philosophy as

[1] *Philosophical Review*, vol. xxv, p. 241, May, 1916.

vision.   From the professional point of view it is not sufficient
that a man should believe in free will, absolute chance, or the
survival of consciousness beyond death.   To be worthy of being
called a philosopher, one must have a logically reasoned basis
for his belief.   James was aware of the importance of technique,
and was, in fact, extraordinarily well informed as to the substance and main tendencies of all the diverse technical schools.
But he was wholly interested in philosophy as a religious vision
of life, and he had the cultivated gentleman's aversion for
pedantry.   His thoughts ran in vivid pictures, and he could not
trust logical demonstration as much as his intuitive suggestions.
Hence his philosophic writings are extremely rich in the variety
of concrete factual insight, but not in effective answers to the
searching criticisms of men like Royce, Russell, and Bradley.
James was aware of this and asked that his philosophy be judged
generously in its large outlines; the elaboration of details might
well be left to the future.

"The originality of William James," says one of his European
admirers, "does not appear so much in his cardinal beliefs,
which he took from the general current of Christian thought, as
in the novel and audacious method by which he defended them
against the learned philosophies of his day."[1]   This, also, is not
true without qualification.   James took almost nothing from
current Christian philosophy.   Nor do any of the great historic
Christian doctrines of sin and atonement or salvation find any
echo in his thought.   Orthodox Christianity would condemn
James as a confessed pantheist who denied the omnipotence of
God.   But though James is far from Christian theology, he
gives vivid utterance to the ordinary popular Christianity which
believes, not in a God who expresses himself in universal laws,
but in a God to whom we can pray for help against our enemies,
whom we can please and even help by our faith in Him.   This
is due to James's deep sympathy with common experience
rather than with the problems of the reflective-minded.   But
the modern sophisticated intellect is certainly tickled by the
sight of a most learned savant espousing the cause of popular
as opposed to learned theology, and by the open confession of
belief in piecemeal supernaturalism on the basis of spiritistic

[1] Flournoy, *William James*, p. 16.

phenomena. James's antipathy to the Hegelian and Roycean attempts to prove the existence of the Absolute certainly plays a more prominent part in his writings than does his antipathy to popular unbelief. But the method of the absolutist he rejected, not only because of its insufferable pretension to finality of proof, but mainly because it is in the way of one who prefers an anthropomorphic universe that is tingling with life through and through and is constantly meeting with new adventures.

The union of religious mysticism with biologic and psychologic empiricism is characteristic of James's work from the very beginning. He grew up in a household characterized by liberal culture and mystic Swedenborgian piety.[1] The teacher who made the greatest impression upon him, Louis Agassiz, was a pious opponent of Darwin but a rare master in the art of observing significant details. More than one American naturalist caught the fire of his enthusiasm for fact. The companionship of Chauncey Wright and the writings of Renouvier weaned James from his father's religio-philosophical monism. The empirical way of thought of Hume and Mill proved most congenial to one who was par excellence a naturalist and delighted in the observation of significant detail.[2]

James began his career as a teacher of physiology and gradually drifted into psychology. His *Principles of Psychology* (2 vols., 1890) contains the substance of his philosophy. Having, despite the influence of Agassiz, become converted to Darwinism, he was led to adopt as fundamental the view of Spencer that thought is something developed in the course of evolution and must, therefore, have a biologic function. The great idealistic argument against the old associationist psychology of Hume, Mill, Bain, and Spencer was to the effect that the sensational elements can at most account for the qualities of things, but not for their relations or connections; and when it was once granted that the relations between things were of a non-sensational or non-empirical character, very little of the world was

---

[1] His father, Henry James, Sr., was a Swedenborgian philosopher and a cultivated gentleman of ample means, who united to genuine originality of thought a remarkable insight into human character and a delightful freshness and pungency of language.

[2] James studied art and was a proficient draftsman before he finally decided to study medicine.

left to the empiricist. James early became convinced of the force of this argument and, following certain suggestions of Peirce and possibly Hodgson, tried to save empiricism by making it more radical, by giving the connecting relations themselves a psychologic status on a par with the things they connect. Thus he thought to restore the fluidity and connectedness of our world without admitting the necessity for the idealist's transcendental glue to keep together the discrete elements of experience. Radical empiricism thus becomes a metaphysic which holds the whole world to be composed of a single stuff called pure experience. This sounds monistic enough, and James's adherence to the view of Bergson re-enforces this impression. Nevertheless, James insisted that the world as experienced does not possess the degree of unity claimed for it by Royce and other monists, but that things are essentially many and their connections often external and accidental. At times James professes the dualistic realism of common sense. "I start with two things, the objective facts and the claims." But ideas and things are both experiences taken in different contexts, so that his position has not inaptly been called neutral monism, and thus assimilated to the philosophy of Ernst Mach.

It has been claimed that this view eliminates most of the traditional problems of metaphysics, such as that of the relation of mind and body, and also eliminates the need of the Spencerian unknowable and Royce's or Bradley's absolute. But just exactly what experience is, James does not tell us, except that it is something to be lived rather than to be defined.

The exigencies of controversy as well as James's generous desire to give all possible credit to Peirce, have led the public to regard pragmatism and James's philosophy as identical terms. To James, however, pragmatism was but the method of philosophic discussion, the vestibule to his radical empiricism. The controversy, however, which arose about pragmatism enabled James to elaborate from different approaches his account of the nature of truth. The meaning of ideas is to be found in their particular experimental consequences. Abstract ideas are not copies of things but their substitutes or derivatives, evolved in the process of evolution to enable us to deal more adequately with the stream of immediate experience. An idea is, therefore, true if it enables us to deal satisfactorily with the concrete experiences at which it aims. An idea is said to work satisfactorily if it leads us to expected facts, if it harmonizes with other accepted ideas, if it releases our energies or satisfies emotional craving for elegance, peace, economy, or any kind of utility.

So anxious was James to overthrow the view that the truth of an idea consists in its being an inert copy of reality, so anxious to substitute for it the more activist view that an idea is true if it works or leads to certain results, that he neglected to indicate the relative importance of these results. This led to a great deal of misunderstanding and caused considerable scandal. Those brought up in the scientific tradition and trained to view the emotionally satisfactory consequences of ideas as having nothing to do with their scientific or theoretic value were scandalized by James's doctrine of the will or right to believe anything the acceptance of which made us more comfortable. This was in part a tragic misunderstanding. Most of James's life was a fight against accepting the monistic philosophy simply because of its æsthetic nobility. He rejected it precisely because it was "too buttoned up and white chockered, too clean-shaven a thing to speak for the vast slow-breeding, unconscious cosmos with its dread abysses and its unknown tides." It is true, however, that absorption in the psychologic factor, personal or æsthetic, which actually does make some people prefer a narrowly classic universe and others a generously romantic one, made him obscure the distinction between the causes of belief and the evidence for the truth which we believe. We may all start with a biassed or emotional preface, but that is neither evidence nor guaranty of our arriving at scientific truth. Like other violent opponents of intellectualism, James himself falls into the intellectualistic assumption that we must either wholly believe or wholly disbelieve, just as one must either go to church or stay out. He ignores the scientific attitude of suspended judgment and the fact that men may be compelled to act without being constrained in judgment. We may vote for X or Y and yet know that owing to the absence of adequate information our choice has been little more than a blind guess. His interest in vital preferences and his impatience with the emotionally thin air of purely logical argumentation led James, towards the end of his life, to the acceptance of the extreme anti-logical view of Bergson that our logical and mathematical ideas are inherently incapable of revealing the real and changing world.

James's interest in philosophy was fundamentally restricted to the psychological aspect of things. He therefore never elaborated any systematic theory of morals, politics, or social organization. His temperamental preference for the novel, the unique, and the colourful re-enforced his traditional American liberalism and made him an extreme individualist. He attached scant value to the organized or fixed channels through which the fitful tides of ordinary human emotion find permanent expression. This shows itself best in his *Varieties of Religious Experience* (1902). He is interested only in the extreme variations of religious experiences, in the geniuses or aristocrats of the religious life. The religious experience of the great mass, or even of intellectual men like Chief Justice Marshall, who go to church without troubling much about matters of belief, seems to James "second-hand" and does not solicit his attention. Neither does the whole question of ritual or ceremony. He is interested in the beliefs of extraordinary and picturesque individuals. Hence his book on religion tells us almost nothing to explain the spread and vitality of the great historic religions, Buddhism, Confucianism, Judaism, Islam, and Christianity. This extreme individualism, however, is connected with an extraordinary democratic openness and readiness to admit that it is only the blindness in human nature that prevents us from seeing the uniqueness of every individual. Unlike any other philosopher, William James was entirely devoid of the pride of the intellect. He was as willing as Jesus of Nazareth to associate with the intellectual publicans and sinners and learn from the denizens of the intellectual underworld.

James's position in the history of metaphysics is still a matter of debate, but as a seer or prophet he may fitly be put beside Emerson. Like Emerson, he preached and nobly exemplified faith in one's intuition and the duty of keeping one's oracular soul open. In spite of a note of obscurantism in his attitude to logic and "over beliefs," there is no doubt that the main effect of his work was to raise the American standard of intellectual honesty and courage: Let us stop this miserable pretence of having at last logically proved the comforting certainties of our inherited religion. Let us admit that we have no absolute assurance of the complete success of our ideals. But the fight is on. We can all take our part. Shame on the one who sulks and stays out.

CHAPTER XII

The English Language in America

O N 22 February, 1917, the American Academy of Arts
and Letters sat to consider its duty toward the English
language in America. The published reports of the
session proclaim its "academic" character in that nothing resembling a plan of action was proposed. It was less to be expected, perhaps, that no problem should be clearly formulated,
but this may be accounted for partly by reason of the fact that
much of the discussion turned not on the problem itself but
on the duty of the Academy in the face of a problem of which
everyone more or less definitely assumed the existence without
attempting to state it, and partly because the company contained among many skilful users of the English language
hardly more than one qualified to speak from any extended
study of the problem, a lack which was expressly noted. It is
not so surprising that to the mind of an assembly of this sort
English as written was more constantly present than English
as spoken. But from so many men of accomplishment in
various forms of artistic expression there could hardly fail to
emerge various points of view, prejudices, agreements and dis-
agreements, which further discussion of the subject would do
well to begin by taking into account.

To the reader of these proceedings it is made abundantly
plain, taking what was said with what was implied, that in the
minds of an overwhelming majority of the members, though not
of all, the English language in America is in a very bad way.
That this should have been their opinion might easily have been
predicted. English is the most bewept of the tongues. From
the days of Caxton its uncertain syntax, its perplexing variety
of forms, its exotic and luxuriant vocabulary have brought dis-

tress to most of those who have taken thought of it.   Compunctious visitings of an idealized Latinity have caused some to strive to regulate an apparent chaos, but all, or nearly all, to despair of stopping a heedless journey to destruction.   Historically, the question turned first on matters of vocabulary, later on points of form and meaning, and at present, though the other questions are not forgotten, alarm is felt chiefly, as Henry James puts it, on account of "those influences around us that make for the imperfect disengagement of the human side of vowel sound, that make for the confused, the ugly, the flat, the thin, the mean, the helpless, that reduce articulation to an ignoble minimum . . . a mere helpless slobber of disconnected vowel noises."   It is because of a growing slovenliness in uttering the unstressed vowels that the British poet-laureate, Robert Bridges, is inclined to believe that English pronunciation, even in Britain, is on the road to ruin.

It seems impossible for a student of language to refuse to be stampeded by these alarms, to maintain a certain serenity before so doleful a picture of things, pending some effort to assure himself that the picture is drawn to scale, without being accused in his turn of proclaiming with a sort of blatant cheerfulness that whatever is, linguistically, is right.   Such extremes of optimism and pessimism are, of course, absurd.   If they seem to exist, it must be because people are talking from different points of view about different sets of facts.   To attempt to steer a rational middle course between these extremes, however, demands for its success some rehearsal of the facts.   And at once, to show the existence of a middle ground, over against centuries of forebodings may be placed the fact that since Chaucer's day there has been continuously evolving, step by step with the widening experience of men, an English in which men of education everywhere in the far-flung English-speaking world could write and converse together in a way highly agreeable to any but a most inflexibly provincial taste.   Amid much confusing detail it is as well not to lose sight of this central fact, that the thing we all are talking about exists.   But where, and in what form?

Variety is of the essence of language.   Uniformity and consistency are inventions of philosophical grammarians whose efforts are most successful when they deal with a language no longer used to satisfy elementary social needs. A living language is one of the *mores* of a social group; it is neither a biological growth unaffected by human intervention nor a work of art given its form for all time by a single act of human creation. Consequently it will vary within the group somewhat according to the variation in other respects to be found in the individuals comprising it, and between groups it will vary still more. Like other *mores* it will be subject to modification by time. But the necessity for mutual intelligibility within the group will greatly restrict the play of individual whim; between groups this force will operate somehow in proportion to the immediacy of their contacts. In a cultured city like ancient Rome or mediæval Florence a group of people might raise and maintain a literary standard around which literary people of other groups would rally. Or, again, a convenient dialect might be somewhat arbitrarily chosen for a particular literary task, as Luther chose the dialect of the Saxon chancellary for his translation of the Bible, and this dialect, with more or less conscious modification from time to time, might remain the standard literary language. In all these cases the great mass of people, not wholly uninfluenced by the literary language perhaps, would go on speaking their own dialects, just as the Romans did until their language of the street, of the camp, and of the provinces broke up into the larger groups, such as French, Spanish, and the rest, each containing within itself many smaller groups; or just as the Italians and the Germans have gone on speaking their dialects to the present day, learning their literary language as best they can besides.

The history of English is somewhat different from any of these. In origin, Modern English, as it appears everywhere in books and as it falls from the lips of the vast majority of speakers, is the dialect of a city, London. But unlike the case of Rome, there was at the outset presumably no great difference between the language of literature and the language of every day, and, unlike Florence, London was the chief city of a steadily unifying country. With the changing language of the city, its gradual loss of Southern, or Saxon, forms and its gradual acquirement of Northern, or Anglian, forms, the language of literature kept closely in touch. By the early sixteenth century, though details are shifting, the outlines of

Modern English are fairly clear.   Then came a period of great
expansion.   The language was carried, farther than the Roman
legionaries carried theirs, into the remotest parts of the world;
it came to be spoken by more people than ever before in the
history of the world could hold comfortable converse together.
The really surprising thing is not that the result exhibits some
variety but that, when the lapse of time afforded opportunity
for, and indeed effected, so much change, when groups widely
scattered might so easily have completely lost contact when
there was so little external compulsion of any kind to keep
even the literary language true to itself, there should have
resulted a literary language that is almost uniform and a number of spoken dialects which never become unintelligible one
to all the rest.   In 1789 Noah Webster prophesied that there
would develop, ''in a course of time, a language in North America, as different from the future language of England, as modern
Dutch, Danish, and Swedish are from German or from one
another.''   When it was made this was not a foolish guess;
all analogy supported it.   That it has not come about, that
every passing day adds to the unlikelihood of its realization,
is one of the things that the observer of the ways of language
thinks about when he is invited to be very miserable.   Clearly,
matters are not so bad as they quite easily might have been.

But this is speaking in the large.   What of details?   Excellence is largely a matter of details.   A literary language ''almost uniform''—why not entirely so?   ''A number of spoken
dialects''—why any dialects at all?   Confronted with a demand for perfect uniformity—one of our academicians very
expressly makes it and deplores the fact that Americans us
''back of'' and ''toward'' and ''spool of thread'' instead of
British ''behind'' and ''towards'' and ''reel of cotton''—what
can we say?   Obviously, such a demand more nearly concerns
the literary English of books than the vernacular of daily intercourse; no one seriously hopes to see us all regimented into
speaking exactly alike.   But even in the former case it is proper
to ask not only how far uniformity may be possible, but also
how far an absolute uniformity, as opposed to something fairly
close to it, is really desirable.   On what ground shall this
agreement be effected?   Few would now feel, as some did in

¹ *Dissertations*, pp. 22–23.

the early days of the Republic, that the dignity of the nation requires that it should have a language entirely its own.   More would be ready to assent to the implication of one of our academicians that American usage conform itself as far as possible to the practice of British writers.   It is an old notion; Franklin and Webster both gave reverent expression to it, but neither, it should be noted, made any special effort to live up to it, and Webster at other times professed quite a different ideal.   They made no more effort, that is, than any educated man does who allows his best reading to be reflected in his best writing.   The simple fact is that such differences as exist between English in America and English in Britain are not mainly due to ignorance or perversity.   The days are long past when the British reviewer branded as an "Americanism" every word and every construction which, during a period of enormous growth in the demands made upon the language, he could not remember having met with before.   Such differences as there are, it is now well recognized, are due to the historical evolution of the language.   It will be well to look at this for a moment before casting up the losses and gains and before pointing out a possible, indeed a very real, danger involved in attempting to alter too drastically the record with which history presents us.

The literary dialect of London never, as has been said, got wholly out of touch with the other dialects of the island. They continued to affect it in many ways; it was a "natural" growth in that it was not consciously regulated by groups of literary men in the way that German or French has been regulated.   In company with the British Constitution it muddled along, obtaining surprisingly good results, all things considered.   Of the spoken language, apart from many rustic dialects of a pedigree as honourable as it is ancient, there are at least two recognized standards in England, a Northern British and a Southern British, and, in addition, educated Scots and Irishmen and Welshmen have ways of speaking that are quite distinctly their own.   The farther one travels from London the less noticeable becomes the difference between British English and American.   If it be urged that the literary language is largely uniform throughout the British Isles—leaving out works that are frankly in dialect—this can in great part be accounted for by the fact that political and literary life centre in the great commercial city of London. But the varieties that characterize spoken English today were probably even greater—less subdued to a literary medium—in the seventeenth century when the language was transplanted to America. And American authors have seldom written with an eye to the London book market. It is not, therefore, surprising that the English in America, cut off from the British at home by an estranging sea and feeling for them an affectionate regard in about the same degree as it was accorded, should not have followed precisely the same lines of change. Some of the resulting differences it will help matters to glance at.

The early colonists in America brought their English with them. They were for the most part plain people and their language must have had all the characteristics of the several dialects which they spoke at home. How far their original dialectical peculiarities are reflected in later American speech it might be hard to determine; probably so far as the later educated speech goes, not much. But the old New England plural *housen*, *clever* = *good*, *mad* = *angry*, *I be, you be, they be, shet* (*shut*), *becase* (*because*), *sich* (*such*), *wrastle, mought* (*might*), *ax* (*ask*), *ketch* (*catch*),[1] *guess* = *suppose*, and many others more certainly came over in the *Mayflower* than much else reputed a part of that seemingly miraculous cargo. Some of these forms are not often heard today, though *guess* has become a sort of shibboleth.[2] If they were once more common, it should be remembered that the situation in America was not wholly unlike that of England after the Norman Conquest; with the relaxation of literary standards, dialect forms, no longer repressed, gained recognition they could not have had in conflict with a strong literary tradition.

But it is not chiefly here that we are to look for the causes of such differences as gradually separated American and British speech. New conditions of life, to be sure, called for new words: *wigwam, tomahawk, squaw, papoose, prairie, canyon,*

---

[1] *Ketch*, Spenser's form of the word, is, to many educated people, the only natural pronunciation, and *catch* a purely literary affectation. There is a certain pleasant irony in the fact that in the strictly analogous word *keg* it is the pronunciation *kag* that is regarded as a vulgarism.

[2] The real objection to such expressions as *guess* and *right away*, as to *quite so* and *I mean to say*, lies not in themselves but in their monotonous employment as catch-words.

and all the others that have become a part of the general stock of English.   *Stores* in the Western world (the usage is not confined to the United States) really were stores and not shops. Our most common *corn* was maize, and it naturally became *corn* par excellence.   *Fall* (*autumn*) and *rare* (*underdone*) are "Americanisms" only in the sense that they have retained a vitality here which even in England they have not wholly lost. Political life, sport, changed economic conditions, have all furnished the language with new words, or old words in new senses.   The most striking differences, however, have come about, not through the retention of dialect words or the introduction of new words for new ideas, but because American English, in its comparative isolation, has not followed step by step the many changes that have occurred in British English since the seventeenth century.   American English is in some respects archaic.   It has never developed, for example, the swooping diphthongs that, since the end of the eighteenth century at least, have characterized the British pronunciation of $\bar{e}$, $\bar{\imath}$, $\bar{o}$, $\bar{u}$,[1] to represent which the British phoneticians write *say*, *be*, *boat*, and *do* [sei], [bij], [bout], [duw].   The American diphthongs, so far as they exist, are much less noticeable.   The characteristic American unrounding of [o] to [a], *got*, *not* [gat], [nat], occurs in some of the British dialects and was an elegant affectation in the days of Charles II.   The palatal *g* and *c* still sometimes heard in the Virginia pronunciation of *garden* and *card* (written "gyarden," "cyard") were held by many in eighteenth-century England to be the height of refinement. The old distinction between *hoarse* (vowel of *no*) and *horse* (vowel of *law*) is still preserved by many Americans, especially outside the Middle States.   Elizabethan *gotten* and the old preterite *ate* are heard oftener in America than in Britain. Americans, indeed, look on a pronunciation "et" as vulgar. They have either never lost or have, for the most part, successfully recovered the ancient distinction between the voiceless initial in *which* and the voiced in *witch*, where the South Briton pronounces them both *witch*.

Finally, the so-called broad or Italian *a*, which began to be fashionable in England near the close of the eighteenth century, never established itself outside of New England and, to some

[1] In phonetic notation vowels should be given their Continental sounds.

extent, in Virginia, except in *father*, before *r* (*car*, *arm*), and somewhat uncertainly before *lm* (*calm*, *psalm*).   The American, then, who pronounces *pass*, *dance*, *aunt*, with the vowel of *hand* does only what all the authorities before the last quarter of the eighteenth century told him to do, and what apparently everybody in England did do who wished to avoid an appearance of vulgarity.

Certain anomalous British forms, of comparatively recent origin, have never become established in America.   The pronunciation of *wrath* as if *wroth*, and the occasional pronunciation of the latter with long ō, are seldom (one dare not say never) heard in America.   *Wrath* (with the vowel of *law*) does not seem to be older than the end of the eighteenth century, and *wroth* (with the vowel of *no*) is a recent attempt to distinguish anew between the words.   Another anomaly is *schedule*, commonly pronounced by the British with *sh*.   The earlier pronunciation of this French word was *sedyul*, and it might have retained this pronunciation in spite of its classical spelling, just as *schism* has done.   But the spelling suggests other classical analogies like *scholar* and *scheme*, and this pronunciation followed by American English seems to offer the only reasonable alternative to *sedyul*.   What analogy the British pronunciation follows is not easy to see; one hesitates now to urge afresh the old suggestion that in this word, as in *schist*, the determining influence is German.

The pronunciation of *either*, *neither*, with the diphthong of *eye*, which is not recorded before the eighteenth century, has met with better reception in America.   It was Franklin's pronunciation.   But with many of the persons who use it it is a conscious affectation.   The Elizabethan pronunciations, it may be noted, were "ayther," "nayther," just as the Irishman still says it, and "ether," "nether," to rhyme with *leather*. The ordinary American pronunciation is the representative of the former type; the latter seems to have left no modern descendants.

Besides being in some respects more conservative, American English has in still other respects grown apart from British English through following different analogies.   The question how an English word shall be pronounced breaks up at once into a whole set of queries.   Shall it be pronounced as a Latin word, a French word, or as a more or less domesticated form of either? What other word is it like? Shall the spelling be allowed full weight? In general, of two forms already in existence which shall be preferred? To such questions it is only to be expected that the two countries should in many instances make different responses.

British English frequently makes more effort to imitate a modern French pronunciation in *trait, chamois, turquoise, charade, imbecile,* and *vase,* where Americans frankly accept them as native words. It is, however, the French tradition rather than the Latin which Americans follow in preferring [i] to [ai] forms in the terminations-*ide,-ine,-itis,-ique.*

Dr. Johnson's spelling has undergone some simplification in both countries: *almanack, musick, errour, horrour, interiour, successour, emperour, oratour,* have everywhere dropped unnecessary letters. The abandonment of the French *-our* for Latin *-or* has gone a little further in the American printinghouses; *honour, humour, vigour, harbour, labour, neighbour, valour, clamour, clangour, saviour,* and a few others have joined the overwhelming majority of *-or* words. British men of letters could be cited who have employed the same simplification. Other French spellings like *theatre* and *centre* are less common in America than in England. Parallel to the simplification of *almanac(k)* are *wag(g)on, travel(l)er.* Of the British attempts to distinguish by the spelling *story,* narrative (plural *stories*), from *storey,* floor (pl. *storeys*), and *curb* (bit) from *kerb* (stone), the first has some etymological argument in its favour, but neither has commended itself to American usage. Britons themselves are quite as likely to spell *cider* and *pajamas* in the fashion always employed in America as they are to write *cyder* and *pyjamas.* [1]

The spelling book has exerted a powerful influence in America, where so many speakers have learned their language in the school and looked to it as a more compelling authority than the sometimes uncertain tradition of the home. The notion that all the letters of a word are entitled to a certain respect, reinforced by the native slowness of utterance, has led to the retention of unstressed vowels in *tapestry, medicine, venison,* and

[1] The spelling used in this chapter, as of this history in general, conforms ordinarily to British usage.

produced a secondary stress in such words as *secretary*, *extra-ordinary*. The eighteenth-century refinement of "dropping the *g*" in *going*, *seeing*, which still persists as a "smart" pronunciation in England, almost all Americans, though they use it oftener than they could be got to confess, would regard with horror because it violates what seems to them the obvious principle that all the letters should be pronounced. The same state of mind leads to the retention of *h* in *hotel*, *hostler*, reinforces the distinction between *w* and *wh*, and induces many to persist in pronouncing an *r* final and before consonants, in spite of the frankly expressed disgust even of their own countrymen of the East and South. *Figure* has lost its fine old pronunciation ("figger") for a spelling pronunciation "figyure." As for *lieutenant*, Coxe (1813, p. 36) notes that "*lef-tenant* prevails most generally, but *lew-tenant* appears to be becoming more popular"; spelling has now completely carried the day. Out of deference to spelling Americans pronounce a *g* in *physiognomy*, *recognizance*, and sometimes even in *suggest*.[1]

Enough has been offered in support and illustration of the contention that the roots of American speech lie deep in history. The same might be done for less literary speech. Lowell established the antiquity of much in the Yankee dialect of his Hosea Biglow, and it is to be presumed that research, of which there has been far too little in this field, may establish the antiquity, if nothing more, of many other dialectical peculiarities. There is not an oddity in the "coarse, uncouth dialect" of the Deerslayer and Hurry Harry (*The Deerslayer*, 1841) that has not its root deep in the soil of the eighteenth and preceding centuries.[2] Cooper has Noah Webster's own *creatur'*, *ventur'*, *f'erce*. *Sarpint*, *desarted*, *vartue*, *larned*, *s'ile*, *app'inted*, *expl'ite* can all be found recommended in grammars of the eighteenth century. *The Oxford Spelling Book* (1726) says that *sigh* is pronounced *sithe* "according to the common way of speaking," just as Natty Bumppo pronounces it. His *ven'son* is still good English. His *consait* (*conceit*), *ginerous*, *fri'nd*, *'arth* sound Irish, but that is as much as to say that they belong to the old,

---

[1] Spelling, of course, increasingly influences pronunciation in England.

[2] An interesting list of "vulgar errors" may be found in Elliot and Johnson's *A Selected Pronouncing and Accented Dictionary*, Suffield [Conn.], 1800, p. 16.

authentic vernacular; they cannot be made to serve as illustrations of any wanton perversity on the part of Americans.

But cannot all these historical reasons for American English being what it is be granted (and they pretty generally are) and still leave us facing a very desperate situation about which something should be done? History, after all, brings no solution to the problem which it helps to define. It does not furnish a standard, it can only show us the steps by which all present English has gone very badly astray. But a standard is precisely what is wanted; lack of standard, our academy was quite persuaded, is what ails American English. Enough has been said already to suggest the hopelessness of finding such a standard in literary South British. Just what sort of folly that leads to may be seen in the case of the academician who lamented that Americans wrote *toward* when an Englishman, "following the established usage of prose," wrote *towards*. *Towards* is not the established usage of prose, and quite as many Englishmen write *toward* as *towards*. All that the academician can mean is that he personally prefers *towards*. No one could deny him the privilege of choosing, but no one would attach the slightest significance to his choice either way. Much the same can be said of most of the differences of detail between literary English in America and the same thing in England; they are too trivial to be worth much trouble in trying to remove them.

But even the attempt to remove these peculiarities of American English in deference to some standard outside itself may work harm vastly greater than it is proposed to help. If English had remained the literary language of a small homogeneous group, who like the Athenians could consent instantly in the pleasure of jeering a misplaced accent, the single and precise kind of standard which some critics of English seem to have in mind might have been successfully applied to it. But English has become the common possession of many scattered peoples. It is quite possible that this involves some sacrifice with some gain. English can hardly become the adequate expression of so varied a human experience, the medium of so many diverse men, without losing something in the direction of perfect uniformity as against its gains in range. This expansion has its too evident dangers, but to try to correct them by a single narrow standard is not only impossible; it is harmful in its results just so far as it breeds in the mind of speakers and writers an uneasy feeling that really good English is something vaguely and beautifully beyond them, something they can never hope to attain to, something so high and delicate that they would not care to use it if they could get it, certainly not for even the best moments of every day.

This brings us to the very centre of the problem. The trouble with American English, it might reasonably be urged, is that it has been so constantly disparaged in comparison with a standard so vague, so remote, so "superior," but of so little practical guidance, that the fine sense of possession, the feeling that the way one goes about one's *mores* is inevitably the right way, has been in many cases completely lost. "I say 'dawg,'" said an American teacher of English, "but I know 'dahg' is correct and I make my pupils say it." We can be sure that her pupils do not say "dahg" outside the classroom, and carry away with them only a conviction that "good English" is something with which they can and will have nothing to do.

"All this is very different in English English," says another of our academicians. "They believe in English and have the ideal of good usage." But the standard, it should be noted, is a native standard; it is fairly well defined; it is not impossible of attainment; and it is not flagrantly at variance with the practice of the linguistic environment in which the fortunate young Britisher is being fitted by governesses, tutors, and public-school masters to take his place. Conditions so favourable must be somewhat limited in their occurrence even in England. In America those who inherit a sound native tradition in their homes are more than likely to spend large parts of their lives in regions of quite other language habits. In school they will encounter many who have been brought up in an environment distinctly foreign, the teacher even may have an unsure control of the language, and he—or more generally she—is sure to have some very extravagant and ill-informed notions of what constitutes good English. In the university they may learn a good deal about correctness in composition but will encounter no very definite standards of speech, for both teachers and students are usually drawn from all parts of the country and represent every sort of social opportunity.

All this sounds much worse than it actually turns out to be.

26

For English is the authentic speech of free peoples and it is endowed with an innate energy for getting along, going into strange places on strange errands, but never quite losing its sense of identity. It breeds surprisingly true, in the main, even amid the most unpromising conditions. Franklin, the cosmopolitan, said "air" for *are;* "hev" and "hez"; sounded the *l* in *would* and *calm,* and in the latter used the vowel of *hat;* uttered *new* with the vowel of *too,* and *bosom* as who should write "buzzum." Noah Webster, father of American lexicography, advocated the pronunciations "creatur," "natur," "raptur"; *angel* with the vowel of *hat, chamber* with that of *father; fierce* and *pierce* were to rhyme with *verse, beard* with *third,* and *deaf* with *thief;* the present pronunciation of *heard* and *wound* he regarded as new and objectionable. With such a start what might not American English have become? Without any external compulsion, without any very clearly expressed ideals, however, American English has kept pace step by step in these particulars with the development of British English.

The problem of American English resides, then, not in its differences from British English, nor yet in its own infinite variety—here history is both enlightening and consoling—but in the attitude which it adopts toward itself. It is not as good as it might be—no language is so in its entirety, because people are not so wise and well-bred, so sensitively in touch with the best of literature and of life as they might be—but to make itself better it has no reasonable standards to look to. It has held up to it silly ideals, impossible ideals, ignorant dogmatisms, and for the most part it wisely repudiates them all. But in so doing it is left with a diminished self-respect. Excellence is not for it. Why bother about the impossible? We shall get along. Not thus, however, is bred that subtle atmosphere of linguistic authenticity, the inevitableness of the thing rightly said, which is the peasant's by inheritance and to which the man of letters attains by giving his toilsome nights to much else beside Addison. The great mass of men lies between, the many who write and are not great writers, the many who talk not so well as they might; where in irritation and bewilderment may they look?

"All this is very different in English English." Here, quite possibly, is a hint of some value. One can hardly suppose that there is any very determined effort to make Scottish boys and girls acquire what Arnold Bennett calls a Kensingtonian accent.   There is a distinct and well recognized standard of North British, as well as South British.   American English has a history that entitles it to consideration.   It has certain peculiarities of vocabulary.   Let them be kept; half of them will be adopted by the rest of the English-speaking world, the other half will be liked by them if the American who uses them is otherwise likable, and above all if he uses them as if they were authentically his.   The well of English has never mistaken increase for defilement.   The American is traditionally supposed to have a "nasal twang."   If any allow air to leak through the nasal passage when it should be closed (a characteristic of unrefined English outside of America); if any speak with a certain constriction of the muscles of the nose and upper lip, with a certain shrillness and thinness of voice (and many do), let them be taught not to do it.   That is something worth making a fight for.   But let them not give up the cool, deliberate, level tone, with half a laugh in it, which shall be the mark of the American in whatever part of the world his destiny calls him.   Let his restrained speech keep to the unemphatic forms of the verb *to be* which it has instinctively preferred.   *Were* ("wear") and *been* ("bean") are emphatic forms that sort well with the highly energized speech of South Britain, with its sudden changes of speed and pitch, its great expenditure of breath.

American English is not uniform.   But neither is British English uniform.   Only a dead language, or the language of a highly centralized country, or a more or less artificial literary language, can approach uniformity.   But American English falls into clearly recognizable groups that are not too many to handle in the sensible way in which the British regard the several types of English of their own islands.   By all means recognize an English of New England, an English of the Middle States, of the South, and of the West.   To attempt to harmonize them in an impossible unity is only to confirm them in their several peculiarities.   It would be wiser to direct the attack against those peculiarities which are a little too peculiar.   If the New Englander shortens his long *o*'s, if the New Yorker confuses *voice* and *verse* in an absurd diphthong that both misleads and

offends, if the Southerner loops and curls the diphthong of
cow, if the Westerner in pronouncing *r* retorts the tongue so
far back upon itself that no clear vowel can be made before it,
each can be told, with some hope of affecting both his belief and
his practice, that such extremes have no appropriateness, are
not indulged in, indeed, by the best speakers of his own region.
If many Americans tend to lengthen the vowel in *frost* and
long, that is something that can be effectively discouraged
without resorting to the equally objectionable extreme of saying "frahst" and "lahng." But it is just as useless to tell a
Westerner that he must not use an *r* as to tell a New Englander
that he must furnish himself with one.

It is, then, not a question of one standard that does not
exist against no standards at all; it is a question of sensibly
recognizing several standards that do exist and making the best
of them, criticizing the language of each main group according
to its own standard, and not on grounds of right and wrong
but on grounds of what may be regarded as appropriate. The
peasant and the pedant, though one talks like a man and the
other like a book, are alike in that each speaks his language in
only one way; the educated man knows and employs his language in three or four ways. He has only an enlightened sense
of appropriateness to guide him. But it is enough.

How to get such a sense of appropriateness widely diffused
among people of widely various opportunities, is the problem
of American English. It is a serious problem. With Italian-
American, Yiddish-American, Scandinavian-American, Ger-
man-American yammering in our ears, it is not a time for
academicians to regret that we write *toward* and not *towards*,
or for teachers of "oral" English to endeavour to make broad
our *a*'s. Such scribal pharisaism, if it were harmless, would be
amusing. But it is chiefly owing to such folly that sound and
reasonable standards for American English have never come
into recognition. What is needed is some knowledge of the
facts, a willingness to face them with a sympathetic and rational criticism, and above all a belief that life as lived in
America has a value and an atmosphere of its own. It is
distinctly to be desired that British authors should write *whilst*
and *different to;* we rejoice when the hero begins his dinner with
"an" oyster, talks about "coals," takes "in" the *Times*, says

"directly" and "expect,"[1] and knows exactly what he means when he says "sick" and "bug," or rather knows exactly why he does not say them.   We should be "very disappointed" if he did not do these things; it is all part of the British atmosphere; it goes with the very smell of the book.   These things are not good or bad, right or wrong, in themselves; they are merely appropriate, or the reverse.   And Americans will generally speak well when they are taught to look for the best in the speech of their neighbours, pruning the more luxuriant growths of dialect and tempering their speech in the glowing heat of the common literary tradition; no longer reluctant to speak well because "good" English is unnatural and unattainable, but conscious that a really good English, such as the world will value according to their worth as individuals and as a nation, is their rightful heritage to enter upon and enjoy.

Great things have been expected of American English in the past.   A Frenchman, Roland de la Platière (1791), saw in America, a land so fortunately situated, so happily governed, with a people so constituted that they "fraternized with the universe" and presumably to be trusted to benefit by association with the primitive virtues of Indians and negroes, the country which was most likely to develop its speech into a universal language.   Whitman, in the notes published as *An American Primer*, dug deep in the recesses of language for a word-hoard that should be distinctly American, and rolled the aboriginal names—Monongahela—with venison richness upon his palate.   He saw an America cleared of all names that smack of Europe, an American vocabulary enriched with many words not in the print of dictionaries.

American writers are to show far more freedom in the use of words. . . .   Ten thousand native idiomatic words are growing, or are today already grown, out of which vast numbers could be used by American writers, with meaning and effect—words that would be welcomed by the nation, being of the national blood— words that would give that taste of identity and locality which is so dear in literature.

No such drastic Americanization of the language as was prophesied has come to pass, or is likely to come to pass.   The

[1] In the senses of *as soon as* and *suppose*, not unheard, indeed, in America.

old dream of an America *penitùs divisa* was grievously troubled at Manila Bay and ended for ever at Château Thierry. A literary America apart was never even a possibility. Henceforward there is less excuse—if there ever was any—for emphasizing differences merely as differences. The burden of this chapter has been to crave a certain intelligent respect for what exists. And it is directed mainly, perhaps, at the theorizings of men of letters, of all amateur critics of language, and at the practice of most school teachers, who so peculiarly hold the destinies of American speech in their hands. American writers have generally been bold enough. Emerson, Whitman, Mark Twain—but that is the subject of this whole work and needs no recapitulation in a final chapter. The wish to see things afresh and for himself is indeed so characteristic of the American that neither in his speech nor his most considered writing does he need any urging to seek out ways of his own. He refuses to carry on his verbal traffic with the well-worn counters; he will always be new-minting them. He is on the lookout for words that say something; he has "a sort of remorseless and scientific efficiency in the choice of epithets," which the hypercritical authors of the "King's English" ascribe to Kipling, who is "americanizing us." The American's slang is not made up of words that look like words, as is the case with much British slang, but words that are things, images; grotesque, preposterous, perhaps, but born of a quick fancy. He has an Elizabethan love of exuberant language. The highfalutin' spread-eagleism of the old-fashioned Fourth of July oration, the epistolary style of Lorenzo Altisonant in his *Letters of Squire Pedant*, who "merged his plumous implement of chirography into the atramented fluid," the sort of polysyllabic eloquence of which Holmes and Lowell made such excellent fun, now linger perhaps only in the columns of the rural weekly newspaper and in a Congressional speech which is delivered to be heard a long way off.

There is in this view of the American speech a good deal of carefully cherished tradition. No American writer has perhaps played with words as daringly as Meredith or expressed himself as whimsically as Carlyle. There is in American speech and writing a good deal of timidity, as well as audacity, quite as much colourlessness as picturesqueness. A British critic

wrote somewhere the other day of the "whitey-brown" style
of American college professors.   Such a charge is not directed
against too great linguistic daring.   A lack of pith, of raciness,
an insecure hold on idiom in some of its more slippery turns
might very properly be remarked in not a little American
writing; in short, an anxiety to play safe in a dangerous game.
There is nothing unnatural in an association of boldness and
timidity.   Both, however, represent excess.   The discovery of
the mean is the problem, and that will move toward a solution as the standards which express it are more zealously and
intelligently sought within the history and present practice of
American English itself.

BIBLIOGRAPHICAL NOTES

For extended bibliographies of all the writers discussed in this volume consult *The Cambridge History of American Literature* (1917–21) issued in four volumes by the publishers of this abridgment.   In the following lists the name of the publisher is given only when the book is still in print.

General Authorities

Anthologies: *Library of Southern Literature*, compiled by E. A. Alderman, C. W. Kent, and others, 1908–13, 16 vols.; *Anthology of Magazine Verse for 1913* [1914, 1915, 1916, 1917, 1918, 1919, 1920, 1921] *and Yearbook of American Poetry*, edited by W. S. Braithwaite, 1913—(Small, Maynard); *American Orations*, edited by A. Johnston and J. A. Woodburn, 4 vols. (Putnam); *American Familiar Verse*, edited by B. Matthews, 1904 (Longmans, Green); *The Oxford Book of American Essays*, edited by B. Matthews, 1914 (Oxford); *Representative Plays by American Dramatists*, edited by M. J. Moses, 1917—, 3 vols. (Dutton); *American Literary Criticism*, edited by W. M. Payne, 1904 (Longmans, Green); *Representative American Plays*, edited by A. H. Quinn, 1917 (Century); *An American Anthology 1787–1900*, edited by E. C. Stedman, 1900 (Houghton Mifflin); *A Library of American Literature from the Earliest Settlement to the Present Time*, edited by E. C. Stedman and Ellen M. Hutchinson, 1889–1890, 11 vols.; *Poems of American History*, edited by B. E. Stevenson, 1908 (Houghton Mifflin); *Colonial Prose and Poetry*, edited by W. P. Trent and B. W. Wells, 1901, 3 vols. (Crowell); *Southern Writers*, edited by W. P. Trent, 1905 (Macmillan).

History and Criticism: *A Dictionary of American Authors*, by O. F. Adams, 5th edition, 1905 (Houghton Mifflin); *A Critical Dictionary of English Literature and British and American Authors*, by S. A. Allibone, 1857–71, 3 vols., and *Supplement*, by J. F. Kirk, 1891, 2 vols. (5 vols., Lippincott); *American Prose Masters*, by W. C. Brownell, 1909 (Scribner); *Cyclopædia of American Literature*, by E. A. and G. L. Duyckinck, 1855, 2 vols., *Supplement* 1866, revised edition of entire work by M. L. Simons, 1875, 2 vols.; *Leading American Novelists*, by J. Erskine, 1910 (Holt); *A History of the Theatre in America*, by A. Hornblow, 1919, 2 vols. (Lippincott); *The Spirit of American Literature*, by J. Macy, 1911 (Boni and Liveright); *American Lands and Letters*, by D. G. Mitchell, 1897–99, 2 vols. (Scribner); *A History of American Literature Since 1870*, by F. L. Pattee, 1915 (Century); *American Literature 1607–1885*, by C. F. Richardson, 1887–89, 2 vols. (Putnam); *American Thought from Puritanism to Pragmatism*, by W. Riley, 1915 (Holt); *A Manual of American Literature*, edited by T. Stanton, 1909 (Putnam); *Poets of America*, by E. C. Stedman, 1885 (Houghton Mifflin); *A History of American Literature 1607–1865*, by W. P. Trent, 1903 (Appleton); *Great American Writers*, by W. P.

Trent and J. Erskine, 1912 (Holt); *A History of American Literature during the Colonial Period 1607–1765*, by M. C. Tyler, 1878, 2 vols. (Putnam); *The Literary History of the American Revolution 1763–1783*, by M. C. Tyler, 1897, 2 vols. (Putnam); two preceding works also in 2 vols. (Putnam); *The American Novel*, by C. Van Doren, 1921 (Macmillan); *A Literary History of America*, by B. Wendell, 1900 (Scribner); *Chronological Outlines of American Literature*, by S. L. Whitcomb, 1894 (Macmillan); *America in Literature*, by G. E. Woodberry, 1903 (Harper); also various histories for the use of schools and colleges, notable among them being those by Katherine Lee Bates (Macmillan, 1897), P. H. Boynton (Ginn, 1919), W. C. Bronson (Heath, revised edition, 1919), W. B. Cairns (Oxford, 1912), W. J. Long (Ginn, 1913), B. Matthews (American Book, 1896), F. L. Pattee (Silver, Burdett, 1909), B. Wendell and C. N. Greenough (Scribner, 1904).

CHAPTER I

Edwards: *Works*, edited by S. Austin, Worcester, 1808, in 8 vols., and frequently reprinted; *Benjamin Franklin and Jonathan Edwards: Selections from Their Writings*, edited by Carl Van Doren, 1920 (Scribner); *Jonathan Edwards*, by A. V. G. Allen, 1889 (Houghton Mifflin).

Franklin: *Works*, edited by John Bigelow, 1887, 10 vols. (Putnam); numerous editions of the *Autobiography*, the best of them being that edited by John Bigelow, 1900 (Putnam); *Benjamin Franklin and Jonathan Edwards: Selections from Their Writings* (see under Edwards), *Benjamin Franklin Self-Revealed*, by William Cabell Bruce, 1917, 2 vols. (Putnam); *The True Benjamin Franklin*, by S. G. Fisher, 1899 (Lippincott); *Benjamin Franklin as a Man of Letters*, by J. M. McMaster, 1887 (Houghton Mifflin); *Benjamin Franklin*, by J. T. Morse, Jr., 1889 (Houghton Mifflin); *Life and Times of Benjamin Franklin*, by James Parton, 1864, 2 vols. (Houghton Mifflin).

CHAPTER II

Irving: *Works*, published complete in various editions by Putnam; also various separate works in many editions (Putnam); *The Life and Letters of Washington Irving*, by P. M. Irving, 1862–64, 4 vols. (Putnam); *Washington Irving*, by C. D. Warner, 1881 (Houghton Mifflin).

Bryant: *Life and Works*, 1884–89, 6 vols.; *Poems*, Roslyn Edition, 1903, 1910 (Appleton); *William Cullen Bryant*, by John Bigelow, 1890 (Houghton Mifflin); *William Cullen Bryant*, by W. A. Bradley, 1905 (Macmillan); *Bryant and His Friends*, by J. G. Wilson, 1886.

Cooper: *Works*, 33 vols. (Putnam); various editions of separate novels (Putnam), (Houghton); *James Fenimore Cooper*, by T. R. Lounsbury, 1883 (Houghton Mifflin); *James Fenimore Cooper*, by Mary E. Phillips, 1913 (Lane).

CHAPTER III

Poe: *Works*, edited by Charles F. Richardson, illustrated, 1902, 10 vols. (Putnam); also edited by E. C. Stedman and G. E. Woodberry, 1914, 10 vols. (Scribner); *Poems*, edited by J. H. Whitty, 1911 (Houghton Mifflin); *Poems*, Illustrated, 1910, 1 vol. (Putnam); *Tales*, Illustrated, 1910, 1 vol. (Putnam). *Selections from the Critical Writings*, edited by F. C. Prescott, 1909 (Holt); *Life and Letters of Poe*, by J. A. Harrison, 1903, 2 vols. (Crowell—actually revision of vols. 1 and 17 of *Works* edited by Harrison); *Edgar Allan Poe: How to Know Him*, by C. Alphonso Smith, 1921 (Bobbs-Merrill); *Edgar Allan*

Poe, by G. E. Woodberry, 1885 (Houghton Mifflin); *The Life of Edgar Allan Poe*, by G. E. Woodberry, 1909, 2 vols. (Houghton Mifflin).

CHAPTER IV

Emerson: *Works*, 12 vols. (Houghton Mifflin); *Journals*, 1909–14, 10 vols. (Houghton Mifflin); various editions of separate works by various publishers; *A Memoir of Ralph Waldo Emerson*, by J. E. Cabot, 1887, 2 vols. (Houghton Mifflin); *Ralph Waldo Emerson: How to Know Him*, by S. M. Crothers, 1921 (Bobbs-Merrill); *Ralph Waldo Emerson*, by O. W. Firkins, 1915 (Houghton Mifflin); *The Teachers of Emerson*, by J. S. Harrison, 1910; *Ralph Waldo Emerson*, by O. W. Holmes, 1885 (Houghton Mifflin); *Ralph Waldo Emerson*, by G. E. Woodberry, 1907 (Macmillan).

Hawthorne: *Works*, 13 vols. (Houghton Mifflin); various editions of separate works by various publishers; *Personal Recollections of Nathaniel Hawthorne*, by Horatio Bridge, 1893; *Life of Nathaniel Hawthorne*, by M. D. Conway, 1890 (Walter Scott); *Nathaniel Hawthorne and His Wife*, by Julian Hawthorne, 1885, 2 vols. (Houghton Mifflin); *Hawthorne and His Circle*, by Julian Hawthorne (1903); *Hawthorne*, by Henry James, 1879 (Macmillan); *Memories of Hawthorne*, by Rose Hawthorne Lathrop, 1897; *Nathaniel Hawthorne*, by G. E. Woodberry, 1902 (Houghton Mifflin); *Nathaniel Hawthorne: How to Know Him*, by G. E. Woodberry, 1918 (Bobbs-Merrill).

Thoreau: *Works*, 11 vols. (Houghton Mifflin); *Works*, including *Journals*, 20 vols. (Houghton Mifflin); various editions of separate works by various publishers; *Thoreau the Poet-Naturalist*, by W. E. Channing, 1873, 1902; *The Life of Henry David Thoreau*, by F. B. Sanborn, 1917 (Houghton Mifflin); *Henry David Thoreau: A Critical Study*, by Mark Van Doren, 1916 (Houghton Mifflin).

CHAPTER V

Longfellow: *Works*, 11 vols. (Houghton Mifflin); *Poetical Works*, Cambridge Edition (Houghton Mifflin); various incomplete editions and editions of separate works by various publishers; *Henry Wadsworth Longfellow*, by G. R. Carpenter, 1901 (Small, Maynard); *Life of Henry Wadsworth Longfellow*, by S. Longfellow, 1891, 3 vols. (Houghton Mifflin); *Henry Wadsworth Longfellow*, by T. W. Higginson, 1902 (Houghton Mifflin).

Whittier: *Works*, 7 vols. (Houghton Mifflin); *Poetical Works*, Cambridge Edition (Houghton Mifflin); various incomplete editions and editions of separate works by various publishers; *John Greenleaf Whittier*, by G. R. Carpenter, 1903 (Houghton Mifflin); *John Greenleaf Whittier*, by T. W. Higginson, 1902 (Macmillan); *The Life and Letters of John Greenleaf Whittier*, by S. T. Pickard, 1894, 1907, 2 vols. (Houghton Mifflin).

Holmes: *Works*, 14 vols. (Houghton Mifflin); various editions of separate works by various publishers; *Poetical Works*, Cambridge Edition (Houghton Mifflin); *Dr. Holmes's Boston*, edited by Caroline Ticknor (Houghton Mifflin); *Life and Letters of Oliver Wendell Holmes*, by J. T. Morse, Jr., 1897, 2 vols. (Houghton Mifflin).

Lowell: *Works*, 11 vols. (Houghton Mifflin); *Poetical Works*, Cambridge Edition (Houghton Mifflin); various incomplete editions and editions of separate works by various publishers; *James Russell Lowell*, by F. Greenslet, 1905 (Houghton Mifflin); *James Russell Lowell*, by H. E. Scudder, 1901, 2 vols. (Houghton Mifflin).

Melville: *Works*, 4 vols. (Dana, Estes); various editions of *Typee, Omoo, Moby Dick*, by various publishers; *Herman Melville: Mariner and Mystic*, by Raymond Weaver, 1921 (Doran).

Mrs. Stowe: *Works*, 15 vols. (Houghton Mifflin); various editions of *Uncle Tom's Cabin*, by various publishers; *Life and Letters of Harriet Beecher Stowe*, by Annie Fields, 1897 (Houghton Mifflin); *Harriet Beecher Stowe*, by C. E. and L. B. Stowe, 1911 (Houghton Mifflin).

CHAPTER VI

Lincoln: *Works*, edited by Arthur Brooks Lapsley, Introduction by Theodore Roosevelt. With Essay on Lincoln by Carl Schurz, and Address on Lincoln by Joseph H. Choate, 1905, 8 vols. (Putnam); also edited by J. G. Nicolay and John Hay, 1894, 2 vols. (Century); various collected editions, Lincoln-Douglas *Debates*, edited by E. E. Sparks, 1908 (Illinois Historical Society); various editions by various publishers; *Speeches and Letters*, edited by James Bryce, 1907 (Dutton); various volumes of selections; *Uncollected Letters*, edited by G. A. Tracy, 1917 (Houghton Mifflin); *Six Months at the White House with Abraham Lincoln*, by F. B. Carpenter, 1866; *Abraham Lincoln*, by Lord Charnwood, 1916 (Holt); *Herndon's Lincoln*, by W. H. Herndon and J. W. Weik, 1889, 3 vols.; suppressed and later issued as *Abraham Lincoln*, 2 vols. (Appleton); *Abraham Lincoln*, by J. T. Morse, Jr., 1893, 2 vols. (Houghton Mifflin); *Abraham Lincoln: A History*, by J. G. Nicolay and John Hay, 1890, 10 vols. (Century); *Abraham Lincoln*, by Carl Schurz, 1891 (Houghton Mifflin); *Abraham Lincoln and the Union*, by N. W. Stephenson, 1918 (Yale); *Abraham Lincoln, the People's Leader*, by G. H. Putnam, 1909 (Putnam); *Every Day Life of Lincoln*, by F. F. Browne, 1915 (Putnam); *Personal Recollections of Abraham Lincoln*, by H. B. Rankin, 1916 (Putnam); *Abraham Lincoln, Man of God*, by J. W. Hill, 1920 (Putnam).

CHAPTER VII

Whitman: *Complete Writings*, 1902, 10 vols.; *The Gathering of the Forces*, early writings previously unpublished, edited by John Black and Cleveland Rodgers, 1920, 2 vols. (Putnam); *Leaves of Grass*, 1917 (Putnam) (Doubleday, Page); *Complete Prose Works* (Doubleday, Page); *The Uncollected Poetry and Prose of Walt Whitman*, edited by Emory Holloway, 2 vols., 1921 (Doubleday, Page); *Walt Whitman*, by Leon Bazalgette, 1920 (Doubleday, Page); *Whitman: A Study*, by John Burroughs, 1867, 1896 (Houghton Mifflin); *Walt Whitman*, by G. R. Carpenter, 1909 (Macmillan); *Walt Whitman: A Critical Study*, by Basil de Selincourt, 1914 (London: Secker); *Walt Whitman: His Life and Work*, by Bliss Perry, 1906, 1908 (Houghton Mifflin); *Walt Whitman: A Study*, by J. A. Symonds, 1893 (Dutton); *With Walt Whitman in Camden*, by H. L. Traubel, 1906–14, 3 vols. (Doubleday, Page); *In Re Walt Whitman*, edited by H. L. Traubel, R. M. Bucke, and T. B. Harned, 1893.

CHAPTER VIII

Mark Twain: *Works*, 18 vols., 25 vols. (Harper); *The Ordeal of Mark Twain*, by Van Wyck Brooks, 1920 (Dutton); *My Mark Twain*, by W. D. Howells, 1910 (Harper); *Mark Twain: A Biography*, by A. B. Paine, 1912, 3 vols. (Harper).

Howells: *Works,* never collected but published for the most part by Houghton Mifflin and Scribner; *William Dean Howells,* by A. Harvey, 1917 (Huebsch).

Henry James: *Works,* New York Edition, 1907–17, 26 vols. (Scribner); 35 vols., 1921—(London: Macmillan); *Letters,* 1920, 2 vols. (Scribner); *The Method of Henry James,* by J. W. Beach, 1918 (Yale); *Henry James,* by Rebecca West, 1916 (Holt).

Lanier: *Works* not collected but chiefly published by Scribner; *Poems,* edited by Mrs. Lanier (Scribner); *Sidney Lanier,* by E. Mims, 1905 (Houghton Mifflin).

Harris: *Works* not collected but chiefly published by Houghton Mifflin; *Life and Letters,* by Julia Collier Harris, 1918 (Houghton Mifflin).

CHAPTER IX

The Short Story: *The Short Story in English,* by H. S. Canby, 1909 (Holt); *The Philosophy of the Short Story,* by B. Matthews, 1901 (Longmans, Green); *The American Short Story,* by C. A. Smith, 1912 (Ginn); *Our Short Story Writers,* by Blanche Colton Williams, 1920 (Moffat, Yard); *Representative American Short Stories,* by A. Jessup (an anthology of over seventy stories to be published by Allyn and Bacon during 1922); *The Best Short Stories of 1915* [1916, 1917, 1918, 1919, 1920 and 1921] *and The Year-book of the American Short Story,* edited by E. J. O'Brien, 1916—(Small, Maynard); *Century Readings for a Course in American Literature* [contains over thirty short stories], edited by F. L. Pattee, 1919 (Century).

CHAPTER X

Prescott: *Works,* 16 vols. (Lippincott); various editions of separate works by various publishers; *William Hickling Prescott,* by R. Ogden, 1905 (Houghton Mifflin); *William Hickling Prescott,* by H. T. Peck, 1905 (Macmillan); *Life of William Hickling Prescott,* by G. Ticknor, 1864 (Lippincott).

Motley: *Works,* 17 vols. (Harper); various editions of separate works by various publishers; *Correspondence,* 1889, 2 vols. (Harper); *John Lothrop Motley: A Memoir,* by O. W. Holmes, 1879 (Houghton Mifflin).

Parkman: *Works,* 12 vols. (Little, Brown); *A Life of Francis Parkman,* by C. H. Farnham, 1900 (Little, Brown); *Francis Parkman,* by H. D. Sedgwick, 1904 (Houghton Mifflin).

Henry Adams: *Works* not collected, but chiefly published by Houghton Mifflin and Scribner; *The Education of Henry Adams,* 1907, 1918 (Houghton Mifflin); *Letters to a Niece and Prayer to the Virgin of Chartres,* 1920 (Houghton Mifflin); *A Cycle of Adams Letters 1861–1865,* by Charles Francis Adams, Charles Francis Adams, Jr., and Henry Adams, 1920, 2 vols. (Houghton Mifflin).

Ticknor: *History of Spanish Literature,* 3 vols. (Houghton Mifflin); *Life, Letters, and Journals,* 2 vols. (Houghton Mifflin).

Whitney: *Works* never collected and for the most part highly technical monographs and articles; *Language and the Study of Language,* 1867 (Scribner); *The Life and Growth of Language* (Appleton).

CHAPTER XI

Beecher: *Works* never collected; *Lectures and Orations,* edited by N. D. Hillis, 1913 (Revell); *Henry Ward Beecher,* by L. Abbott, 1903 (Houghton Mifflin).

Brooks: *Works* never collected; *Twenty Sermons* (also called *Visions and Tasks*

(Dutton); *Life and Letters*, by A. V. G. Allen, 1900, 3 vols.; *Phillips Brooks*, by A. V. G. Allen, 1907.

Royce: *Works* never collected but published chiefly by Houghton Mifflin and Macmillan; *The World and the Individual*, 1900–02, 2 vols. (Macmillan); *Character & Opinion in the United States: With Reminiscences of William James and Josiah Royce and Academic Life in America*, by G. Santayana, 1920 (Scribner).

William James: *Works* never collected but chiefly published by Holt and Longmans, Green; *Principles of Psychology*, 2 vols. (Holt); *The Varieties of Religious Experience* (Longmans, Green); *Selected Papers on Philosophy*, Everyman series (Dutton); *Letters*, 1920, 2 vols. (Atlantic Monthly); *William James*, by E. Boutroux, 1911 (Longmans, Green); *William James and Henri Bergson*, by H. M. Kallen, 1914 (University of Chicago); *William James and Other Essays*, by J. Royce, 1911 (Macmillan); see Santayana, under Royce.

CHAPTER XII

The Pronunciation of Standard English in America, by G. P. Krapp, 1918 (Oxford); *Americanisms and Briticisms*, by B. Matthews, 1892; *The American Language*, H. L. Mencken, 1919, revised 1921 (Knopf); *An American Glossary*, by R. H. Thornton, 1912, 2 vols. (Lippincott).

INDEX

27

For EU product safety concerns, contact us at Calle de José Abascal, 56–1°, 28003 Madrid, Spain or eugpsr@cambridge.org.

www.ingramcontent.com/pod-product-compliance
Ingram Content Group UK Ltd.
Pitfield, Milton Keynes, MK11 3LW, UK
UKHW042139130625
459647UK00011B/1099